The Social History of Post-Communist Russia

This book tells the untold story of how ordinary Russian people experienced and coped with Russia's transformations after the end of communism. Unlike most studies of the subject, which focus on high politics, developments in the elite and events at the centre, this book, which includes findings from interviews, memoirs, public opinion surveys and press articles and documents from the regions, portrays a multi-ethnic, multi-confessional society with different groups affected by the deep and varied changes in diverse and different ways. The book covers economic developments, social changes, how official policies played out at the grass-roots level, the psychological impact of the changes and the impact on public opinion, and how individual regions were affected differently. Overall, the book reveals the hidden dynamics of Russian society, including its formal and informal mechanisms and rules for relating to the state and other citizens, and shows how millions of Russians coped, despite all the odds, and maintained the integrity and stability of the country.

Piotr Dutkiewicz is a Professor of Political Science and Director of the Centre for Governance and Public Policy at Carleton University in Ottawa, Canada.

Richard Sakwa is Professor of Russian and European Politics at the University of Kent, UK.

Vladimir Kulikov is Associate Professor and Deputy Head of the Department of State Politics, Faculty of Political Science, Lomonosov Moscow State University.

The Social History of Post-Communist Russia

Edited by Piotr Dutkiewicz,
Richard Sakwa and
Vladimir Kulikov

Routledge
Taylor & Francis Group
LONDON AND NEW YORK

First published 2016 by Routledge

2 Park Square, Milton Park, Abingdon, Oxfordshire OX14 4RN
711 Third Avenue, New York, NY 10017

Routledge is an imprint of the Taylor & Francis Group, an informa business

First issued in paperback 2017

British Library Cataloguing in Publication Data
A catalogue record for this book is available from the British Library

Library of Congress Cataloging in Publication Data
The social history of post-communist Russia / edited by Piotr Dutkiewicz, Richard Sakwa and Vladimir Kulikov.
pages cm. — (Routledge contemporary Russia and Eastern Europe series; 67)
Includes bibliographical references and index.
1. Russia (Federation)—Social policy—1991– 2. Social change—Russia (Federation) 3. Economics—Russia (Federation)—Sociological aspects. 4. Russia (Federation)—Politics and government—1991– 5. Elite (Social sciences)—Russia (Federation) I. Dutkiewicz, Piotr, editor. II. Kulikov, V. V. (Vladimir Vladimirovich) editor. III. Sakwa, Richard, editor.
HN530.2.A8S63 2016
306.0947—dc23
2015024659

ISBN: 978-1-138-91920-4 (hbk)
ISBN: 978-1-138-47711-7 (pbk)

Typeset in Times New Roman
by Swales & Willis Ltd, Exeter, Devon, UK

Contents

Figures

Tables

Contributors

Piotr Dutkiewicz is Professor of Political Science and the Director of the Center for Governance and Public Policy at Carleton University in Ottawa, Canada. He is editor-in-chief of a 19-volume series on *Local and Regional Development in Poland and Eastern Europe* (1986–1989) and editor (or co-editor) of 12 other books, the most recent of which are *Eurasian Integration: The View from Within* (co-edited with Richard Sakwa, 2015), *22 Ideas To Fix the World* (co-edited with Richard Sakwa, 2013), *Democracy versus Modernization: A Dilemma for Russia and for the World* (co-edited with Vladislav Inozemtsev, 2012) and *Russia: The Challenges of Transformation* (co-edited with Dmitri Trenin, 2011). He has received a doctorate honoris causa from the People's Friendship University, Moscow, in 2006 and the Russian Academy of Public Administration (2007) for his contribution to the development of Canada–Russia relations and academic achievement.

Valery Fyodorov has since 2003 been the Director of the All-Russian Centre for the Study of Public Opinion (VTsIOM), the largest polling and survey agency in Russia. In addition, since 2013 he has been the academic director of the Political Science and Sociology department of the RF government's Finance University, and he also teaches at Moscow State University and is a professor at the Higher School of Economics. He is the author of numerous publications on Russian public opinion and political sociology. His latest books are *The Putin Era* (2003) and *Russian Choice: An Introduction to the Choice Behaviour of Russians* (2010).

Mikhail G. Gorshkov is Director of the Institute of Sociology of the Russian Academy of Sciences, and one of the most prominent contemporary Russian sociologists. He was elected a Full Member of the Russian Academy of Sciences in 2011. In 2002 he was awarded the title of Laureate for the Russian Federation State Prize in the sphere of science and technology. He is a member of numerous state and academic advisory committees. He is the author of more than 25 books and more than 250 articles, published in Russian, English, German, Chinese, Mongolian and other languages. He is chief editor the *Bulletin of the Institute of Sociology*, an academic e-journal, and the chairman of the editorial council of the journal *Vlast*. He is the coordinator of

Russian and international research projects. His most recent book publications include *Perestroika Through the Eyes of Russians: Twenty Years Later* (2005), *The Youth of Russia: Sociological Portrait* (2010, co-author), *Uninterrupted Education in the Context of Modernization* (2011), *Russian Society as It Is: Experience of Sociological Diagnostics* (2011), *Socio-Cultural Factors of Russian Society's Consolidation* (co-author, 2013), *Civil Society and Civil Culture in Modern Russia: Experience of Sociological Diagnostics* (2013) and *National and Civil Identity under the Context of Global Processes* (2014).

Galina Gribanova is the Head of the Political Science Department at the Herzen Pedagogical University and a Professor of Political Science at St Petersburg State University. She has worked as a visiting professor at Tallinn University in Estonia and Helsinki University in Finland. She has published widely on a range of topics dealing with sub-national levels of governance, federalism, regionalism and local government. Recent publications have focused on the relationship between territoriality, ethnicity and religion in the context of system transformation in post-communist countries.

Leonid Grigoryev is a professor of economics, Head of the Department of Global Economy at the Higher School of Economics, Moscow. Currently he is a Chief Adviser to the Head of the Analytical Centre of the RF Government and a member of the Board of Trustees of WWF-Russia (Chairman of the Board 2006–2014). He has published more than three hundred research works, edited a dozen books and produced numerous scientific media pieces. He is co-author of the '500-Days Plan' of the Russian government in 1990, and served as a deputy Minister of Finance in the transition government in 1991–1992. In the last two decades he has worked extensively on global growth and energy, as well as on elites, the middle class and inequality. He is an active member of the National Research Council on the BRICS and has lectured extensively in Russia and internationally. His most recent books include *Middle Class after the Crisis: Express-Analysis of its View on Politics and Economy* (in collaboration with A. Salmin, 2010), *Global Economy at the Beginning of the Twenty-First Century* (editor, 2013), *Global and Russian Energy Outlook up to 2040* (co-author, 2014), *Energy Subsidies in G-20 Countries* (editor, 2014).

Boris Kapustin teaches political philosophy at Yale University and is senior research fellow at the Institute of Philosophy, Russian Academy of Sciences. He has published widely on a range of topics, such as political morality, civil society, capitalism and democracy, and post-communist transformations in East-Central Europe and Eurasia. His recent publications include *Critique of Political Philosophy: Selected Essays* (2010), *Citizenship and Civil Society* (2011), 'Capitalism and Russian Democracy', in Per-Arne Bodin et al. (eds), *Power and Legitimacy: Challenges from Russia* (2013).

Vladimir G. Kulikov, PhD, graduated from the Institute of Asian and African Countries (Moscow State University) in 1977. From 1977 to 1991 he worked as a researcher in the Institute for Oriental Studies (Russian Academy of

Sciences) and from 1991 to 1995 he was Deputy Director of this Institute. Since 2003 he has worked in the Executive Committee of the World Public Forum (WPF) 'Dialogue of Civilizations' as the Executive Secretary and Head of the Scientific Department; he also holds a position as a Deputy Department Head at the Faculty of Political Science of Moscow State University. He served as project manager of several projects that resulted in publications (supported also by WPF), the most recent of which include Craig Calhoun and Georgi Derluguian (eds), *Possible Futures*, Volume I, *Business As Usual: The Roots of the Global Financial Meltdown*; Volume II, *The Deepening Crisis: Governance Challenges after Neoliberalism*; Volume III, *Aftermath: A New Global Economic Order?*; Piotr Dutkiewicz and Dmitri Trenin (eds), *Russia: The Challenges of Transformation*; and Piotr Dutkiewicz and Richard Sakwa (eds), *22 Ideas to Fix the World* (2013).

Andrey Margolin is Vice-Rector at the Russian Presidential Academy of National Economy and Public Administration. He has more than 30 years' experience teaching economics and has published more than 120 papers on investment policy and evaluation, regional development, and natural resource management. He has implemented a wide range of domestic and international research and training projects, including the first MPA programme in Russia and a series of study tours for senior federal government officials. As an expert, he has participated in a number of research projects funded by the World Bank and the European Commission, as well as assessment reviews of Russian federal targeted programmes. He is a doctor and professor of economics, and holds the title of Honorary Economist of the Russian Federation.

Boris Mezhuev, PhD, has since 1998 taught the history of philosophy at Moscow State University (MGU), where he holds the position of professor. From 2002 until 2006 he was a deputy editor-in-chief of *Cosmopolis* journal. Since 2013 he has been a deputy editor-in-chief of the *Izvestia* newspaper and regular columnist there. He is also a member of the editorial board of the political science journal *Polis*. He writes about problems of American political culture, the different aspects of Russian-American relations and about the transformations of Russian political culture. He is the author of approximately 200 articles in different journals and collections of works. His most recent books include *Political Critique by Vadim Tsymbursky* (2011) and *Perestroika-2: the Experience of Repetition* (2014), a book analysing the influence of Mikhail Gorbachev's perestroika on the shaping and trajectory of Dmitry Medvedev's politics of modernization.

Vladimir Popov is currently an Interregional Adviser in DESA, UN and professor emeritus at the New Economic School in Moscow, professor (on leave) at the Graduate School of International Business at the Russian Presidential Academy of the National Economy and Public Administration in Moscow, and an adjunct research professor at the Institute of European and Russian Studies at Carleton University in Ottawa. He has written extensively on various issues of the economics of development and transition. He is the author and editor of 11 books and numerous articles in the *Journal of Comparative Economics*, *Comparative Economic Studies*, *World Development*, *Post Communist Economies*, *New Left Review* and other academic journals, as well as essays in the media. His books and articles have been published in many languages. His new book *Mixed Fortunes: Economic History of China, Russia and the West* was published in 2014 by Oxford University Press. His personal website is: http://http-server.carleton.ca/~vpopov/

Richard Sakwa is professor of Russian and European Politics at the University of Kent, an Associate Fellow of the Russia and Eurasia programme at Chatham House, an Honorary Senior Research Fellow at the University of Birmingham's Centre for Russian, Eurasian and East European Studies (CREES), and a Fellow of the Academy of Social Sciences. His main research interests are Russian domestic and international politics, European international relations and comparative democratization. His recent books include *The Crisis of Russian Democracy: The Dual State, Factionalism, and the Medvedev Succession* (2011), *Putin and the Oligarch: The Khodorkovsky – Yukos Affair* (2014), *Putin Redux: Power and Contradiction in Contemporary Russia* (2014) and *Frontline Ukraine: Crisis in the Borderlands* (2015).

Elena Shestopal is Professor and head of the Chair of Sociology and Psychology in Politics of the Political Science faculty of Moscow State University. Her area of expertise includes political perception, problems of personality in politics and leadership. She is the author of over 400 scholarly publications. Her most important publications include *Personality and Politics: Contemporary Conceptions of Political Socialization* (1988), *Essays in Political Psychology* (1990), *A Handbook of Political Psychology* (2012), *Political Profile of Russian Politics in the 1990s* (1999), *Political and Psychological Problems of Mass Mentality* (2002), *Political Socialization and Resocialization of Russian Citizens in Post-Soviet Russia* (2009) and *Psychology of Political Perception in Contemporary Russia* (2012), *Human Capital of Russian Political Elites* (editor, 2013), *Citizens and Leaders in a Comparative Perspective* (2013). She is a member of the governing council of the Russian Academy of Political Sciences, member of the Executive Committee of the Russian Political Science Association, 1994–2000, and Vice-President of IPSA (1997–2000). In 1993 she founded the Russian Association of Political Psychology.

Natalya E. Tikhonova is professor-researcher at the Higher School of Economics and a leading researcher at the Institute of Sociology of the Russian Academy of Science. She is a member of editorial boards of the journals *Social Sciences and Modernity*, *Bulletin of the Institute of Sociology*, *Journal of Social Policy Studies* and others. Her main spheres of interest include the social structure of Russian society and the impact of reforms on various social groups. Her major publications include *Factors of Social Stratification in Conditions of Transition to Market Economy* (1999), *Work and Welfare in the New Russia* (co-author, 2000), *Phenomenon of Urban Poverty in Modern Russia* (2003), *Poverty and Social Exclusion in the New Russia* (co-author, 2004), *Social Stratification in Contemporary Russia: Empirical Analysis* (2007), *Health and Health Care in the New Russia* (co-author, 2008), *Middle Class: Theory and Reality* (co-author, 2009) and *The Social Structure of Russia: Theory and Reality* (2014).

Natalya Zubarevich is a Professor of Moscow State University, Department of Geography, Director of Regional Programmes of the Independent Institute for Social Policy. She is a member of the Expert Board of the federal government. She was an Expert of the UN Development Programmne (Russia) in 1997–2012. She is a specialist in the field of the socio-economic development of regions, human geography and urban development. She is the author, co-writer and scientific editor of several monographs, including *Russian Regions: Inequality, Crisis, Modernization* (2010), *Social Development of Russia's Regions: Problems and Trends in Transition* (2003, 2005 and 2007), *Russia's Regions: What Is the Social Space We Live In?* (2005).

Acknowledgements

Many people and organizations contributed to this volume in a variety of meaningful ways. The editors are most grateful to the World Public Forum (WPF) 'Dialogue of Civilizations' for co-sponsoring this project and making its progress relatively smooth and efficient.

Our personal thanks go to Professor Andrei Shutov, Dean of the Political Science Faculty of Moscow State University (MGU) for supervising and facilitating the Russian version of this book. We are in debt to Kinross Gold Corporation for their generous support in making such a high-quality professional translation of this book possible. A big thank you also goes to the Magna Fund for supporting a special seminar in Ottawa to discuss changes in social structure in Russia. We are most grateful to a team of outstanding translators from Russia Today, headed by Natalia Shavlak. We were very glad to work on the Russian version of this volume with its Russian literary editor, Dr. Katerina Dobrynina. The Russian version of the book was published by Moscow State University Press in 2015, with a Foreword by Vladimir Yakunin, which is reproduced at the end of this volume.

We are grateful to all the contributors to this volume for making work with them so vibrant, smooth, pleasant and educational. It is also a pleasure to acknowledge the support, encouragement and professionalism received from Peter Sowden at Routledge.

Piotr Dutkiewicz is grateful to Vincent Della Sala and Trento University for the opportunity to finalize collecting the chapters to this book in the wonderful setting of Trento. Many genuine thanks go to our families. Piotr Dutkiewicz's wife Ewa Hebda-Dutkiewicz was always ready to assist when needed, and Richard Sakwa is most grateful to the support and assistance of Roza Sakwa.

This book is devoted to the Russian people who – by living, working, parenting, adapting, persevering and acting daily in many social and economic incarnations, against many odds – are truly shaping Russia's reality.

1 Introduction

The evolution of Russian society since 1991 – actors, attitudes and practices

Piotr Dutkiewicz

This is the story of millions of Russians who – despite all odds – maintained the integrity and stability of the country in the context of a long, turbulent, socially costly and multi-faceted transformation from a centrally planned to a market economy, from socialism to capitalism and from the empire to a regional power.[1] So far, most of the countless books on Russia's transition have been written from a high-politics perspective, with a narrative focused on elite-level developments (such as changes in the top leadership[2] or changes in key legal and institutional aspects of the Federation[3]) or from a formulaic binary-comparative perspective focusing on the success/failure of 'transition to democracy' and 'liberalization of the market'.[4]

Contributors to this volume believe that there is an untold history of Russia that remains to be written from its citizens' perspective, both about and set against the backdrop of major political and economic events. This book will obviously follow key political and economic developments of federal importance, but will inject a significant component of original, interdisciplinary research that will show societal change and the evolution of public opinion and values in Russia presented simultaneously in two dimensions: spatial (spanning the Russian regions) and longitudinal (covering the period of 1991 to 2014).

Content and methodology

This book presents the evolution of Russian society and state since 1991. This story will be told not by outside commentators, but by Russian experts representing different disciplines (philosophy, sociology, economics, regional studies, history, public opinion pollsters and political science). The editors believe that such a 'Russian made' volume has a certain comparative advantage in that it provides the reader with an insider, culturally specific, at times emotional, and overall more nuanced view of this unique society during this fateful historical juncture.

One of our key tasks was to show the complexity and dynamics of Russian society and its formal and informal mechanisms and rules, including in its relations to the state. The information presented is based on multi-regional field research performed over the last twenty-five years. The Russia this book presents is socially complex,[5] multi-ethnic and multi-confessional,[6] and one whose civilization is both deeply rooted historically and simultaneously representative of the post-modern system of unconstrained reconstruction (an ability to transform almost anything into an object of capitalization). One of the key goals of this project is to provide evidence for the book's guiding thesis that Russian society is, in fact, not merely an object of high-level political processes, *but an adaptive, dynamic and – at times reluctant – subject of its own history.*

This book was inspired by two central questions:

- Why is there no serious public discourse in Russia on social needs, social change and social structures? Or – in other words – why in many narratives on Russian society in the last twenty years is there a marked absence of a character that could be called 'the people'?; and
- Why is Russian society ('*narod*') not prominently featured in books and articles published in both Russia and the West, while at the same time there exists a rich literature on *civil society* in Russia?

It seems that the basic answers to these two questions are the following. First, Western literature focuses almost exclusively on the question of *civil society* in Russia rather than society as whole.[7] Civil society, defined as the politically mobilized, independent from the state, and active network of organizations and people, has been the direct focus of Western research and discourse about Russia. Western academics, funds and projects have flowed into Russia in order to establish why Russia is so different from Southern Europe and Latin American states in introducing and – potentially – consolidating democracy, how Vladimir Putin's regime might be changed and how its authoritarian tendencies might be checked. At the same time, it seems that almost no one was interested in the *politically inactive majority* of Russian society. This is likely because this aspect of Russian society could lend no answers on how to influence or challenge the current political regime in Russia.

Russian elites (both pro- and anti-Kremlin) seemed likewise uninterested in having access to research on their own society, as for most of them real politics is located in the higher echelons of power. Involving society at large in their politics seemed to them both improbable and useless. Thus, the structure and evolution of Russian society became the focus almost entirely of Russian researchers in the niches of sociological and regional research (including such scholars as M. Gorshkov, E. Shestopal, N. Zubarevich, N. Tikhonova and some others mostly associated with the Institute of Sociology of the Russian Academy of Sciences).[8]

Second, not having systemic studies on Russian society (with the notable exceptions of the scholars mentioned above) simultaneously triggered two processes. The first was a lack of *popular debate* about the key elements of social change such as social structure, income distribution and societal perception of its own trajectory of development. Simultaneously, this lack of information was conducive to the deliberate strategy of the political elite of depoliticizing Russian society. This was done by actively precluding widespread debate involving different social strata on key domestic policies and deciding 'what is best for the society'.[9] Thus a selective Western interest in the politicized sections of Russian society coincided with the Russian elite's disinterest in involving society *at large* in a dialogue with those in power. This resulted in a narrowing of the scope of both research and societal dialogue to elite groups.[10]

This volume combines chapters that represent five disciplines: sociology (macro-sociology, political polling, and socio-psychology), philosophy, economics, political science and political economy (in its version of regional studies). In this way we sought to present Russian society from a multidisciplinary perspective in order to reflect the complex and multi-dimensional process of the last twenty-five years of social transformation.[11]

Russian society: actors

Perceptions matter. On the train from Moscow to St Petersburg in 2005, a fellow traveller, an older worker at a machine building plant (the famous Kirov Factory), who was visiting his family in Moscow, told me that for him there are two classes in Russia – one that flies in their own jets and another that walks below. Even if this is obviously – as our book shows in detail[12] – a gross simplification, it seems to indicate a relative impossibility of dialogue between the social layers that make up Russian society today. When I tested this quite frightening proposition on my Russian colleagues, I was quite surprised that it was shared (albeit in degrees that significantly varied from person to person) by most. Behind each 'perception' – like the one presented above – there is always a reason (even if highly subjective) that points to a specific direction in search for the answer to why it is placed in someone's mind. Let me try to decipher that 'reason behind this perception'.

Let me start this section from the generalization and then – deductively – present a more substantiated explanation. It seems that the *nature* (or deep structural backbone) of the current Russian political system is a complex, intertwined hybrid of three components: pre-modern (Dionysian/Byzantine)[13] mixed with (neo)realism and a high dose of post-modernism. From this 'nature' we can trace the relations between society and those in power (or a broadly defined ruling group).[14]

The 'pre-modern' aspect embraces intrigue and manipulation as a surrogate of politics, expects subordination to the leader and assumes de-politicization of society. The (neo)realist component embraces the idea of power as the most important factor in domestic/international relations, sovereignty as the most valuable treasure of the nation and anarchy as the main feature/threat of the system (the 'neo' aspect of realism). Finally, post-modernism is key to understanding the system as it draws on a highly constructivist belief that everything is possible and permitted, for everything seems to be only a question of either desire or fear, and desire and fear are merely technical problems of will, resources and power. In other words 'reality' is what is to be constructed and the system is determined by the ability to transform virtually anything into an object subordinated to its own will. If the above is correct, then this mix of three modes of 'systemic being' becomes a structural barrier in state–society relations.

A second obstacle is the model of relations with society based on the concept of *trusteeship*. Let me explain. Putin's 'new ruling group' started to construct a new edifice using a mix of old bricks inherited from the Boris Yeltsin period as well as some new ones to rebuild a Russia that, in the early 2000s, was deeply traumatized after a series of a crises.[15] This group became engaged in a form of *étatization*.[16] For that task, they needed not only more power than Yeltsin had as president but, most importantly, a different kind of power. The current rulers in the Kremlin are convinced that they needed to restore, at the very core, what was traditionally the central engine of social development throughout Russian history: the state. In order to accomplish this project, they had to link the state and accumulation into one undivided complex of social power.

If one looks for a single explanation of 'Putin's idea', most probably this is the closest we can get. In fact, power and resources are synonymous with accumulation (as power derives from capital and – at the same time – provides capital with its most important instrument, power/protection). So what the ruling group was really looking for was a different mode of accumulation, one that would not differentiate between 'economic' and 'political' power, and where money would not be 'separated' from social institutions, law, culture and so on. This new type of accumulation would be totalizing in its capture of economy and society. It would epitomize power. They also probably felt that along the way they would have to reconstruct the elite itself in order to control the process of modernization and to 'reconcile national and liberal opinion once again; and so create the first government in Russian history to enjoy a broad political consensus' and achieve – at least for some years – what Perry Anderson aptly observes as a 'hegemonic stability'.[17]

At this point comes an important question that was at the very beginning of our book's conceptualization. Who can lead society in a truly revolutionary time of transformation? What should be a model for state–societal interactions? Is conversation with your own society necessary and useful for development? It seems that Russian leaders[18] made a conscious decision on what Boris Kapustin calls in our book an 'absence of the people' in a national discourse and what Boris Mezhuev – in a concluding chapter – describes as the 'strategy of self-isolation' from the people by both ruling group and its nascent opposition.[19]

Society, the argument goes, cannot be trusted entirely as it has lived too long in an entirely different system, and so it cannot grasp the 'goal of the transformation'.[20] Society is also susceptible – as the 1990s showed – to massive media and political manipulations. Oligarchs and high-level officials were not the best option in 1998 for a ruling group either, as they were engaged in stripping assets and moving them abroad. They were, after all, business people, not interested in the wealth of society or the future of the state. So who was to lead Russia to its revival? From the utopian socialists through to Hegelian principles of development, Marx's debate on the role of the 'individual man', the Fabian's Society ideal of correcting the socio-economic change in the British colonies, the League of Nation's institution of trusteeship, the ideas of Sergei Witte, and Lenin's notion of a 'vanguard party', theorists and practitioners of all stripes and colours have struggled with the answer to this very question: who is to lead society towards development and progress? Who can be entrusted to lead the change? Will it be Hegel's 'spiritless mass' or someone else? In their brilliant book on development, Michael Cowen and Robert Shenton observed that 'a "handful of chosen men" could now assume the mantle of the "active spirit" to become the inner determination of development', regardless of the system of governance and its ideological stamp.[21]

Putin's version of trusteeship is thus given its philosophical justification. The notion of the trusteeship, I believe, explains a lot about Putin's leadership. It may explain, for instance, the Kremlin's partial distrust of society (which – in turn – explains why only very limited change via grassroots social movements was permitted and why restrictive laws on NGOs were introduced), as well as their desperate need to 'have society engaged' (for instance in the convoluted form of the Social Chamber and other forms of popular '*kontrol*', or supervision).

On the other side of this power–society spectrum, one of the modern world's most grandiose social experiments, called the 'transformation from communism' and probably comparable in scale only to the socialist revolutions in Russia and China, reshuffled the social positions and status of 150 million people in just under a quarter of a century. Natalya Tikhonova and Mikhail Gorshkov in this volume analyse the evolution of the social structure of modern Russia and provide an explanation of the ways society was influenced by the introduction of market relations. Simultaneously, 'society' had a direct impact on the speed and depth of economic restructuring by creating structural (social) constraints on reforms (by making policies in that area welcome or unwelcome or 'adjusting' them to their own, individual survival strategies).[22] The novelty of our approach is to show how different types of resources (such as education, position in the administration, access to decision makers, participation in private business, access to capital, etc.) have influenced the process of social stratification along 'geographically based' sources of stratification (such as regional and local sources for and obstacles to vertical and horizontal mobility).

Our position – at this point – is that without changing the modus operandi towards dialogue with the 'people', revitalizing politics as a means to engage the 'silent majority', and making politics more transparent, moral and understandable (as well as opening up new channels for vertical mobility), the system risks facing stronger societal opposition than anticipated (most likely not in one or another form of the so-called 'colour revolutions') as it may come not from the politically awakened minority of the Russian self-proclaimed 'creative class', but from the currently politically passive majority.

Russian society: attitudes

For Russian politicians society 'exists' mostly in opinion polls, and rarely do they make significant decisions that run against the preferences of the majority. Equally, rarely do politicians become hostage to societal ambitions, expectations, worries and hopes represented in public opinion polls.[23]

In this volume we divide the chronology of the evolution of the opinions of the Russian public into six periods: (1) 1989–1993, covering the collapse of the system and the beginning of new institutional reforms; (2) 1994–1997, describing attempts at stabilization of the Yeltsin regime; (3) the systemic crisis of 1998–2000; (4) stabilization and consolidation of Putin's rule, 2000–2008; (5) the world economic crisis and political destabilization of 2009–2012; and (6) conservative mobilization, from 2012. This periodization allows us to group (and show the evolution of) quite dramatic changes in public reactions to key events, the main challenges that public opinion created for decision makers and their policies and their attitudes to political personalities in many Russian regions since 1989–1990. In that sense, our authors paint a broad picture of the collective state of mind of Russian society over the last twenty-five years across two dimensions: time and space.

As these chapters will speak for themselves, I would like to offer just a few reflections on their rich content to situate them and connect them to other parts of this volume. First, there is a close correlation between changes in the social structure (Natalya Tiknonova's chapter) and the reflection of these structures in public opinion (Valery Fyodorov's chapter). The more complex the social structure becomes, the more clearly visible are potential social conflicts, both structural (related to how social groups constituting society are structured and relate to each other) and situational (related to a societal reaction to concrete events or personalities). Thus politicians are facing more sophisticated challenges in properly calibrating their reactions to polls. In that sense – as Valery Fyodorov explains – opinion polls not only serve to detect 'reaction to events' but may also provide substantive pointers to a longer term 'social needs assessment' strategy embracing the 'silent majority' of the Russian population.

Second, extensive research conducted over more than twenty years presented in the chapters by Mikhail Gorshkov and Elena Shestopal shows how, despite dynamic changes in Russian society, certain expectations and disappointments from those in power seems to have stayed the same for last 10–15 years (two issues in particular seem to worry most people – corruption and social disparities). This indicates some level of inefficiency or unwillingness or lack of state capacity to deal with these issues.

Third, data (our book provides information up to the beginning of 2014, so before the crisis in Ukraine and all changes in public opinions related to it) show a high level of support (particularly in the age group above 40–45) for transforming the country away from Yelsin's chaos to the relative economic stability, reduction of poverty, increased social spending and increased military strength of Russia. These are considered the main systemic achievements of the recent period.

Fourth, to our surprise, even if economic transformation provoked several semi-criminal redistributions of property and the significant material diversification of Russian society (in other words, major inequality), these processes were (as Vladimir Popov's chapter shows) still supported by the majority of the population. This may be explained by a general willingness to turn the page from the socialist economy, initial trust in the market (as an antidote to socialist inefficiencies), the role of the mass media in presenting no alternatives, over-evaluation of one's own place on the 'income ladder' (supported by the study by Natalya Tikhonova that shows Russians consistently placing themselves in the higher brackets of the middle class, failing to appreciate their lower, measurable material status) and excessive expectations regarding liberal economic policies.

Fifth, Russian society – in the relatively short period of the last two decades – became pluralistic in terms of openly declared and/or followed values and reflects a very wide spectrum of political, religious, ethical, ideological and cultural values. This is a dramatic departure from the artificially constrained 'one size fits all' model of Soviet society. This is a new type of 'open' pluralism in which ethnic/religious/regional-social/cultural diversity is openly expressed and – if necessary – defended. Two chapters in this book (by Natalya Zubarevich and Galina Gribanova) convincingly show that surge of a 'new Russian pluralism' is encouraged by (sometimes) overlapping growing economic and social diversification of the Russian regions (with several cleavages dividing main four groups of regions), access to IT technologies, social media and 'politicization of ethnicity' (particularly among the non-Russian population, and aimed mainly at 'over-centralization' at the regional level and the politics of local elites).

Sixth, all the research presented in this book confirms the strong societal demand for 'Russian values' to act as the basis of the state's culturally based domestic and international policy. This presents a real challenge to those in power to establish a balance between the plural and multi-ethnic aspects of Russian society and the contribution of 'Russian values' as policy determinants. The main dilemma for policy makers is to maintain support of the majority of the Russian population in which according to 2010 data ethnically Russians constitute 80.9% (of which 66% – according to another survey from 2013 – strongly support the statement 'Russia shall be for Russians') and not creating a backlash among ethnic minorities (and immigrants).

Finally, this book shows that there is the uncharted (in terms of the predictability of their political and social behaviour) territory of the young population (aged 18–25) who grew up during the transformation period. They are angry and disappointed and, from various ideological perspectives, demand a more 'moral' politics: a politics that is less corrupt, less nihilistic, less selfishly oriented by regional and national power elites and more transparent, and which takes into account issues of social justice.

Russian society: practices

Retrospective evaluations of transformation – as much as they have to be conducted as part of the learning process on 'what went right and what went wrong' – usually tell us little about the decision-making process of the time when they were taken, the available alternatives, the motives behind particular policy choices or the level of information and intellectual preparedness for making decisions among decision makers.[24] Also, because of the lack of past models which can be used as a model for systemic change, an important part of the process was imitation of policies and institutions that came to Russia from abroad, mainly from the West.

To add to the list of transformational constraints, Russian reformers faced enormous regional diversity in social and economic levels of development, which meant that the Soviet-style 'one size fits all' model of systemic change had vastly different effects on the ground. As our book shows, the unintended consequences of federal policies were quite significant as people reacted to them by trying to maximize their short-term interests. People did – depending on regional conditions as we present in this book – respond to change from above by adapting their survival strategies to the level of regional or local economic development, level of urbanization, structure of the local labour market, educational opportunities, distance to the regional centres, and other factors. In this collection of essays we sought to address these issues in three chapters by those who either participated in these processes (Leonid Grigoryev) or acted as expert advisers (Natalya Zubarevich and Andrei Margolin).

Finally, this book is devoted to the Russian people who are – by living, working, parenting, adapting and acting in many social and economic incarnations – shaping Russia's transformation and thus making the people's history of Russia since 1991. In particular, we tried to give a voice to the 'silent majority' (the Russian middle, lower-middle and underprivileged classes), the people with little political representation and empowerment, who are demographically dominant and yet politically almost invisible. We hope that this book will help bring society back to its proper place in the mainstream of political and economic discourse.

Notes

1 There are a few but excellent works written in the last fifteen years covering the post-communist period from the 'people's perspective', for example: Linda J. Cook, *Postcommunist Welfare States: Reform Politics in Russia and Eastern Europe* (Ithaca: Cornell University Press, 2007), Andrea Chandler, *Democracy, Gender and Social Policy in Russia: A Wayward Society* (London: Palgrave Macmillan, 2013), and Linda Edmondson (ed.), *The Soviet Social Contract and Why It Failed: Welfare Policy and Workers' Politics from Brezhnev to Yeltsin* (Cambridge, MA: Harvard University Press, 1993).

2 For instance: Timothy J. Colton, *Yeltsin: A Life* (New York: Basic Books; 2008), Richard Sakwa, *The Crisis of Russian Democracy: The Dual State, Factionalism and the Medvedev Succession* (Cambridge: Cambridge University Press, 2011); idem, *Putin Redux: Power and Contradiction in Contemporary Russia* (London & New York: Routledge, 2014), and various works by Archie Brown, Fiona Hill, Marshall Goldman and Stephen White; and in Russia A. Chirikova, Oksana Gaman-Golutvina, Olga Kryshtanovska, Gleb Pavlovsky and Nikolai Svanidze.

3 See works by William E. Butler, Kathryn Hendley, Stephen Holmes, Eugene Huskey, Peter Solomon, Peter Reddaway, Gordon B. Smith; and in Russia, for example, Alexei Avtonomov, Gadis Gadzhiev, Sergei Kabyshev, Andrei Medushevsky, Gary Minkh and Valery Zorkin.

4 This multi-disciplinary group of economists, political scientists and macro-sociologists includes, inter alia, Alexander Dynkin, Leonid Grigoryev Alexei Kudrin, Vladimir Mau, Vladimir Popov and Anatoly Torkunov.

5 See the chapters in this volume by Gorshkov, Shestopal and Tikhonova.

6 See Gribanova's chapter in this volume on the evolution of ethnic and religious relations in Russia since the 1980s.
7 Some authors from this very numerous camp include Andrew Arato, Timothy Garton Ash, Laszlo Bruszt, Valerie Bunce, Elena Chebankova, Grzegorz Ekiert, M. Steven Fish, James Gibson, Mark Howard, Zdenka Mansfeldova, Michael McFaul, Aryeh Neier, Guillermo O'Donnell, Philippe Schmitter, Sabrina Ramet and Stephen Whitefield.
8 A sample of authors writing from that perspective include Mikhail Gorshkov, Natalya Tikhonova, Elena Shestopal, Natalya Zubarevitch and, outside of Russia, Alena Ledeneva and Jessica Pisano.
9 Alexander Dugin, one of the most active critics of V. Surkov, who was 'responsible' for 'state–society relations' during Putin's first presidency, went as far as to say that 'So he had an idea about society and its views on it. It was a pretty vulgar representation – in the spirit of social Darwinism. People seemed to him vain, selfish, unprincipled and corrupt animals seeking pleasure and pride of the slave. Quite in keeping with the liberal philosophy of Hobbes and Spencer', in A. Dugin, 'Good Bye, Golden Boy. The First Thought about Surkov's Departure', http://evrazia.org/article/1876 [Accessed on: 17 June 2015].
10 I am aware of the argument that elites play a leading role in transformation but they need a far reaching consensus among population to make sustainable change.
11 It was our deliberate choice – except for the two co-editors – that all the authors are Russian scholars (either living or working in Russia or involved actively in Russian academia while living abroad) to present an insider view based on many years of their field research, much of which not known to a larger public.
12 See in particular the chapters by Fyodorov, Gorshkov, Shestopal and Tikhonova in this volume.
13 A more detailed explanation of that aspect may be found in Teresa Rakowska-Harmstone and Piotr Dutkiewicz (eds), *New Europe: The Impact of the First Decade* (Warsaw: Polish Academy of Science, 2006), pp. 207–35.
14 For the purposes of this chapter I define a ruling group as a social construct whose representatives(s) make key decisions on the national scale (or securing the confidence in obedience by the majority of people) and/or decisively influence those decisions by their dominant position in the economy, culture or/and administration.
15 For a more systematic explanation, see Popov and Dutkiewicz's chapter in this volume.
16 Etatization is defined here as the accumulation of the state's capacity to develop and implement modernization/'developmental' strategies; it describes the state as the fundamental instrument of accumulation and nationally defined social change. See Piotr Dutkiewicz and Robert Shenton, 'Etatization and the Logic of Diminishing Reproduction', ROAPE 13, no. 37 (1986): 108–15; and Piotr Dutkiewicz and Gavin Williams, 'All the King's Horses and All the King's Men Couldn't Put Humpty Dumpty Together Again', *IDS Bulletin*, No. 18, 1987, pp. 1–6.
17 Perry Anderson, 'Russia's Managed Democracy', *London Review of Books*, 25 January 2007, p. 20.
18 Some political scientists interviewed by the author (2005–2008) pointed to the critical role of Vladislav Surkov in devising that approach.
19 See the chapters by Kapustin and Mezhuev in this volume.
20 The 'Hobbesian sovereign – was used [. . .] to convert people into human integers who are interchangeable with one another as units of a unified and contentless compact', from Waller R. Newell, *Tyranny: A New Interpretation* (Cambridge: Cambridge University Press, 2013), p. 80

21 Michael Cowen and Robert Shenton, *Doctrines of Development* (New York: Routledge, 1996), p. 397.
22 See Tikhonova in this volume.
23 In this book we present four chapters that reflect people's attitudes to transformation during the last twenty years: those by Fyodorov, Gorshkov, Popov and Shestopal.
24 See Grigoryev in Chapter 4 of this volume.

2 A people in the absence of the people, or a view of post-communism from below

Boris Kapustin

If we take 1991 as our point of departure, the post-communist 'new Russia' is not yet 30 years old, and already there are enough works of history dedicated to making sense of this period (many of them entitled *A History of Modern Russia*) to fill a small library. All of them are about the 'reforms'[1] inspired by what Katherine Verdery called 'the troika of Western self-identity', 'privatization', 'marketization' and 'democratization',[2] as well as their consequences. Of course, these narratives differ, sometimes diametrically, in how they interpret the nature of the 'reforms' and evaluate their results – intermediate or final[3] – or even understand the historical trajectory on which they have placed Russia. The more apologetic accounts of the 'reforms' portray them as a pragmatic and necessary, if painful, method of dealing with the late Soviet crisis, modernizing the country and transitioning to a market economy.[4] János Kornai describes it as returning to the path of capitalist development from the socialist dead end imposed on countries by Communism.[5]

Similarly liberal, albeit unapologetic, appraisals (as a rule, methodologically supported by a critique of neoclassical economics) hold that the setbacks encountered in the course of the reforms – primarily their failure to create an efficient market economy – are due in the first place to their being theoretically untenable.[6] The non- and anti-liberal criticisms of the 'reforms' are even more unsparing. According to conservatives, the 'reforms' are synonymous with the merciless destruction of Russia's distinctiveness and the very foundations of its historical existence, casting all of its material and moral values into some sort of 'black hole'.[7] For leftist authors, the 'reforms' are a 'second edition' in Russia of an 'uneven and combined' capitalism – dependent, economically inefficient, politically authoritarian and ruinous for science and culture – that retains considerable elements of pre- and non-capitalist forms of economic activity. In a word, the 'reforms' by and large were a return to the type of social order that was characteristic of the Russian Empire before the Bolshevik revolution.[8]

The purpose of this chapter is not to evaluate critically these narratives for accuracy or theoretical soundness. My interest lies elsewhere. For all their diversity, these narratives have one feature in common: they lack a character that could be called the 'people'. In this case I use the notion of 'people' simply to describe the unprivileged mass of society. I have attempted to separate the term, as much as possible, from its own philosophical connotations in order to render 'people' amenable to translation into the language of applied sociology, while at the same time keeping consideration of the term focused on the range of problems revealed by philosophical inquiry. Those problems should not be 'forgotten' in even the most 'empirical' approaches to 'people'. The interplay of the philosophical and sociological components of the notion 'people' (which is important to understand whenever this notion is being used) will be considered in a separate section of this article ('digression') that follows directly after the introduction. For the time being, we will abide by the abovementioned, rather modest, definition of 'people'.

As noted, a character named the 'people' is practically absent from the historical accounts of modern Russia that seek to elucidate the country's path and meaning. More precisely, the majority of these works regard people as an object or material for manipulation by the elites. Changes in the life of the people reveal the operation of what could be called the 'laws of history', to use an old-fashioned term, or 'modernizing imperatives', if translated into today's newspeak.[9] The title of a book by the British historian Robert Service – *Russia: Experiment with a People* – captures the modality of 'people' in the majority of narratives on 'new Russia'.[10] It is only in rare cases that researchers shift the focus from elites and 'imperatives' to 'social history' or socio-cultural practices.[11] But this likewise devolves into speculation about poll respondents' 'attitudes' to certain aspects of the experiments being conducted on them – their commitment to certain 'values' and their 'assessments' of various institutions.[12] In other words, people remain the passive material of history, the only distinction being that they are now capable of conveying 'views' on what it has to endure. However, these views are of no consequence politically, because the very possibility of a liberal reformation of post-communist societies is predicated on the prevailing view – the 'majority' opinion by definition – *not* coming across in the process of political decision making.[13]

The 'absence of the people' (as anything other than material for experiments) from the narratives on Russia's post-communist transformation needs to be explained in theoretical and political terms. Analysing the whole of modern democratic theory – while it would be useful to understand the 'absence of the people'[14] – is beyond the scope of this article. Instead, I will focus on two points: first, the notions of the *temporal organization* of history that underlie, often unconsidered, the narratives on the Russian post-communist transformation and determine their *trajectory*; and second, the empirical reasons that make it impossible to detect the 'presence of the people' in the Russian transformation using standard methods of political science. These issues will be covered in the first part of this article.

The criticism contained in the following section 'A digression on the history of the concept "people"' is not an end in itself but a means of preparing the ground for a different way of viewing Russia's post-communist transformation – a view of history from below, from the point of view of the 'absent people', or what some historians call 'people's history'.[15] The second part of this chapter will shed light on the concept of 'people's history' and identify the theoretical and methodological aspects of applying this type of historical analysis to recent Russian history. For this we need to relate 'people's history' to the so-called 'event-based history' as opposed to 'teleological history' (determined by laws and 'imperatives' and oriented towards predetermined goals) or the 'history of great people' (or 'elites').

In the third section, I will attempt to show that the *content* of a people's history of post-communist Russia is primarily determined by finding out how the *capitalist* transformation of Soviet society was reflected in the everyday practices of 'ordinary people' and, conversely, how these changing practices influenced the form and function of macrostructures (economic, political and others) that came into being in the course of the 'reforms'. This approach shifts the investigative focus from 'democracy' and the 'market' to 'capitalism', and specifically to 'historical capitalism' as a 'concrete unique reality', to use Immanuel Wallerstein's dictum. This is distinct from the deductive definition of 'pure capitalism' that postulates and establishes its immutable essence.[16] Although this discussion lies beyond the scope of this chapter, it is quite possible that capitalism lacks such an essence and can be understood in its many manifestations only as different forms of embedding capital accumulation regimes in various socio-historical contexts. If so, democracy and the market – again, in their concrete forms – will appear as specific elements of the embedding of a particular capital accumulation regime in a particular socio-historical environment, that is as elements of Wallerstein's 'historical capitalism', whose importance varies depending on the context.

But this non- or anti-essentialist understanding of 'capitalism' requires a brief account of the nature of Soviet society whose capitalist transformation set into motion the dynamic interaction of macrostructures and microprocesses, an interaction forming the content of a people's history of post-communist Russia. Setting aside propagandistic clichés about 'totalitarianism' and the 'command-administrative system' on one hand, and about 'the planned economy' and the 'state of all people' on the other, the nature of Soviet society, particularly in the late Soviet era, is the *main riddle*. The lack of a solution to this riddle stands in the way of a theoretical understanding of the post-communist transformation. In fact, it is clear enough that capital accumulation and even overaccumulation was a defining feature, if not the driving force, of the Soviet economy and that the different types of markets (not only 'black' and 'grey' but also 'bureaucratic', used for exchanging even the means of production, among other things) were inalienable elements of the Soviet economy from the start. Nor can we doubt that a considerable part of the national product existed and circulated in commodity form; and that labour was mostly hired and showed all the signs of being 'alienated' and subordinated to capital as 'previously accumulated labour', as Marx described in relation to 'classical capitalism'. From this it follows that the USSR was a capitalist, or state-capitalist, society (despite its 'ideology' or possibly even owing to it), and that consequently there could be no *capitalist* transformation in the post-Soviet period. We can only speak about the natural swing of a pendulum from one mode of capital accumulation to another, from state capitalism to (mostly) private capitalism, not an epochal shift.[17] Contrary to this argument, I will try to show that the capitalist transformation of Soviet society was epochal if examined as 'people's history'.

A digression on the history of the concept 'people'

The concept of 'the people' is certainly a 'history laden' concept.[18] History is impressed upon it and cannot be ignored even in attempting to effect the concept's applied operationalization. On the contrary, in its applied use, 'people' should retain some traces of its former usage, if only for the sake of asking what the people of today is *not* and *what* it can become under different circumstances. It is for this reason that, even when using 'people' as a collective term to simply denote the unprivileged strata of society, I am not prepared to substitute seemingly more easily operationalized notions like 'the masses', 'the lower and middle strata', 'non-elite groups' and so on. Such notions are not similarly 'history laden' and, therefore, do not readily lend themselves to critical reflection on their contents.

The concept of 'people' in the grand political-philosophical tradition, which goes back to the early modern age, is firmly associated with unity, determined by the unity of the will, and therefore what in modern parlance is called agency ('the people', according to Hobbes, is the opposite of 'the masses' because the latter lack this unity and therefore agency).[19] But if in Hobbes this unity is predetermined by the subjection of private individuals to the sovereign (voluntary subjection based on a social contract), in Rousseau the same unity and agency is the result of the people's *self-constitution.* This means, literally, that everyone concludes a contract 'with oneself' and with others, thereby turning a conglomerate of private individuals into a political association, a 'body politic' or the People in the proper sense of the word.[20]

The sociological explication of 'the people', which means projecting the notion onto groups existing in a society and deciding which of them belong to 'the people', presented considerable difficulty even before the French revolution, which revealed the full tragic significance of this issue.[21] These problems led Charles Montesquieu, possibly the greatest Enlightenment 'sociologist', to what Louis Althusser called the differentiation of 'two peoples within a people' in an essay dedicated to the author of *The Spirit of the Laws*.[22] In fact, Montesquieu, in describing democracy, characterizes it as a regime under which 'power belongs *to the whole people*' while also noting the critical importance of 'how, by whom, for whom, and on what the voting is to be held' in a democracy.[23] As he analyses this problem (discovering in the process that a people cannot function politically – even for its own good – unless it is 'guided by a council or a senate'), Montesquieu comes to the conclusion that in a democracy everything depends on *how* 'the people are divided into certain classes' and what *rights* of democratic participation they are endowed with. This is the origin of the idea that 'the low people' (*bas-peuple*) should be excluded from 'the whole people' because their 'status is so low that they are regarded (*sic*!) as people incapable of having a will of their own'. This will cause no damage to democracy as the rule by the 'whole people': 'The whole people' as a philosophical concept simply comes to stand for the sociological result of 'the low people' being subtracted from 'the whole people'. This operation's political corollary is that 'under rule by the people, power should not be transmitted to the lower elements of the population'.[24] The theoretical conclusion is precisely Althusser's concept of 'two peoples within a people', that is the subtracted 'low people' and the remaining 'good people' that in the France of that time was represented by the bourgeoisie, and the identification of 'the whole people' with its 'good' part.[25]

During the French revolution, Montesquieu's divergent convergence of 'the whole people', or the universal, and the 'good part of the people', or the particular, transpired as a political formula of 'the people's party' (a term coined by Saint-Just), destroying 'the non-people', that is 'the King's party'.[26] Of course, there was a radical change in the *content* of the sociological reference of both 'the good people' and, in the sense described above, 'the whole people'. Ultimately, 'the low people', whom Montesquieu had subtracted from 'the whole people', have largely comprised 'the whole people', rather than the respectable bourgeoisie. During the stormy period of the Jacobin terror, however, this sociological content continued to change rapidly and *evaporate* as it did. What was left by July 1794 of the wise, kind, patriotic and virtuous 'people', 'the world's premiere people' (Maximilien Robespierre) created by the Revolution? If conspiracies, intrigues, betrayals, cliques and vices are all around, if 'the majority itself is paralyzed and deceived', if Robespierre admits in his last speech before his execution that 'the time has not yet come for decent people to serve their homeland with impunity', is there any recourse but to conclude that under these circumstances 'the people' shrunk to just several members of the Committee of Public Safety and was eventually beheaded on the scaffold along with them?[27] There is nothing absurd in this assumption if we follow the logic of the convergence of 'the whole people' and 'the good people'.

The scope of this article does not allow me to trace the further historical evolution of the concept 'people'. I will confine myself to an observation that the trajectories it followed were determined, wittingly or unwittingly, by the movement of that fundamental and ineradicable contradiction that I termed the divergence-convergence of the universality of 'the whole people' and the particularity of the 'good people'. The above is also typical of a series of theoretically and historically untenable attempts to retreat from this contradiction by cementing it in a perpetual unity of 'the people'.[28] I think there is no particular need to explain that the historical trajectories of the evolution of 'the people' and its philosophical and sociological metamorphoses reflected not just the competition and filiation of theoretical ideas but primarily the political conflict practices (differently conceptualized by philosophers and sociologists) in which certain social groups – successfully or otherwise in related historical situations – laid claim to being 'the people' and *in fact* conflated 'the whole people' with 'the good people'.[29] The evolution and historical transformations of 'the people' can be summed up as follows.[30]

1. A 'people' is always a constructed rather than an 'organic' or 'substantial' community. Hobbes and Rousseau already understood this much. More generally, this means that a 'people' comes into being (or does not in certain situations) as a product of historical practices and as 'the spontaneous distillation of a complex 'crossing' of discrete historical forces'.[31] In a narrower sense, this means that the construction of a 'people' always involves, in some way or other, 'figments of the imagination' of several social groups as well as those of individual ideologues and, as a subtype, what Jacques Derrida called 'fictions'. The latter have to be understood not as idle imagination, let alone deception, but as performative-contestatory statements on behalf of what is actually nonexistent but what is being brought into existence and asserted as an element of reality by these statements.[32] While stressing the creative force of these 'figments of imagination' and these 'fictions', we should beware of confusing 'discourse' with reality and of attributing to imagination and 'fictions' an independent capacity to change reality. A methodological antidote to this 'discourse idealism' can be found in a well-known Marxian formula: 'It is not enough for thought to strive for realization, reality must itself strive towards thought.'[33]
2. A 'people' is always 'imagined' as universal, as 'the whole people' (in contradistinction to a 'nation', which is always 'imagined' as limited, as something particular like other nations). Its universality, however, is *constituted by exclusion*, that is transforming a certain part of 'the whole people' into 'the non-people'. It is only through this opposition-exclusion that it is possible to mark the limits of the universal 'whole people'. Thus it can acquire (as long as this opposition-exclusion is *effective*) political agency and achieve the practical resolution of the logically impossible paradox of the identification of the universal and the particular, of the whole and its part, of 'the whole people' and 'the good people' (although this is precisely what dialectic logic does).
3. In the modern political imagination, a 'people' is the sovereign, even when it has no real agency and becomes dissolved in depoliticized conglomerates, such as 'populations' or 'electorates'. In other words, a 'people' is *constantly present* in contemporary political life as 'the whole people' and 'unity', which fact is not only enshrined in crucial political and legal documents but is also present as an organizing principle of its most important practices (such as electing its representatives and thus filling the respective bodies of governance). To be sure, this presence is neither chimerical nor deceptive, even if Schumpeter's conclusion regarding the people's inability to rule under modern democracy (see footnote 14) is true. This is the real presence of the politically *significant* 'empty signifier' that *is still capable* of 'filling' itself with the sociologically tangible 'signified' in the form of certain concrete social groups and their coalitions.[34] This real opportunity (whose realization, of course, by no means is guaranteed) will drop out of our field of vision, if in our search for concepts that can be operationalized more easily in applied research we discard the term 'the people' in favour of something like 'the masses', 'the lower and middle strata' and so on.

4 When a 'people' lacks real political agency and exists in reality only as an 'empty signifier', the focus of research tends to be on identifying the conditions of its existence and the activity of social groups, which we *can expect* to turn into the people-as-agency filling an 'empty signifier'. Of course, this expectation is nothing more than a hypothesis of ours and its only basis in reality is the observed lines of tension between different social groups, which potentially might be transformed into divisions between 'the people' and 'the non-people', with both likely to later acquire political agency. (Since 'being the people' has a considerable legitimizing value, the right to 'be the people' is prone to be contended for, and sides to the conflict will seek to exclude each other from the 'people' as 'the non-people'. During the French revolution, not only the Parisian revolutionaries but also the Catholic and Royal Army of Vendée claimed the right to 'be the people'.) Moreover, it is important to understand which particular lines of tension will lead to divisions between the people and 'the non-people', for this directly determines the moral and political quality of the resultant people. For example, from 31% of the 'poor' to 38% of the 'non-poor' in today's Russia believe that the most important fissure dividing Russian society is that between Russians and non-Russians, whereas only 26% and 27%, respectively, see it as the divide between oligarchs and the rest of the public.[35] Is not this a reason to suppose that a *Völkisch* type of a 'people' with a potential for radical right-wing action is more likely to emerge in Russia than a 'people' with a more democratic leaning toward social justice?

The absence of the people

The 'absence of the people' is the result of empirical observations intertwined with a particular theoretical framework and a specific understanding of how history is organized. Let us start with the former. It is a well-known fact that political activism in Russia declined markedly after the failed coup in August 1991 and particularly after the commencement of the liberal reforms in 1992. This trend was interrupted by several upsurges of protests, including before and during the bloody events of October 1993, the financial catastrophe in 1998 and the 2008 crisis, as well as following the parliamentary elections in 2011, which many people believed to be rigged and undemocratic. However, long-term sociological surveys and political statistics point to the overall stability of this trend.[36] Compared with the early 1990s, fewer Russians believe that mass protests against falling living standards and violations of their rights in their city/region are possible and fewer still would be willing to join such protests.[37] Russia, it must be acknowledged, experiences astonishingly little political turmoil[38] given the scale and acuteness of the economic, political and everyday problems confronting ordinary Russians, their low – by European standards – quality of life, and the enormous gap between rich and poor.

Protests are not the only form of political participation that has petered out. All the institutional channels and forms of political engagement – political parties, trade unions, civil society organizations – look inefficient, feeble, devoid of a solid social base (with the exception, perhaps, of the Communist Party of the Russian Federation, CPRF), or thoroughly bureaucratized (like United Russia or the Federation of Independent Trade Unions). The ascendancy of a political and civil society expected at the start of Russia's post-communist transformation has not occurred, to say the least. The interest in politics *as such* is so low that Russian society can be described as fundamentally *depoliticized*.[39] Moreover, it looks like Russians themselves identify 'power' with the 'great people' in power ('personalization of authority') and, to a lesser extent, with 'institutions' (like the presidential administration, law enforcement, parliament, etc.) rather than with 'the people'.[40]

All of this shapes the view – an absolutely legitimate one by the standards of mainstream political science – that the people, save for ritualistically coming to the polls from time to time, stay out of politics, that politics is a business for the elites, and that government institutions, including the legislature, are just mechanisms for elites to manipulate 'their' people. It is this view that creates optics which preclude the possibility of a perspective on public life 'from below'.

Of course, a very important question is what caused that depoliticization and what explains the limited scope of popular movements in Russia, which are typical (or were until recently) of 'normal' capitalist societies, such as the workers' movement in the first place but also women's organizations, peasant and farmers' associations, cooperatives, religious-political movements of different stripes (with radical Islamism being perhaps the only exception)? The most general answer would be lack of faith that an alternative to the status quo is feasible or even conceivable. This lack of faith is the consequence of twin historical traumas: the disappointment of socialism and the collapse (in Eastern and Central Europe) of socialist regimes, on the one hand, and the establishment of the (seemingly) indivisible and indisputable dominance of neo-liberal global capitalism, on the other. Does it make sense to act if there is no alternative? And conversely: If there is no alternative, the hardships and disorder of our life are *natural*. How can you rebel against what is natural?[41]

A more concrete approach might point to the conformism and 'acceptance of capitalism' of trade union leaders and heads of other popular organizations, and people's ill-formed understanding of their specific (class and other) interests due primarily to their limited experience with the market, the legacy of 'real socialism' that emphasized the 'unity of society' and thereby prevented the emergence of group identities and group consciousness, and so on.[42] There is certainly some truth in these explanations. But the fact that they remain at the level of consciousness and ideology, as 'Western Marxism' did in attempting to explain why there was no explosion of proletarian revolutions in the West, should give us pause. Such explanations again fail to reach the level of everyday practices of popular life, practices that determine the people's *non-participation* in the formal and institutionalized sphere of politics created by the post-communist transformation (the formal sphere being synonymous with politics as such in a view of Russia 'from above'). Likewise, they are unable to shed light on how the people *do* influence what is going on in the formal sphere of politics despite, or because of, their non-involvement in it. To be sure, this influence is communicated via channels that official politics and its ideological reflections and underpinnings (e.g. political science) do not recognize as 'political' and, therefore, fail to conceptualize. But the presence of the 'absent people' can only be discovered by examining these practices and their influence on 'official politics'.

As mentioned, the 'absence of the people' is a function of a certain kind of empirical observation of Russia's political life *and* certain methodological frameworks, including the principle of organizing a narrative based on the 'logic of history', characteristic of many accounts of the 'new Russia'. In keeping with these frameworks and principles, history is organized according to the logic of what William H. Sewell, Jr. called 'teleological and experimental temporality'.[43] 'Teleological temporality' means that phenomena and processes under study are treated as instances of a movement towards a preset goal or as impediments to this movement. 'Experimental temporality' reduces real historical causality, which always includes the 'accidental', the 'reverse', discontinuity, and a selective attitude to the past and to the future forming the changing meanings of both of them, to pure logic operating applying the *timeless* formula 'if *X* then *Y*'.[44] Properly speaking, historical time in this case is reduced to an 'empirical' manifestation of timeless logic.

In many 'teleological' narratives of the 'new Russia', the 'market' and 'democracy' usually appear as *the* goals Russia should strive after. The corresponding 'experimental temporality', as it manifests itself in theoretical tracts as well as in reform programmes ('shock therapy') and specific political decisions, roughly speaking boils down to the following cause-effect connections between *X*s and *Y*s. If we deregulate/liberalize prices (*X*), we will get the market (*Y*); if we privatize public assets, we will get an 'efficient economy' (and its social accompaniments, such as a 'middle class' and a 'responsible proprietor'); if we eliminate the Communist Party's monopoly on power, we will get a vibrant democratic political system and 'civil society'. These views were attacked from different perspectives. We, for our part, will approach them only from the angle of their teleology.

I can hardly imagine a single theorist or practitioner of liberal reforms in the entire post-communist world who would subscribe to the Aristotelian concept of teleological causality. But if, as implied by teleology, a goal is unable to *cause* – that is, to literally 'drag towards itself' the object for which it is the goal as the result of the object's immanent striving toward it – then why *should* Russia or any other country become a 'market' and a 'democracy' at all? If a goal *does not cause*, then *what* is it that determines the object's movement along the trajectory leading to this goal? After all, we cannot seriously assume that the late-Soviet society possessed an immanent teleological striving for the market and democracy, as liberal theorists perceive them. Anyway, such an assumption would have been incompatible with the deepest convictions held by such theorists (and executors of liberal 'reforms') concerning the nature of the system they condemned and set out to 'reform'.

Absent the metaphysics of the Aristotelian teleological causality, there has not been, is not, and cannot be *theoretical* answers to the above questions about why and in what sense the 'market' and 'democracy' should be Russia's goals. The answers can be either entirely dogmatic or entirely empirical, if you will. The dogmatic answer boils down to establishing a dichotomy between the market and the planned economy (by analogy, between democracy and totalitarianism), which is meant to make us think that we are left with an inescapable either–or choice between them. Accordingly, if we move away from a planned economy (totalitarianism), we necessarily move towards the market (democracy). It is at this point that the logic of 'experimental temporality' comes into play. It is hardly necessary to argue that this dogmatic position is untenable. History has known nothing other than different combinations of the 'plan' and the 'market' (the USSR was one such combination) and there is no teleological reason or any other form of predetermination behind movements from one combination to another.[45]

The empirical answer is even simpler: The market and democracy are our goals *because* 'they', that is the 'civilized world', have them. According to this logic, it is the *imitation* that sets the 'ought' rather than any theoretically meaningful definition of the 'market' and 'democracy' as our goals. Indeed, not only do the 'market' and 'democracy' currently come in various forms in the 'civilized world', they have also metamorphosed throughout history.[46] If, therefore, we are still to consider (one or another version of) the 'market' and 'democracy' to be our goals, rather than a slavish imitation of what just happens to be somewhere to the west of Russian borders, it will be necessary to answer several questions that the 'reformers' never even posed. Which particular historical and organizational model of market (and democracy) do we want to reproduce? Why does precisely this model suit Russia best? Which potentialities inherent in Russia's economy and culture will this model help actualize? The logic of imitation, on the contrary, renders these questions superfluous. In plain terms, it means the following: meet the requirements of the *acquis communautaire*, then the status of 'modern capitalist democratic state' will be conferred on you.[47] The embarrassing and difficult questions raised by the left *and* right critics of the status quo across Europe, such as in what measure, on what grounds, in what theoretical frameworks and so on, the European Union's own practices can be regarded as 'capitalist' and 'democratic', are also ignored. What else but the imperious might of the ideological, political and economic hegemony of the centres of global capitalism make it possible to ignore them?[48]

The non-Aristotelian 'teleological temporality' of the post-communist transformation is, in fact, a tremendous social engineering venture. We can also call it a 'revolution from above'.[49] A classical teleology of history, such as Hegelian, instrumentalizes human beings and their activities, reducing them to the moments and means of the 'providential plan' of history. It is, however, more democratic than the social engineering teleology of post-communism because it instrumentalizes not only 'ordinary people' but also 'historic personalities' (they are the first to be *used* by the Spirit in its self-motion, which usually is done cruelly, with these personalities forced to exist 'beyond good and evil' and often meeting with a tragic end). In the post-communist teleology, insofar as it lacks a 'providential plan', the 'great people' and the elites are the creators (or the transmitters of such 'laws' that come from their real sources like the IMF, the European Commission, and the like), not disposable executors, of the 'laws of history' and only the people are a means.[50] The people were urged to repent (of the 'original sin' of their Soviet background and generally 'of being corrupted by socialism'), to become purged (of the filth of old habits), and to accept spiritual renewal (in order to 'blend in' with the grandiose plans of the 'reformers'). Moreover, it was assumed from the outset that far from all would make the mark, something that was imposing on society a new divide between the 'deadweight' and the 'creative classes'.[51] This is the modern post-communist subtraction of 'the non-people' from 'the people' (see the corresponding paragraph in the 'Digression') as carried out by today's wielders of power and wealth. To be sure, the calls for repentance, the accusations of 'moral depravity' (caused by the 'ineradicable' traces of Sovietism), and appeals for purification do not apply to the elites and the new 'masters of the land' themselves, who, almost in the spirit of Calvinist predestination, were redeemed from the socialist filth 'from eternity to eternity'.

No type of teleology needs a living and concrete people. Any teleology reduces this living plurality to an abstraction, be it the Hegelian '*Volksgeist*', or 'population', 'labour resources', and 'electorate' – the last being more characteristic of the social engineering teleology of the post-communist transformation.[52] Moreover, this teleological presentation of the people as a functionalized abstraction is not a worthless figment, nor philosophical or transitological nonsense that should only be denounced in theoretical criticism. No, it quite accurately reflects the *real* political economy of dominance that reduces the people – to the extent to which it 'works' efficiently – to the role of material and tool of the 'laws of history' (ditto the laws of consolidated dominance systems) and the plans conceived by the 'great men'. The *validity* of the teleological presentation is confirmed empirically by the observations concerning the 'absence of the people' in politics we mentioned earlier. But the question is whether this is the whole truth. Is there not an element of the political economy of dominance, which is not represented in and by the teleological representations of that political economy of dominance? Is there not an element which is the inverse of dominance but at the same time its *sine qua non*, so that dominance is as incomprehensible without it as love is without hate or action without counteraction or peace without war? Will we not discover in this unrepresented element the presence of the people, which could not, in principle, be identified through observation of the existing and consolidated products of dominance, such as the institutionalized sphere of politics or existing market mechanisms?

The presence of the 'absent people': general remarks

The people's presence begins to reveal itself once we ask a seemingly naive question: Why do the elites have to act at all? This is indeed a difficult question to answer if we dismiss the patently apologetic claims that they selflessly serve the people, the common good, or 'modernizing imperatives'. To proceed further, it would definitely be helpful to furnish ourselves with David Hume's healthily cynical 'political maxim' – 'in contriving any system of government and fixing the several checks and controls of the constitution, every man ought to be supposed a *knave* and to have no other end, in all his actions, than private interest'.[53] The private interests of the elite 'knaves' are most immediately served by the preservation of what Richard Lachmann calls their 'organizational autonomy' and 'exploitative relationship' with non-elites.[54] Why does this enterprise of 'preservation' involve so much arduous and oftentimes perilous activity, which may include carrying out dramatic structural reforms, implementing contentious social policies, venturing in uncertain and potentially high-risk integration processes, and so on?

Once again, apologetics – represented this time by the ideology of 'representative democracy' – offer us an easy and ready answer. Let the elites be selfishly concerned with preserving their dominance, but in a situation when they have to compete for votes they will be able to preserve it only by answering the needs of the majority of the electorate. The implication is that in order to preserve their 'organizational autonomy' and reproduce their 'exploitative relationship' with non-elites, elites are compelled to satisfy certain needs of certain politically influential groups of people and thereby limit and relativize both the 'autonomy' and the 'exploitative relationship'.

The real picture is certainly much more complex than this ideological cliché. The really difficult question is, to what extent voter 'demand' is 'rational' and independent of the elite 'supply' (analogous to the 'rationality' and autonomy of demand relative to supply in the economy). Of course, empirical observations performed in functional democracies demonstrate that 'when a majority of citizens disagrees with economic elites and/or with organized interests, they generally lose'.[55] One 'big issue' that determines the very existence of the political and economic system is that (supposedly) rival elites act in unison without considering the views of the electorate, as was clearly demonstrated by both the Republican and Democratic administrations in the 2008–2009 financial crisis, when it became necessary to save the bankrupt US financial behemoths. Of course, democracy is powerless to change the most unfavourable trends affecting the masses of voters, if these trends are determined by the operation of the fundamental mechanisms of capitalist evolution. To grasp what this means in reality, one can look at the four-decade deepening of the gulf between the rich and the poor in nearly all OECD countries, the wage stagnation of fully employed American males that has persisted since 1973, or the explosion in household debt.[56] We can even view representative democracy, in the spirit of left-wing criticism, as an efficient mechanism for co-opting the popular masses into the political economy of bourgeois society.[57] Yet they *are* able to use it, albeit to a limited extent, in order to bring pressure to bear on the upper strata and achieve at least some of their goals.

It is clear that one of the elites' most important activities is co-optation of the lower strata, a specific technique of which is representative democracy. But *why* should elites engage in these and other types of activities aimed at 'mediating' and 'harmonizing' relations between social groups and classes in order to maintain the 'integrity' of modern bourgeois society? (These include the juridification of societal relations through and by the law, under which 'all are equal'; social protection of 'the weak'; the shifting and redirecting of social conflicts and divisions from areas where explosions would threaten the status quo to safer areas; the extraction by taxation and other methods of 'additional surplus labour' over and above what is extracted through the direct labour–capital relationship, etc.).[58] The episodic incursions of the lower strata into the sphere of 'official' politics, such as industrial actions and massive demonstrations, let alone more radical and open forms of disobedience and resistance, are relatively infrequent and in themselves can hardly explain the elites' relentless and indefatigable efforts to maintain the 'integrity' of modern society in all the ways laid out above. Moreover, the episodes of direct political protest by the lower strata evidence the failures and setbacks in the elites' continuous labours to integrate society and 'debug' its functional ties.[59]

Open protests, however, are but visible political splashes of the magma simmering beneath the surface of official political life and uncontained by society's formal institutions. Unsurprisingly, it normally falls outside the scope of sociological and political observation. Generally, the formal political institutions are suitable for channelling the activities of those strata that possess sufficient material, organizational and cultural resources and skills to express themselves in this way, that is for the elites and, to a certain extent, the middle class. In some societies such strata are, needless to say, more numerous than in others. In post-communist Russia, they comprise the tip of the iceberg. It is difficult for the lower, working strata to cross the resource and skill threshold and enter the sphere of formal politics; their protest activities *typically* take place outside of its framework, in the sphere of informal relations,[60] and predominately at the level that Vaclav Havel described as 'pre-political'.[61] Besides, the protests of the lower strata are customarily very prosaic. They are not motivated by 'principles' or sparked by 'ideology'; they are directed at resolving some concrete 'issues' affecting people's everyday life and usually expressed in 'malfunctioning' of the *existing* order; they are directed at known 'culprits' rather than abstractions like the 'bourgeoisie' or 'partocracy', 'capitalism' or 'totalitarianism'. As a result, they are generally anything but revolutionary and their aims could fit easily into the logic of the status quo, provided there are some slight improvements. Eric Hobsbawm aptly noted that these kinds of protests intend to minimize the damage inflicted on 'ordinary people' by the status quo; they do not demonstrate a desire to blow up the existing order.[62] The path from these protests – which originate in the undercurrents of everyday life and could be more accurately called *resistance to injustices* (or what is perceived as such) – to overt actions in the sphere of formal politics is long, arduous, uncertain and dependent on many 'contingencies'. This means that it is not determined by any essences (be it the essence of this particular social order, class struggle, 'modernization', or anything else).[63]

The causes of resistance are as innumerable and 'trivial' as the forms in which they manifest themselves. Such causes could be low pay and arrogance of superiors, 'excessive' fines and the master's encroachments on 'legitimate' leisure, 'exorbitant' performance demands and deteriorating sanitary conditions, imposed conformism and inadequate housing, and so on and so forth. The forms of resistance might include (pretended) obtuseness and lack of initiative, 'work-to-rule' and dissimulation, mismanagement and pilfering, folklore of mocking 'higher-ups' and withdrawing within oneself or one's inner circle. Each of these acts of resistance per se is negligible. In their totality, they determine society's key political and economic parameters as well as the volumes, conditions and forms of social wealth generation and distribution. James Scott offers this take in his brilliant description of acts of peasant resistance: 'Everyday forms of resistance make no headlines. But just as millions of anthozoan polyps create, willy-nilly, a coral reef, so do the multiple acts of peasant insubordination and evasion create political and economic barrier reefs of their own. It is largely in this fashion that the peasantry makes its political presence felt. And whenever, to pursue the simile, the ship of state runs aground on such reefs, attention is usually directed to the shipwreck itself and not to the vast aggregation of petty acts that made it possible.' Understanding this fact explains the reasons of the collapse of the state.[64]

The presence of the people remains invisible as long as social life is observed from above and humans are treated as the material for social engineering experiments. It reveals itself precisely in the connection between macro-structural changes (such as the collapse of the state, which is just a specific 'case' thereof) and micro-processes (of everyday life and resistances typical of it).[65] From the point of view of the upper strata, overcoming the 'rigidity' of the material is what drives the elites to engage in their incessant labours described earlier. What is demanded from the unyielding popular material involves something more than the lower strata's 'acceptance' of the existing order (or of the ways in which it is modified by the 'reforming' elites). In principle, it is possible to obtain this 'acceptance' by means of overtly repressive methods, possibly accompanied by ideological brainwashing, that is, by something that vulgar theories portray as the trademark of 'totalitarianism'. But what has to be more importantly exacted from a people, what the viability of each society depends on is more than its mere 'acceptance'. A people *must* invest itself in the perpetuation of a society in question. The last task is of particular importance for the elites and presents the greatest difficulty, for which reason they sometimes have to compromise even on the purity of their 'autonomy' or, which is the same, on the consistency and thoroughgoingness of their 'reform' policies.

As to the transition from the 'invisible' and informal practices of resistance to an open revolt, it cannot and should not be looked at through the prism of 'ought'. In the normative sense, *a people owes nothing to anyone*: a people has no obligation before the avant-garde revolutionaries to flock into the battalions capable of 'storming the skies', nor does it have any duty to supply a sufficient contingent of compliant, brainy and deferential Fridays for the dominant capitalist or bureaucratic Robinson Crusoes. The dictates of duty are a classical gesture and means of imposing or reproducing dominance, which Arthur Schopenhauer sagaciously discerned even in its most refined form of Kant's moral theory of duty, which he aptly described as 'slavish'.[66] Confidence in the people's sound judgment as to *what* is better for it in different situations is the only possible *democratic* stance an intellectual can adopt both in his/her research and in his/her practical involvement in political life. A people may choose to 'storm the skies', or to become Fridays or, what happens most often and without taking any explicit decisions, to imperceptibly form the 'reef' on which, to use James Scott's simile, its masters' dominance will eventually run aground. It only remains to be said that in the larger scheme of things, the course of history and its dramatic twists and turns, whose visible markers are precisely the 'sky storming' and the emergence of new contingents of Fridays, are nevertheless determined by the invisible consolidation of 'reefs' of popular resistances.

The presence of 'the absent people' in the post-communist transformation

Visualizing the post-communist transformation as a transition from plan to market, or from totalitarianism to democracy, means playing a hypostasizing game, in which abstract notions and ideas are objectified and given an independent existence. Of course, such ideas do not simply 'conceal' real practices, as vulgar theories depict the operation of 'ideology'. Ideas, including those mentioned above, do participate in the formation of reality, if only in the sense of Max Weber's interpretation: 'Not ideas, but material and ideal interests directly govern men's conduct. Yet very frequently the "world images" that have been created by "ideas" have, like switchmen, determined the tracks along which action has been pushed by the dynamic of interest'.[67] But what this means is that we should abandon the speculations about the transition from plan to market and its 'distortions' and engage in an analysis of the concrete practices of the so-called reform process in which different strategies pursued by different actors clash, intersect, combine and resonate. 'Ideas' the actors adhere to, whatever they can be, do play their roles in shaping such strategies and thereby do contribute to 'determining the tracks' along which a society in question proceeds. In this case, both the market and democracy (as well as the planned economy and totalitarianism) will appear not as hypostasized entities but as concrete networks of interactions maintained by concrete agents. A specific, 'context-dependent' structure of such networks has to be uncovered as well as a trajectory of their evolution. Particular attention should be paid to how such networks form the respective types of 'rationality' of the individuals involved in them (their 'calculating competences'), as well to how those individuals define 'competition' and to what they mean by it (to how they specify its limits, forms, terms and the very social entities to which it can extend). Given this approach, we cannot speak about universal laws of the market (or democracy), nor, consequently, about 'transitional economies' that are perceived to be in the process of 'implementing' these laws but so far have not attained this perfectly.[68] Of course, this does not mean that we deny the existence of certain parallels in how markets (and democracy) change and function in the modern world. However, they are explained not by the immanent laws of the market (and democracy) in general, but by the global domination of certain organizational types of markets (and democracies) sustained by the power of concrete nations, their alliances and international organizations responsible for relevant policies (US, EU, IMF, etc.).[69]

So what are the strategies of the main actors of the post-communist transformation, whom we have designated as the people and the elites?[70] To answer this question, we must take a closer look at the political economy of the *ancien régime*, or the old Soviet system, in order to see how it shaped relations between the people and the elites and to understand the logic of its transformation after the collapse of the USSR.

Despite the persistent difficulty in providing a clear-cut sociological description of the USSR's dominant class known as the *nomenklatura*, there is no doubt that the political economy of Soviet society was based on this class alienating the surplus product turned out by the working people. It was also organized around capital accumulation and reproduced the main forms of inequality and submission that are characteristic of capitalist societies. Simultaneously, many Soviet labour control methods were cruder and less efficient than those typical of 'normal' capitalism, to say nothing about the barbarous oppression of the peasantry and their forced 'bond-service' (eased only in 1974, when internal passports were issued to collective farmers). The same goes for the mass exploitation of the prison population, particularly during the time of the Gulag system. Under these conditions, the working people's reaction involved the same forms of 'concealed' resistance, ranging from apathy and sluggishness to pilfering, which are well known from antagonistic forms of economy in general (see note 64). There is every reason to believe that the resistance was even more pervasive, recalcitrant and economically noxious in the USSR than under 'normal' capitalism. Partly this was due to the impossibility of open forms of political protest, and partly to the fact that the disciplining mechanisms of the market and the 'law of value' were seriously constrained in the Soviet environment (as will be discussed later).

It would hardly be an exaggeration to say that the string of economic reforms, carried out nearly continuously in the USSR since the 1960s without ever reaching their goal, were, in the final analysis, aimed at solving the *systemic politico-economic problem* of relations between the world of labour and the *nomenklatura*. The microeconomic problems, such as organizational inefficiencies, technological decline, economic disincentives and so on, highlighted by the official explanations of such reforms, were for the most part the consequences and symptoms of the insolubility of the aforesaid systemic problem.[71] Without resolving the core political economy problem, any microeconomic or technological successes proved at best palliatives incapable of saving the country from the plagues of (relatively) low labour productivity, mismanagement, pilfering of 'socialist property' and much more.

But Soviet society was not 'capitalist'. Nor was it 'authoritarian capitalist', if by this we want to underscore its salient *political* distinctions from those societies which are classified as 'democratic capitalist'.[72] Soviet society was 'dual'. I am modelling the 'duality' of Soviet society on the concept of 'duality' Otto

Kirchheimer used to describe the contradictory character of the Nazi party following its accession to power in Germany. On the one hand, it was undoubtedly a tool of bureaucratic domination over the masses (and a means to keep the format of this domination from dissolving into conflicting 'special interests'). On the other hand, it was a successor to a broad-based party of the period of its struggle for power. As such, the ruling Nazi party retained a number of its organizational characteristics and ideological commitments determined by its past, and had to address at least the economic concerns of its numerous supporters and followers to some extent.[73]

The 'duality' of Soviet society stems from the combination of oppression and 'the legacy of October' (the October Revolution), which the authorities never quite reduced just to the ritualistic legitimization of the status quo. The working class had never been the 'hegemon' or 'the leading force', but its 'socialist primogeniture' appeared as something more than just a cynical figure of speech employed by its oppressors. In the politico-economic sense, labour's immunities and securities, as expressed in the absence of unemployment and the set of universal social rights, meant that the working person was never reduced to the abstraction of 'personification of workforce', which is the key condition of capital accumulation in the specific capitalist sense of the term. Correlated to this is, of course, the fact that labour's antagonist had never been the abstraction of 'personified capital', something that accounts for the main difficulty in providing a clear-cut sociological description of the dominant Soviet groups. The relations between the oppressors and the oppressed, the working people and the 'higher-ups', therefore, had never reached the level of *universality* conveyed by the term 'capital', denoting universal, necessary and *abstract* (in the sense of the Hegelian 'real abstraction') ties between people. On the contrary, in the Soviet milieu these relations were decidedly *particularistic*, meaning by this that they were the relations between people in their *specific* political, ideological, administrative and other roles.

The particularistic nature of these relations was responsible for the ease with which they transformed into interpersonal relations – their 'informalization', if you will. Not only did this cause the widespread proliferation of networks of informal relations, but also their integration into the formal structures and their ultimate replacement by the former. (For a brilliant description of this process, read Alena Ledeneva's book on *blat*.[74]) Meanwhile, although Soviet leaders were obsessed with capital accumulation, it never turned into a self-referential system of *autopoesis* (as Niklas Luhmann would say), or 'production for the sake of production' (the production of capital, of course, not its concrete material carriers). In the USSR, capital accumulation did not distinguish itself from its social environment in recurrent acts of abstraction, which would have constituted both capital as *autopoetic* system and its own environment. It is in this way that 'normal' capital-as-value abstracts itself from all of its materializations, whether in production factors or in the use-values of commodities. On the contrary, certain particularistic aims dictated by the environment (or, more precisely, by how the *nomenklatura* interpreted that environment) always trumped the logic of 'production for the sake of production'. At different stages in history, such particularistic aims included 'building socialism in one single country' and the defence of the 'besieged fortress of socialism' from the imperialist encirclement, Khrushchev's unwritten 'social contract' with the people during the 'thaw', the notorious stability of 'stagnation' under Brezhnev, and so on. In any case, capital accumulation – at times ruthlessly achieved through terror – has never followed its 'immanent logic', has never been something 'self-propelling' and, ideologically speaking, 'self-explaining' and, therefore, has never been, strictly speaking, 'capitalist' accumulation.

The regime's duality, combining oppression with the 'legacy of October', made the position of the *nomenklatura* as the dominant class inherently contradictory and 'unsecured'. The very material basis of its domination, the so-called 'people's property', was the embodiment of the main contradiction in Soviet society. Leaving aside the fact that it blocked private capitalization of income (whatever form it was created in), the degree and the forms of the protection of labour implied by 'the property of all people' made labour's resistances that much easier, drastically restricting the chances of its exploitation, or, if you will, of 'the rational utilization of 'human capital'.[75] It also dramatically circumscribed the social space where capital accumulation could take place at all, pushing to the outside the entire so-called social sphere (education, healthcare, many types of leisure etc.) as well as practically the whole of real estate and land. No matter how ruthlessly the Soviet elites oppressed the people in certain historical periods, in their role of 'masters' they were hamstrung by a number of obligations to the people that were dictated by the legitimizing role of the 'legacy of October'. Ironically, the same 'legacy' served as the justification of their predominance and of the very existence of 'people's property' as its material foundation.[76]

The post-communist transformation was a project designed to remove the duality of Soviet society by annihilating the 'legacy of October'. The decisive damage to its legitimizing role was done during *perestroika.*[77] A set of new ideological constructs, such as 'democracy', 'universal human values' and 'entering the common European home', supplanted the 'legacy of October' as the foundations of legitimacy of the ruling elites. That much was achieved at an early stage in the transformation. Later those constructs were replaced by the great-power spirit, nationalism and the uniqueness of Russian (Eurasian) civilization. The material component of the 'legacy of October' was wiped out by a series of 'market' reforms. Hyperinflation essentially expropriated working people's savings, leaving them literally at the winners' mercy. Dismantling the Soviet version of the 'welfare state' has taken longer and is being completed right now with reforms/commercialization of public education, healthcare and the housing and utilities sector.[78] Still earlier, businesses 'dumped' their 'social infrastructure' (sanatoria, clubs, sports facilities, health centres, subsidized canteens etc.), which had made a sizable contribution to working people's 'social wages' in the Soviet period.[79] Finally, the privatization of the 'people's property' created an 'expropriated' proletariat in the proper sense of the word and as the abstraction of 'personification workforce', on the one hand,

and the masters personifying capital, on the other. ('People's capitalism' of the voucher privatization period was certainly an ideology in the most primitive sense of the word, that is, it was good for nothing, except for concealment and misrepresentation of reality).

Many observers rate the results of the project of the elimination of the duality of Soviet society extremely low. Writers describe them in the categories of the criminal and predatory form of Russian capitalism and of the kleptocratic regime, which has taken root in Russia. The regime has failed to guarantee the main rights and freedoms, including the right of private property. The Russian economy is becoming increasingly backward and turning into a mere supplier of raw materials for the centres of world capitalism. There are growing authoritarian trends in internal politics and a widening rift between the impoverished many and the affluent few. The list of Russia's maladies and failures can be continued and it is increasingly difficult to write them off as just the collateral damages of the otherwise benign process of transition. They look more and more like elements of the existing system's *modus operandi*. Unsurprisingly, a tendency has appeared to promote theories that look to history to explain Russia's current woes. Such theories emphasize something called the 'Russian "cultural code"' that 'is constantly pushing Russia into a revolution only to recreate a modernized copy of the political regime that was destroyed by the revolution . . . '. In this reading, the new Russia embodies the 'old Soviet past' and its future is certain to be 'Soviet' as well.[80] To express the idea in a better 'academic' fashion, '[t]he institutional solutions that emerged in distant Muscovy have been reproduced over time. . . . For all their outward appearances of radical departure, in a more fundamental institutional sense the Yeltsin and Putin regimes have been manifestations of deep-rooted continuity rather than change'. This is what is known as 'path dependence', which determines the recurrent reproduction of such phenomena as unaccountability of authorities, mutual cover-up, clientelism, nepotism and the like.[81]

'Path dependence' becomes yet another hypostatized concept unless it is translated into practices and strategies of concrete actors in concrete historical situations. In our case, this situation involves the dismantling of Soviet society's duality. In this situation, the practices and strategies of the elites and their liberal-intellectual allies were determined by the goal of capitalizing (and multiplying) the resources at their disposal. At the same time, their strategies were shaped by two important facts. First, the resources at their disposal were limited and unreliable due to the dramatic decline in the state's capacity to the point where it started to resemble a 'failed state'. Second, there was no chance to legitimate the project of 'capitalizing Russia' in the eyes of the great majority of its population.[82] At the same time, popular practices and strategies seek to offset, at least in some measure, the damage done to the security, status and relative prosperity ensured in the past by the 'legacy of October'.[83] These include concealed 'sabotage' and the creation of informal self-support networks. For their efficiency, both need to be 'hidden' from official observations. They should stay beyond the formal institutions' reach.

Under these circumstances, is there any need for the invariable 'Russian cultural codes' or the 'legacy of Muscovy' to explain the fact that the developments follow anything but the scenarios copied from the (ideologically dissected and 'sublimated') Western path to a modern society? After all, the actual logic of Russia's post-communist transformation is the *opposite* of what guided the progress of the sociologically representative West over the last two centuries. While what characterizes the latter is the *universalization* and *expansion* of the content of rights, with social rights gradually supplementing and enriching the freedoms and possibilities enshrined in political and civil rights (at any rate, until the recent 'neoconservative revolution' and the rise of financialized capitalism), the post-communist transformation in Russia implements the opposite logic.[84] What determines it is precisely the *particularization* and *contraction* of rights and their conversion into privileges that can be enjoyed by some or other groups under certain conditions and their *dilution* as regards the amount and quality of benefits guaranteed by these rights.[85]

Is it in any way surprising, then, that in the context of the post-communist transformation, networks of informal relations – far from shrinking relative to the Soviet period – have, on the contrary, proliferated both 'at the top' and 'at the bottom', with all the ensuing consequences for the economic and political-legal modernization prescribed by Russian liberals?[86] But how else can the elites exercise power and capitalize their incomes, given the country's uniformly unreliable and ineffective government institutions, unless they organize their own informal networks inaccessible to outsiders?[87] How can the people survive in Russia's post-communist environment without the informal economy producing about 40% of national GDP?[88] Why, finally, should all these survival strategies obey the capitalist logic of capital accumulation? Why should not being *excluded* from capitalist development or being pressed down by this development lead to the emergence of non-capitalist forms of economic activity and exchange, which are the proper products of this development and offshoots of its own contradictions in the current historical situation, rather than 'unprocessed' relics of the past?[89] What Lenin described as 'multistructurality' with regard to a different epoch seems to be manifesting itself as an essential characteristic of the *necessarily* 'wrong' post-communist transformation of Russia.

The particular dynamics and specific form of modern Russian capitalism and, accordingly, its political, cultural and ideological aspects, are determined by the conflicting interaction of the full range of practices and strategies developed by the elites and the popular strata. The only way to change these dynamics and this form is to change the alignment and configuration of popular and elite forces. For now, these changes seem unrealistic. Expecting them or even contemplating them can be described as utopian. But, according to Karl Mannheim, utopias ('relative' not 'absolute' utopias, in his words) in general are only condensed forms expressing the 'unrealized and unfulfilled tendencies which represent the needs of each age. These intellectual elements later form the explosive material for bursting the limits of the existing order.'[90] Is the idea of changing the alignment and configuration of forces determining the current order of the Russian post-communist transformation a utopia of this kind?

Notes

1 I have to put this term in quotation marks because far from all authors of these narratives recognize the pre- and post-1991 processes in Russia as 'reforms', even though they describe the same events and processes as those that their opponents do accept as 'reforms'. See, for example, Boris Kagarlitsky, *Restavratsiya v Rossii* (*Restoration in Russia)* (Moscow: Editorial URSS, 2000), p. 5 and *passim*.
2 Katherine Verdery, 'Whither Postsocialism?' in Chris Hann (ed.), *Postsocialism: Ideals, Ideologies and Practices in Eurasia* (London & New York: Routledge, 2002), p. 20. It should be noted, however, that for Verdery this 'troika' is an 'outdated' image of 'us' that has little to do with the current reality of Western societies and is imposed on 'them', that is post-communist Europe and Eurasia, as part of the continuing Cold War and the effort to assert the West's political and ideological hegemony (see pp. 20–21).
3 The understanding of these results as intermediate or final is, in itself, an important distinction between the narratives on 'new Russia'. Certain authors believe that the transition period is over. The reforms resulted in a 'specific type of economy possessing a logic of its own, which is not just a sum of its parts or a mixture of features of a planned economy and a modern market economy', with this 'specific type' being *essentially* different from both the Western 'democratic capitalism' and the (destroyed) Soviet system. See Grigory Yavlinsky, *Periferiynyi kapitalizm* (*Peripheral Capitalism*) (Moscow: Integral-Inform, 2003), p. 26 and *passim*.
4 See Andrei Yanik, *Istoriya sovremennoi Rossii: Istoki i uroki poslednei rossiyskoi modernizatsii* (*A History of Modern Russia: Sources and Lessons of Russia's Latest Modernization*) (Moscow: Moscow University Press, 2012), p. 593.
5 See Janos Kornai, *Highways and Byways: Studies on Reform and Post-communist Transition* (Cambridge, MA: MIT Press, 1995), pp. vii–ix.
6 For example, Joseph Stiglitz writes: 'I believe that the failures of the reforms in Russia and many republics of the former USSR stemmed from causes other than poor implementation of what was generally sound policy. The causes of these setbacks are much deeper and rooted in the reformers misunderstanding the very foundations of the market economy and the institutional reform process.' J. Stiglitz, 'Kuda vedut reformy?' ('Where Are the Reforms Leading?'), *Voprosy Ekonomiki*, No.7, 1999, p. 6.
7 See Nikolai Leonov, *Krestny put Rossiyi 1991–2000* (*Russia's Calvary 1991–2000*) (Moscow: Russkii Dom, 2002), Epilogue.
8 See Alexander Tarasov,'Vtoroye izdaniye kapitalizma v Rossii' ('The Second Edition of Capitalism in Russia'), *Levaya Politika*, Nos. 7–8, pp. 33–68; Boris Kagarlitsky *Periferiynaya imperiya* (*A Peripheral Empire*) (Moscow: EKSMO, 2009), Chapters 15–16.
9 See Francis Fukuyama, 'The Modernizing Imperative: The USSR as an Ordinary Country', in *The National Interest*, Spring 1993, pp. 10–18.
10 Robert Service, *Russia: Experiment with a People* (Basingstoke: Macmillan, 2002).
11 See, for example, Rudolf Pikhoya, Sergei Zhuravlyov and Andrei Sokolov, *Istoriya sovremennoi Rossii: Desyatiletiye liberalnykh reform 1991–1999* (*A History of Modern Russia: A Decade of Liberal Reforms 1991–1999*) (Moscow: Novy Khronograph, 2011), p. 22.
12 A happy exception is the 'ethnography of post-communism', which focuses on the interconnection between changes in macrostructures and everyday practices or microprocesses. See Michael Burawoy and Katherine Verdery, 'Introduction', in Michael Burawoy and Katherine Verdery (eds), *Uncertain Transition: Ethnographies of*

Change in the Postsocialist World (Lanham, MD: Rowman & Littlefield, 1999), p. 2. I will discuss this theoretical and methodological point later.

13 Adam Przeworski illustrates this point well using the Polish example. In May 1991, more than 80% of respondents regarded unemployment as the biggest social problem. But the thrust of the reforms at the time was to bridle inflation *at the expense of employment*. Once this objective was more or less achieved, the reforms lost mass support as no longer relevant, both because inflation was now under control and because the reforms had led to higher unemployment. Nevertheless, the reforms continued. Since the burden of inflation and unemployment was borne primarily by the 'poor', that is underprivileged groups, attitudes to reforms began crystallizing along traditional *class divisions in society*. See Adam Przeworski, 'Public Support for Economic Reforms in Poland', in Susan C. Stokes (ed.), *Public Support for Market Reforms in New Democracies* (Cambridge: Cambridge University Press, 2001), p. 125.

14 Briefly, the 'absence of the people' from mainstream democratic theory is implied in Schumpeter's seminal definition of democracy – the theme on which most Western political science has been, in effect, a variation: ' . . . Democracy does not mean and cannot mean that the people actually rule in any obvious sense of the terms "people" and "rule". . . . Democracy is the rule of the politician'. Joseph Schumpeter, *Capitalism, Socialism and Democracy* (New York: Harper Perennial, 1975), 284–285.

15 See Howard Zinn, *A People's History of the United States* (New York: Harper Perennial, 1990); Chris Harman, *A People's History of the World* (London & New York: Verso, 2008); cf. Orlando Figes, *A People's Tragedy: The Russian Revolution 1891–1924* (London: Random House, 1996).

16 See Immanuel Wallerstein, *Historical Capitalism* (London: Verso, 1983), p. 7.

17 See Stephen Resnick and Richard Wolff, 'Between State and Private Capitalism: What Was Soviet Socialism?', in *Rethinking Marxism*, 1994, Vol. 7, No.1, pp. 9, 11; Paresh Chattopadhyay, *The Marxian Concept of Capital and the Soviet Experience* (Westport, CT: Praeger, 1994), Chapter 8. The classic of this genre is Charles Bettelheim's theory of 'Soviet capitalism'. See Charles Bettelheim, 'The Specificity of Soviet Capitalism', in *Monthly Review*, September 1985.

18 I have borrowed this term from Margaret Somers; readers interested in its importance for the methodology of sociological research should consult her work. See Margaret Somers, '"We're No Angels": Realism, Rational Choice, and Relationality in Social Science', in *American Journal of Sociology*, Vol. 104, No. 3, 1998, pp. 731ff.

19 See Thomas Hobbes, *On the Citizen*, ed. Richard Tuck (Cambridge: Cambridge University Press, 1998), Chapter 6.

20 See Jean-Jacques Rousseau, *The Social Contract*, trans. by Maurice Cranston (London: Penguin, 1968), Book. I, Chapter vii. According to this logic, a people's submission to any superior master is the people's destruction. See ibid., Book II, Chapter I, p. 168.

21 To Rousseau himself, with his emphasis on the transformation of people's social existence and their recovery of (lost) authenticity, this issue appeared to be inverted: How can social groups that have no concept of the 'common will' be transformed into 'the people' and subsumed within it? Rousseau's grappling with this particular issue produced a host of aporias in his philosophy and led him to the blind alleys of 'civil religion', miracles worked by the god-like Legislator, and nostalgia for the (imaginary) past, or society as yet untouched by the depravity of the modern civilization and *therefore* capable of consummating a fair social contract.

22 Louis Althusser, 'Montesquieu: Politics and History,' in *Politics and History*, trans. B. Brewster (London & New York: Verso, 2007), p. 63.

23 Charles Montesquieu, *The Spirit of Laws*, trans. and edited by Anne M. Cohler, Basia Caroline Miller and Harold Samuel Stone (Cambridge: Cambridge University Press, 1989), pp. 10–11.
24 Montesquieu, *The Spirit of Laws*, pp. 12, 160, 262.
25 To repeat, 'people' in Montesquieu is a *political category* that differs qualitatively and quantitatively from the demographic presentation of 'population' (as we know it these days). It goes without saying that the nobility and the financial oligarchy, that is, 'those distinguished by the advantage of birth, wealth or honours' are *not* 'the people' and relegating them to the category is tantamount to subverting the freedom of 'a free state,' such as England under the Hanoverian dynasty in the 18th century. See Montesquieu, *The Spirit of Laws*, p. 160.
26 See Louis Antoine Saint-Just, *Esprit de la revolution et de la constitution de France*, https://classiques.uqac.ca/classique/saint_just/esprit_revolution/saint_just_esprit_revol.pdf, p. 7. [Accessed on: 17 June 2015]
27 See Maximilien Robespierre, *The Ninth of Thermidor: The Fall of Robespierre*, ed. by Richard Bienvenu (New York: Oxford University Press, 1968), p. 174.
28 These attempts are characteristic of conservative and particularly radical conservative currents of thought. For example, 'the people' for the conservative revolutionaries in the Weimar Republic is not derived from the classes created by modern (industrial, capitalist) society, but what is beyond them. 'The people' is the antipode of modern society, 'the great Nothing from the point of view of the world of public interests', the *subjectification* of a certain original substance and force of history and 'statutes of the Absolute', and an expression of 'spirits that are very close to nature'. See Hans Fryer, *Revolution von Rechts* (Jena: Eugen Diederich, 1931), quoted from the Russian edition of the book: *Revolutsiya sprava* (Moscow: Praxis Publishers, 2009), pp. 59, 69–70. It is not surprising that in Fryer's work, for example, the philosophical definition of 'the people' in terms of *Volkstum* and *Volksgeist* is superimposed on its *double* sociological explication. On the one hand, it is a purely *negative* description of 'the people' that seems to correspond (in its negativity) to the philosophical universality of 'the people' (it is not a social class, nor is it 'associated with a neglected and powerless interest,' etc.). On the other hand, 'the people' overlaps with the sociological *particular*, such as the world of 'the peasantry and countryside,' as the 'eternal foundation of history' (see Fryer, *Revolutsiya sprava*, pp. 70, 73, 63–64.
29 In the current literature, one or other version of the concept of 'hegemony' is often employed to describe what I am talking about. See Ernesto Laclau and Chantal Mouffe, *Hegemony and Socialist Strategy* (London & New York: Verso, 1987). In this chapter, we cannot dwell on this concept's heuristic potential for describing 'the people'. For insight into this theme, see Ernesto Laclau, *On Populist Reason* (London & New York: Verso, 2007).
30 To be concise, I will base this summary on the logic behind Benedict Anderson's description of 'nation'. Of course, 'nation' and 'people' are not identical. Moreover, the relationship between these terms is a separate and difficult problem in its own right. I will borrow from Anderson his logic alone, not the content of his description. The shared feature of 'people' and 'nation' as 'imagined communities' makes this borrowing possible. Anderson writes that 'in fact, all communities larger than primordial villages of face-to-face contact (and perhaps even these) are imagined. Communities are to be distinguished, not by their falsity/genuineness, but by the style in which they are imagined.' Benedict Anderson, *Imagined Communities* (London: Verso, 1991), p. 6.

I would only add that they are also distinguished by the functions that they realize or do not realize in public life.

31 Anderson, *Imagined Communities*, p. 4.

32 For a brilliant analysis of these 'fictions' and their role in political practices (as exemplified by Nelson Mandela's liberation struggle to create a 'South African people'), see Jacques Derrida, 'The Laws of Reflection: Nelson Mandela, in Admiration', in J. Derrida and M. Tlili (eds), *For Nelson Mandela* (New York: Seaver Books, 1987). For the same, in application to the rhetoric of the Declaration of Independence and the constituting of the 'American people', see Jacques Derrida, 'Declarations of Independence', in Elizabeth Rottenberg (ed.), *Negotiations: Interventions and Interviews, 1971–2001 (*Stanford, CA: Stanford University Press, 2002), pp. 46–54.

33 Karl Marx, 'A Contribution to the Critique of Hegel's Philosophy of Right', in *Early Writings,* trans. by Rodney Livingstone and Gregory Benton (London: Penguin, 1992), p. 252.

34 See Ernesto Laclau, 'Why Do Empty Signifiers Matter to Politics?' in Ernesto Laclau, *Emancipation(s)* (London & New York: Verso, 1996).

35 See Vladimir Petukhov 'Bednye v Rossii: Otnosheniye k vlasti, politicheskoye uchastiye, protestnyi potentsial', in Mikhail Gorshkov and Natalya Tikhonova (eds), *Bednost' i bednye v sovremennoi Rossii* ('The Poor in Russia: Attitudes to Power, Political Participation, and Potential for Resistance', in *Poverty and the Poor in Contemporary Russia*) (Moscow: Ves Mir Publishers, 2014), p. 243, Table 11.2.

36 See Mikhail Gorshkov's conclusions based on a national sociological survey conducted by the Institute of Sociology of the Russian Academy of Sciences in 2013. What is so characteristic and indicative (in connection with our speculations on 'the people' in the 'Digression') is Gorshkov's denial of the *political agency* of the poor in Russia. See Mikhail Gorshkov 'Zaklyucheniye' (Conclusion), in *Bednost' i bednye v sovremennoi Rossii*, p. 293.

37 Relevant data for the period from 1994 to 2013. See 'Protestnaya aktivnost' v Rossiyi poshla na spad: Levada-tsentr' ('Protests Are on the Decline in Russia – Levada Center')', http://www.levada.ru/eng/protests-and-peace-marches. [Accessed on: 17 June 2015]

38 This lack of turmoil cannot be explained by a growing crackdown on protests since the early 2000s, and came as a surprise to foreign observers even in the 'liberal' and muddled 1990s, which were marked by the unprecedented degradation of government institutions and a general regression of governance. See Steven Fish, 'Postcommunist Subversion: Social Science and Democratization in East Europe and Eurasia', in *Slavic Review*, Vol. 58, No. 4, 1999, p. 812.

39 According to Levada Center, only 1% of respondents displayed active interest in politics in November 2013, which is within the margin of error (compared to 4% in 1996), 'somewhat interested,' 28% (31% in 1996), 'fairly uninterested in politics,' 41% (43% in 1996), 'totally uninterested,' 26% (21% in 1996), and 'don't know,' 4% (2% in 1996, http://www.levada.ru/16-12-2013/interes-k-politike. [Accessed on: 15 June 2015]

40 See Yuri Levada's seminal article, 'Obshchestvennoye mnenie v politicheskom zazerkalie' ('Public Opinion behind the Political Looking-Glass'), originally published in *Vestnik Obshchestvennogo Mneniya*, 2006, No.2, particularly Table 1. But for all the 'personalization' of authority, the prevailing attitudes in Russia are criticism, scepticism and even irony towards the 'great people' in power and official institutions. See Table 3 and 8, http://polit.ru/article/2006/06/06/pubopinion/. [Accessed on: 15 June 2015]

41 In his time, Jean-Paul Sartre demonstrated the *opposite*, that is the transformative potential of the alternative. He wrote: 'For it is necessary here to reverse common opinion and on the basis of what it is not, to acknowledge the harshness of a situation

or the sufferings which it imposes, both of which are motives for conceiving of another state of affairs in which things would be better for everybody. It is on the day that we can conceive of a different state of affairs that a new light falls on our troubles and our sufferings and that we decide that these are unbearable', Jean-Paul Sartre, *Being and Nothingness* (London: Methuen, 1957), pp. 434–435. Of course, Sartre's formula leaves unanswered the most important question (on which grounds it was criticized by Pierre Bourdieu): *What* opens our eyes to the alternative and *how* does this recovery of sight materialize in our practices?

42 See, for example, David Ost, 'Social Forces and the Post-communist Transition: Why Labour Turns Right', in David Lane (ed.), *The Transformation of State Socialism: System Change, Capitalism or Something Else?* (New York: Palgrave Macmillan, 2007), pp. 80–81.

43 See William H. Sewell, Jr., *Logics of History: Social Theory and Social Transformation* (Chicago: University of Chicago Press, 2005), pp. 83ff.

44 As Niklas Luhmann expresses the idea: 'By history we do not simply mean the factual sequence of events, according to which what is present is understood as the effect of past causes or as the cause of the future effects. What is specific to the history of meaning is that it enables optional access to the meaning of past or future events, and thus leaps within the sequence. History originates in the release from this sequence.' Niklas Luhmann, *Social Systems*, trans. by John Bednarz, Jr. (Stanford, CA: Stanford University Press, 1995), p. 79.

45 For all the rigour of the *analytical* differentiation between the two main types of order, which Friedrich Hayek calls 'spontaneous order' and 'made (or abstract) order' (or simply 'organization'), he emphasizes that 'the two kinds of order will regularly coexist in every society of any degree of complexity'. Every 'organization' relies, to some degree, on the rules of 'spontaneous order'; every type of 'spontaneous order' includes certain elements of 'organization'. See Friedrich A. Hayek, *Law, Legislation and Liberty*. Vol. 1 (Chicago: University of Chicago Press, 1973), pp. 46, 48–49.

46 There is a vigorous debate, especially among sociologists and economists, about the variability of capitalism and on the multiplicity and changeability of its synchronic and diachronic forms. For a good overview of the discussions of these issues and the latest contributions to them, see Uwe Becker, *Open Varieties of Capitalism* (New York: Palgrave Macmillan, 2009); and Christel Lane and Geoffrey Wood (eds), *Capitalist Diversity and Diversity within Capitalism* (New York: Routledge, 2012), particularly Chapters 2, 5, 7 and 8.

47 See David Lane, 'Introduction: Outcomes of Transformation' in Lane (ed.), *The Transformation of State Socialism*, p. 2.

48 Were it not for this protective hegemony, *what* would the Brussels-based EU bureaucrats say to the following invective from so passionate a liberal as Friedrich Hayek: '(s)o far as much of current government action is concerned, there is in the present world very little reason for the liberal to wish to preserve things as they are. It would seem to the liberal, indeed, that what is most urgently needed in most parts of the world is a thorough sweeping away of the obstacles to free growth'. Friedrich Hayek, 'Why I am Not a Conservative,' in *The Constitution of Liberty* (Chicago: University of Chicago Press, 2011), p. 521. Hayek's uncompromising criticism of all forms of state interference in economy, of the 'mirage of social justice', of democracy's degeneration into what he calls 'bargaining democracy' and the plaything of lobbies and 'special interests', suggests that present-day Western Europe is indeed one of the places in the world that makes the 'true liberals', like Hayek, deeply grieve.

49 See David Kotz and Fred Weir, *Revolution from Above: The Demise of the Soviet System* (London & New York: Routledge, 1997).

50 Anders Åslund, a sober-minded economist who is not given to philosophical metaphysics, came up with this precise formula: 'Russia's history is that of its leaders and their ideas'. See Anders Åslund, *Russia's Capitalist Revolution: Why Market Reform Succeeded and Democracy Failed* (Washington, DC: Peterson Institute for International Economics, 2007), p. 285.

51 Gil Eyal uses the Czech post-communist transformation as an example to show how such ideological practices of the subjugation and manipulation of the people are carried out and how they become embodied in specific political decisions and strategies. See Gil Eyal, 'Anti-Politics and the Spirit of Capitalism: Dissidents, Monetarists, and the Czech Transition to Capitalism', in *Theory and Society*, Vol. 29, No. 1, 2000, pp. 54–57. Russia was distinct only in that these practices assumed more coarse forms and proved less effective from the point of view of the ruling classes.

52 However paradoxical this may seem, radical criticisms of the liberal teleology of transitioning to the market and democracy occasionally prove a mere 'inverted teleology' rather than a negation of teleology as such. In Michael Burawoy's work, for example, an evolution towards the market and democracy turns into an involution towards archaic forms, and modernization into de-modernization. All of this is caught by the concept of 'transition without transformation'. The concept itself makes sense only as a reflection of and as an attempt to explain the frustrated expectations of Russia's transition to 'a modern capitalist economy' that remains a kind of landmark and a starting point in any analysis of the disconcerting and unpalatable Russian post-communism. Of course, this approach reduces the people to the suffering and dispossessed masses rather than a tool in the hands of the elites. See Michael Burawoy 'Transition without Transformation: Russia's Involuted Road to Capitalism,' in *East European Politics and Society*, Vol. 15, No. 2, 2001.

53 David Hume, 'Of the Independence of Parliament' in Eugene F. Miller (ed.), *Essays Moral, Political, and Literary* (Indianapolis: Liberty Fund, 1987), p. 42.

54 See Richard Lachmann 'Agents of Revolution', in John Foran (ed.), *Theorizing Revolutions* (London & New York: Routledge, 1997), p. 97, note 2.

55 Martin Gilens and Benjamin Page, 'Testing Theories of American Politics: Elites, Interest Groups, and Average Citizens' in *Perspectives on Politics*, Vol. 12, No. 3, 2014, p. 576.

56 See David Prindle, *The Paradox of Democratic Capitalism* (Baltimore, MD: The Johns Hopkins University Press, 2008), pp 238–248; Jeffrey Sachs, 'Why America Must Revive Its Middle Class, *Time*, 10 October 2011, p. 30; David Harvey, 'The Enigma of Capital and the Crisis This Time' in John C. Calhoun et al. (eds), *Business as Usual: The Roots of the Global Financial Meltdown* (New York: New York University Press, 2011), p. 100; 'Not So Frugal,' *Time*, 14 March 2011, p. 18.

57 See Goran Therborn, *What Does the Ruling Class Do When It Rules?* (London: NLB, 1978), p. 230. Therborn, with good reason, emphasizes the point that modern democracy historically appeared as an achievement of the people's struggles *against* the bourgeoisie rather than as the latter's creation, which was crafted to co-opt the lower strata. How the bourgeoisie has mastered democracy and transformed it into a co-optation mechanism is a separate issue, which we cannot address in this chapter.

58 We cannot consider these types of activities. For their detailed analysis, see Therborn, *What Does the Ruling Class Do When It Rules?*, Part II, Chapter 5.

59 As is obvious, this work is dependent on numerous concrete circumstances and can be more or less successful; the tools and methods used in the process are determined by

the existing institutional and cultural context and therefore its efficiency always has certain limits.

60 See Frances Fox Piven and Richard Cloward, *Poor People's Movements: Why They Succeed, How They Fail* (New York: Vintage, 1977), pp. 5ff; James Scott, *Weapons of the Weak: Everyday Forms of Peasant Resistance* (New Haven, CT: Yale University Press, 1985), p. 299.

61 See Vaclav Havel, 'The Power of the Powerless', Vaclav Havel et al., *The Power of the Powerless: Citizens against the State in Central-Eastern Europe*, ed. John Keane (Armonk, NY: M.E. Sharpe, 1985), p. 50.

62 See Eric Hobsbawm 'Peasants and Politics' in *Journal of Peasant Studies*, Vol. 1, No. 1, 1973, p. 7. Barrington Moore notably extends this observation to great modern revolutions: 'Indeed I would hazard the suggestion that in any of the great revolutions that have succeeded, the mass of the followers has not consciously willed an overturn of the social order. . . . To the extent that angry little people want something new, it generally amounts to their perception of the old order minus the disagreeable and oppressive features that affect them'. Barrington Moore, Jr., *Injustice: The Social Bases of Obedience and Revolt* (White Plains, NY: M.E. Sharpe, 1978), p. 352.

63 To borrow Laclau's terminology, this path can be conceived as a transformation of 'requests' into still particular 'demands' and on into universal 'claims', expressing the *rights* to what has originally been just a desired concession on the part of the wielders of power and wealth. According to Laclau, the same logic (which in reality is only a string of contingent events) underlies the formation of a 'people' as a 'universal historical actor whose aims will necessarily crystallize around empty signifiers as objects of political identification'. See Ernesto Laclau 'Why Constructing a People Is the Main Task of Radical Politics', *Critical Inquiry*, Vol. 32, No. 4, 2006, pp. 654–657.

64 Scott, *Weapons of the Weak*, p. xvii. Scott's metaphor, with some adjustments, could be extended to modern capitalist industry, looking at it through the prism of what Pierre Dubois calls 'sabotage in industry'. See Pierre Dubois, *Sabotage in Industry* (Harmondsworth: Penguin, 1979), esp. pp. 21–59.

65 Of course, these connections are mediated by various phenomena at the meso-level of political and economic life, from which we in this case have to abstract.

66 See Arthur Schopenhauer, *The Basis of Morality*, trans. Arthur Brodrick Bullock (London: Swan Sonnenschein & Co, 1903), p. 5. For a brilliant, multifaceted and truly historical study of the phenomenon and the very idea of duty as a mechanism of domination, see David Graeber, *Debt: The First 5,000 Years* (New York: Melville House, 2011).

67 Hans Heinrich Gerth and Charles Wright Mills (eds.), *From Max Weber: Essays in Sociology* (New York: Oxford University Press, 1958), p. 280.

68 See Michel Callon, 'Introduction: The Embeddedness of Economic Markets in Economics' in Michel Callon (ed.), *The Laws of the Market* (Oxford: Basil Blackwell, 1998), pp. 41, 47. Generally speaking, 'the market' as it exists in the discipline of economics is such an underdeveloped concept that it is impossible to discuss the 'laws of the market' seriously. Douglass North noticed long ago an extremely curious circumstance, which is by no means accidental, that '(i)t is peculiar that the literature on economics contains so little discussion of the central institution that underlies neoclassical economics – the market', Douglass C. North, 'Markets and Other Allocation Systems in History: The Challenge of Karl Polanyi', *Journal of European Economic History*, Vol. 6, No. 3, 1977, p. 710. Precious little has changed since that time and what one can still find in standard economics textbooks is nothing but intellectual

pabulum like the following: 'A market is an institution or mechanism which brings together the buyers ('demanders') and sellers ('suppliers') of particular goods, services or resources', C.R. McConnell and S.L. Brue, *Microeconomics: Principles, Problems, and Politics* (New York: McGraw – Hill/Irwin, 2005), p. 39. Described in this way, this 'mechanism' can be a feature of prehistoric times just as much as of today's 'postmodern' global financial capitalism, telling us equally little about either of them. Employing this vacuous concept, we would never know what in particular distinguished the former from the latter, apart from that substance-wise different sets of goods and services were exchanged then and now. But the substance of goods and services cannot help us explain the structural polarity between the 'stone age' economy and the contemporary one. For an analysis of the very sparse 'classical' definitions of the market (in Antoine Augustin Cournot, Alfred Marshall and others) see Callon, *The Laws of the Market*, pp. 1–2, 52.

69 See Neil Fligstein, 'Markets as Politics: A Political-Cultural Approach to Market Institutions', *American Sociological Review*, Vol. 61, No. 4, 1996, p. 663.

70 This 'enlarged' presentation of the 'main actors' of the post-communist transformation is clearly a huge simplification. It is obvious that different factions of the post-communist elites used different, and even competing, strategies to attain their goals and that the reactions by different groups comprising the people were extremely diverse. Yet I think that this simplification is fair for two reasons. First, the current literature contains a sufficiently thorough accounting of the diverse strategies used by the post-communist elites in their different configurations; the study of these strategies has even reached the stage where a typology of historical trajectories of post-communist societies, as determined by the composition and behaviours of their elites, can be formed. Significant credit in this respect goes to the so-called neoclassical sociology. For its 'manifesto', see Gil Eyal, Ivan Szelényi and Eleonor Townsley, 'On Irony: An Initiation to Neoclassical Sociology', *Thesis Eleven*, No. 73, 2003, pp. 5–41. For an expanded presentation of neoclassical sociological theory, see Gil Eyal, Ivan Szelényi, and Eleonor Townsley, *Making Capitalism Without Capitalists: Class Formation and Elite Struggles in Post-Communist Central Europe* (London: Verso, 1998). Second, what is common to these otherwise different strategies used by post-communist elites and what is dictated by their attitude to the people is too often left 'off screen,' as is the common element of resistance in the various strategies used by different non-elite groups. My 'enlargement' makes it possible to focus on these points of overlap in the strategies of the elites and underprivileged social groups, respectively.

71 See Bob Arnot, *Controlling Soviet Labour* (Armonk, NY: M.E. Sharpe, 1988), pp. 2ff.

72 For a survey of different approaches to defining the political economic nature of Soviet society, see Arnot, *Controlling Soviet Labour*, p. 268.

73 See Otto Kirchheimer, 'Changes in the Structure of Political Compromise' in Andrew Arato and Eike Gebhardt (eds), *The Essential Frankfurt School Reader* (New York: Continuum, 1987), pp. 66–68.

74 See Alena Ledeneva, *Russia's Economy of Favours: Blat, Networking and Informal Exchange* (Cambridge: Cambridge University Press, 1998), esp. Chapters 1–5.

75 Suffice it to say that for all the above reasons, labour resources in the USSR were always in short supply, and whatever labour market we can speak of in the Soviet Union was certainly a seller's, not a buyer's, market. Testifying to this is the long-term trend towards the levelling of white-collar and blue-collar salaries in the Soviet industry. While in 1955, the former category earned 1.68 times more than the latter, by 1977 this indicator shrank to 1.21, Arnot, *Controlling Soviet Labour*, p. 35.

76 A political – as opposed to politico-economic – explanation of the Soviet elites' 'insecurity' points to a menacingly growing alliance between the liberal intelligentsia and specialists on the one hand, and the working class, on the other. The working class' positions were strengthened by demographic changes, primarily by the depletion of rural human resources in the course of Soviet urbanization and industrialization. Against this background, the leadership under Brezhnev allegedly had to be 'nice' to the working class and bribe them *at the expense* of the intelligentsia, enabling the growth of private consumption and turning a blind eye to inefficient management. See Georgi Derluguian, 'What Communism Was' in Immanuel Wallerstein, Randall Collins et al., *Does Capitalism Have a Future?* (Oxford: Oxford University Press, 2013), p. 116. To me, this does not seem a convincing explanation, even if we disregard the fact that the intelligentsia, commonly grouped together as the 'shestidesyatniki' ('men of the sixties') cannot be considered 'liberal'. Moreover, there are hardly any signs of its alliance with the working class (as distinct, for example, from Poland's case), an alliance that could present at least some threat to the *nomenklatura*. Besides, recruitment to the *nomenklatura* was the normal path of upward mobility for the intelligentsia at that time. In retrospect, this is confirmed by the fact that the intellectual recruits of this sort emerged as the main drivers of the *perestroika* movement in the late 1980s.

77 A thorough and colourful description of this process is provided by Leon Aron, who portrays it – in the best liberal tradition – as a heroic push towards 'truth' and freedom. See Leon Aron, *Roads to the Temple: Truth, Memory, Ideas and Ideals in the Making of the Russian Revolution* (New Haven, CT: Yale University Press, 2012).

78 The once widely publicized 'national projects' (in healthcare, affordable housing, education and agriculture) were meant to cushion to a certain extent the negative consequences that these reforms entailed for working people. Today there is a consensus among experts that the 'national projects' proved to be nonstarters. See Anastasia Bashkatova, 'Zabytye natsproekty' ('The Forgotten National Projects'), *Nezavisimaya Gazeta*, 29 December 2009.

79 In the 1980s, 'social wages' made up almost a quarter of urban workers' incomes (19% in the countryside). In the late Soviet period, social wages grew at a much higher rate than cash wages (between 1971 and 1981, the former increased by 81%, while cash wages in the cities grew by 45%). See Arnot, *Controlling Soviet Labour*, p. 36.

80 Vladimir Pastukhov, *'Restavratsiya vmesto reformatsiyi: Dvadtsat let, kotorye potryasli Rossiyu* (*Restoration Instead of Reformation: Twenty Years that Shook Russia*) (Moscow: OGI Publishers, 2012), pp. 7, 8 and 9.

81 See Stefan Hedlund, *Russian Path Dependence* (New York: Routledge, 2005), pp. 263, 274–281.

82 It is for this reason that the market reforms could only be 'sold' to the public as a package deal including democracy. The salesmen's strategy necessarily involved the concealment of the fundamental tension between the two, which, in the specific situation of the post-communist transition, was so severe that it made many of the more astute theorists doubt at an early stage of the process that a market transition was feasible at all in a political democracy environment. See Jon Elster, 'When Communism Dissolves', *London Review of Books*, 25 January 1990, pp. 3–6; Claus Offe, 'Capitalism by Democratic Design? Democratic Theory Facing the Triple Transition in East Central Europe', *Social Research*, Vol. 58, No. 4, 1991. For more on what, in my view, made the juxtaposition of democracy and capitalism possible in post-communist countries, see Boris Kapustin, 'Capitalism and Russian Democracy'

in Per-Arne Bodin, Stefan Hedlund and Elena Namli (eds), *Power and Legitimacy: Challenges from Russia* (London & New York: Routledge, 2013), pp. 85–89. The fundamental impossibility of justifying capitalism (at least the variety that existed in the West until recently) is explained, according to Luc Boltanski and his colleagues, by the gap between the real forms of capital accumulation that enrich very few and its normative substantiation as serving the 'common good'. It is the collapse of 'classical' capitalism's legitimacy that compels it (under the pressure of criticism) to develop a new 'spirit of capitalism' emphasizing individualism, autonomy, authenticity, self-expression and so on as its justifications. See Luc Boltanski and Eve Chiapello, 'The New Spirit of Capitalism', *International Journal of Politics, Culture, and Society*, Vol. 18, Nos. 3/4, 2005, esp. pp. 162–171. It is questionable to what extent the new 'spirit of capitalism' really manifests itself in Western societies. No less disputable is its capacity to establish a basis for legitimizing capitalism. What is, however, quite clear is that this 'spirit' is absolutely unrelated to the capitalist reality in the present-day Russia, possibly with the exception of its privileged zone occupied by CEOs in the financial, commercial and energy sectors.

83 Is it in any way surprising that a considerable part or possibly even the majority of people both in Russia and in Central and Eastern Europe during the period of anti-communist revolutions in the late 1980s to early 1990s and later *did not* reject the 'socialist path of development?' Of course, in the popular mentality – unlike the mentality of the elites – it was associated with egalitarianism and social protection of labour, rather than with one-party regimes and the official ideology of Marxism-Leninism. See Robin Okey, *The Demise of Communist East Europe: 1989 in Context* (London: Hodder Arnold, 2004), p. 76.

84 For a classical presentation of this developmental logic, see Thomas Humphrey Marshall, 'Citizenship and Social Class' in *Class, Citizenship, and Social Development*, with an Introduction by Seymour Lipset (Garden City, NY: Doubleday, 1964).

85 Peggy Watson brilliantly illustrates this offering the example of healthcare in post-communist Poland. See PeggyWatson, 'Inequalities in Health and Health Care in Post-Communist Europe' in Lane (ed.), *The Transformation of State Socialism*, esp. pp. 191ff.

86 See Alena Ledeneva, 'From Russia with 'Blat': Can Informal Networks Help Modernize Russia?' *Social Research*, Vol. 76, No. 1, 2009, pp. 266–267.

87 As an example of this, in 2010, no more than 20% of all presidential executive orders and ordinances were carried out in time. But this was perceived as considerable progress compared with previous years, when this figure stood at 15%. Note that the case in question is unrelated to the Yeltsin period of 'institutional chaos'. See Alexei Petayev, 'Eto upravlencheskiy nonsens' ('This Is So Much Managerial Nonsense'), Slon.ru, 12 June 2010, http://slon.ru/articles/414962. [Accessed on: 17 June 2015]

88 See Jeremy Morris and Abel Polese, 'Introduction: Informality – Enduring Practices, Entwined Livelihoods' in Jeremy Morris and Abel Polese (eds), *The Informal Post-Socialist Economy* (London & New York: Routledge, 2014), p. 2.

89 For an analysis of these non-capitalist forms as exemplified by modern-day Ukraine, see Colin C. Williams, 'Beyond a "Varieties of Capitalism" Approach in Central and Eastern Europe', *Employee Relations*, Vol. 33, No. 4, 2011, pp. 413–427.

90 Karl Mannheim, *Ideology and Utopia: An Introduction to the Sociology of Knowledge* (New York: Harcourt, Brace and Co., 1949), p. 179.

3 A time of transition

Changes in reality and perceptions

Vladimir Popov and Piotr Dutkiewicz

This chapter seeks to explore as objectively as possible the milestones along the path of economic and social development in Russia in the 1991–2014 period. This time of transition from a centrally planned to a market economy, from socialism to capitalism, from authoritarianism to new forms of individual freedoms was, as is any turning point, brimming over with action. It was a blur of events, from which it is not always so easy to sift out the really important moments. In this chapter, we attempt to draw as unbiased a picture of the economic and social changes as we can, anchoring the discussion in the central theme of this work, which is how economic transformations and transition affected the social structure of society and public opinion.

The economic and social dimensions of transition

It is well-known that production dropped in the 1990s in Russia; what is less known is that this decline was of a magnitude unparalleled in the twentieth century. Neither the First World War nor the revolutions of 1917 and the subsequent bloodshed of the Civil War, nor the horrors of the Second World War brought about such a dramatic drop in output as was seen in the 1990s. National income fell by more than 50% between 1913 and 1920, but had rebounded by 1925, 12 years later, surpassing the pre-war 1913 level. In 1998, at the lowest point in the transformational recession of the 1990s, Russia's GDP was 55% of the pre-crisis peak of 1989 – slightly more than the percentage of the 1913 level achieved in 1920. However, the current recession is lasting much longer.[1] GDP had only achieved the 1989 pre-crisis performance in 2008; but then the new crisis of 2008–2009 dealt another blow and it was only in 2012 that GDP significantly exceeded the 1989 level (Figure 3.1). By way of comparison, national income never once fell that far during World War II. In 1942, it was 80% of the 1940 prewar level, then climbed back up to the prewar level in 1944, and then once again descended to the 80% mark in 1946 during the conversion of the defence industry. But, by 1948, it had already substantially exceeded the 1940 level. The economic losses from the 1990s recession were exceptional in scale, greater than those suffered as a result of world wars and revolutions.

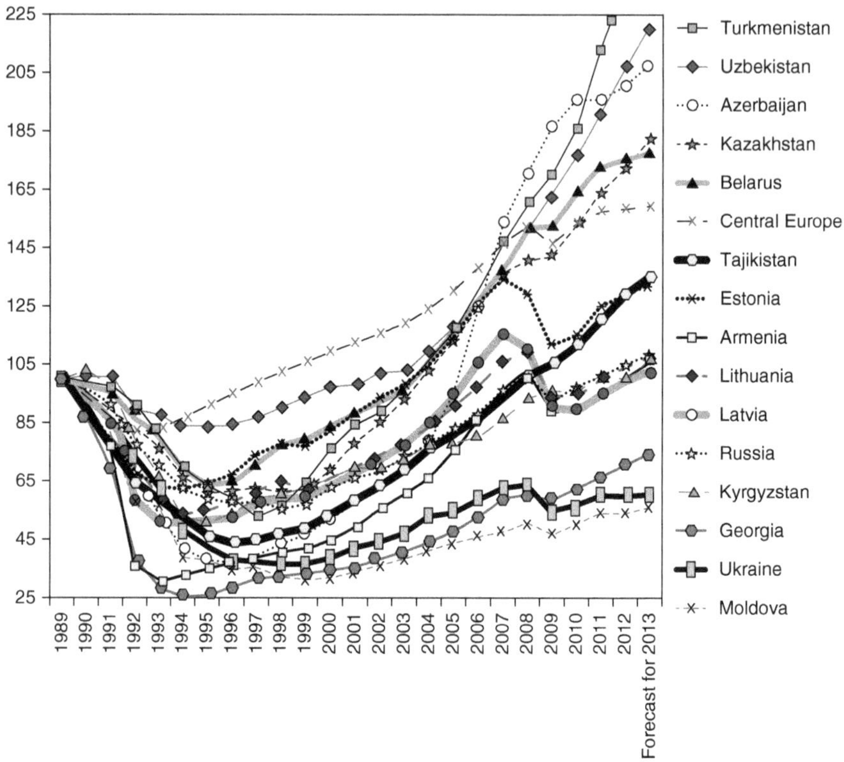

Figure 3.1 Changes in the GDP of FSU Economies (1989 = 100%).

Source: EBRD Transition Report for various years. See also EBRD macroeconomic statistics: http://www.ebrd.com/downloads/research/economics/macrodata/sei.xls.

The transformational recession of the 1990s in Eastern Europe and the countries of the former USSR was a phenomenon truly unprecedented in world economic history. The scale of the decline in production in Central European countries is comparable to the losses of the Great Depression of the 1930s – 1929–1932 saw an approximate 30% drop, with output restored by the late 1930s (Figure 3.2). However, the world had never before seen output plummet by 50% or more and take a full 15–20 years to recover, as was the case in the majority of the countries of the former USSR. Some, like Ukraine, are still not back to the level they had at independence. It is technically possible to find examples of deeper and even more prolonged decline in production in certain countries, but only in times of war, epidemics or natural disasters, and never as a result of economic policy. The drop in output in the countries of the former USSR is described in economics textbooks as the biggest manmade economic crisis in the history of mankind, a crisis manufactured by economic policy makers.

Leaving aside the question of why the recession occurred or how it could have been avoided, let us only point out that such an unprecedented plunge in production brought an equally unprecedented tension in the social sector.[2] In the 1990s, real household incomes and consumption decreased by at least a third, which was very significant, despite being less than the drop in production (the recession was more pronounced in the defence and investment sectors, while imports of consumer goods expanded). Moreover, due to the drastic increase in income inequality, the real incomes of the absolute majority – 80% of the low-income population – were approximately cut in half. As for wealth inequality, redistribution of national wealth occurred on a hitherto unseen scale during privatization. In only a few years, well-nigh a third of all state property passed into the hands of a few dozen oligarchs at knockdown prices.

In 2005, Andrei Shleifer and Daniel Treisman published the article 'A Normal Country: Russia After Communism', in which they compared Russia with Brazil, China, India, Turkey and other developing countries, arguing that Russia is nowhere near the worst from the point of view of crime, income inequality, corruption, macroeconomic instability and other typical third-world ills.[3] In reality, Russia is somewhere near the middle of the list, above Nigeria, but below China. In short, Russia is a *normal* developing country. By contrast, the Soviet Union was an *unusual* developing country, one that had sent the first man into space and was home to approximately twenty Nobel Prize winners in the natural sciences and literature. Of the approximately 40 living winners of the Fields Medal (awarded since 1936, it is often called the Nobel Prize of Mathematics), eight hail from the former Soviet Union (whose population made up less than 5% of the world's population). In the Soviet Union and other socialist countries, health care and education were universal and free of charge, as well as being the best among the developing countries; the level of wealth and income inequality was low, and the level of crime and corruption was relatively low. By 1965, the average life expectancy in the USSR had increased to 70 years of age, which is only two years less than in the USA, although the per capita income in the USSR was only 20–25% of that in the USA.[4]

The transition to a market economy in the 1990s led to the dismantling of the Soviet state: government services, from healthcare to law and order, deteriorated drastically. The shadow economy, whose share under the Brezhnev regime stood at between 10% and 15% of the GDP (by the most generous of assessments), increased by the mid-1990s to 50% of the GDP.[5] In the 1980–1985 period, the Soviet Union was placed in the middle among 54 countries in the rankings for corruption: Soviet government officials were less corrupt than those in Italy, Greece, Portugal, South Korea and practically all of the developing countries. In 1996, after the market economy had been established and democracy had won the day, Russia was placed 48th in the same rankings out of 54 countries, between India and Venezuela.

The income gap widened significantly with the Gini coefficient increasing from 26% in 1986 to 40% in 2000 and 42% in the 2006–2013 period (Figure 3.2). The decile dispersion ratio (the ratio of the incomes of the wealthiest 10% to the

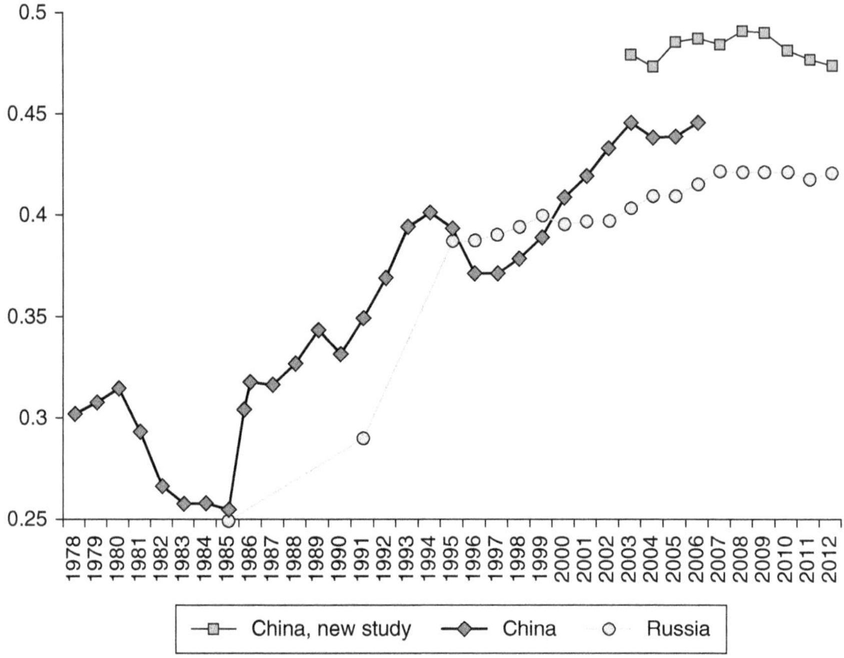

Figure 3.2 The Gini coefficient for income distribution in China and Russia, 1978–2012.

Source: Popov, 2014.

incomes of the poorest 10%) increased from 8 in 1992 to 14 in 2000 and then to 16–17 in the 2006–2013 period (Goskomstat). However, income inequality grew much faster at the very top. There was no one with wealth exceeding 1 billion US dollars in Russia in 1995; while, according to *Forbes* magazine, there were 53 billionaires in Russia in 2007, moving the country into second or third place in the world, right after the USA (415) and Germany (55). Russia trailed Germany by only two billionaires, but the Russian billionaires possessed a total wealth of 282 billion dollars, which was 37 billion dollars more than the German billionaires were worth. In 2008, the number of billionaires in Russia was up to 86 with a total worth of more than 500 billion dollars (a good third of the country's GDP). By 2013–2014, Russia's absolute billionaire count had increased to more than 100; however, China came out ahead of Russia in 2014 with 162 billionaires. In contrast, the Soviet Union was indeed an unusual developing country: it had no billionaires at all, and hardly any dollar millionaires either.

The criminalization of Russian society also intensified drastically in the 1990s. Crime in the Soviet Union had been gradually on the rise, starting in the mid-1960s; but after the collapse of the USSR there occurred an unprecedented surge in crime levels. In the space of only a few years in the early 1990s, crime rates doubled and murder rates tripled, placing Russia among the world's top rankers in these areas. By the mid-1990s, the murder rate had risen to more than 30 people per 100,000 population (Figure 3.3) in contrast to 1–2 per 100,000 in Western and Eastern Europe, Canada, China, Japan, Mauritius and Israel. Only in two other countries (not counting war-torn and crumbling developing countries) were the murder rates higher in the same period, and that was in South Africa and Colombia.[6] In such countries as Brazil and Mexico, the rate was half of that in Russia in the same time period. Even the USA, with the highest murder rate among the developed countries at 6–7 people per 100,000 population, paled in comparison to Russia.[7]

By the early 21st century, the mortality rate for external causes of death (accidents, murders and suicides) soared to 245 people per 100,000 population. It was higher than in any of the 187 countries for which a WHO evaluation was done for 2002 and is equal to 2.45 deaths per 1,000 for one year, or 159 deaths per 1,000 over 65 years, which was the life expectancy at birth in Russia in 2002.[8] In other words, if this murder rate were to be maintained over a human lifetime, one out of every six citizens of Russia born in 2002 would die an 'unnatural' death. Of course, in the 1980s, the murder, suicide and accident mortality rates

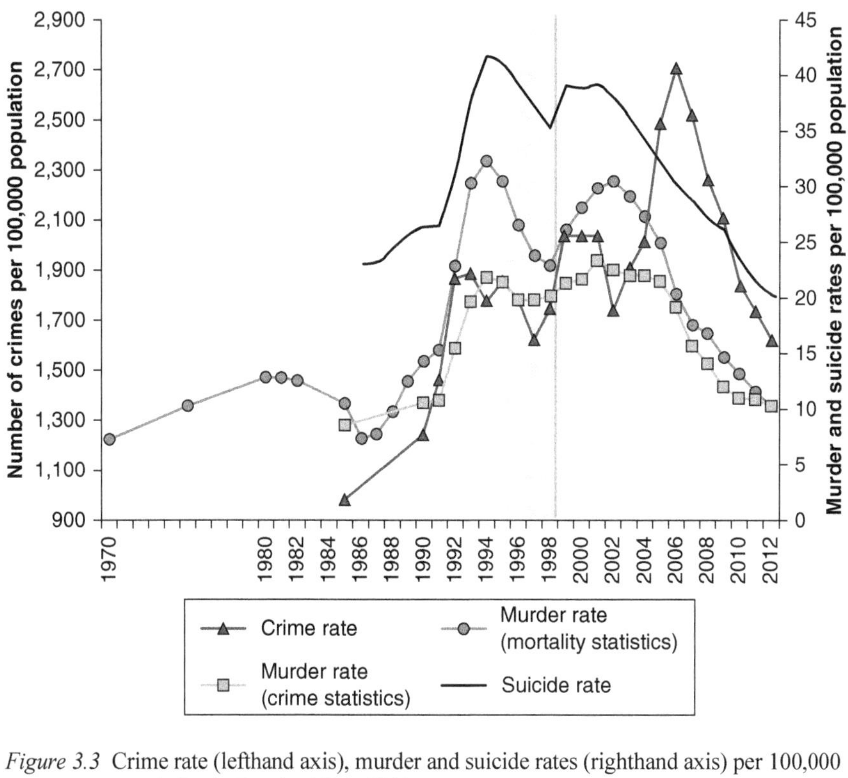

Figure 3.3 Crime rate (lefthand axis), murder and suicide rates (righthand axis) per 100,000 population in Russia, 1970–2012.

Source: Rosstat.

in Russia, Ukraine, Belorussia, Latvia, Estonia, Moldavia and Kazakhstan were already fairly high. They were several times higher than in the other former Soviet republics and the Eastern European countries. At the same time, they were fairly comparable to the indicators for other countries with a similar level of development. In the 1990s, these levels grew precipitously and substantially exceeded the indicators for the rest of the world.

The mortality rate rose from 10 people per 1,000 in 1990 to 16 in 1994 and fell within the range of 14–16 deaths per 1,000 population up to and including the year 2010.[9] This was a veritable mortality crisis – the only example in all of history where the mortality rate increased by 60% in only five years in the absence of wars, epidemics or volcanic eruptions. The mortality rate in Russia had never skyrocketed the way it did in the 1990s, not since the famine of 1947. Even in 1950–1953, during the last few years of Stalin's reign, despite the high mortality rates in the penal forced-labour camps and the effects of wartime malnutrition and war injuries, the mortality rate was only 9–10 deaths per 1,000 population, and not 14–16, as was the case in the 1994–2010 period (Figure 3.4).

Special studies have shown that the increased mortality rate was, for the most part, not caused by reduced real household incomes and the resulting deterioration in diet, not by smoking or alcoholism, not by the breakdown of the health care system or environmental pollution, and not by an upswing in the

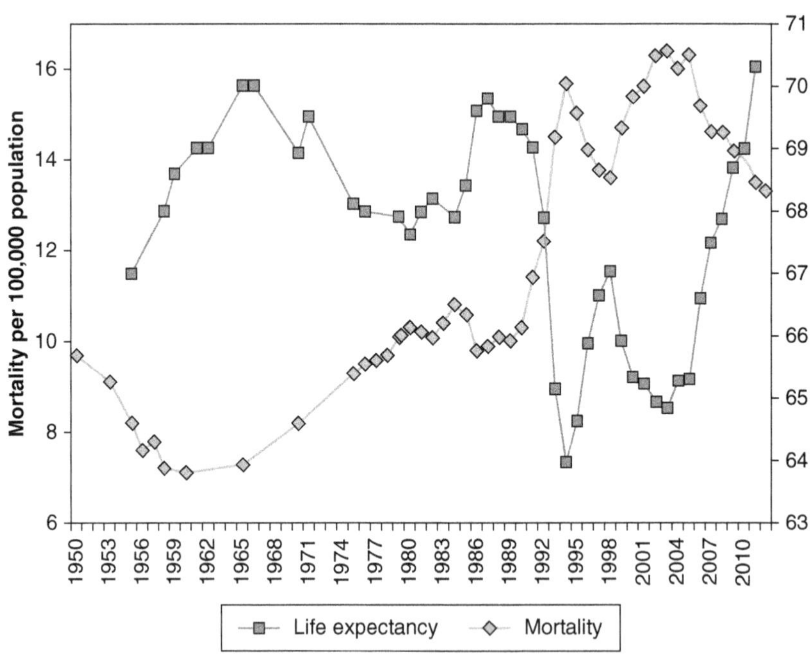

Figure 3.4 Mortality rate per 1,000 population and life expectancy at birth (years).

Source: Rosstat.

crime and accident rates.[10] No, the main cause of the rising mortality rate was cardiovascular diseases in 40–50-year-old males, who could not deal with the shock of the instantaneous transition to a market economy. The stress index, determined by the unemployment rate, the frequency of changes in employment (hirings and firings) and place of residence (migration), the marriage and divorce rates, as well as income inequality, is an index that very closely correlates with the mortality rate both in countries with economies in transition, as well as in certain Russian regions. In China, where reforms were undertaken gradually, life expectancy has risen from 65 (immediately after the death of Mao Zedong) to its current level of 73 years, while in all other former socialist countries, including the GDR, the transition to a market economy has generated considerable stress, resulting in a great many premature deaths. Despite an influx of migrants from other former Soviet republics, Russia's population dropped from 148 million in 1991 to 143 million in early 2005.

The Human Development Index for the population of Russia (calculated as the average value of three indicators converted to a scale of 0 to 100 – GDP per capita based on purchasing power parity, average life expectancy and level of education) did not increase throughout the 1990s, leaving Russia behind Belarus and on a par with Cuba for that index (Figure 3.5). Russia became a typical resource-based

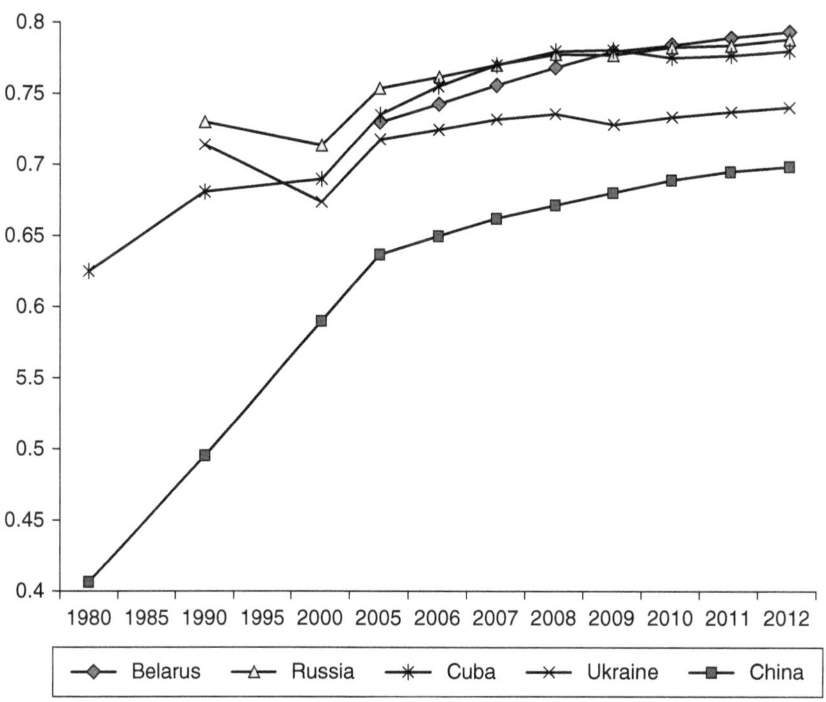

Figure 3.5 Human Development Index for China, Cuba, Belarus, Russia and Ukraine.

Source: Human Development Report (for various years).

economy. Very few experts would call the Soviet Union a resource-based economy; however, the structure of the Russian economy was substantially transformed after the transition to a market economy. For the Russian economy, the 1990s were truly a time of rapid deindustrialization and transitioning to the 'resource track', and the trend appeared to intensify with the rise in global fuel prices after 1999. The share of the leading resource industries (fuel, power, ferrous and non-ferrous metals) in Russia's overall industrial output increased from approximately 25% in 1991 to more than 50% by the mid-1990s, and has remained this high ever since. In part, this was the result of changing relative prices (prices for resource commodities experienced a greater increase), but was also due to lower real rates of growth in production outside the resource sector. The share of minerals, metals and diamonds in Russian exports increased from 52% in 1990 (Soviet Union) to 67% in 1995 and 81% in 2007, while the share of machinery and equipment in the exports decreased from 18% in 1990 (Soviet Union) to 10% in 1995, and then dropped below 6% in 2007.

The percentage of government spending on R & D in the Soviet Union in the late 1980s was 3.5% of GDP. That share has dropped to about 1% in present-day Russia (for the sake of comparison, it is 1.3% in China, 2.5% in the USA and

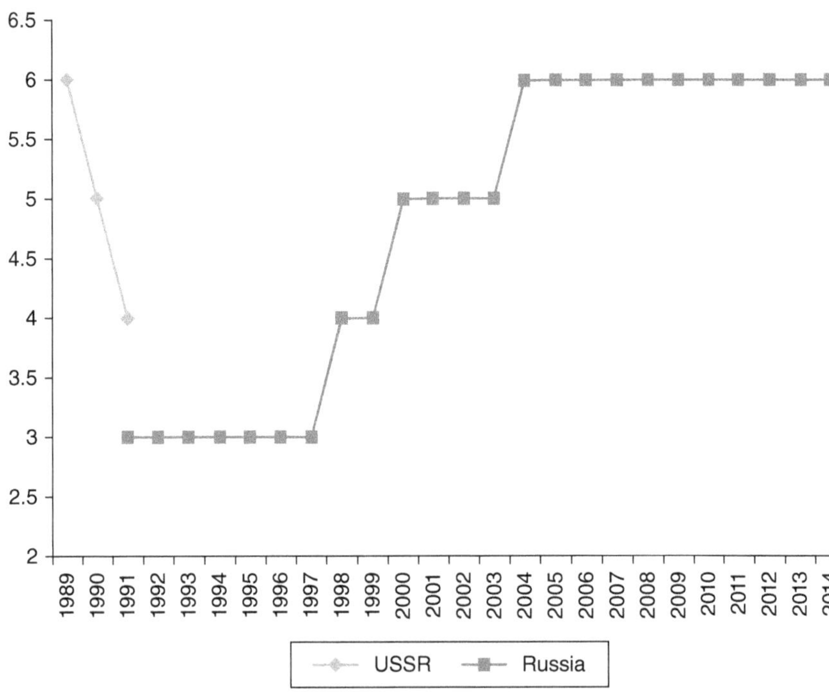

Figure 3.6 Political rights rating for the USSR and Russia, 1989–2014.

Source: Freedom House.

Germany, 3.5% in Korea, Finland and Japan, and 4–5% in Israel). That is why Russia today genuinely looks like a 'normal' developing country with rich natural resource reserves. Moreover (at least, according to Freedom House), the initial progress achieved in the areas of democracy and human rights in the early 1990s was then followed by regression. The Freedom House political rights rating, which ranges from 1 (absolute democracy) to 7 (absolute authoritarianism), after dropping to 3 in the 1991–1997 period, returned to its pre-reform value of 6 in the 2004–2014 period (Figure 3.6).

Diagnosis: state institutions in crisis

The post-reform recession was brought on more by the weakening of the political institutions due to the de facto collapse of the state than by market liberalization. Those countries that successfully prevented government revenues and expenditures from plunging (Central Europe, Estonia, Uzbekistan, Belarus) experienced a less significant drop in output. In contrast, in Russia and other FSU countries, with the exception of those mentioned above, the current public spending for 'ordinary everyday needs' (exclusive of spending on defence, investments, subsidies and debt servicing) decreased three-fold or more in real terms.[11] Purely government functions – from the collection of customs duties to law enforcement – essentially passed into private hands or were de facto 'privatized'.[12]

The State Capture Index, calculated by the EBRD through polling of enterprises in the late 1990s as a measure of the degree of subordination of government policy to private interests, showed that Russia and other new CIS democracies were much worse off than the Central European democracies and even the authoritarian regimes of Uzbekistan and Belarus.[13] In the first half of the 1990s, Russia was faced with a wave of regional separatism that was rapidly gathering force. In August 1990, in an attempt to win the Russian regions over to his side in his battle with the Gorbachev government, Yeltsin promised them as much sovereignty 'as they could swallow'. As a result, the share of the regional budgets in the consolidated budget revenues and expenditures increased, while the federal government was forced to haggle with the subjects of the federation over the division of powers, including financial powers. Many of them directly blackmailed the federal government, threatening to withhold monies owed to the federal treasury. In 1992–1994, agreements were signed with many of the Russian Federation's constituent units, establishing different levels of federal tax to be paid in each specific case. One of the Russian regions, Chechnya, separated de facto from the federation.

The voucher privatization of 1993–1994 and the 'loans for shares' auctions of 1995–1996 led to state property being sold off for a pittance, and this at a time when the state needed money more than ever. Throughout the entire 18 months that the vouchers were valid, they were never quoted at more than $20 a piece, so the approximately 150 million vouchers issued, one per resident, were worth less than $3 billion, all told. This was enough to buy up about a third of all assets in a country with an annual GDP of about 1 trillion dollars (purchasing power parity). At 'loans for shares' auctions, companies with an annual output worth several billion dollars were sold on the auction block for hundreds of millions. Of course, the privatization was mostly carried out in accordance with the legislation, but the laws were such that the supply of property was tens of times greater than the solvent demand, so plants, factories and banks were going for a song. As a result, anyone who could call themselves the least bit well-to-do at the time not only gained unlimited opportunity for incredible enrichment, but literally took control of the economy of the former superpower. As journalists so aptly put it, the country ended up under the thumb of the Seven Bankers ('semibankirschina') along the lines of the rule of the Seven Boyars ('semiboyarschina') during the Time of Troubles of the early seventeenth century,[14] which was the most anarchic period in Russian history, sandwiched between the reign of two tsarist dynasties.

During Gorbachev's perestroika in the late 1980s, the Soviet Union had sought to become one of the world's richest democratic countries. Instead of achieving this status, Russia experienced a transformational recession of unprecedented magnitude and in the following decade plummeted to the level of an ordinary developing country, considered to be undemocratic and unable to lay the groundwork for rapid economic growth. Certain foreign observers believe that 'an ordinary developing country' may, in fact, be better than a fearsome superpower that poses a threat to Western values. However, the Russian public sees things differently. The majority of Russian citizens want the country modernized in such a way as to make it a prosperous and democratic state. However, they also feel that major errors were made during the market reforms and that the economic policy and political leaders of the 1990s have been completely discredited.

An indispensable attribute of any state is that there be a minimum of three monopolies in place – a monopoly on force, on tax collection and on issuance of currency. All three were torpedoed in the 1990s. The unprecedented rise in crime and the notorious contract killings of leading politicians, journalists and businessmen testified to the bankruptcy of the law-enforcement agencies. The decline in tax revenue resulting from the growth of the shadow economy to all intents and purposes meant the 'privatization' of government revenues by the bureaucracy and the criminal element, which took the place of the state as the 'protectors' of business. The increased circulation of monetary substitutes (bills of exchange issued by regional governments) in 1994–1996 and the staggering increase in barter and non-payment (peaking in the summer of 1998, right before the August crisis) virtually forced the Central Bank of Russia out of the business of regulating monetary circulation.

In the period of macroeconomic stabilization in 1995–1998, it finally became possible to bridle inflation by pegging the exchange rate of the rouble to the dollar, and it seemed that things were getting better. A small increase (1%) was detected in 1997 after seven years of unabated decline in production. The mortality, crime and suicide rates began to drop. However, there was no healthy underpinning to this stabilization – the pyramid of government debt and non-payment continued to grow, the real exchange rate of the rouble rose, undermining the competitiveness of Russian goods, the balance of payments deteriorated and production slumped once again in 1998 due to the stubborn unwillingness of the authorities to devalue the rouble. As a result, the short-lived stabilization ended in stunning failure in 1998, after only three years, with the August devaluation of the rouble and debt default. Real incomes calculated on a month-to-month basis fell by 25% in the fall of 1998, only climbing once again to the pre-crisis mark in 2002.

It was in this period that the crisis of the state reached its culmination: federal government revenues and expenditures fell in 1999 to 30% of GDP at a time when GDP itself was almost half of what it had been 10 years before (Figure 3.7). The national and foreign debt had hit a maximum, and currency reserves had shrunk to $10 billion, less than in the Czech Republic and Hungary with populations numbering 10 million. It would certainly be a challenge to find countries with a developmental level like Russia's where the state could have lost so much of its independence in its relationship with 'big capital' in the 1990s. A virtual merging of big business and the middle management levels of the bureaucracy occurred in Russia, and their interests became practically indistinguishable.[15] Neither the civilian ministries, nor even top government officials were able to counter that kind of might. Even the so-called 'power ministries' – the Ministry of the Interior, the army and the security services – underwent 'privatization'.

At the turn of this century, Russia was to be found somewhere in the middle between the developing and the developed world as regards the concentration of corporate ownership and control. According to a World Bank study, in 2003, 23 oligarchs controlled 35% of industrial output (the state had 25%) and 17% of the banking system assets (the state had 26%). In the late 1990s, the 15 richest families controlled around 3% of GDP in the USA, 2% in Japan, but 62% in Indonesia, 38% in South Korea and 53% in Thailand.[16] However, it is unlikely that there are many countries where the oligarchs, first of all, started with nothing and became 'world leaders' in only 10 years and, secondly, openly pitted themselves against the state, in effect demanding its privatization.

As a result of these processes, the division between private and public became blurred and the interests of the mid-level bureaucracy and the business elite merged. Thus, the state, having been almost completely privatized, took on neo-patrimonial (feudal) features. In such an environment, it became 'incongruous' to conduct policy interventions to improve the situation (as it would be virtually impossible for any intervention to counter such a powerful fusion of interests). Economic and social collapse served the elite remarkably well. One would perhaps have to look to Latin American history for analogies: the overthrow of the Jacobo Árbens government in Guatemala by the American corporation United Fruit Company in 1954, or the toppling of the Salvador Allende government in Chile with the involvement of Anaconda and ITT in 1973, in both cases with the support of the CIA. True, the challenge to the state in Russia came from home-made oligarchs and not American transnationals, and the army did remain on

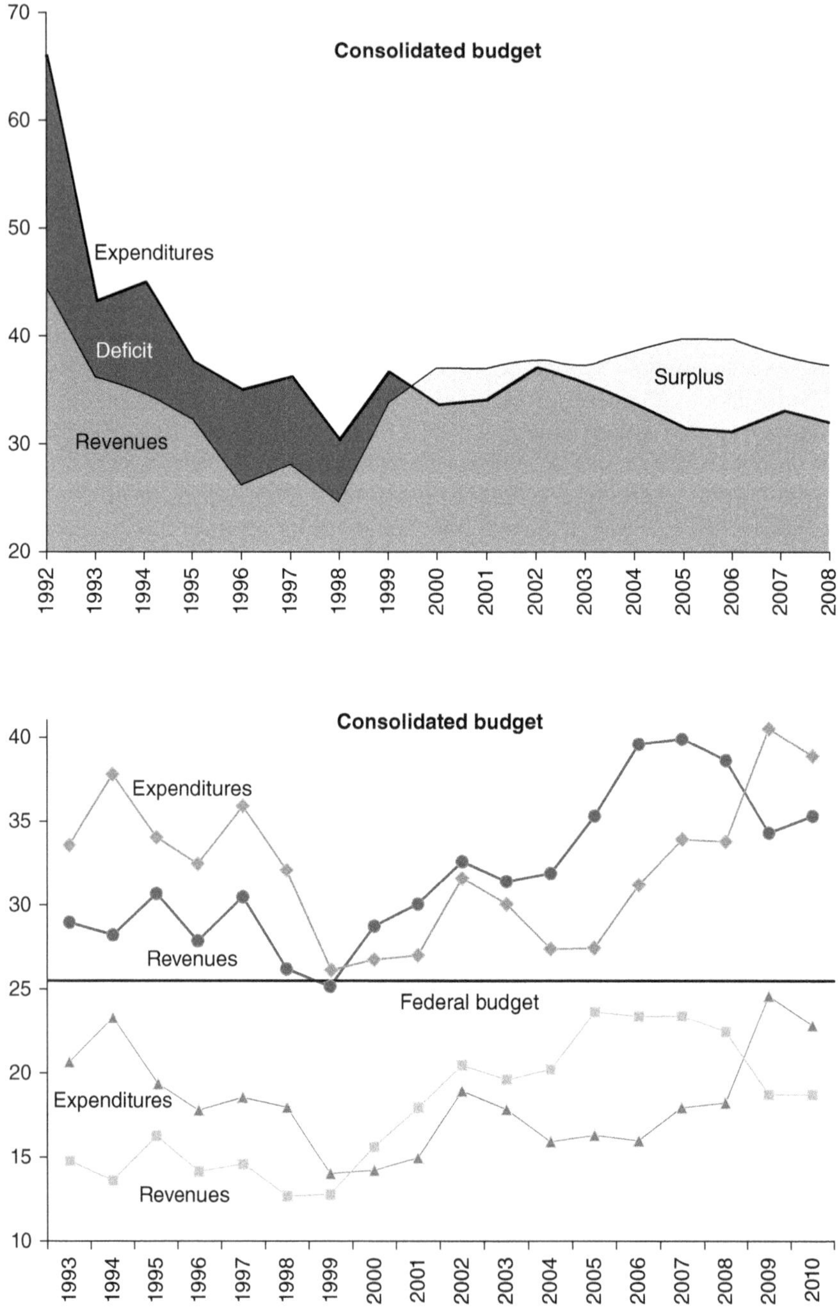

Figure 3.7 Government expenditure, percentage of Russia's GDP.

Source: EBRD Transition Report, Rosstat.

the side of the government, a valuable legacy of the Soviet past, whose merit the historians of the future will come to re-assess.

Even on 31 December 1999, when Boris Yeltsin handed the presidency over to Vladimir Putin, who had only been Prime Minister for five months, and, even in March 2000, when Putin was elected President for his first term by a majority of 52.5% of the vote, the federal government was weaker than it had been at any time since the Civil War of 1918–1921. In August 2000, the Ostankino television tower in Moscow went up in flames and the nuclear submarine Kursk sank – the feeling was that the federal government might as well be done away with, it was so useless. It is easy to imagine what would have happened in Russia if the trends of the 1990s had continued. Further criminalization of the country, complete 'privatization' of the machinery of government by the oligarchs, the collapse of civil society, the weakening of the federal government as real power shifted to the regions, and a battle between criminal groups and the oligarchs and regional governors for the remaining power in an ocean of anarchy.[17] In short, not the 'wild west', but the 'wild east'.

To paraphrase Marx, you could say that the worst state differs from the best oligarchs in that it has a longer planning horizon. The oligarchs, despite being so 'civilized' and committed to democratic ideals, are, nevertheless, more concerned with their profits in the here and now than they are with long-term national interests. During and after the currency crash of 1998, the oligarchs were 'siphoning off' the assets of their banks into 'clean' companies, leaving only debt in the bankrupt banks. In the end, most personal deposits were returned, but only under pressure from the government and only following five years of litigation. Is it at all surprising that the people supported Putin and not the oligarchs?

Restoring institutions

The victory of Unity (Yedinstvo), the 'party of power', in the 1999 parliamentary elections was, among other things, a victory of the have-nots (subsidized regions) over the haves (donor regions), the latter having joined forces in the Yevgeny Primakov–Yury Luzhkov bloc called Fatherland – All Russia. Putin tried to limit the all-powerful regions by changing the principles of fiscal federalism, appointing presidential 'viceroys' in seven federal districts, each combining a dozen or so regions, and reforming the Federation Council, the upper chamber of the Russian parliament, which represented the interests of all the 89 regions in existence at that time. In September 1999, Putin began the second Chechen war, refusing to negotiate with the separatists in any way, shape or form. He launched court proceedings against the oligarchs, all the while staying within the law: they were accused of failing to pay taxes and engaging in financial machinations. Some of them emigrated; others were arrested. The only non-governmental television channel, NTV, was shut down (incidentally, also on totally legal grounds, as oligarch Gusinsky had refused to pay off debt owed to the state-owned Gazprom, having seemingly decided that freedom of speech was not worth that much money).

Meanwhile, the Russian economy was continuing to revive: economic growth reached 6% in 1999, 10% in 2000 and 4–6% annually in 2001–2008 (Figure 3.1). Unemployment dropped from 13% in 1999 to 6% in 2008, and inflation fell from 84% in 1998 to 12% in 2003–2005. The budget deficit turned into a surplus, and government revenues and expenditures as a percentage of GDP slowly began to rise (Figure 3.7). Foreign debt as a percentage of the GDP decreased, capital flight decelerated and currency reserves expanded. The state began to regain ground.

But then, the global economic crisis of 2008–2009 struck Russia. The GDP slipped almost 8 percentage points in 2009 (largely because of the exodus of capital), more than in the majority of countries, but real household incomes did not decrease. And, post-crisis recovery was sluggish – the growth rate was 3–4% in 2010–2012 and 0–1% in 2013–2014. The slowdown was to all intents and purposes caused by an excessively restrictive monetary policy (inflation slowed to 6–7% per year in 2011–2014) and an increase in capital flight in 2014 related to the annexation of Crimea, the conflict in Ukraine and Western sanctions. Nonetheless, the social climate did not deteriorate during or after the 2008–2009 crisis – the level of inequality remained high, yet stable, while the crime rate, the number of murders and suicides, and the mortality rate all dropped (Figs. 3.2–3.4). The birth rate, which had hit a 50-year low in 1999, began to rise, as did the number of marriages registered (although this is partly a result of the demographic wave of the 1970s); the number of divorces, having reached a maximum in 2003, then began decreasing. Russia's population bottomed out in 2009 (142.7 million people, compared to 148.3 million in 1991) and then began to inch its way back up. In 2013, the rate of natural increase (the birth rate minus the death rate, or the population increase minus net immigration) was positive for the first time in 20 years. In effect, this means that Russia is gradually backing away from the edge of the abyss of anarchy and chaos, into which it was plunging, seemingly irrevocably, in the 1990s.

It is these improvements in the social sector since the early 2000s that have given rise to a feeling of stability and led to government popularity. Economic growth and low inflation alone cannot prevent the disintegration of the country if social inequality and crime are on the rise. Building the vertical power structure and intensifying centralization may not even help surmount the state's decline, if these measures do not strengthen the rule of law and limit the shadow economy. In fact, Putin has been criticized in the past precisely for concentrating power in the hands of one person without greater order resulting. At any rate, it is now possible to detect signs of a real, rather than an ephemeral, stabilization: the crime and suicide rates are falling, the mortality rate is dropping, the number of marriages and the birth rate are rising, and the divorce rate is down.

Putin's popularity throughout his 15 years as president (2000–2008 and 2012 on) or prime minister (2008–2012) never dropped below 50%, despite all of the ups and downs.[18] Even before the annexation of Crimea in March 2014, polls indicated that his popularity was even greater than the 71% of voters who cast their ballot for him in 2004 and the 64% who did so in 2012 (many of his supporters simply did not turn out to vote, as they were certain that he would win anyway). A confidence rating of this magnitude can be explained primarily by his ability to stop the decline of the state in the wake of the reforms of the 1990s. All other problems pale in contrast to the threat of social and national disintegration. The majority of Russian citizens are prepared to forgive Putin his hard-handed tactics in dealing with the oligarchs and even with entrepreneurs of a lesser stature, his 'purges' in Chechnya and the constraints placed on democracy and freedom of speech, all in the interests of strengthening law and order and putting limits on a situation that knows no bounds. The Happiness Index for the people of Russia (the percentage of happy people minus the percentage of unhappy people) has almost always been on the rise, except during the 2008–2009 crisis, with the annexation of Crimea catapulting the index to the highest level it had been in 24 years (see Popov's chapter later in this book).

The legacy of the hard times of the 1990s remains embodied in multiple challenges, and economic and social policy could naturally be better in many respects. Russia's economic growth is relatively unstable and, on average, advances at a rate that is far below China's. The percentage of the oligarchs' wealth to GDP – 'oligarch intensity' – is one of the highest in the world. High tech industries have deteriorated, the structure of the economy and exports is increasingly resource-oriented, and education and health care are no longer universally free nor universally high-quality. However, in contrast to the 'turbulent 1990s', progress is evident in practically all areas, from social development to foreign policy. Therefore, despite the crisis of 2008–2009 and the post-crisis economic downturn, it must be acknowledged that Russia's socioeconomic situation today (in 2014) is not just satisfactory; it is, in fact, rather successful.

Conclusion

The almost quarter of a century that is objectively analyzed here (1991–2014) naturally separates into two timelines – the Yeltsin era (1991–1999) and the Putin era (2000–2014). All indicators (with the exception of the Freedom House democracy ratings) point to the socioeconomic situation deteriorating in the first, while improving in the second. This does not mean that Yeltsin was solely responsible for the collapse of the 1990s, and that Putin can take sole credit for the recovery of the 2000s. After all, energy prices were much lower in the 1990s than in the 2000s. Moreover, and most importantly, the Yeltsin policies of the 1990s, just like the Putin policies of the 2000s, were supported by the majority of the elite at the time and by the majority, or at least a considerable portion, of the public. In fact, this is the main question posed by this book: why was the public no less supportive of the policy of economic and social destruction in the 1990s than it was of its antithesis in the 2000s. In subsequent chapters, we try to answer this question with respect to policies in various areas of public life – in the economy, social sector, state-building, regional development and international policy.

Notes

1 Vladimir Popov, 'Life Cycle of the Centrally Planned Economy: Why Soviet Growth Rates Peaked in the 1950s', in Saul Estrin, Grzegorz W. Kolodko, and Milica Uvalic (eds), *Transition and Beyond* (New York: Palgrave Macmillan, 2007).

2 Vladimir Popov, 'Shock Therapy versus Gradualism: The End of the Debate (Explaining the Magnitude of the Transformational Recession)', *Comparative Economic Studies*, Vol. 42, No. 1, 2000, pp. 1–57, available at http://http-server.carleton.ca/~vpopov/documents/TR-REC-full.pdf. [Accessed on: 19 June 2015].

See also Vladimir Popov, 'Shock Therapy versus Gradualism Reconsidered: Lessons from Transition Economies after 15 Years of Reforms', *Comparative Economic Studies*, Vol. 49, No. 1, 2007, pp. 1–31, available at http://http-server.carleton.ca/~vpopov/documents/Shock%20vs%20grad%20reconsidered%20-15%20years%20after%20-%20CES,%202007.pdf. [Accessed on: 19 June 2015].

3 Andrei Shleifer and and Daniel Treisman, 'A Normal Country: Russia after Communism', *Journal of Economic Perspectives*, Vol. 19, No. 1, 2005, pp. 151–74.

4 Vladimir Popov, 'Mortality Crisis in Russia Revisited: Evidence from Cross-regional Comparison', NES and CEFIR Working Paper No. 157, 2001 (http://http-server.carleton.ca/~vpopov/documents/Mortality-regions-MPRA_paper_21311.pdf. [Accessed on: 19 June 2015].

5 D. Kaufmann and A. Kaliberda, 'Integrating the Unofficial Economy into the Dynamics of Post-Socialist Economies', World Bank, *Policy Research Working Paper*, No. 1691, 1996; Simon Johnson, Daniel Kaufmann, and Andrei Shleifer, 'The Unofficial Economy in Transition', *Brookings Papers on Economic Activity*, 1997; Michael Alexeev and William Pyle, 'A Note on Measuring the Unofficial Economy in the Former Soviet Republics', *Economics of Transition*, Vol. 11, No. 1, 2003, pp. 153–75.

6 UNODC (United Nations Office on Drugs and Crime), UNODC Homicide Statistics, available at: http://www.unodc.org/gsh/en/data.html. [Accessed on: 19 June 2015].

7 WHO (World Health Organization), 'Global Burden of Disease Database', 2000–2012, available at: http://www.who.int/healthinfo/global_burden_disease/estimates/en/index2.html. [Accessed on: 19 June 2015].

8 Ibid; and Vladimir Popov, 'Russia Redux', *New Left Review*, No. 44, 2007.

9 Vladimir Popov, 'Strategies for Economic Development', Higher School of Economics Publishing House, 2011, http://http-server.carleton.ca/~vpopov/documents/NDS-April%202011/Vvedeniye.pdf. [Accessed on: 19 June 2015]

10 G. A. Cornia and R. Paniccia (eds), *The Transition's Mortality Crisis* (Oxford: Oxford University Press, 2000); Popov, 'Strategies for Economic Development', op. cit.

11 Popov, 'Shock Therapy versus Gradualism'.

12 Piotr Dutkiewicz, Marketa Geisler and Vladimir Suchan, 'Postcommunism and Globalization', in I. Suchanek (ed.), *From Global Security to Transborder Initiative* (Cambridge/Kielce, 2000), pp. 81–91.

13 J. Hellman, G. Jones, and D. Kaufmann, 'How Profitable Is Buying the State Officials in Transition Economies?', *Transition: The Newsletter About Reforming Economies*, April 2000, pp. 8–11.

14 Piotr Dutkiewicz, 'Democracy After Collapse', *Russia in Global Affairs*, No. 4, October/December 2011, pp. 144–54.

15 Piotr Dutkiewicz, 'Russian Developmental State' (in Russian), *Russia in Global Affairs*, No.5 September–October 2009, pp.73–86.

16 S. Guriev, A. Rachinsky, 'The Role of Oligarchs in Russian Capitalism', *Journal of Economic* Perspectives, Vol. 19, No. 1, Winter 2005, pp. 131–50, available at http://econ.sciences-po.fr/sites/default/files/file/guriev/GurievRachinsky.pdf. [Accessed on: 19 June 2015]. S. Claessens, S. Djankov, L. Lang, 'The Separation of Ownership and Control in East Asian Corporations', *Journal of Financial Economics*, Vol. 58, 2000, pp. 81–112.

17 Piotr Dutkiewicz, 'Asymmetric Power, Heresy and Post-Communism', *Politex*, Journal of St. Petersburg University, Vol. 2, No. 4, 2007, pp. 40–50 (in Russian).

18 Vladimir Popov, 'China's Rise, Russia's Fall: Medium Term Perspective', *TIGER working paper*, No. 99, Warsaw. Published subsequently in *Historia e Economia Revista Interdisciplinar*, Vol. 3, Nos. 1–2, 2007.

4 Transformation

For the people or for the elite?

Leonid Grigoryev

Russia's transition from a Soviet state, Communist ideology, and planned economy to democracy and a market economy (which have become a new ideology) is replete with critically important questions. We will try to address some of them, but to begin with, we need to answer the following question: what are the criteria that have determined the success or failure of Russia's transformation over the past 25 years? Prior to drawing any conclusions, we need to define a basic frame of reference: the results, the stages of transformation, the approaches used to analyze and assess the conditions faced by the country and its main social groups at the beginning of its transformation, at various stages and at present, in 2014–2015. The key aspects of the transformation are reform of property relations, governance and rule of law (and the availability of effective legislative power).

While macro-economic stability, about which so much has been said, is crucial for economic growth and investment, ultimately it is property owners who determine the rules of the game within any macro-economic framework. Still, the outcome of the transformation reforms is not determined by laws, which politicians can cite in their memoirs, or by the approval of international financial institutions, and even less so by favourable coverage in scholarly journals. The outcome of historic reforms of such magnitude as the transition of a great power from socialism to democracy and a market economy (and a successful transition, in particular) is first and foremost determined by the destiny of the people who lived in that period and who unwittingly became 'engines of progress'. The verdict of history on the success or failure of the transformation will be based not on the opinions of future generations or historians, but on the fortunes and misfortunes of these people and their children.

Unlike the Bolsheviks, who promised happiness in a distant future, today families, companies, entrepreneurs and intellectuals make immediate online judgments on the success or failure of political and economic reforms. While certainly important, fiscal stability, low inflation, stable GDP growth, taxes and bankruptcy laws are only instruments of reform. In the end, it is not the specific reforms that will matter, but the interaction among the key features of the new social and economic system, including the type of property relations, the quality of governance, the unemployment level and the availability of well-paying jobs, work for intellectuals and, accordingly, the increased or maintained development level (intellectual development, in particular) of the country, and the quality of its financial and political elites. We believe that it is absolutely necessary to apply the well-known principle that an object does not exist without an observer. The assessment of Russian reforms, including economic growth, public welfare and the position and type of the elites, is to a large extent based on the initial expectations, their success or failure, the changing interests and goals in various stages of the transformation, and finally, the conditions faced by various groups at the end of the transformation process, that is, today.

Transformation can be considered successful if it results in the creation of a new system of institutions, maintains the society's intellectual level and public welfare (the main goal of the reforms), and restores the country's competitiveness in the new conditions. The course of the transformation, its phases and the conditions of various social groups over the last 25 years have been determined by the position of a certain group of people known as reformers. Depending on the observer's beliefs, the reformers are either heroes or villains. During transitional periods (in times of active reforms) we observe two types of state: a *regulatory state* and a *reformer state*. The first type is prevalent in countries with a mature institutional foundation. Reforms implemented in these countries (e.g. the OECD countries) are of a limited scale and do not usually affect the nature of their economies. The regulatory state ensures compliance with the rules and their adjustment when necessary. The reformer state is a special and temporary group of high ranking officials that develops and tries to systemically introduce new institutions. They implement reforms using the legislative and executive branches of power, but within a very tight timeframe, very energetically and without regard for the interests of those groups and social strata that were the beneficiaries of the old institutional system.

The success of the reforms depends on the basic conditions of the period, the information available to the reformers, their goals, the instruments of analysis and implementation at their disposal, what can be anticipated and promised to the public, and, finally, the resistance level of the old institutions, or the new ones that have acquired an independent role and power and are preventing further evolution of the system. In relation to major reforms that are painful for the population, three normative reform principles (regardless of who the reformer was) have been used in the process of transition from a planned to a market economy during the first 10–15 years, but especially in the first critically important years: first, a return to the development path in the framework of the European-Christian tradition; second, minimization of the negative impact of the reforms on the public; and third, continuation of the reform for a sufficiently long period.

These three goals clearly contradict each other, as their simultaneous implementation is impossible: an ideal and proper goal; appropriate implementation methods with limitations on available (allowed) resources and instruments (with limitations on counter-productive shocks); plus the reformers' lengthy stay in power and a stable policy of reforms. Obviously, these conditions would be extremely difficult to meet, although positive examples are available. We believe that these are the benchmark criteria, based on which the transformation process should be assessed. Accordingly, the results should be compared with the intentions, strategies and promises of the reformers and the expectations of the 'reformed', although tracing them at each step of the process is hardly possible, and it would be more feasible to review the results at each phase of the transformation.

We believe that 1990 should be taken as the starting point of the reforms for several reasons: Russian GDP was down by only 3% (the overall decline of the Soviet GDP was 2.4%). The start of the reforms in 1990 still offered a chance to avoid the collapse of the Soviet economy and disintegration of the country. The 500-Days economic programme was launched on behalf of two leaders, Mikhail Gorbachev and Boris Yeltsin (although this unity did not survive the drafting of the programme), and was the first such document to proclaim the goal of transformation, as opposed to reforming socialism.[1] Mikhail Gorbachev lost power in autumn 1991, following a failed coup. His reforms lasted from 1988 to 1991 (beginning with the laws On Enterprises and On Cooperatives). Not much was accomplished, and it was too late and absolutely insufficient to avert the crisis. Trade liberalization and other free market reforms were only launched in 1992, in an extremely difficult economic situation.

Economic data for 2015 will accurately demonstrate the transformation results over the past 25 years (Figure 4.1). Obviously, responsibility for the late launch of the democratic and market reforms lies with the Soviet elites. Fearing to lose their privileged position in society, they failed to initiate less radical and more gradual reforms and ended up by 'giving up' everything. They 'lost everything' and were replaced by fifteen (or more) new counter elites, which were willing to take power without adequately considering the realities in their countries and the consequences for public welfare. Clearly, in this case the elites acted based on their drive for power, which was the dominant factor, while being disguised by the rhetoric of public benefit (in the new narrow sense). We do, of course, admit the existence of individual cases of altruism and actions motivated by public benefit, but do not see them driving political behaviour.

It is equally obvious that that a transformation of such complexity should not have been implemented in conditions of economic downturn (in 1991 and 1992 GDP was down by 6.3 and 14.5% respectively). Under such circumstances and facing such a variety of obstacles, much higher demands are placed on the government to thoroughly develop the methods and instruments of reform, to secure public support and, most importantly, to seriously examine and find a solution to the issue of strategic goals and objectives. In this sense, the starting conditions and the existing realities for transformation in the Soviet Union and the post-Soviet space were significantly less favourable than in the countries of Central and Eastern Europe. Only a few experts realized the existence of the differences in the starting conditions, while most enthusiasts viewed the Polish experience of reforms in 1988–1990 as a model, and the likely outcome of the transformation in Russia (see the Programme for the Expansion of Reforms of June 1991).

The expectations of rapid economic recovery in 1992 as a result of the barely started reforms proved counterproductive to the sustainability of these reforms and the political fortunes of those who initiated them. We have always viewed transformation not merely as a replacement of old institutions, both formal and informal, with new ones, but as a multi-tier reconstruction of government and public institutions, including a new rational (different and conscious) form of public behaviour. It is precisely for this reason that rapid transformation of various formal rules cannot be sustainable without prescribing and enforcing a certain type of behaviour for economic agents, households and the public in general.

The pace of transformation is determined by the 'lame camel', which can block evolution, and the distribution of the new dominant institutions and behaviour, rather than progressive politicians or business people. A pilot project successfully implemented for several years will lead to 'transformation' only when the majority of the population (the proportion of the majority is also an important factor) accepts the new system and consistently complies with its rules. In general, this means that without adequate reconstruction of the social system and political institutions in all three branches of power, economic reforms can hardly be sustainable and are likely to be either partially reversed or, more likely, start deviating from the appropriate course instead of returning to it.

The transition of a country-economy-society from condition A to condition H includes several stages and implies qualitative shifts – transitions between levels – of all actors or social groups, which can block further transformation. Considering that at each intermediate B-C-D stage these key players were fated to change (and actually did change) their interests, priorities and behaviour, transformation becomes extremely difficult in this model, which takes the same form as in real life. The first clarification that needs to be made is how we divide (division level) the stages through which the country has passed since the late 1980s, and how we determine them.

Figure 4.1 gives us concise macro-economic information on the country's development stages since the start of the reforms. Later, we will consider additional indicators, including the price of oil, the fiscal situation, the rouble's exchange rate, average income in USD and the unemployment rate, in order to present a broader statistical picture of the country's socioeconomic development during this period.

The scope of this chapter is not sufficient to discuss all of these data, and therefore we invite readers to verify our findings independently, which is a good opportunity to look at the country's economy from the perspective of the government (or the reformers, depending on the period), different interest groups and the population. For a qualitative analysis, let us consider the issue of institutional reform. The following discussion on the periodization of transformation over the past 25 years is largely based on our 2010 work, in which we tried to provide a more detailed step-by-step analysis of this period. However, due to the limited scope of this chapter, longer periods will be considered.[2]

The most difficult question is how many actors should we consider for a country like Russia, and at what level of fragmentation, given the tremendous regional differences, over-concentration of assets and very limited experience of

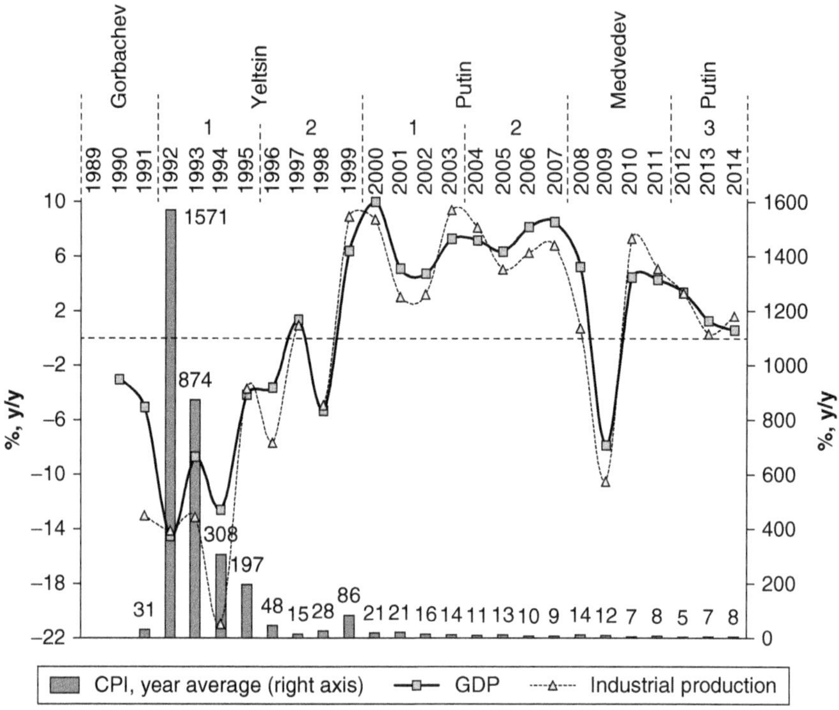

Figure 4.1 Russia's macro-economic indicators, 1989–2014.

Source: IMF, World Bank, Euromonitor.

self-organization in civil society. As mentioned, our approach is based not on statistics, but on an analysis of actors and interest groups and the evolution of their interests as they experienced disappointments and radical changes in their objective conditions.[3] However, in this case, we are constrained by the limited scope of this chapter, the increasingly complicated view of the past and the continued fragmentation of interest groups as more time passes since the start of the reforms. Therefore, we will have to reduce to the minimum the number of actors and periods for consideration, although the task objectively remains extremely complex and multifaceted.

In each new period, actors pursue their objectives (modified at each step) under new external conditions facing the interests (competition) of other groups with modified objectives. However, we will try to set the task correctly, so that in the future these cases may be verified according to actors and stages (Figure 4.2). In the sections below we will consider the various milestones, with adjustments for traditional macro-economic turning points and related major reforms, to which the reader will be accustomed. We have to make additional clarifications regarding the categories of actors (interest groups), although it is clear that with time the composition and type of these categories will change. The political elite (unless otherwise stated) refers to the authorities in control of the executive, and to a greater or lesser extent, legislatives bodies.

While we distinguish five elite categories in Russia, we believe that in this case the military and religious elites can be conditionally merged with the political elite, although we realize the limitations of this approach due in part to the lack of space.[4] Law enforcement agencies (the so-called *siloviki*), with their rising influence, have been classified as the support base of the political elite, and not as part of the middle class, intelligentsia or working class. The financial elite include the high propertied class, owners of major privatized assets and senior managers of state companies, which make most economic decisions. New business comprises the new post-Soviet industries (IT, advertising, consulting and other new sectors), small and medium-sized businesses in conventional industries and some not very large companies. The working class includes the lower middle and lower classes (about 70–80% of the population in this period of the country's history). The regional aspect is an enormous problem in its own right.[5] Finally, the intelligentsia includes educated people of modest means, who, for the most part, do not own privatized assets. Here we should distinguish between the upper segment of the intellectuals (an important but small group), which lives in the capital cities and is able to 'export its services', from the rest of the intelligentsia. To clarify, we believe that a relatively stable middle (middle and upper-middle) class made up about 20% of the population in the late 1990s, and currently totals about 30%.

Before the start: hopes

The Gorbachev period (1988–1991) before the start of the reforms and transformation exemplifies the failure of the old elite to ensure effective government in the country and implement a soft transformation of the economy and society in general.[6] Failing to curb the systemic crisis, which has been thoroughly analysed by Yegor Gaidar,[7] they placed the country, which they created, in a perilous situation, threatening its very existence. It is clear that in the late 1980s, the Soviet Union faced serious developmental failures.[8] The central government's inability to effectively redistribute resources to the republics and regions (and the soaring budget deficit), combined with declining consumer spending and decreased investment rates, further aggravated the situation, resulting in the country's disintegration.[9] It seems 1990 was the last chance to try to implement a successful economic and social transformation from above. Regardless of different political attitudes toward the process of 'imperial collapse', the enormous economic cost of potential disintegration was not obvious to the Soviet republics at that time.

In this regard Russia, like all former socialist countries (depending on the level of ideological penetration), has undergone three institutional transformations: change in the type of government, collapse of ideology and collapse of the plan-based economy. In addition, Russia has also experienced territorial changes, which were so ‘simplified in procedure’, sudden and ill-conceived that they resulted in a transition crisis significantly more severe than in other countries, the consequences of which we are still facing today. The crisis in Ukraine is one of its delayed manifestations.

A number of issues that have subsequently affected the transformation process in Russia and are still important today first emerged in that period. The first problem was the macro-economic crisis, including production decline, increased foreign debt, budget deficit, high inflation and bankruptcy of the Bank for Development and Foreign Economic Affairs (VEB). The second issue involved the delay in reforming and negotiating with the republics a new type of relations within the Soviet Union, and the false belief (including in Russia) that independence would immediately result in prosperity. The third problem was the launch of widespread chaotic privatization, which often took the form of asset seizure by managers, who became the owners of privatized enterprises. Finally, even in this economic analysis, we have to mention the infamous broken promise by the West not to expand NATO, which Gorbachev was given in the context of German unification. For the central elites, this meant the loss of their previous status, whereas the elites in the republics gained independence and the regional elite received almost feudal rights.

For the newly formed market actors, who were to become the future financial elite, this was the period when they prepared for their leap into power. For the working class, the period was associated with anticipation of imminent changes and the belief that the situation could not get any worse, which, of course, was far from the case. For democratic forces – the intelligentsia, the educated working class and a significant portion of the government and Communist Party bureaucracy – this was a period of free speech, the first democratic elections, growing hopes and interesting discussions, although they were very vague as far as their practical implementation was concerned.[10]

It is clear that the proto-middle classes in the Soviet Union (at least in Russia and major cities in the republics), to use modern terms, hoped that following these changes, they would still be living in their large and respected country. What they sought were democratic freedoms and significantly more social justice in the broadest sense, without a major socioeconomic crisis. For them, the disintegration of the Soviet Union was not something imminent or inevitable in that period. The understanding of the main economic issue facing the country (as articulated in the discussions of 1990) was rather simplistic and naive: the transition to the market was a means of coping with the systemic crisis and stimulating individual initiative and private enterprise. There was hardly any discussion of the costs associated with the transformation, while the proposed alternatives to voucher privatization were limited to populist ideas like ‘people’s capitalism’. This point is particularly important, given that privatization, as a means of ensuring development through more effective private ownership, failed to become the central theme of the economic discourse at the time, overshadowed by the political necessity of privatization as a means of ensuring a speedy transition from socialism to capitalism.

Table 4.1 Stages and actors

	Political elite	*Financial elite*	*Intelligentsia*	*New business*	*Working class*	*Great powers*
Gorbachev	Failure	What will happen?	Naive belief in democracy and market economy	Becoming legal	Extremely bad	Promise, praise
Yeltsin 1	Struggle and reforms	What to do?	Excited by the reforms without privatization assets	Formation and growth	Even worse	Observe, praise
Yeltsin 2	Control	Control	Tiredness and poverty	Macro disaster	Even worse	Advise
Putin 1	Attempts at reform	Still peace	Accessing option to emigrate	Growing corruption	At least we won the war	Can pay themselves
Putin 2	Rent for great power	Yukos as a lesson	Problem of statism returning	Corruption and oligarchs	Improvement from oil revenue	Russians have too much oil money
Medvedev	Global economic crisis	Need to share	Some return to liberalism	Used to corruption	Crisis, but there is a reserve fund	We are busy dealing with the crisis, don't have time for them
Putin 3	Stay home	Pay at home	Emigration or?	Less corruption outside	Rent is still available	What is 'he' doing?
Results	Consolidation	Dependence and waiting for the next crisis	Disappointment and expectation	Two capitals, one here and one there	Quiet until there is oil	New reality – Putin wants status

In Table 4.1, we have included the same periods as in Figure 4.1 but will try to use more succinct institutional characteristics and will reduce to a minimum the number of generalized groups whose position, self-perception and behaviour are important for the state of the economy and society. In this case, the phased changes and the final position of the main actors and interest groups determine the perception of the success or failure of the transformation process.

Before the start: practice

It is essential to clarify the goals, interests, and expectations of the groups at the start of the reforms in 1988–1991, as these are usually concealed behind the rhetoric of transition to a market economy and democracy. The political elite was disoriented and split between the central authorities and a temporary coalition of Russia's regional elite and the elite in the constituent republics of the Soviet Union, which saw an opportunity to obtain statehood for themselves. This was too tempting an incentive to resist. The old industrial elite of Soviet enterprise directors tried to manoeuvre in this critical situation to maintain operational control and evade the oversight of the ministries and regional (republican) authorities as the quasi-owners of the enterprises.[11] Taking advantage of the conditions presented by the Law on the Enterprise, they set the process in motion, at the end of which the enterprise managers were to emerge as the de facto owners.

In the 'management–control–ownership' sequence of property acquisition steps, they made the crucial move from 'management' to 'control' and were preparing for the possible next step: ownership. In the meantime, they tried to maximize their current gains, as the state controllers were no longer able to fully extract the due rent and profits. So the cash flows were privatized even before the assets. They were prepared to undertake certain limited responsibilities, associated with their old functions, to secure their newly acquired control, as was the case with other managers. The future financial elite did not yet exist. It was still engaged in the primitive accumulation of capital through cooperative shops, profiteering on computer sales and later, the first banking activities, making enormous profits from high inflation. Consisting of a broad spectrum of small groups, ranging from entrepreneurial Komsomol members to the Soviet criminal underworld, they promoted liberal ideas and radical reforms while earning their first purely financial capital. Their hopes and interests were obvious: maximum liberalization without any liabilities or responsibilities. But claims to political power were still in the distant future.

The intelligentsia (doctors, mid-level bureaucrats and officers, teachers, and engineers: the proto-middle class) was in a state of 'half-starved hope' for freedom and a decent life. It naively believed that discarding Soviet bureaucracy would free market forces, which would help bring about an era of prosperity and allow Russia to catch up rapidly with the West in terms of living standards, political freedoms and other criteria. The intelligentsia was certainly the main bearer of liberal-democratic ideas, but it lacked access to assets, experience in civil society activities, and skills and interest in entrepreneurship. Later, this group would split (in addition to the division along national borders) into those who had something to 'export' and the rest, which included public sector workers, defence industry workers and those who were 'uncompetitive': the future victims of the social and economic crisis. The former would gain access to international contracts, employment at universities and so on, and, in general, would benefit in the long term, significantly improving their financial wellbeing, although without owning major assets. At the same time, the bulk of the educated class would experience a severe crisis of transition together with the rest of the working population.

Individual and public expectations are generally based on a certain amount of information. In this case, we should acknowledge the extreme scarcity of reasonable and comprehensive information on the market economy, both in the scientific and practical sense of the word, which was available in that period.[12] In this regard, emulating the Polish reforms played an important role, although the initial conditions in the two countries were completely different. This is particularly important since in Russia the transformation reforms were led not by the political elite (as was the case in China, despite the internal differences), but rather by individual intellectuals (even though they lacked sufficient information and experience). Of course, at the time all of this was still 'anticipation of crisis and transformation'.

At the end of the Gorbachev period, the new economic system was just emerging. It gradually created an inflow of goods and services, taking advantage of inflation and international trade, made possible by the opening of borders. The main problems faced by businesses were security, extortion and the survival of families. Everything became mobile and new, while expectations significantly exceeded the reality. The great powers were quite happy to see the Soviet Union sliding into internal chaos and unrest. With the fall of the Berlin Wall, countries in Central and Eastern Europe began breaking free from socialism and the Warsaw Pact, hoping to join the 'world of freedom and prosperity'. There, too, a crisis was in the making, with China able to obtain technologies at a cheaper price. NATO started reducing military spending (although not yet expanding), reaping the benefits of peace. However, the political elites of the West had no plans for helping the Soviet Union transform itself into one of their own. For them, the elimination of a political competitor turned out to be more important than long-term global stability. Western intellectuals, however, were indeed quite supportive of the Soviet transformation reforms, although the results of their technical assistance are still a subject of debate.

The working classes in the late 1980s and early 1990s were exhausted by endless queues for basic goods. They had a very vague idea of the prospects of transformation, but at the time, any change gave hope for a better future. The first free elections brought to the forefront opposition figures and young people, which was a good indicator of public preferences. At the household level, the most burning problems were the consumer goods deficit, inflation (which essentially meant forced savings) and a pronounced mood of injustice. Justice in Russia did not just include the need to ensure genuine meritocracy, but also very strong conscious and subconscious elements of equality.

Figure 4.2 Wages and unemployment in Russia, 1990–2014.

Source: IMF, Euromonitor.

The foundation of the social and economic system was crumbling. The macroeconomy in 1990–1991 was on the brink of collapse, which was to become a reality in subsequent years. The republican elites were becoming counter-elites, and were weighing the possibility of exiting the Soviet Union, while the political elite acted slowly and indecisively. The refrain from Viktor Tsoi's song: 'Change! We are waiting for change!' became a popular slogan for both the youth and adults. All of this prepared the ground for the dramatic events which swept the country in the following decade.

Boris Yeltsin, 1992–1999

The 1990s saw diverse trends in macroeconomics, people's wellbeing and the nature of reforms. In this section we will examine various sub-periods. However, the length of the period we selected for analysis was determined by the transition crisis, Yeltsin's presidency, relatively low oil prices and, last but not least, the overall domination of liberal solutions for the tasks facing the country. The first, though not the most important factor of that decade, was the failure of the macro-stabilization and growth policies. The depth and nature of the transition crisis of the 1990s were discussed often and at length. In our case, it is sufficient to point to the general decline in GDP by 43% by 1998, with a minor respite in 1997. In terms of dynamics, this period can be divided, if necessary, into several sub-periods that could be discussed separately. The overall picture is clear: it is hard not to feel sorry for the Russian governments of that period, with their never-ending budgetary crisis.

The government as national regulator did its best to stabilize the economy, but almost all of its efforts failed. The IMF programmes did not help either, and debates on the expediency of endless borrowing and supporting the rouble at six roubles per $1 in 1996–1998 continue to this day. The plunge of oil prices in 1998 against the backdrop of the Asian crisis knocked the bottom out of the efforts taken in the preceding eight years to ease the budget crisis and bring about macroeconomic stabilization. The government was left without revenues, but with bankrupt state treasury bills, a paralyzed banking system and huge old and new debts. By 1999, unemployment reached 13%, and hourly earnings fell below $1 (Figure 4.2). The GDP investment rate – an objective indicator of the success of reforms (not to be confused with ticks in the reform success tables) – did not rise above 15–17%, and the country has not climbed out of its investment hole to this day. The situation was so unusual that it is difficult to place the blame squarely on the period's governments. It is possible that a solution to those problems simply did not exist. However, the optimism of government plans and the naïve hope that the proposed macroeconomic methods would improve the situation raise serious doubts.

The second notable factor of the period was the large-scale institutional reforms, including in the constitution, laws and new institutions and regulations. That huge job was accomplished in 1992–1996 under Boris Yeltsin. This survey is too short to assess the totality of these institutional changes, but we will focus on property, which was a crucial element of the transformation, because it is the owners who ultimately determine the conduct of managers, investment policy, the attitude toward laws and politicians, support for civil society institutions, and the import and export of capital. At the privatization stage, the future owners were heavily dependent on the reformers and the rules they set for acquiring assets and turning one's managerial powers into full ownership rights. But as soon as the transition of property rights is complete, the new owners formulate independent views of the socio-political processes and economic policies, which differ from the views of the political forces that made the acquisition of assets possible. In terms of path dependence theory, the influence of the 1992–1996 institutional reforms was possibly even larger than dependence on the Soviet past.

Earlier, I assessed the privatization process in Russia as extremely complicated, even before it began.[13] The unresolved problems of that period forced us to focus on the voucher privatization of 1993–1996 (including the infamous shares-for-loans scheme). The privatization of 45,000 enterprises amid a deep fiscal crisis increased budget revenues by only about $9 billion (calculations based on official data) in 1992–1999, which is several times less than comparable privatizations yielded in Brazil or Argentina. There are grounds to suspect that privatization revenues were smaller than administrative spending on privatization (with the possible exception of 1997), which rendered the process irrational.[14] Essentially, and according to those responsible for it, privatization was carried out for political purposes ('greed' versus communism). But it failed to create efficient owners, corporate governance and quality market institutions, or to attract foreign capital, because these goals were not formulated as crucial elements of reforms.[15]

We believe it is of crucial importance that privatization, re-privatization, corporate raiding, fraudulent bankruptcies and asset snatching by the state have not stopped even 20 years after the implementation of the first blitz privatization scheme. It was subsequently sharply criticized by many authors, for example: 'Russians themselves do not distinguish sharply between voucher privatization (in which most received worthless shares) and the corrupt sales of the largest enterprises. Both have left a residue of popular distrust of privatization and a market economy that has already slowed other reforms and will affect future market reforms for decades to come. That is a heavy price to pay for the uncertain economic benefits of fast privatization.'[16]

One of the key problems is that people refuse to recognize the legality of large-scale property, and all attempts to solve this problem, even at the theoretical level, have failed.[17] Moreover, the political importance of privatization and its influence on the people were largely negative, while the development of trade and the gradual saturation of the consumer market mostly had a positive effect. Of course, privatization is never fair, but at the least it could be used as an instrument of political influence to bolster the position of the reforming government. The idea was thoroughly considered, and it turned out that this policy was implemented during five of the six analysed privatization programmes (two French, two British, one Czech and one Chilean).[18] The authors did not include the Russian privatization programmeme in their survey, because it did not aim to support pro-reform groups and the reform governments, with the policy modified to facilitate get-rich-quick schemes.

In fact, large groups of educated people did not have to read economic articles or even the media to see from their personal experience that privatization was not only unfair, but also split society into the very rich and the very poor virtually overnight. Everyone saw the gaping difference between the '*nomenklatura*' and the people in the Soviet Union, but at least it was officially criticized, smoothed over and, most importantly, was not a fully inherited benefit. But in the case of privatization, the new riches created by the work of millions of people (across 45,000 enterprises) were divided among the chosen few in just three to four years. The contrast between reality and the people's naïve understanding of a market economy (let alone fairness) was too strong not to affect the reformers, who sustained serious image and political losses. The reformers' pragmatic (or political) task was to encourage people to believe for as long as possible that they owned shares in the new companies. The hasty privatization, the accumulation of huge assets in the hands of non-qualified individuals (defined as those without adequate knowledge of the business) and failure to increase budget revenues had a strongly counterproductive effect on the leading reform principles: the stability of the pro-reform movement, mutual reliance on allies and the consistency of reforms. It turned out later that this type of privatization (by an enterprise in a given geographical area) also tends to increase unemployment. The government did not win any short-term political advantages or long-term revenues from the new effective owners of the privatized assets. Not all problems of that hasty privatization have been resolved to this day. The overall feeling about that huge project was one of disappointment, and of problems that continued to damage Russia for decades.[19]

The third important factor of that period is the establishment of new business, which was a formidable challenge in the midst of a crisis and growing corruption. But it was the main achievement of the reforms, although due to the lack of market institutions the system of small and midsized business did not prosper. People's wellbeing decreased over the course of the decade, compared to the start of the reforms. Until 2003, the hourly wage rate (Figure 4.2) was about $1 or even less, which was in huge contrast to the incomes of the newly rich. The feeling of freedom and the ability to influence developments were also limited. The time factor was crucial for families' ability to weather the crisis. The crisis lasted four or five years although it was weaker in the Central and Eastern European countries, where GDP fell by 20–25%. This difference became an additional factor of disappointment starting in the second half of the 1990s. Figure 4.2 shows the pressures of the crisis on poor Russian families in the 1990s, including unemployment and inflation. A crisis that lasted 10 years, structural unemployment, an unemployment rate of 13%, the growing suicide rate and the impoverishment of pensioners and the professional class: all these issues have been discussed at length by politicians and journalists. But we want to point to a deep feeling of failure and loss and huge social outlays, because the promise of wellbeing and an efficient market economy did not materialize.

The severe and lengthy crisis created a deep divide between the new rich and the majority of the people, and deprived people of their traditional sources of income. Some became 'suitcase traders' (*chelnoki*), others emigrated, while others joined the criminal underworld. In the 2010s, over half of Russians were worse off in terms of personal consumption than in the late 1980s, when life was extremely difficult and with long queues for products that were in short supply.[20] But a new system of institutions, even if imperfect, was created in the 1990s. People were fighting the crisis, numerous new businesses were started, social support was inadequate, the regions were pulling through despite a kaleidoscope of governors, and new big companies were taking over the market, elbowing out independent businesses. It is unclear if even one of the main interest groups (excluding oligarchs and new businesses) was satisfied with Yeltsin's socioeconomic reforms. On the other hand, businesses did not complain as much about corruption as they did later.

The development of the financial oligarchy was almost complete within a decade, and it laid its first claim to power. Its position improved consistently throughout the 1990s due to several factors, such as legal protection of ownership (offshore areas, lawyers), improved asset management, and the growing market value of assets (the improvement of financial markets as distinct from the efficiency of companies). Some of the professional class opted for emigration, not so much to resolve immediate problems as to give their children a better future (this factor has not changed to this day), because their education allowed them to consider the situation in the country realistically. The political elite was either weak or did not have its own funds, and hence depended on the financial elite.

The change began with reforms launched in the government and the political elite under Yevgeny Primakov's premiership between September 1998 and May 1999, which was an instance of change initiated at the top. The period of liberal reforms ended amid an economic crisis, heavy debts, a weary population, unresolved socioeconomic problems and a lack of government resources needed for changing all of this. In a way, the elites of other countries could be pleased with Russia's obvious political, economic and military weakness. Many reforms, some of them necessary but many more questionable, were launched in that period. Freedom of speech and movement, the liquidation of one-party rule and oppressive ideology, and withdrawal from international confrontation were clear achievements of that period. Some good and reasonable things were accepted right away, unlike the issues of general welfare and fairness. Compared to expectations ten years before, the situation in the country at the end of the key transformation period as seen by working people and professionals was lamentable.

The basic institutions, especially in the area of property, were created in the first four or five years of reforms and determined the type of Russian capitalism. The crisis of 1997–1999 forced the authorities to admit the failure of macropolitics and reliance on foreign advice and credits from international financial organisations. But there was nothing much they could do, as property had been distributed, unemployment had peaked and more and more professionals were emigrating. There was no light at the end of the crisis tunnel in the late 1990s, with foreign assistance insufficient and not provided on time or for the required purpose. The authorities needed a new source of income, but it was also necessary to carry on the reforms and to improve property relations and the oversight system.

The oil-based growth model, 2001–2008

This period between crises can be divided into two stages, not so much corresponding to Vladimir Putin's two presidential terms, but rather according to oil prices and government policy. In late 2003, with oil prices rising, a criminal case was launched against Yukos. The logic of this move was not something extraordinary, as under similar circumstances many governments try to squeeze oil companies for as much revenue as possible (through modifying production sharing agreements, for example). In Russia's case, the difference was not so much in the ends, but in the means. However, the first reform attempts undertaken by Putin's government in 2001–2003 were based on several objective and subjective factors. In fact, at the time, the importance of these factors was viewed differently by observers. We will present our own assessment. Russia's emergence from the 1998 crisis was relatively quick for the following reasons ('main boosters'):

1. the sharp devaluation of the rouble, which boosted exports and limited imports;
2. the gradual rise in oil prices above the threshold of $30 per barrel in 1999–2000;
3. the reserve of production capacity and labour; and
4. the sharp decline in the dollar value of exporters' debts to the tax authorities (Solon's reforms, Russian style) and a significant restructuring of tax liabilities.

In 1999–2000, the Russian economy crawled out of the crisis without any clear prospects in sight for high oil prices. It was under these conditions that German Gref's economic programme was unveiled. This was not the last liberal economic programme to be written, but it was probably the last one that was attempted to be realized. The programme had its backers and played a positive role in reducing bureaucratic obstacles for businesses, which, however, were subsequently reinstated by a bureaucratic backlash. We believe that this period between the crisis and the rise in oil prices was the last chance during the transition period to implement a major overhaul of Russian capitalism. However, the key issues like property relations, business freedom, competitiveness development and improved corporate, federal, and regional governance remained unresolved.

The GDP growth rates were quite decent at the beginning of this period, (averaging about 7%), although the baseline of the growth was very low. Most importantly, the government failed to increase capital investment on a broad scale to start overcoming the gap formed over the previous decade.[21] Figure 4.3 shows that consumer spending and housing construction grew at the beginning of the decade (reaching their highest levels in 2008), but not significantly enough. Investment grew at about the same rate as GDP and was not sufficient for technical modernization. It is still worth noting in this regard that for the general public this was the first period since the middle of 1980s to see improvement in living conditions. The political and financial elites maintained their differences and a certain level of independence in decision-making. The political elite 'already' had it, while the financial elite 'still' had it. The emergence of high oil prices freed the hands of the political elite, providing it with an enormous and independent source of budget revenue, which allowed it to introduce a flat 13% income tax rate.

From 2004, in addition to the changes in the relations between the state and business, it became possible to support the poor classes (like pensioners) and the regions. The strengthening of the state's executive capabilities got underway, helped by financial contributions from taxpayers and federal assistance to the regions and pensioners. Often only the material or psychological aspects of Putin's first two presidential terms are considered in this process. For the vast masses of impoverished families, which made up about 70% of the population, this period was characterized by the sudden emergence of stability and confidence in the future. We should not overestimate the ability of the masses to differentiate between their views on the economy and the role of the state. The opinion polls, of course, demonstrated households' preference for state patronage, despite the absence of any serious opportunities for upward mobility.

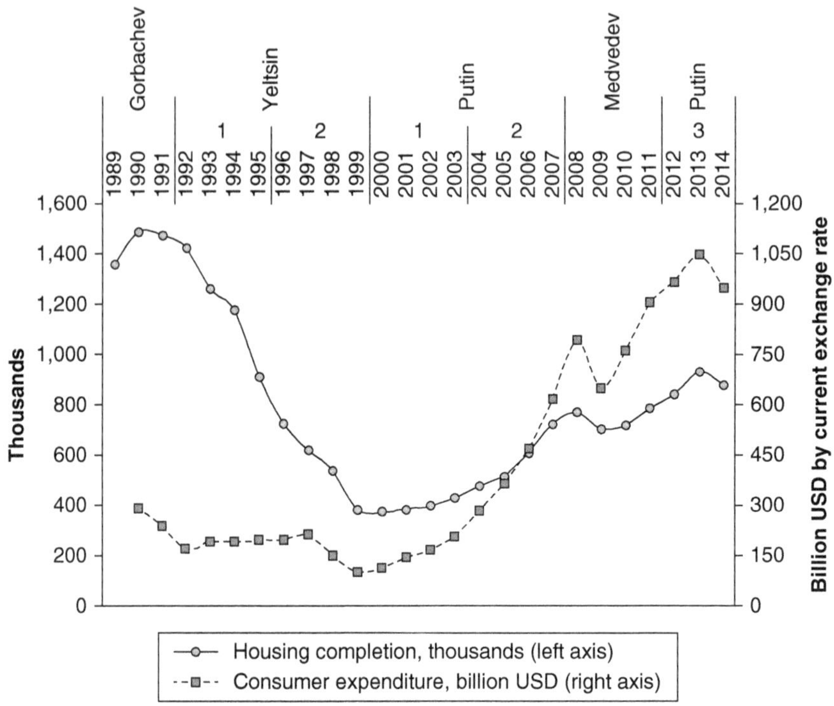

Figure 4.3 Housing completion and consumer expenditure in Russia, 1989–2014.

Source: Euromonitor.

However, stable subsistence of households is important when major decisions are being planned, particularly concerning the future of children, business operations and in general, when various social and government institutions are being tested. It should be noted that during the seven pre-crisis years, the average retail sales growth rate was 11%, an unattainable dream for almost any country. As a result, oil revenue first facilitated the consumption boom and then was used to repay debt, increase defence expenditure and various prestige projects. It goes without saying that the consumer welfare achieved in the 2000s underlies the stability and the relative wellbeing of households in the country. New business, strange as it may seem, failed to improve its position significantly, as regional and local authorities followed the example of the federal government in increasing pressure on entrepreneurs. Throughout this period, the federal authorities continued to strengthen their role in financing and decision-making. The financial elite felt the pressure of the political elite and tried to safeguard itself through compromises within the country and expansion of contacts abroad.

The country's internal economic development model was based on achieving stability and survival rather than modernization. The rapid consumption growth, the consistent strengthening of state companies and the concentration of resources in the budget took place against the background of the lack of a serious basis for the process of capital formation. Income inequality, which first emerged in the 1990s, reached Latin American proportions, close to Argentinean numbers. During the years of booming consumption growth, the investment rate never surpassed the threshold of 25% of GDP. Over these 25 years, Russia did not experience an intense investment boom.

Foreign powers observed with interest Russia's unexpected strengthening, although the bulk of the oil revenue initially went toward private consumption, support of the regions and repayment of the foreign debt. During this period, the West was dealing with the aftermath of the 9/11 attacks and the war in Iraq, mostly with Russian support. The reaction of the Western elite was prompt and simple: instead of accommodating the Russian elite for the solution of long-term global problems, it sided with the some East European elites and pushed for NATO and EU enlargement. Conflicts ensued immediately. The fundamental rule was already in place and was simple: Russia could mimic the role of a Great Power provided that it did not act like one.

Overall, prior to the crisis of 2008–2009 the Russian economy, business and society evolved an increasingly bureaucratic and paternalistic development model, with growing levels of nationalization. In fairness, it should be noted that the economy's development model did not allow for rapid acceleration of the country's development in key aspects: technology, modernization and levelling and evening out of the main economic differences and gaps (provided that it was a matter of concern at all). The issue of accumulating resources for the next stage of growth remained unresolved. The growth and paternalistic development model, based on oil revenue, became a reality. And the lack of success in the sphere of accumulation and modernization has left enormous financial reserves in government hands, which became very useful during the global recession.

Growth slow-down and the crisis of the oil-based model, 2009–2014

This period can be viewed through the lens of two sub-periods: the crisis of 2009–2010 and the exit from it as a separate event; and the sluggish growth of 2011–2014. Before the crisis of 2008, an attempt was made to draft a package of ideas to initiate more radical modernization, including elements of social modernization in addition to a technocratic one.[22] In our opinion, the chances of this being implemented were not very high from the outset, and in the end the idea fell through, not least due to the global recession. The way the 2008–2009 crisis was handled in Russia demonstrated that the political elite was mainly concerned with maintaining stability. Overall, the country emerged from the crisis without depositors losing their savings (due to the increased deposit insurance limits), poor regions were supported by the federal government, and unemployment consequences, especially in single-enterprise cities, were kept in check through payment of unemployment benefits and other measures.

The country came out of the crisis having lost some of its industrial capacity, even more dependent on the exports of hydrocarbons and reliant on budget resources rather than private initiative.

Despite the high oil prices in subsequent years, it should be acknowledged that the oil-based development model has exhausted itself. Under this model, it is possible to exist, and to support certain programmes and areas, such as defence, nuclear energy and energy in general, pensioners and poor regions. It is, however, unable to ensure development and economic boom as befits a young country seeking to take its place at the forefront of global progress.

With declining oil revenues, the political elite focused its support (as evidenced by the structure of the federal budget) on its political base: pensioners, regions and major development projects. In addition, the country is trying to maintain its status as a great power, particularly a great military power, which requires significant resources. The financial elite is trying to survive between two stools, seeking accommodation in the country and recognition as an equal partner abroad through investing, as with previous generations of the nouveau riche, in 'local' projects. The concentration of wealth (in just over two decades) is indecently high: 111 billionaires account for 20% of the country's GDP, which is only slightly better than in Ukraine, where nine people own 15% of GDP.[23] The intelligentsia and new business have found themselves in the most complicated position. Liberalism is no longer the dominant ideology, and as a result, the intelligentsia's role has faded. The protests following the December 2011 parliamentary elections demonstrated that only the capital or the two capitals are really concerned with this issue, while the majority of the population is more preoccupied with corruption, rule of law and illegal enrichment of the few.

These preferences are typical not of a developed, educated and democratic country, but of a country with a vast income gap and unstable democratic institutions, experiencing problems with law, excessive nationalization of public life and a weak civil society. This characterization resembles the one prior to the start of the reforms 25 years ago. It appears that the circle has closed up in various key issues that are highly important for the country's modernization and future competitiveness. The liberal path has failed not because it was faulty, but because appropriate conditions did not exist for it, and innovative solutions were not sought and not found. Still, the country has some leeway (about 20 to 30 years) to implement modernization, at least technical modernization, using oil revenues.[24]

Thus, by the end of the first phase of Putin's renewed presidency the elite was surviving, but was not very confident about the long term. The intelligentsia and new business were silent, with some sending their capital and their children abroad. All of this was observed by two completely different actors: the working classes and foreign elites. The former were not faced with any significant unemployment, while the birth rate in the country remained rather low and the inflow of migrant workers rather high. While oil revenue continues to trickle down from the oligarchs, everything remained relatively quiet, although lower corruption and better rule of law would have greatly improved the situation in the country.

The outside world (the United States, the European Union and NATO), however, was no longer interested in understanding what was happening in Russia, but sought to limit Putin's influence on world affairs. This became all the more clear by the end of 2014. The Ukrainian events and the halving in the price of oil from a high of $115 per barrel in early 2013 to a trough of $45 in January 2015 before stabilizing at around $60 drastically changed the situation. The political elite and Putin were faced with sharply reduced energy rents, sanctions and an economic recession.

Conclusion

Our analysis demonstrates that for an intelligent observer, the transformation of Russian (Soviet) society has followed a very strange path. The goals of gaining the status of a great power and financial domination by a hundred billionaires have been fully realized, and a 'power elite' has been created. At the same time, the intellectual elite and the intelligentsia in general have suffered enormous losses. Some have emigrated, while others have adapted somewhat to living in a country where talented youth have difficulty finding employment and the quality of education is not improving fast enough. The dependence on a number of factors and phenomena of the Soviet period still persists, just as the dependence on the features of transformation in the first half of the 1990s.

The financial and political elites do not get along with each other, and potential reformers lack any breakthrough ideas. The overall results of the transformation period can be seen in Figure 4.4, which compares Russia's GDP growth with that of the world's leading countries and organizations. The results of the comparison are rather obvious. From the viewpoint of the transformation objectives of a relatively developed country with an educated population, these are very unfortunate results.[25] Neither the Russian elite nor intellectuals can consider this a success. The country has lost 25 years and two million educated immigrants in the global competition for long-term prosperity. Of course, as far as their families are concerned, these people, who have been lost to the Russian middle class, have opted for a stable life without politics but with material wellbeing, which in the foreseeable future will not be available in this country. They have given up on politics and enjoy quiet work and, together with our students and tourists, museums, beaches and exotic places.

Across the globe, passive people stay at home, while the more active and adventurous ones travel and explore the world. In Russia, it is the other way around, with the quiet middle class leaving the country.[26] Today, reformers are debating who is to blame for this, without analysing how realistic the objectives and instruments of reform were from the beginning in the existing conditions. The world around Russia has become more complicated and less sympathetic to the idea of national identity and statehood. In fact, it is much more sceptical, or even hostile, to the strengthening of the 'resurrecting empire'. Summing up by interest groups the results of the 25 years of transformation, from the fall of the USSR to the growth slowdown of the current model, this is what we get:

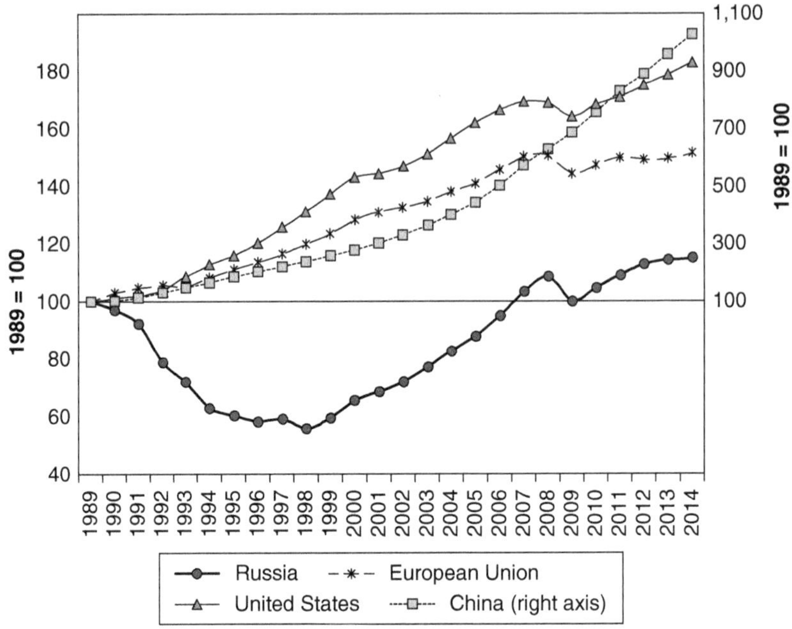

Figure 4.4 The GDP growth of various countries in 1989–2014 (1989 = 100).

Source: World Bank.

- The political elite have changed twice in two decades; the new elite dominate, but are facing the problems of sustainability and Russia's great power status.
- The financial elite, partly controlled by the state and partly rooted in offshore areas, are barely trying to maintain maximum financial independence from the state, holding a significant portion of its assets offshore, and manoeuvring in the long-term game.
- The great powers of the West are not ready to accept the Russian political elite as an equal. They have been able to achieve only one objective of the two. They have weakened Russia, but have failed to turn it into a 'normal' state.
- The new business, weak and heavily dependent on corruption, is creating safety reserves in offshore areas.
- The working classes and poor regions have led a relatively stable existence since 2004, but only thanks to enormous oil revenues with a strong dependence on the distribution of budget resources.
- The intelligentsia has shrunk, lost its positions in society and is buying apartments in Europe and sending its children abroad. While the older generation is still able to reproduce knowledge, the transformation has forced close to two million law-abiding young educated people (according to expert estimates) to emigrate, and this process is continuing. They will either disappear in the global middle class, losing their identity in the process, or will survive outside the country they still love, but which lacks decent jobs for them.

The main issue is how to ensure genuine qualitative progress in Russia following 25 years of transformation processes under the current form of social and economic institutions, given the seriousness of the existing problems and the incredibly complicated external environment. So far, there is no definite answer to this question.

Notes

1 Leonid Grigoryev, '500 dnei na revolyutsiyu soznaniya?' ('500 Days to Revolutionize Thinking?'), *EKO*, No. 5, October 2010, pp. 6–19.
2 Leonid Grigoryev, *Ekonomika perekhodnykh protsessov* (*The Economy of Transition*) (Moscow: International University in Moscow (MUM) Publishers, 2010), two volumes, Volume 1, 'Preface', pp. 8–13.
3 Leonid Grigoryev, Sergei Plaksin and Marsel Salikhov, 'Poslekrizisnaya struktura ekonomiki i formirovanie koalitsii dlya innovatsii' ('The Post-Crisis Structure of the Economy and Formation of Innovation Coalitions'), *Voprosy Ekonomiki*, No. 4, 2008.
4 The political, financial, intellectual, military and religious elites – Leonid Grigoryev, 'Elity i srednii klass' ('The Elites and the Middle Class'), *Spero*, No. 13, 2010; idem, 'Elites – A Choice for Modernization', in Piotr Dutkiewicz and Dmitry Trenin (eds), *Russia: the Challenges of Transformation* (New York: New York University Press, 2011).
5 See chapter by Natalya Zubarevich in this volume. Its existence is specified; residents of poorer regions will be classified as 'workers' (although this is not always accurate). See also Leonid Grigoryev, Natalya Zubarevich and Gabibulla Khasayev (eds), *Rossiiskie region: Ekonomicheskiy krisis i problemy modernizatsii)* (*Russian Regions: The Economic Crisis and the Problems of Modernization*) (Moscow: TEIS, 2011).
6 The author personally took part in the presentation of the 500-Days programme to Gorbachev at his office on Old Square in August 1990. I presented the part on privatization. There was no reaction on Gorbachev's part.
7 Yegor Gaidar, *State and Evolution: Russia's Search for a Free Market* (Seattle, University of Washington Press, 2003); idem, *Russia: A Long View*, translated by Antonina W Boius, Foreword by Anders Aslund (Cambridge, MA: MIT Press, 2012).
8 See Leonid Grigoryev, O. Ivanova and O. Korchagina, 'Ekonomika SSSR: novaya faza krizisa' ('Soviet Economy: New Phase of the Crisis'), in 'Tendentsii mirovogo ekonomicheskogo razvitiya' ('Trends in Global Economic Development'), supplement to the journal *Mirovaya Ekonomika i Mezhdunarodnye Otnosheniya* (Moscow: Nauka, 1991). On the political, financial, intellectual, military and religious elites, see Leonid Grigoryev, 'Elity i sredniy klass' ('The Elites and the Middle Class'), *Spero*, No. 13, 2010; idem, 'Elity – Vybor dlya Modernizatsii' ('Elites – A Choice for Modernization'), in Piotr Dutkiewicz and Dmitry Trenin (eds), *Russia: the Challenges of Transformation*, op cit.
9 Leonid Grigoryev, 'Soviets Need a Unified Free Economy', *New York Times*, 12 September 1991.
10 On 26 March 1989 Boris Yeltsin was elected deputy of the USSR Supreme Soviet from Moscow electoral district number 1 by a majority of 91.53% of the votes and with a turnout of 90%.
11 Janos Kornai, *Defitsit* (Moscow: Nauka, 1990).
12 To the author's knowledge, most reformers in 1990–1992 either did not speak English at all, or spoke it at a level that could not have allowed them to read serious Western scholarly literature.

13 Leonid Grigoryev, 'Ulterior Property Rights', in Anders Asland (ed.), *The Post-Soviet Economy* (London: Pinter, 1992); Leonid Grigoryev, 'Raspredeleniye sobstvennosti i kontrolya v protsesse privatizatsii: posledstviya dlya inostrannykh investorov' ('Property and Control Distribution During Privatization: Consequences for Foreign Investors'), in *Inostrannye investitsii v Rossii: tendentsii i perspektivy* (*Foreign Investment in Russia: Trends and Perspectives*) (Moscow: Informat, 1995), pp. 62–74.
14 See Leonid Grigoryev 'Programmy privatizatsii 90gg' ('Privatization Programmes of the 1990s'), Chapter 8 of *Sravnitelny analiz stabilizatsionnykh program 90-godov* (*Comparative Analysis of Stabilization Programmes of the 1990s*) (Moscow: Carnegie Foundation, 2003), Table 2.
15 See Leonid Grigoryev, *Ekonomika perekhodnykh protsessov* (*The Economy of Transition*) (Moscow: MUM Publishers, 2010), pp. 19–26.
16 B. Black, R. Kraakman, and Anna Tarassova, 'Russian Privatization and Corporate Governance: What Went Wrong?' *Stanford Law Review*, July 2000, p. 1,788.
17 V. Tambovtseva, *Prava sobstvennosti: privatizatsiya i nationalizatsiya v Rossii* (*Property Rights, Privatization and Nationalization in Russia*) (Moscow: Liberal Mission Foundation; Novoye Literaturnoye Obozreniye, 2009).
18 Bruno Biais and Enrico Perotti, 'Machiavellian Privatization', July 2000, available at http://www.aeaweb.org/articles.php?doi=10.1257/000282802760015694. [Accessed on: 17 June 2015].
19 Leonid Grigoryev, 'Sobstvennost i kontrol: 20 let spustya' ('Property and Control: 20 Years After'), *EKO*, No. 7, July 2011.
20 'Uroven i obraz zhizni naseleniya v Rossii v 1989–2009 godakh' ('Standards of Living and Lifestyles in Russia in 1989–2009'), a report for the 12th international research conference on economic development and society, Moscow, 5–7 April 2011, in G. Andrushchak, A. Burdyak, V. Gimpelson et al., Project Director Ye. Yasin (Moscow: HSE Publishers, 2011).
21 Leonid Grigoryev, 'Investitsionnyi protsess: nakoplennye problemy i interesy' ('Investment Process: Accumulated Problems and Interests'), *Voprosy Ekonomiki*, No. 4, 2008.
22 Leonid Grigoryev, 'Konflikty interesov i koalitsii' ('Conflicts of Interests and Coalitions'), *Pro et Contra*, September 2007; Leonid Grigoryev, Alexander Auzan, Sergei Afontsev et al., *Koalitsii dlya budushchego: Strategiya razvitiya Rossii* (*Coalitions for the Future: A Development Strategy for Russia*) (Moscow: RIO, 2007).
23 'Billionaires putting on weight each year', *Areppim*, 12 March 2014, AG, Bern, Switzerland.
24 Leonid Grigoryev (co-author), 'Prognoz energetiki mira i Rossii do 2040 goda' ('Energy Forecast for Russia and the World until 2040'), Analysis Centre, Energy Research Institute, Russian Academy of Sciences, 2014.
25 Leonid Grigoryev, 'Stsenarii razvitiya i ekonomicheskie instituty' ('Development Strategies and Economic Institutions'), *Ekonomicheskaya politika*, No. 3, 2013, pp. 33–60.
26 Leonid Grigoryev, 'Obitayemy ostrov' ('Inhabited Island'), *Sotsialnoye Partnyorstvo* (*Social Partnership*), No. 4, 2013, pp. 38–41; 'Otdat rodine vse, nichego ne teryaya' ('Give the Homeland Everything, Without Losing Anything'), *Nezavisimaya gazeta – Stsenarii*, 25 February 2014.

5 Puzzles of public opinion

Popular support for the transition to capitalism

Vladimir Popov

In the late 1980s, during the time of Gorbachev's *perestroika*, the majority of the population in the Soviet Union was displeased with the socialist system, and wanted it to be reformed. They hoped that the reforms would enhance living standards, ensure progress in the social sphere, strengthen law and order, promote democracy, improve the international situation and bolster the USSR's international standing. In reality the opposite happened: the economy sunk into a protracted recession, over 90% of people saw their living standards plummet, pensions and benefits shrank, free education and healthcare were mostly replaced with paid services, corruption, crime and a shadow economy proliferated, and NATO expanded eastward, coming close to Russia's borders.

This chapter traces how these changes were reflected in the public consciousness. It's commonly known that objective changes are not always adequately reflected in public opinion. People are more likely to overestimate rather than underestimate their abilities. They forecast situations on the basis of past experience (adaptive expectations) and are far from rational in their decision making. The transition from socialism to capitalism, like other turning-points in history, provides rich material for an analysis of the patterns in the evolution of public consciousness. A look at how public preferences in the USSR and Russia have shifted since the late 1980s can reveal at least several puzzles.

1. The political class and the intelligentsia mostly supported the market reforms in the late 1980s and the early 1990s and managed to convince large masses of the population of their relevance, even though earlier the majority of them had been committed to socialist ideals.
2. The majority, or at least a considerable minority, of the population supported the shock therapy of 1991, even though this version of reform led to a dramatic decline in their living standards and social status (in the 1990s, the reforms benefitted between 5 and 10% of the population).
3. Even today, despite the emergence and rapid enrichment of 'oligarchs', along with a surge in inequality, this majority doesn't support an alternative economic policy (left-wing or social democratic) that could improve the living standards and social status of large masses of population.

This chapter attempts to explain these 'puzzles.'

How the elite became disappointed with the planned system: the loss of social dynamism (1970s–1980s)

The Soviet planned system reached its peak in the early 1960s. Though the economy continued to grow even after that zenith, its pace was consistently slowing down (Figure 5.1). Life expectancy hit 70 years in 1965 and stopped growing, oscillating between 68 and 70 years until 1991 (Figure 5.2). Crime, homicide, suicide and alcohol abuse began mounting, starting in the 1960s (Figure 5.3). Khrushchev's 'thaw' in public and cultural life came to an end in the mid-1960s, and all hopes for 'socialism with a human face' were thwarted by the invasion of Czechoslovakia in 1968.

To understand the extent to which the 1970s and 1980s were a 'period of stagnation', we should measure the system's dynamism in the preceding period. Previously, Soviet economic growth rates were indeed very high: between the 1930s and 1950s just two countries in the world – Japan and the USSR – were closing the gap between them and the USA. While Russia under the Tsars, like all of Europe, was falling farther behind the United States throughout the nineteenth century, the Soviet Union began catching up rapidly, with its per capita GDP rising from less than 30% in 1913 (and 20% in 1928) to almost 40% of the US level by the late 1960s, despite a wartime fall-off (Figure 5.4).

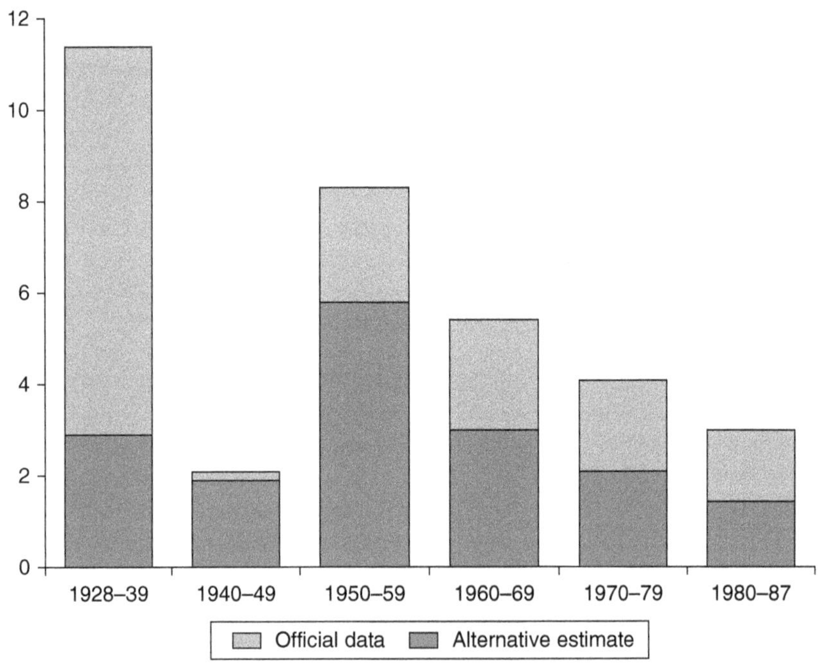

Figure 5.1 Average annual labour productivity growth rates in the Soviet economy.

Source: W. Easterly and S. Fisher, 'The Soviet Economic Decline', *The World Bank Economic Review*, Vol. 9, No.3, 1995, pp. 341–371.

In the mid-1960s, the average life expectancy in the USSR was 70 years, or just a year or two less than in the USA. This was an unprecedented social achievement for a country the per capita GDP of which was under 40% of America's and the per capita consumption of which was even less, hovering at around 30% of the US figure (because of a higher share of investment and defence spending). The USSR's homicide rate in the late 1950s and the early 1960s was much lower than in the early twentieth century, and was approximately the same as in the late nineteenth century (Figure 5.5).

Generally, no matter how you slice it, the Soviet catch-up development model, for all its shortcomings, was certainly highly competitive in the 1950s and 1960s, both in the economy and the social sphere. Actually it was no less attractive than the East Asian (Chinese) model today. It is for this reason that developing countries attempted – with different degrees of success – to imitate this model even when the USSR did not offer any economic aid in exchange. It is another matter where this competitiveness went in the 1970s and 1980s, and what led to the stagnation. Everyone answers this question in their own way.[1] But the loss of competitiveness proved fatal for socialism. The 1970s and 1980s was a time when the Soviet elite, which earlier accepted its restricted consumption as 'temporary teething problems', began turning away from the socialist idea.

As the story goes, in 1964, the Honduran Minister of Communications Rodriguez received minister Ivanov, his Soviet counterpart, in Tegucigalpa. After formal talks, Rodriguez invited Ivanov to his *hacienda*. He showed Ivanov his

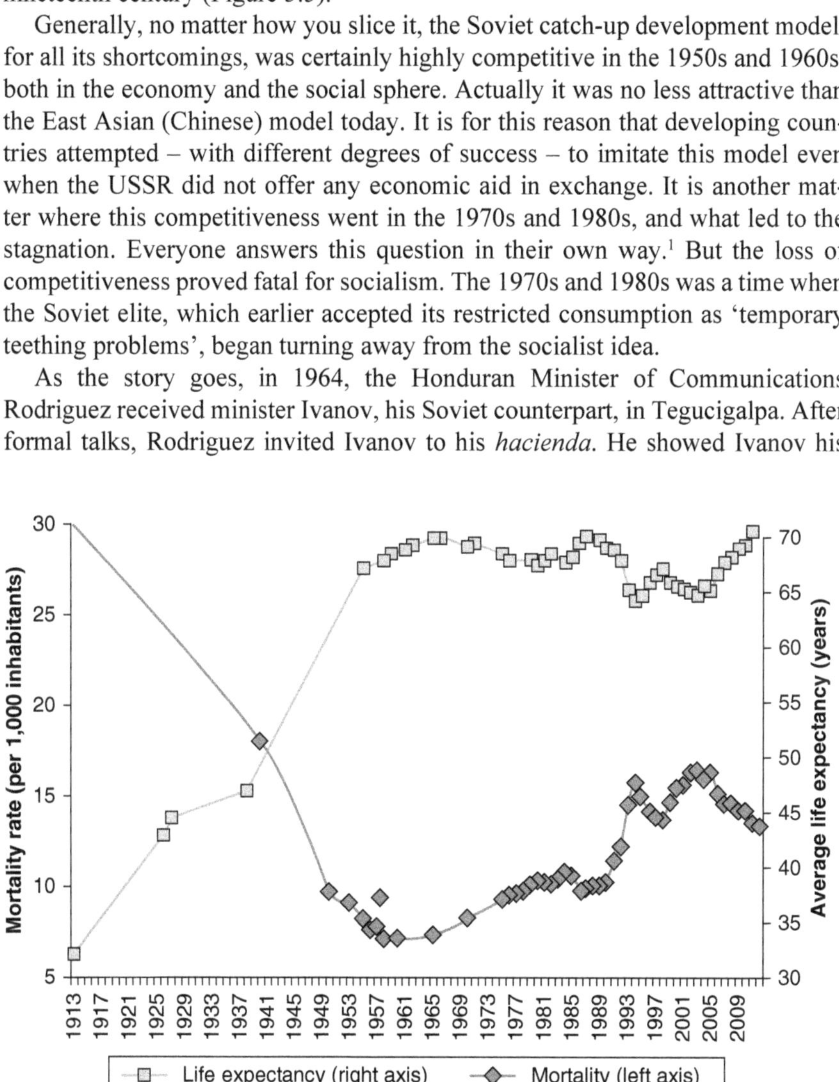

Figure 5.2 Mortality rate per 1,000 individuals and life expectancy (in years).

Source: State Committee for Statistics.

Figure 5.3 Alcohol consumption and mortality rates.

Source: State Committee for Statistics, *Demoscope*, Nos 263–264, October 30–November 12, 2006.

seven bedroom mansion, swimming pool, garages, hectares of orchards, and domestic servants. He took him for a fishing trip on his personal yacht and offered him a luxurious dinner with exotic foods. He gave him a ride in his limousine and told of how his children were studying at Ivy League universities in the United States. Ivanov was not discouraged and not impressed. He knew that the people of Honduras were poor and many were starving. In the Soviet Union, he knew that while living standards were lower than in the West, there was no starvation. He knew that life expectancy in the Soviet Union was twenty years higher than in Honduras. Soviet scientists were receiving Nobel prizes, Yuri Gagarin was the first man in space, the Soviet ballet was the best in the world, and Soviet nuclear submarines could roam the far seas. He was proud that his state was building the most advanced and socially equal civilization in human history.

Twenty years later in 1984, minister Petrov, Ivanov's successor, visited Honduras to talk with his counterpart Minister Gonzales, the successor of Rodriguez. He was unpleasantly surprised and even a little irritated by what he discovered. Over the past two decades, Honduran life expectancy had unexpectedly risen from 50 to 65, whereas Soviet life expectancy showed signs of decline. He realized that even though the USSR was more technologically advanced and economically more developed than Honduras, he would never have the same living

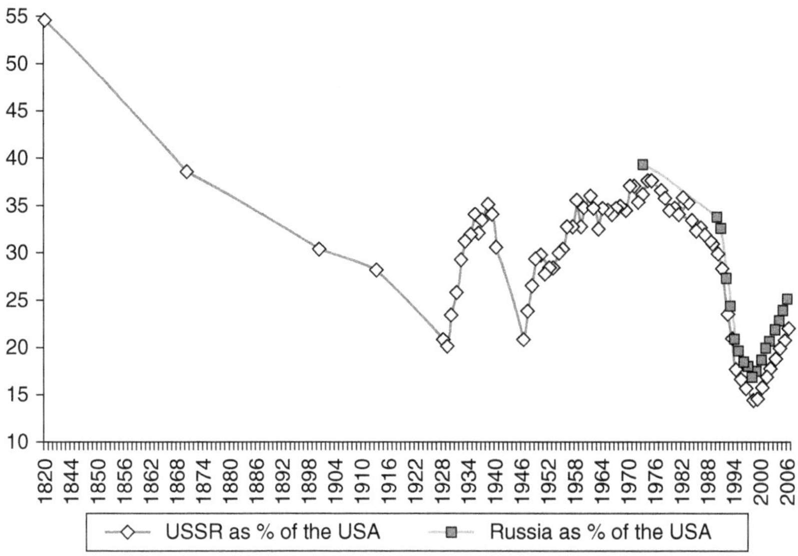

Figure 5.4 Per capita GDP in the USSR and Russia in percentage of the US level.

Source: A. Maddison, Statistics on World Population, GDP and Per Capita GDP, 1–2006 AD (Last update: October 2008, *horizontal file*, copyright Angus Maddison) - http://www.ggdc.net/maddison/

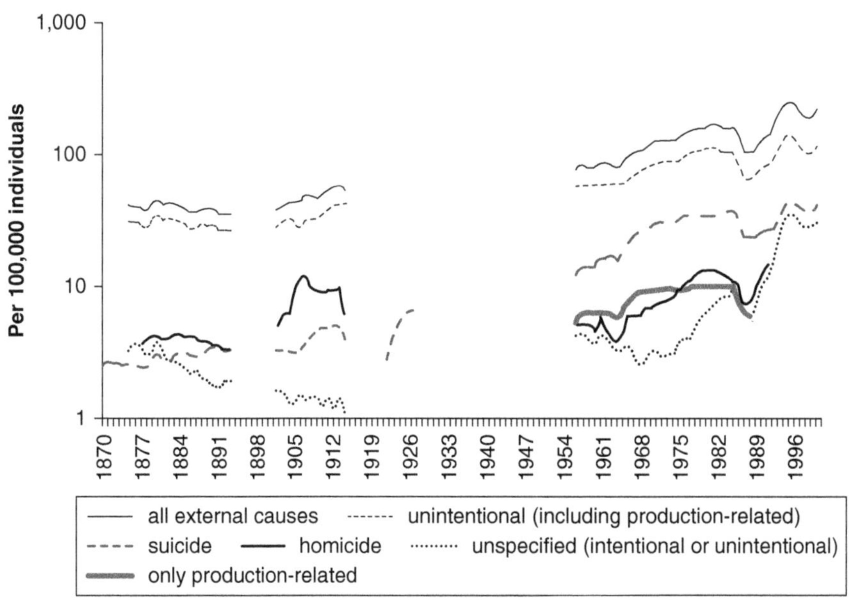

Figure 5.5 Mortality from external causes – various reasons: Russian Empire–RSFSR–Russian Federation, 1870–2000 (logarithmic scale).

Source: *Demoscope*, Nos 29–30, 13–26 August 2001.

standards as Gonzales. Why? Didn't he deserve what Gonzalez had more than Gonzalez? After all, Russian submarines were roaming the oceans and the USSR was leading the world in space exploration, arts, sciences and even ballet. Why should we endure increasing deprivation for the sake of great and noble goals? It dawned on him that even though the Soviet Union was 'growing faster than the West', so were its many contradictions, causing him to think, 'Why bother with socialism? If the USSR had capitalism, I would be far better off than Gonzales!'

Though this story is total fiction, it captures the change in mood of the Soviet elite when the Soviet system had lost its dynamism. The Soviet Union's political, technical and intellectual elites were loyal to the USSR *despite* its lower welfare standards compared to Western countries because they were inspired by the constantly reducing gap with the West in per capita income and life expectancy. These elites believed that socialism as a social system was superior and that it could beat out capitalism once it was 'fully developed'. But when the USSR stopped growing faster than the West in the 1970s–1980s, this belief system was shaken.

Why the public did not vote against market reforms after they led to a collapse of living standards (1990s)

In Eastern Europe in the early 1990s, reformers feared that losses accompanying the market transition could alienate voters from capitalism and bring anti-capitalist parties back to power. It is for this reason that the theorists behind shock therapy spoke about a 'window of opportunities'. They believed that the reform plans should be drawn up almost in secrecy and implemented as soon as possible before the public came to its senses, in order to make the costs of turning back prohibitively high. 'Concentration of political power, limited political competition and rapid implementation enhance the prospects for the successful adoption of economic reforms', was how the EBRD Annual Report 1999 summed up the conventional wisdom of the time.[2]

But the fear that the reforms could be delayed proved groundless.[3] In the first half of the 1990s, Eastern European radical reform parties won three elections out of five, while parties favouring a slower pace of reform lost four elections out of four, and former communist parties lost two elections out of four.[4] Moreover, reforms were not halted in those Eastern European countries where the radical reformist parties (supporters of shock therapy) faced defeat. The aforementioned EBRD 1999 report dedicated to the political economy of reforms shows that the economic reform index correlates with the dispersion of political power:[5] countries with restricted executive powers (presidential and/or prime ministerial), with governments based on coalitions rather than parliamentary majority, with frequently replaced governments or with a higher democracy index were generally ahead of others in the area of economic (pro-market, pro-capitalist) reforms. A study of cases in which reforms were stopped demonstrated that rather than serving as a brake, the frequency of elections helped to promote reforms.[6]

Another study based on panel data for 25 post-communist countries came to the conclusion that political democratization facilitated economic liberalization.[7] Even the heaviest-hit groups (pensioners and the unemployed) voted in Eastern Europe for left-wing (formerly communist) parties, not only while they were in opposition but also when they came to power and continued the reforms.[8] It was the left-wing parties that implemented privatization and austerity programmes, including pension reforms, in Hungary and Poland. In fact, more or less gradual reforms (gradualism) could only be carried out by authoritarian regimes (China, Vietnam before 1989, the USSR under Gorbachev, Belarus, Turkmenistan and Uzbekistan), while states with competitive elections seemed to have no such option at all, because their electorate wanted everything, and right away, regardless of whether it was good for the economy. At any rate, no democratic country was actually able to implement gradual economic reforms.

In Russia's regions electoral preferences also correlated with the economic reform index (Figure 5.6) and remained sufficiently stable (Figure 5.7). The regions that voted more for pro-reform parties and candidates in 1993–1996, and less for the Communists, were as a rule ahead of others in terms of price deregulation, small privatization and abolition of subsidies.[9] The reform efforts of regional governments were supported by the electorate even after controlling for objective factors, such as urbanization and education levels, previous drops in income levels, wage arrears and alcohol consumption.[10]

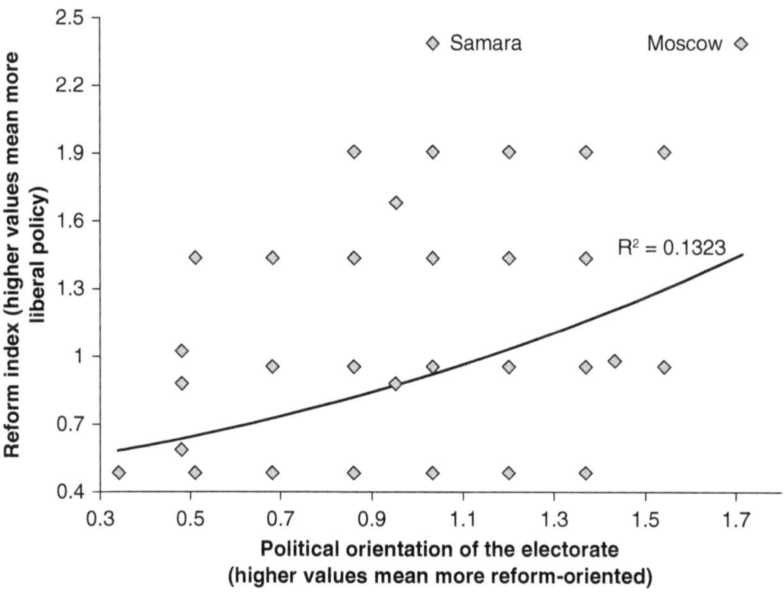

Figure 5.6 Political orientation of voters in 1993–1996 and economic reform index in Russian regions.

Source: Popov, 2001; Popov, 2004.

Notes: Index of the political orientation of the electorate calculated by the Russian Union of Industrialists and Entrepreneurs.

Economic reform index calculated as the average of indices of price liberalization, small privatization and share of subsidies in regional budgets and subsidies for agricultural products (for more detail, see: Popov, 2001).

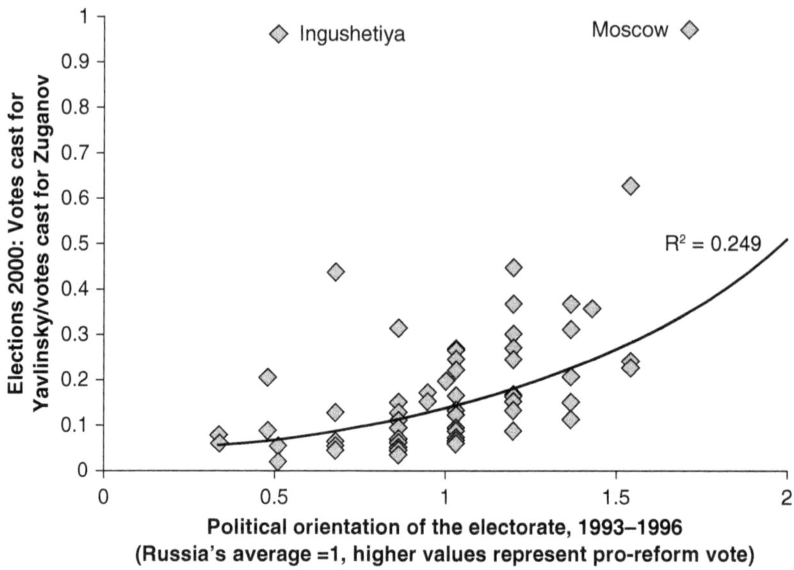

Figure 5.7 The electorate's political orientations in Russian regions in 1993–1996 and in 2000.

Source: Popov, 2001; Popov, 2004.

Note: Index of the political orientation of the electorate calculated by the Russian Union of Industrialists and Entrepreneurs.

Over the course of the reforms, political orientations shifted dramatically to the right regardless of the fact that the reforms led to the deterioration of the economic and social status of the absolute majority of people. Opinion polls conducted in the USSR in 1989–1990 reflected a generally negative attitude toward capitalism: the majority of respondents were clearly against land trade, although they supported family farms, and scorned the cooperatives that sold their products at market prices and served as a cover and euphemism for private businesses. The idea of private businesses was supported by 47%, but over 50% believed that these should be small, family affairs deprived of the right to hire employees. Two-thirds of those polled said that state companies should prevail in the future Soviet economy.[11] A year later (1991), by voting for Yeltsin at the presidential elections, the population effectively approved his radical reform programme that included shock therapy, rapid price deregulation and privatization. Why did the mood change so dramatically?

It is possible to indicate several specific causes that many people seem to have in mind, that are not the main ones. For example, neither the experts, nor the general public were capable of forecasting the future, and the prediction error was simply glaring. Table 5.1 shows that in 1990 the discussion of market transition options was based on predictions that production would grow by 25 to 50% before 1995, whereas in reality production declined by about one-third between 1990 and 1995.[12]

Table 5.1 Two development scenarios submitted by the USSR Government to the Supreme Soviet in May 1990

Year	*Indicator*	*Shock therapy, change in the indicator from 1990 (%)*	*Gradual transition, change in the indicator from 1990 (%)*
1991	GDP	−10 ... −15	−5 ... −9
	Employment	−5 ... −7	−3 ... −5
	Investment	−47 ... −52	−14 ... −19
	Real incomes	−4 ... −7	−1 ... −
1995	GDP	+44 ... +50	+25 ... +35
	Employment	0 ... +2	0 ... +1
	Investment	+47 ... +57	+5 ... +10
	Real incomes	+25 ... +30	+5 ... +10

Source: *Ekonomika i Zhizn*, No. 28. 1990.

Another reason was the inability to forecast the growth in income inequality. Ordinary people seemed to be guided by past experience and by Soviet perceptions of low income inequality and living wage guarantees. In reality, income inequality grew dramatically: in the 1990s, 90% of people saw their real incomes reduced by more than half. The problem was eased somewhat by a significant cut in investment (meaning a greater share of consumption in GDP) and the increase in export revenues with higher oil, gas and metal prices that raised an additional $400 billion a year, or almost $3,000 per capita a year.[13] But even after accounting for these factors, it was not until 20 years later (or by the 2008–2009 crisis) that the majority of people could bring their real incomes to the level of the late 1980s. Thus, the majority was badly affected by the market transition, which they had themselves supported.

But these are not the main factors, and they cannot fully explain why the majority backed the reforms. After all, even the production decline and growing inequality failed to make the electorate swing to the left and demand nationalization of natural resources and introduction of a progressive income tax, let alone more radical leftist measures unsupported by the majority in the twenty-first century. Many countries did not enjoy windfall gains ('money for old rope'), such as oil revenues, but even these countries witnessed a shift towards big business interests in public preferences. The main thing, therefore, seems to be the irrational stereotypes persisting in the mass consciousness despite facts and logic: high taxes and a big state are harmful for economic growth, while the likelihood of getting rich quick is higher than the chance of benefiting from progressive taxes. These stereotypes, in turn, are perpetuated by the media and the political system, which are largely controlled by big business.

Do we all want to be richer than others? (The twenty-first century)

It was observed long ago that social groups often support measures that are at odds with their interests. Even advanced democracies approve decisions that run counter to the interests of the majority. The important book on inequality by Joseph Stiglitz (2012) investigates precisely this paradox: in democratic societies, even modest measures to restrict major fortunes (such as a progressive income tax) are not supported by the majority of the public, even though they are in their own interests.[14] Unless there are special limitations on the involvement of private capital in the media, advertising and elections, the holders of major fortunes would easily impose on the mass consciousness the ideas that promote their own interests and run counter to the interests of the public. Formally, elections are based on the principle of one-person-one-vote, but their results are actually the same as in a joint-stock company, where one vote equals one dollar.

US congressional election studies show that campaign financing is the most significant factor explaining the victories by candidates (particularly new figures, who previously never held elected office).[15] This direct campaign financing, however, is not the whole story: financing of the media, non-profit organizations, political parties and associations, researchers, advertisers, and many other shapers of public opinion matters a great deal. Each voter seeks to increase his or her prosperity, but how to do this and what candidates to support is something that is largely, if not decisively, determined by the prevailing stereotypes formed as a result of financing efforts. The Russian population, like any other, wants better living standards and a better social climate. Growing incomes and longer life expectancies, lower unemployment and crime rates in Russia, as in other countries – all things being equal – lead to greater satisfaction with life and higher evaluation of one's prosperity/happiness (Table 5.2 and Figure 5.8). But the policy that is needed to promote personal incomes and life expectancy is an area where mass consciousness is irrational and reflects the interests of big business and the most well-to-do groups, rather than the middle class, let alone the poor.

It is quite clear, for example, that the majority of the population will benefit from the introduction of a progressive income tax, and that the likelihood of becoming so rich as to be in the highest income tax bracket is slimmer than the chance of benefitting from a high income tax through greater access to public goods (education, healthcare etc.) and better social insurance. Nevertheless, the majority of people are against a steep tax rate progression. It is also patently clear that free education and healthcare is in the interests of the majority of people, but this system is uncommon in developing countries. To maximally increase the average life expectancy, if we consider an oligarch's life to be as valuable as that of a poor person, the limited resources that society is prepared to allocate to the healthcare system should certainly be distributed evenly, or more precisely, in conformity with medical indications. But in all democracies, even if they offer a minimum of medical services for free, the rich are able to receive better medical assistance. Strictly speaking, free healthcare and education was only introduced in poor countries by authoritarian socialist governments (the USSR, China, Cuba), while in democracies at the same development level these were largely paid services, which accounted for their lower life expectancy and education levels.

Table 5.2 Answers to the question 'Are you happy?' (% of total respondents) and Happiness Index in Russia, according to VTsIOM polls

Month, year	*6/1990*	*5/ 1991*	*2/ 1992*	*2/ 1998*	*3/2008*	*3/ 2010*	*9/ 2009*	*3/2010*	*9/2010*	*4/2011*	*9/2011*	*4/2012*	*4/2013*	*4/2014*
Definitely yes	5	8	2	16	22	19	19	20	14	19	15	21	23	25
Basically yes	39	52	40	44	55	50	53	52	56	48	51	56	54	53
Basically no	22	24	31	19	12	16	17	14	19	20	21	16	15	22
Definitely no	5	5	5	6	3	5	4	3	3	5	4	2	3	2
Hard to say	29	12	23	15	8	11	7	11	9	8	9	5	6	8
Index	17	31	6	35	62	48	51	55	48	43	41	59	59	64

Source: Russian Public Opinion Research Centre (VTsIOM) (http://wciom.ru/index.php?id=459&uid=114812).

Note: Happiness Index is the difference between the percentage of respondents who said that they were happy and those who stated that they were unhappy.

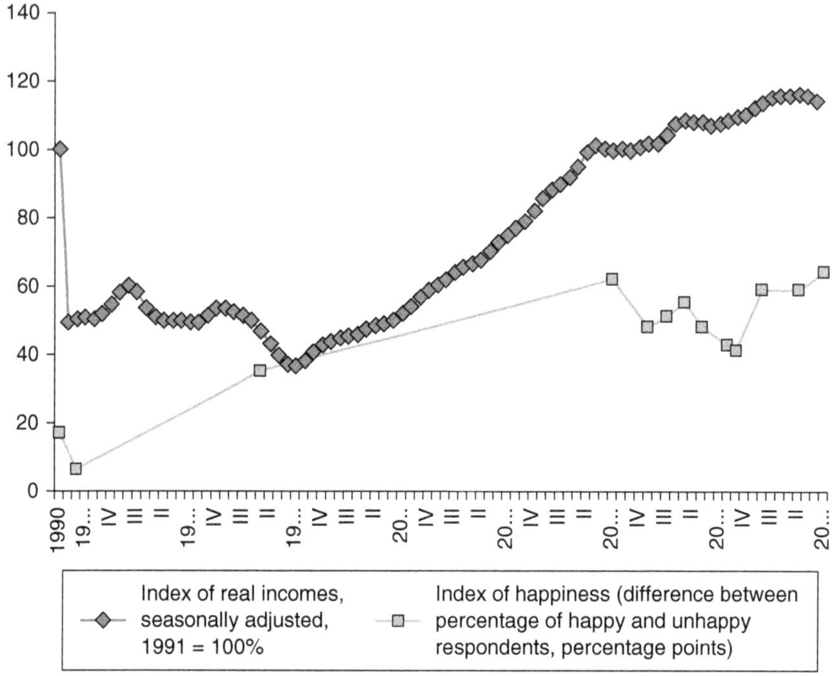

Figure 5.8 Real Income Index and Happiness Index.

Source: State Committee for Statistics (Goskomstat) (www.gks.ru), Russian economic statistics base, HSE website (http://sophist.hse.ru/exes/tables/HHI_Q_I.htm), VTsIOM (http://wciom.ru/index.php?id=459&uid=114812)

It is extremely difficult to alter stereotypes in the public consciousness. One study argues that the press bias is explained by electoral preferences rather than the political orientation of a newspaper owner.[16] In the traditionally Republican constituencies, for example, newspapers hold a Republican orientation, because readers prefer to find confirmation (rather than refutation) of their views, while press earnings (advertising revenues) depend on circulation. So, this creates a vicious circle: conservative voters like information that confirms their views => media concerned with larger circulation are eager to provide this information => voters are even more confirmed in their conservative view.

It would seem this vicious circle can be broken either by reforms from above banning big business involvement in the media and the political process (certain European countries – specifically the Scandinavian countries, with their public funding of political parties and the media – have come closer to this system than others), or by revolutions occurring when the gap between the stereotypes in the public consciousness (opportunities for enrichment) and the reality (impoverishment) reaches a critical level.

Conclusion

Public consciousness in the USSR reflected real economic changes, specifically disappointment with socialism that was felt, albeit with a considerable time lag, by both the Soviet elite and the public following the loss of social dynamism in the 1970s and the 1980s. Views of the future are mostly formed on the basis of an extrapolation of past tendencies (adaptive expectations), while one's own opportunities and abilities are as a rule strongly overestimated (consider the contradictory mass confidence of the 1990s in the preservation of low inequality and personal economic success). However, in undeveloped democracies (which lack effective barriers to big business involvement in politics), the media and election campaigns are controlled by owners of major fortunes and upper-income groups, which results in a vicious circle. Market reforms and privatization bring forth a class of rich proprietors ('oligarchs'), who both have a stake in maintaining their economic and political influence through the media and democratic elections, and possess the necessary leverage to achieve this end. Public preferences can only return to 'normal' – to stereotypes reflecting the interests of the majority – if the media and the political process as a whole are separated from big business and private funding.

Notes

1 Vladimir Popov, 'Life Cycle of the Centrally Planned Economy: Why Soviet Growth Rates Peaked in the 1950s', in Saul Estrin, Grzegorz W. Kolodko and Milica Uvalic (eds), *Transition and Beyond* (Basingstoke: Palgrave Macmillan, 2007); Vladimir Popov, 'Pochemu snizhalis tempy rosta sovetskoi ekonomiki v brezhnevsky period' ('Why Soviet Economic Growth Rates Declined in the Brezhnev Period'), *Neprikosnovenny Zapas*, No. 2 (52), 2007; Vladimir Popov, 'Zakat planovoi ekonomiki' ('The Decline of the Planned Economy'), *Ekspert*, No. 1 (640), 29 December 2008.
2 EBRD, *Transition Report 1999* (London: EBRD, 1999), p. 102.
3 Micael Castanheira and Vladimir Popov, 'Framework Paper on the Political Economy of Growth in Transition Countries', *EERC Working Paper*, 2001.
4 Anders Åslund, Peter Boone and Simon Johnson, 'How to Stabilize: Lessons from Post-communist Countries', *Brookings Papers Economic Activity*, No. 1, 1996, pp. 217–313.
5 EBRD, Transition Report 1999, Chapter 5.
6 Joel Hellman, 'Winners Take All: The Politics of Partial Reform', *World Politics*, Vol. 50, No. 2, 1998, pp. 203–234.
7 Jean-Jacques Dethier, Hafez Ghanem and Edda Zoli, *Does Democracy Facilitate the Economic Transition?*, World Bank, 1999.
8 Jan Fidrmuc, 'Political Support for Reforms: Economics of Voting in Transition Countries', *European Economic Review*, Vol. 44, August 2000.
9 Vladimir Popov, 'Pochemu padeniye proizvodstva v regionakh Rossiyi bylo neodinakovym' (Why Production Decline in Russian Regions was Uneven), *Mirovaya Ekonomika i Mezhdunarodnye Otnosheniya*, No. 9, 2000; Vladimir Popov, 'Reform Strategies and Economic Performance of Russia's Regions', *World Development*, Vol. 29, No. 5, 2001, pp. 865–886; Vladimir Popov, 'Fiscal Federalism in Russia: Rules versus Electoral Politics', *Comparative Economic Studies*, Vol. 44, No. 4, 2004, pp. 515–541.

10 Andrew M. Warner, 'Is Economic Reform Popular at the Polls? Russia 1995', *Journal of Comparative Economics*, Vol. 29, No. 3, 2001, pp. 448–465.

11 *Izvestia*, 26 February 1990; *Argumenty i Fakty*, No. 21, 1990; *Ekonomika i Zhizn*, 2 November 1990.

12 In the late 1980s, practically all experts expected that market reforms would accelerate production growth. In 1989, I wrote an essay entitled, 'Tighten Your Belts, Hard Times Are Ahead', which predicted a 25–30% production decline in the next three to five years. Several Soviet newspapers refused to publish it on the grounds that it was excessively alarmist (it was published in English in *Geonomics Newsletter*, May–June 1991). But even in 1990, when a cutback in production began both in Russia and in Eastern Europe, a market transition programme, 500-Days, predicted the following: A temporary production decline (not defined in quantitative terms) during the first 400 days of the market reform, unemployment growth from 4% in 1990 to 8% in 1991, and a stabilization of the living standards throughout the transitional period, Stanislav Shatalin et al., *Perekhod k rynku: Kontseptsiya i programma* (*Transition to the Market: Concept and a Programme*) (Moscow, 1990). In fact, the production decline continued for almost 10 years, not 400 days, and amounted to 45%, unemployment increased to 13% by 1999, and real incomes dropped by 40% from 1991 to 1998 (Figure 5.8).

13 Russian exports grew from $46 billion in 1992 to $523 billion in 2013, which was mostly due to higher oil, gas and metal prices.

14 Joseph E. Stiglitz, *The Price of Inequality: How Today's Divided Society Endangers Our Future* (New York: W.W. Norton & Co, 2012).

15 Gary C. Jacobson, 'The Effects of Campaign Spending in Congressional Elections', *American Political Science Review*, Vol. 72, No. 2, 1978, pp. 469–491.

16 Mathew Gentzkow and Jesse M. Shapiro, 'What Drives Media Slant? Evidence from US Daily Newspapers', *Econometrica*, Vol. 78, No. 1, 2010, January, pp. 35–71.

6 Twenty years that shook Russia

Public opinion on the reforms

Mikhail Gorshkov

The social history of post-reform Russia is multidimensional and contradictory. In any analysis of this history, the sequence of events is less important than a broad understanding of how people approached changes in society, particularly those that were radical, pervasive and, indeed, systemic in nature. This chapter, therefore, will focus on the key reference points in the transformation processes that engulfed Russian society in the period from the early 1990s to the 2010s. They radically changed people's way of life, values, worldview and behavioural patterns, while actualizing and strengthening the traditional nucleus of the Russian conception of the purpose of life and the world around them.

Hopes and disappointments

By 1992, Russian society had accumulated a mass of varied and even diametrically opposed assessments, judgments, hopes and apprehensions. The events of August 1991 – the coup attempt by the State Committee for the State of Emergency (GKChP), tanks on Moscow's streets, Boris Yeltsin's victory in a show-down with the GKChP, the dissolution of the Communist Party of the Soviet Union, and others – as well as the subsequent collapse of the USSR and the creation of the Commonwealth of Independent States (CIS) on the basis of the Belavezha Accords of December 1991 plunged the overwhelming majority of Russians into a state of permanent socio-psychological stress. Different groups of Russians disagreed about what had happened to their country within just a few months. But everyone agreed that Russia was entering a period of profound crisis. Against this background, the Yeltsin–Gaidar government's move to launch radical market reforms in January 1992 was clearly ill-conceived and ignored the public's psycho-emotional distress.

The very first national poll conducted in April 1992 showed that despite optimistic statements made on television and in the 'democratic' press, the bulk of the population was not ready for such a dramatic change in everyday economic activity, primarily the introduction of free prices of goods and services. The decision to introduce free prices was supported by only 22% of Russians, mostly members of high-income young and middle-age groups. But millions of Russian citizens lost their hard-earned savings and were made destitute virtually overnight.

The prevailing mood was one of profound anxiety. At first glance, it is surprising that a majority regarded the main threat as the prospect of a large-scale armed confrontation in the country, social conflicts and civil war, rather than the consequences of radical economic measures (price and tax hikes etc.). But there appear to be several reasons for that. One of them can be traced back to Russia's history, where almost every period of social transformation (particularly radical and 'revolutionary' changes) was accompanied by clashes, armed conflict and civil war, all of which are indelibly etched in the national memory. Other reasons were largely related to recent events, such as the rift in society following the events of August 1991, with some (Reds) backing the communists and others (Whites) supporting the democrats. Anti-communist hysteria was fomented in the country to play one part of the people off against the other.[1]

There is another important circumstance explaining why *economic* instead of political apprehensions prevailed in the popular consciousness at that time. Radical economic innovations stoked protest sentiment in a considerable segment of the population, but not all of it. For example, the June 1992 national poll (Table 6.1) demonstrated that significant and in some cases overwhelming numbers of Russians expressed support for the federal government's economic reform measures.

As Table 6.1 shows, free pricing and stricter tax rules drew the most opposition. As for other policies, like privatizing state companies or encouraging private enterprise, the majority of Russians supported them. The data further reveal that people who owned shares of their own or another enterprise, bank or company at the time of the poll were much more likely to support privatization, as were groups whose main source of income included not only wages but also property and additional earnings. Among members of different socio-professional groups, the greatest support for privatizing state companies was expressed by specialists employed outside of the public sector, civil servants, engineers and technicians at state companies, and skilled workers at enterprises reincorporated as joint-stock companies, as well as other private industrial enterprises. The least support was found among employees of research institutions, engineers and technicians at companies converted to joint-stock operation, as well as section heads and specialists at public-sector companies. The fact that engineers and technicians were

Table 6.1 Russian attitudes to economic reforms, 1992 (%)

Measures	*Support*	*Unsure*	*Oppose*
Privatizing state companies	53	35	12
Introducing free prices	28	37	35
Encouraging private enterprise	63	28	9
Cutbacks in military production	54	28	18
Land privatization	69	22	9
Stricter tax rules	19	37	44

Source: Mikhail Gorshkov, *Rossiyskoye obshchestvo v usloviyakh transformatsii: sotsiologicheskiy analiz* (*Russian Society in the Face of Transformation: A Sociological Analysis*) (Moscow: Rosspen, 2000), p. 51.

found among both supporters and opponents of privatization was, in effect, the first sign that the transformation of public property was not going to be without conflict and that it was not going the way participants had hoped.

What the first studies conducted at the start of the Yeltsin reforms show is that the reforms carried a certain positive social charge. Even though the public had mixed impressions of the economic transformation, there was a clear trend towards widespread acquiescence to new forms of economic activity that were taking root in practice. For Russia, considering the general state of the country after the collapse of the USSR, this was already a huge moral and psychological achievement. All the government had to do was to retain the people's confidence, confirming with each step that the reforms were in the interests of society and individuals. But there was little confidence in the policies of the new authorities, and above all in the Yeltsin–Gaidar government. In effect, the public was split, with 43% believing the government's economic policies had failed, 30% supporting them, and 27% not expressing an opinion.

The main reason for discontent was the government's decision to go full speed ahead with the most unpopular measures – price liberalization and stricter tax rules. But there were other reasons too. Shortly after the start of the radical reforms, the public became aware of a discrepancy between the strategy and tactics of the economic transformation. While more than a half of the public (54%, as opposed to 23% against) supported the market transition, the overwhelming majority was displeased with how the transition was proceeding in practice and who was benefitting from it. In particular, this applied to the privatization of state companies. Only 8% of Russians believed that privatization 'served the interests of working people' and more than a quarter (27%) claimed that it 'served the interests of the mercantile mafia' and 'the interests of government officials'.

President Boris Yeltsin's base of support began to show cracks as soon as his government embarked on these radical measures. Before August 1991, Yeltsin's support was solid enough (56% against 40%) to bring him to power. Problems inherited from the USSR, combined with the hasty and ill-considered implementation of new socioeconomic policies, turned the majority of the president's former supporters against him. By mid-1992, the original 56% who supported Yeltsin before August 1991 had dwindled to 18%, although 4% of respondents who opposed his policies had come over to his side, for a total of 22% in favour and 73% opposed. These data show that the majority were personally dissociating themselves from the reform policy and were unwilling to share responsibility for its defects or future failures with the government and the president. Public opinion once again settled on one individual as the personification of the new political course. As Mikhail Gorbachev was blamed for the collapse of the Soviet Union, so was the public ready to hold Boris Yeltsin responsible for each and every setback of the economic reforms.

By mid-1992 sociological data showed that views of President Yeltsin were net negative in every regional, social and generational cross-section. His radical economic reform policies lost support among the overwhelming majority of pensioners, agricultural workers, the intelligentsia and industrial workers from the very outset. The decline of support for his political course kept pace with the general impoverishment of the population. In June 1992, for example, the share of Russians rating their material wellbeing as poor (35%) or desperate (11%) while still supporting Yeltsin's policies fell to 12% and 4% respectively from 52% and 46% before August 1991. Nevertheless, Yeltsin could count on the support of people who were satisfied with their material wellbeing. It became absolutely clear during the first year of reforms that their efficacy hinged on political stability. But in Russia political stability requires efforts to coordinate and heed the interests of the main social groups. Given how rapidly Russia's social structure was changing and the fundamental break with the past that had occurred, as well as the volatility of attitudes and worldviews in the main groups in society, such coordination was extremely difficult to achieve. The main values were still 'freedom' and 'good jobs', but the role of material factors grew significantly (Figure 6.1). The available data suggested that economic factors would continue to grow in importance as the crisis deepened in Russia, translating into a greater role for class-based criteria in classifying social groups.

The growing importance of Russians' socio-professional identity was driven in part by the loss of their identity as citizens of a great power, which was painful for many. Polls show that even two years after the collapse of the USSR, more than a third of people (36%) could not find any acceptable replacement for this source of identity (Figure 6.2). This meant that socio-professional status was likely to emerge as the basic criterion of group identity for a broad segment of people.

New poor, new Russians, new schism

While all the different sociological data mentioned above are important in their own right, taken together they signalled the growth of socioeconomic divisions in society as the market reforms gained momentum. This, in turn, made sociologists wonder what social strata and groups the reformers could rely on for support as they pressed forward with their bid to radically transform the country. Regular surveys showed that the base of support for the reforms in 1993 primarily consisted of employees of commercial enterprises (small and medium-sized businesses), researchers, members of the creative class, and mid-level managers at state-owned companies.

The data obtained from these surveys points to the following important conclusion: the way that privatization was handled in Russia eroded rather than strengthened the base of support for reforms and intensified the widely shared feeling that the transformation of the country's economy primarily served the interests of the elite. Far from disappearing, the division in society between the privileged elite and ordinary citizens has become even more pronounced as a result of changes in the economic basis of government power, specifically the sharp increase in the share of property. But these changes had almost no impact on the composition of the ruling elite, and merely differentiated those with status inherited from Soviet society from those with status based on property holdings. The central role in this

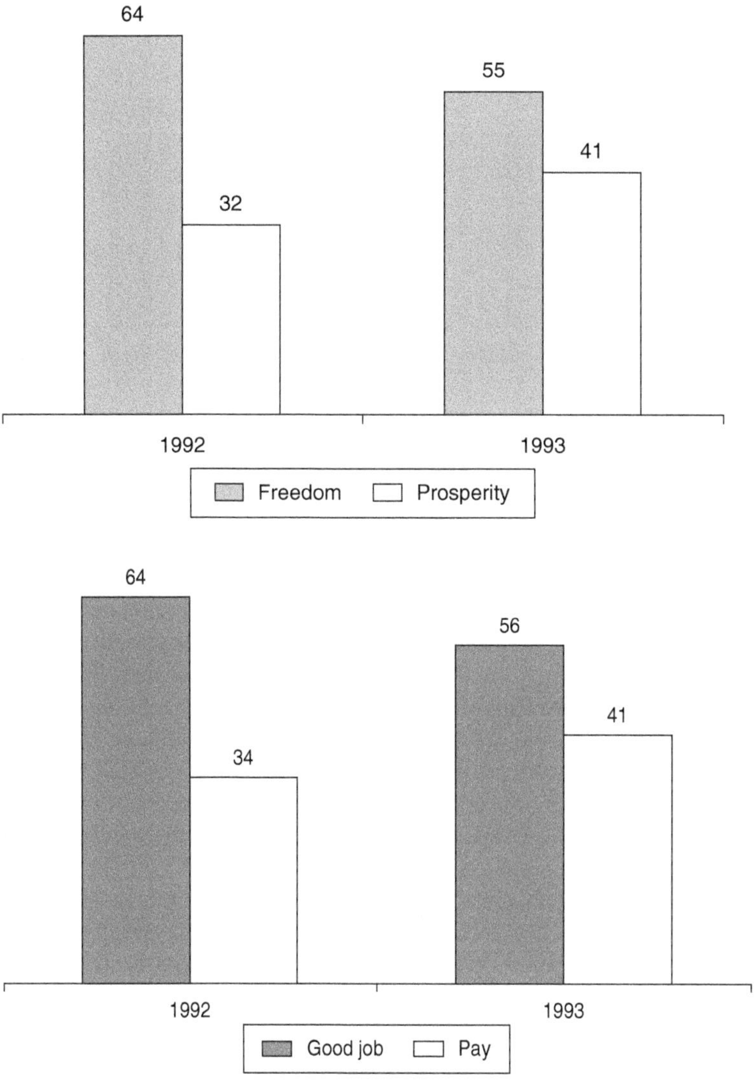

Figure 6.1 Changes in the perceptions of the relative importance of certain values, December 1992–July 1993 (%).

Source: Gorshkov, *Rossiyskoye obshchestvo,* p. 59.

regard was played by a group of Russian entrepreneurs who used their privileged position during privatization to amass property, becoming, in effect, the new dominant class in Russia – the entrepreneur class. But what are the social origins of the members of this class? Table 6.2 clearly shows where public opinion came down on this question at the time.

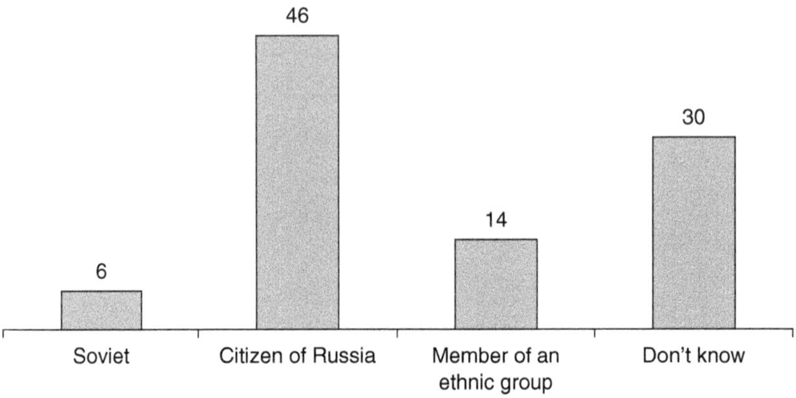

Figure 6.2 How Russians saw themselves in 1993 (%).

Source: Gorshkov, *Rossiyskoye obshchestvo*, p. 62.

As the data make clear, there was little doubt about where Russian entrepreneurs came from. The top three answers in 1992 and 1993 were former Communist Party and Komsomol members, those involved in the trade and distribution network in the USSR, and people with connections to the shadow economy and criminal organizations. Of course, far from all of them became entrepreneurs, but representatives of these groups certainly came to play an increasingly important role in Russia. A particularly powerful group consisted of former top officials of Soviet financial and procurement monopolies. While the bureaucracy was busy fighting for political power, this group – the upper echelon of the new entrepreneurial class – began changing the regime's economic basis in its interests. However, this fact did not go unnoticed.

What this means is that ordinary Russians knew that the old elite retained their status and understood the social composition of the new elite. On its own, this would not have been enough to convince the majority of people to repudiate the reforms as such, had the government sought to create equal opportunities to participate in the reforms for all social groups. But this was not the case. The worst-hit groups after

Table 6.2 Public opinion on the social origins of Russian entrepreneurs, 1992/1993 (%)

Past position/affiliation	*Poll year*	
	1992	*1993*
Former Communist Party and Komsomol members	54	69
Trade and distribution network	52	73
Criminal groups	41	52
Enterprising and ambitious workers and employees	27	47
Heads of state companies or institutions	22	32

Source: Gorshkov, *Rossiyskoye obshchestvo*, p. 65.

two years of reforms were engineers and technicians, researchers, and government employees (doctors, teachers, cultural workers). The data at the time convincingly showed that the bulk of Russia's formerly homogenous population was in a state of ferment that was creating new social groups. Some were transitional, while others became elements of the burgeoning new structure of Russian society (employees of private companies or joint-stock companies, creative intellectuals working in the private sector, specialists employed in the public sector etc.).[2]

In July 1993, just two months before the outbreak of civil conflict (the dissolution of the Supreme Soviet, the shelling of the parliament), the vast majority of Russians held one of three points of view on possible scenarios for the future. The first (held by a quarter of respondents) was based on the assumption that it was possible to maintain stability in the country. To achieve this, in their view, it was necessary to coordinate the interests of different social groups, which would make it possible to avoid conflicts and upheavals in the course of the reforms. According to the second point of view (up to one-third of respondents), the reforms would succeed if modern labour incentives took root, and New Russia would only emerge from its crisis if hard work was adequately compensated. Otherwise, the country was in for mass protests and strikes. The third point of view (up to a quarter of respondents) was based on the assumption that people were losing patience after enduring a succession of political and socioeconomic calamities, and that major social upheavals were inevitable in the near future. The latter view – so indicative of the catastrophism becoming embedded in the popular consciousness at the time – intuitively anticipated the autumn face-off between the legislature and the executive and its violent conclusion.

Indeed, the situation in the country had reached a boiling point by autumn 1993. According to polls, almost 70% of the population characterized the events as a 'crisis' or even a 'disaster'. The public mood was souring. The economic reforms were not benefitting most Russians, and the public stand-off between President Boris Yeltsin and Supreme Soviet Chairman Ruslan Khasbulatov did not inspire confidence. As was the case shortly before the Gorbachev–Yeltsin collision, infighting between the country's new leaders became the focus of national politics, this time ending in the shelling of the Supreme Soviet building.[3] As revealed by polling in the first few months after the events of October 1993, people for the most part realized what sort of a regime they had to deal with and how violently it could respond when its interests were threatened. The profound shock caused by the demonstrative shelling of Russia's White House led many Russians to disconnect from politics and focus instead on family and everyday problems. They also had to get used to the idea that the distinctly Russian version of the market, which had invaded their lives, was there to stay.

Halfway to protest

The protest mood that continued to spread threatened to boil over in 1995. In February, a national poll found that the share of people who viewed the current situation in the country as critical or disastrous had reached 67% (up from 52%

in October 1994). Certainly, one of the main reasons was the aftermath of the grave financial crisis that hit Russia in autumn 1994 and led to a dramatic devaluation of the rouble, high inflation and a decline in commercial activity of Russia's nascent entrepreneurial class. Moreover, this surge of disaffection was observed in all segments of the population (Figs 6.3, 6.4). The share of people willing to join mass protests if living standards continued to decline also increased from 22% in October 1994 to 33% in spring 1995, with the greatest numbers found among the 41–50 age group (38%); industrial workers (36%); engineers and technicians (37%); the cultural intelligentsia (32%); residents of the Stavropol Territory (49%), the Krasnoyarsk Territory (46%), the Komi Republic (41%), the Voronezh Region (29%), St. Petersburg (37%) and the Pskov Region (35%); and mostly people employed at state joint-stock companies or fully state-owned enterprises (44% and 34%, respectively).

Unsurprisingly, the heated public mood, which threatened to erupt in radical mass protests, took a toll on the already low ratings of the leading politicians. In February 1995, just 11% of respondents expressed confidence in Grigory Yavlinsky, compared to 5% for Yegor Gaidar, 4% for Gennady Zyuganov, 3% for Boris Yeltsin, and 1% for Viktor Chernomyrdin. Moreover, a little under 65% of the population was in favour of holding an early election to replace President Boris Yeltsin (with 17% strongly against the idea); 50% wanted new

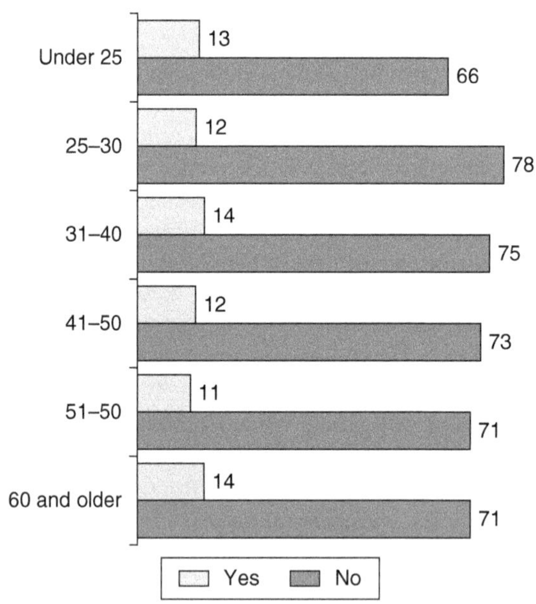

Figure 6.3 Views in different age groups on whether the authorities can halt the country's decline (%).

Source: Gorshkov and Zhuravlyova (eds), *Gorbachev–Yeltsin*, p. 106.

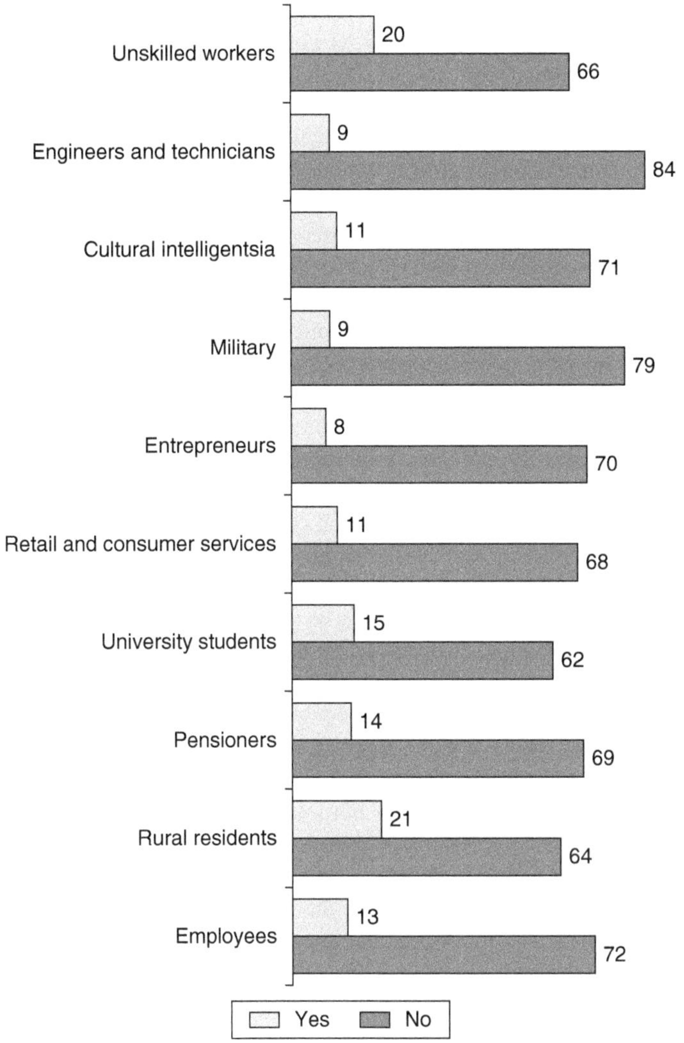

Figure 6.4 Views in different socio-professional groups on whether the authorities can halt the country's decline (%).

Source: Gorshkov and Zhuravlyova (eds), *Gorbachev–Yeltsin*, p. 107.

State Duma elections (19% against); and 37% wanted new local elections (31% against). In October 1994, only 20% of people wanted to see Yeltsin re-elected. As negative public sentiment and impulses continued to mount, many politicians and experts expressed fears that society could backslide to an authoritarian (or even totalitarian) regime. The parliamentary and presidential elections were approaching, and for some the prospect of backsliding was an argument in favour of cancelling the elections altogether, while for others the solution was to hold early elections.

But was there any support in the popular consciousness for another authoritarian regime in 1995 and 1996? The characteristics of public opinion discussed above do not provide an answer to this question. As shown by sociological data, the authoritarian mood in Russian society was in no small measure a reaction to the rapid enrichment of certain groups, which had no moral justification in the eyes of the vast majority of people. It is not surprising that they enthusiastically supported confiscation of the 'ill-gotten' fortunes of some New Russians. But it would be wrong to conclude that society was in the grip of powerful social antagonism caused by the redistribution of property. The majority held moderate attitudes toward those who prospered under the economic reforms. Only 28% of respondents said they had negative feelings toward the new rich (20% expressed suspicion and dislike, while 8% expressed contempt).

Let us take an overview of the authoritarian tendencies among the people who benefited from government economic policies (and could feel the temptation to consolidate their gains with the help of political coercion) and among the losers. The group whose material wellbeing improved considerably during the first years of reforms (7%) tended to equate 'strengthening the state' with the strengthening of the presidency and the president-appointed government more than the average respondent. They likely saw these structures as guarantors of their newly gained social status, whereas the threat of dictatorship, in their view, came primarily from moneyed interests. This group did not want the authorities to target political associations and media outlets calling for the government to be replaced immediately. That said, they also did not have much regard for the idea of a rule-of-law state as the vehicle for the post-Soviet development of Russian society.

People who profited from the reforms but lost confidence in the future (16%) also largely identified 'strengthening the state' with the expansion of presidential and governmental powers. At the same time, unlike the first group, they saw the rule of law as quite capable of rallying the Russian public. The support for political repression in this group was at the average for all respondents, though 150% higher than in the former group. They saw a greater threat of dictatorship coming from the security services and the army (19%), fascist groups (12%) and the president and his allies (10%) than from the financial elite. For the plurality whose wellbeing declined during the reform years (43%), 'strengthening the state' meant primarily a bigger role for the state in the economy and the expansion of the public sector rather than presidential and governmental powers. Like the second group, they believed that the threat of authoritarianism was most likely to come from the president and his allies (16%), the security services and the army (16%), as well as the new *nomenklatura* (11%). They were not particularly enthusiastic about the rule of law and expressed strong support for repressing political opponents of the current authorities.

Thus, after five years of reforms, popular consciousness in Russia was highly contradictory, segmented and ideologically and politically diverse. Two of the main tendencies in society – democratic and authoritarian – had rather complex social origins. In addition to a relatively stable 'nucleus', both democratic and authoritarian tendencies were rooted in similar and sizable segments of the population that were democratic on some issues and authoritarian on others. This seeming paradox was the logical expression of socioeconomic and political processes characteristic of a transitional society during a period of transformation. These authoritarian tendencies were largely a reaction to extreme social stratification, the threat of economic and political instability, and the protracted search for a way out of the crisis. Authoritarian views were held, in varying degrees, both by people who benefitted from the reforms and by people whose material wellbeing markedly deteriorated. The most democratically oriented group enjoyed rising prosperity during the reforms.

The Russian public was essentially prepared to accept a level of government repression that could be classified as moderate authoritarianism. In fact, the public regarded authoritarianism as an alternative to the regime and society returning to totalitarianism, which, under the circumstances, seemed like a more realistic alternative than the strengthening of democratic institutions. The idea that a moderately authoritarian regime, which gave the shoots of democracy a chance to grow and mature, would be better than anarchy, chaos and backsliding into totalitarianism was rooted in Russia's historical memory. This choice was not so much political, let alone moral, as a response to the narrowing range of options for the development of Russian society.

The president of the 'one-third' versus the majority

All the socioeconomic hardships notwithstanding, the country approached the 1996 presidential election with a determination to preserve relative political stability, avoid conflict and maintain social harmony. Boris Yeltsin was re-elected to another four-year term by a mere one-third of all eligible voters. Essentially, this left him with only two options – either preside over the 'one-third' or find a way to make the reforms work in the interests of every 'third' and channel the people's social energy into Russia's renewal.

In the weeks and months following Yeltsin's inauguration on 9 August 1996, it became clear that he lacked the strength to act on either option. The exhausting election marathon had sapped his already frail health. He underwent heart surgery in early November 1996, but his condition did not improve. Yeltsin's third of the electorate began to emerge from the virtual syndrome it was enduring and realized that its votes had brought to power an impotent president incapable of taking deliberate, decisive action and marshalling all economic and political resources to lead the country out of its grave crisis.[4] The grim news was reflected in Russians' views of the outgoing year. As shown by another poll, the overwhelming majority of Russians (74%) rated 1996 as a difficult or bad period for themselves or their families. The year was rated highest by younger Russians, people with college degrees or some college education, and private sector employees. Older Russians, less educated people and employees of state-owned companies expressed the most dissatisfaction. There is a clear dividing line between how people rated the year for themselves and families and for the nation. Figure 6.5 shows that in 1996, 22.5% of respondents said that the year was quite successful in personal terms and generally good, compared to 73.9% of people who described the year as personally difficult. Meanwhile, only 4% called it a good year for the country, with 91.3% of respondents disagreeing.

What might these data signify? At the very least, the fact that Russians were not inclined to link their personal success (relative family prosperity) with the state of affairs in the country. A considerable part of the population had adapted, in some way or other, to the market environment, and their prosperity was not entirely dependent on government policies and activities. This is not to say that people were not dissatisfied with the problems and hardships faced by the country in 1996. In fact, there was a clear tendency to blame personal failures on the unsatisfactory results of the year for the country as a whole. However, it is telling that people for whom the year was bad in personal terms, as well as those who regarded it as good or even excellent, mostly judged the year as difficult and bad for Russia, regardless of age, education, profession or region. Against this background, it is clear why the majority of Russians in 1996 (65–67%) said they often felt a sense of total injustice and shame for the current state of the country.

And yet, even under difficult circumstances, many people found an outlet in family and the simple pleasures of life. Polls showed that Russians took the greatest pleasure in their children's academic or career successes; stability in the workplace; the birth of children or grandchildren, or weddings in the family; the purchase of a car, furniture and so on; get-togethers with family or friends; or just the fact that they managed to take a vacation. In short, they took pleasure in

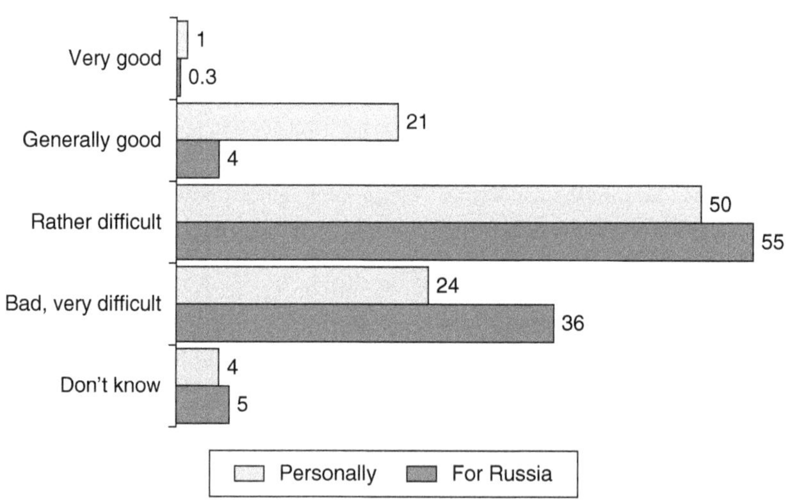

Figure 6.5 Was 1996 a good or bad year for yourself (your family) and for Russia as a whole? (%).

Source: *Ekonomicheskiye i sotsialnye peremeny*, p. 188.

the normal features of human life. On the flip side, the main personal problems reported by people included health problems, illness or death in the family, financial difficulties, loss of job, and family disputes, with women complaining more often than men of poor health and unemployment.

Considering the severity of the hardships and problems facing Russians in their everyday life, you might expect the majority to report feeling apathetic and depressed. But almost two-thirds of employed Russians responded that they usually felt 'calm' or 'cheerful' in the workplace and 76% said that they felt the same at home. Is this just more evidence of the Russian people's 'resilience' and ability to put up with continuous deprivation and poverty? The natural hardiness and adaptability of Russians might have come into play after the presidential campaign in 1996. As for the alleged endless patience of the Russian people, this issue is less clear. A comparative analysis of polling data led to the conclusion that the potential for protests in Russian society was rapidly growing. Almost one-third of Russians were ready to take part in political protests if the economic situation continued to deteriorate: 17% were willing to join a political party; 6% said they would participate in a hunger strike; and 8% said they were ready to take up arms, if necessary. Of course, being willing to protest is not the same as actually protesting. And as protest potential grew, it was accompanied by another extremely negative tendency. As the polling shows, by the end of 1996 public opinion had come to focus less on the crisis of the president's personal rule than the acute national crisis of authority. The declining prestige of all government bodies and political institutions suggested that 1996 would go down in the history of the new Russia as a year that shook the very foundations of the state.

In fact, a mere 3 to 10% of people expressed full confidence in government bodies and political organizations. This applied to federal institutions – the presidency, the State Duma, the Federation Council, federal law enforcement and so on – as well as local governments, including regional and city administrations and legislatures. Even trade unions were trusted by only 7% of people, compared to 5% for political parties. For all its internal problems, the military was the only institution that commanded a meaningful level of prestige (23%). Simply put, after the 1996 presidential elections the gulf between the people and official institutions was larger even than during the worst of the perestroika years. Social expectations fared no better. Polls revealed that Russians were extremely concerned over the state of the economy, the government, law and order, interethnic relations and national defense – in other words, practically all the institutions forming the foundation and superstructure of society. Clearly, these data reflect not only Russians' ordinary, daily mindset but something more fundamental and important – the deeper, contradictory processes at work in the realms of popular consciousness and behaviour. The more dynamic, strong-willed and self-confident Russians were able to adapt to the 'wild market' and learn how to solve problems on their own. But the bulk of the population, including public-sector workers, found the adaptation process much less smooth, as the polling bears out. They were almost entirely dependent on the – frequently empty – public purse.

And yet people of different income levels, ideological persuasions and psychological dispositions were united by a common source of anguish – the depressing state of affairs in the country that threatened the very foundations of the Russian state. It was no coincidence that respondents steadily gave the highest support (41%) to the idea of reviving Russia as a great power as a way to inspire the people and rally them behind a common effort to lead Russia out of its deep crisis. At the same time, the high support for the idea of strengthening Russia as a rule-of-law state (36%) reflected the growing intolerance with the power vacuum in the country and the spread of crime and corruption. According to polls, pervasive corruption remained one of the most serious problems in post-Soviet Russian society throughout the 1990s.

Between 'good' and 'bad'

After the 1996 presidential elections, Russia could be called a society of three thirds, as represented, conventionally speaking, by the 'liberals', the 'conservatives' and the 'indifferent'. But the public underwent a political metamorphosis just half a year later, with all three camps unanimously repudiating all levels of government as incapable of running the country. This was the logical consequence of a tendency revealed by our polls: from year to year, Russians became increasingly pessimistic in their expectations for the country. The financial and economic crisis that erupted in August 1998 only made matters worse, triggering a dramatic decline in living standards. According to a poll at the time, an average family of three subsisted on 1,935 roubles per month in January 1999, or about $90 (at 22 roubles to $1). In June 1998, a few months before the crisis, that figure was 1,750 roubles or approximately $290 (at 6 roubles to $1). This means that the average family budget lost as much as $200 per month.

Average monthly income per family member was at a similarly low level. Two-thirds of the country's population earned less than 500 roubles per month, or slightly more than $20. The situation was further complicated by the growing gap between high- and low-income groups. By that time, the poorest 10% of Russian families earned 22 times less than the top 10% of earners. Naturally, these material disparities generated a groundswell of anger at the government's ineffective social policy. This also explains why three-quarters of the population identified themselves as poor or living below the poverty line (Table 6.3).

But what were the criteria for self-reporting as a member of this or that income group? The threshold for the high-income group started at an average monthly income (for a family of three) of at least 7,860 roubles ($360); the middle-income groups started at 3,330 roubles ($150); low-income started at 1,715 roubles ($80); and 1,100 roubles ($50) or less was considered below the poverty line. Those responding 'don't know' had an average monthly family income of 2,510 roubles ($115). With earnings this low, even for families identified as middle-income, you would expect the majority to report dissatisfaction with many aspects of everyday life. However, the polling data in Figure 6.9 complicates this picture. In spite of being dissatisfied with their level of financial security, more than a half

Table 6.3 Changes in the proportional size of different income groups, 1998/1999 (%)

Income group	*June 1998*	*January 1999*
High-income	1.5	1
Middle-income	34	20
Low-income	53	55
Below the poverty line	10	21
Don't know	1.5	3

Source: *Ekonomicheskiye i sotsialnye peremeny*, p. 284.

of respondents expressed some degree of satisfaction with many other important aspects of their everyday lives.

Over 60% of Russians said their clothing situation was 'satisfactory' or 'good'; over 70% said the same about food, while 80% expressed satisfaction with their housing conditions. Add to this the broad majorities that gave similar marks to health, family relations, opportunities for professional fulfilment, and opportunities for spending free time and socializing with friends, and it becomes clear why three-quarters of Russians rated their general quality of life as 'satisfactory' or 'good'. Given such poor financial security and extreme dissatisfaction with the state of the country, it is perplexing, especially for foreign observers, why people remained satisfied with the conditions they lived in. Could it be that Russians had modest wants and needs to begin with? Or were they helped out by side income that they were unwilling to report even in anonymous polls? Or is it a function of the spirituality of the Russian people and their reluctance to judge life by material metrics alone?

By all evidence, all these aspects of the Russian mentality played a role, as did many others. The polling data operationalize this mentality, to use a sociological

Table 6.4 Rating different aspects of life, January 1999 (%)

Aspects of everyday life	*Good*	*Satisfactory*	*Bad*
Financial security	4	42	54
Food	15	57	28
Clothing	9	55	36
Health	20	56	24
Housing	28	53	19
Family relations	50	42	8
Leisure opportunities	15	46	39
Vacation opportunities	10	35	55
Ability to spend time with friends	41	46	13
Opportunities for professional fulfillment	18	44	38
Opportunities for free expression of political views	35	45	20
General quality of life	12	62	26

Source: *Ekonomicheskiye i sotsialnye peremeny*, p. 285.

term, and help illustrate it more graphically through concrete figures and social facts. In other words, polls help us better understand why the people did not succumb to the temptation of total anarchy and why the country was able to pull itself back from the brink despite a deep crisis and steadily declining living standards.

The start of the Putin era

On 31 December 1999, the first president of the Russian Federation, Boris Yeltsin, announced his decision to resign prematurely. Rumours had been circulating in society and the media, but they were quickly put to rest by assurances that Yeltsin would serve out his term. Whatever the case, his public statement delivered on the New Year Eve was welcomed by the majority of Russians (51%). A little more than a quarter of the population (27%) were surprised by the news, and only 4% expressed regret.[5] The Russian public was divided in their views on the reasons for Yeltsin's decision: 40% believed that he resigned due to poor health and his inability to perform his duties; 28% believed he wanted to make things easier for his official successor, Vladimir Putin, who would face election shortly thereafter; 14% claimed that Yeltsin bowed to criticisms heard from practically the entire political spectrum of Russia; and 13% said he decided to pass the reins to younger politicians capable of leading Russia out of its crisis.

It should be noted that in Russia, all the achievements, failures and distinguishing features of each period in its social history are traditionally attributed to the current leader. (True, Russia is not unique in this respect but here this proclivity is certainly more pronounced than anywhere else.) Therefore, as soon as the distinctive features of the new stage of reforms emerged, the political vocabulary of the country was expanded to include the concept of the 'Putin period' and even the 'Putin era'. Table 6.5, from a poll conducted by the Institute of Sociology, illustrates the scope of the problems Putin faced after being elected president in March 2000.

Half of respondents were most concerned about declining living standards. A large proportion of Russians expressed lack of confidence in the future, while a somewhat smaller group was concerned about unemployment or feared losing their job. One in every four respondents was displeased with the state of health services and almost one in every five was dismayed by the scale of corruption and the arbitrary decisions of officials and civil servants. The data suggested that the research paradigm for post-reform social history needed updating. The 1990s were marked by a plethora of radical and often shocking economic and political measures, and researchers were busy trying to gauge Russian attitudes to these reforms. As the government made course corrections in subsequent years in its efforts to lead the country out of systemic crisis, the goal was to identify sufficiently well-established public attitudes to the radical changes in society.

A number of key questions should be answered in this connection. How does the society in general view the outcomes of a 20-year period of reforms? How did the transformations affect the lives of Russians, their social and financial

Table 6.5 Problems of most concern to people, March 2000 (%)

Problems	
Unemployment or fear of losing a job	21
A minority enriching itself at the expense of the majority	16
State of health services	25
Inadequate environmental situation in a region (city)	9
No chance to get a good education or to provide one to children	13
Housing problems	13
Difficult economic situation in the country (decline in manufacturing etc.)	19
Loss of international standing for Russia	6
Corruption, arbitrary actions by officials	18
Declining living standards	50
Disorder at the top, political instability	15
Lack of confidence in the future, impossible to plan one's life	28
North Caucasus war	14
Crime, lack of security	16
Threat of terrorist attacks	4
Delayed wages and pensions	11
Fear of dictatorship	1
Fear of civil war or interethnic strife	4

Source: *Obshchestvennoye mneniye-1999*, p. 343.

wellbeing, and opportunities for fulfilment? Where and how did the country's transformation influence the evolution of Russians' worldview, opinions on the world around them and their role in society, the state and democratic institutions?

Two seminal studies conducted by the Institute of Sociology – *New Russia: Ten Years of Reforms* (2001) and *Twenty Years of Reforms through Russians' Eyes* – help to answer these questions about the recent period in the social history of Russia.[6] Russians believe that the reforms of the 1990s had led to a disaster in virtually every area of society and national life – the economy, politics and the social sphere (Table 6.6). A certain part of the population tended to see the positive side of processes related to democratization, freedom of speech and human rights. But only the course correction initiated by Vladimir Putin in the reform programme was able to break the unequivocally negative trend of perceptions in the 1990s of the economy, living standards and foreign policy in particular. At the same time, polls conducted in the 2000s registered increasingly negative trends linked to growing corruption, the worst bureaucratic practices and the deterioration of the social sphere.

In parallel, sociologists observed a gradual and subtle rethinking of the main achievements and failures of the reform period in both public and personal terms. Compared to the first decade, respondents placed greater emphasis on the achievements related to creating a 'consumer society' (rising prosperity, greater opportunity and fewer restrictions on making money, market saturation, freedom to travel abroad). At the same time, there was less emphasis on the importance of the

Table 6.6 How Russians rated various spheres of life in the 1990s and the 2000s (%)

Sphere	*Improved in the period*		*Did not change in the period*		*Became worse in the period*	
	1990s	*2000s*	*1990s*	*2000s*	*1990s*	*2000s*
State of the national economy	11	45	15	25	73	29
Living standards	8	34	13	27	77	39
Public morale	5	14	18	34	76	52
Interethnic relations	6	20	23	32	70	47
The country's international standing	17	43	32	36	50	20
Rights and freedoms, democratic development	28	28	36	48	34	23
Anticorruption, law and order	6	14	25	35	68	49
Situation in the social sphere (healthcare, education, culture)	6	19	22	30	71	51
War on terror, situation in the North Caucasus	10	26	27	37	62	37

Source: Mikhail Gorshkov, *Rossiyskoye obshchestvo kak ono est: opyt sotsiologicheskoi diagnostiki* (*Russian Society as It Is: A Sociological Diagnosis*) (Moscow: Novy Khronograf, 2011), p. 133.

Note: The table does not include respondents who answered 'don't know'.

democratic rights and freedoms gained in the early 1990s. Speaking about their personal gains and losses, Russians noted that the reforms opened new opportunities for self-fulfilment, professional and career advancement, doing business, and participating in civic and political life. On the other hand, the majority of respondents said that only a narrow circle of people were able to take full advantage of these opportunities – for many Russians, such opportunities were out of reach or even fewer in number.

Polls show that Russians' socio-psychological state during the reforms was determined less by micro-level conditions (age, income, everyday problems) than by views of the legitimacy of Russia's existing social model and important public events. Indeed, the two decades since the launch of reforms in the 1990s were marked by a large number of momentous national events, the majority of which elicited mixed feelings. The predominately negative views of the 1990s are informed by events like the collapse of the USSR, the dissolution of Russia's Supreme Soviet in 1993, the Chechen war, privatization in the mid-1990s, and economic crisis and default in 1998. The small proportion of the population with liberal views has an unusually positive take on many of these events.

As for the main 'landmarks' of the first decade of the twenty-first century (or the second decade of reforms), they are perceived more positively and less confrontationally. At the same time, a considerable number of Russians hold fairly negative attitudes about such measures as monetization of social benefits, media restrictions, and the government's handling of the 2008–2009 economic crisis. The majority of Russians express some degree of satisfaction with life: 29% rated their lives as generally 'good' and another 62% answered 'fair', while 9% said 'bad'. Recent years have been marked by a gradual improvement in such self-assessments, with the proportion answering 'good' growing from 20% to 29% and 'bad' declining from 13% to 9%. This is a long-term, stable trend. Negative assessments dominated before 2001 (with 26–27% responding 'bad' and 11–12% 'good' between 1995 and 1999). Since 2001, however, the share of positive views has continued to grow (Figure 6.6).

Thus, at the end of the second decade of reforms, social optimism was gradually replacing social pessimism. Polarization was giving way to greater uniformity in self-assessments, which were becoming increasingly positive. Even though Russians are generally wary of optimism and tend to express moderate views, there is a clear upward trend.

How Russia compares to Europe

Compared with foreign countries, primarily Russia's European neighbours, Russians' burgeoning optimism about life looks decidedly modest, as demonstrated, for example, by the European Social Survey (ESS) 2010, in which Russians rank 24th out of a total of 26 places in terms of subjective wellbeing (Table 6.7).

It could be presumed that the sizable gap between Russian and the leading countries (Denmark, Switzerland, Finland, Norway and Sweden) in the subjective wellbeing index is due to the wholesale transformation of its political and economic systems in the recent past. But other post-socialist countries like Poland,

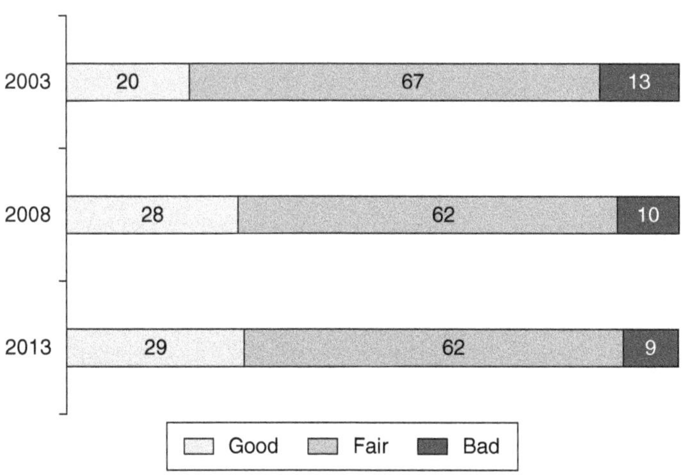

Figure 6.6 Self-assessments of quality of life (2003–2013, %).

Source: Mikhail Gorshkov and Natalya Tikhonova (eds), *Bednost i bednye v sovremennoi Rossii* (*Poverty and the Poor in Modern Russia*) (Moscow: Ves Mir, 2014), p. 186.

Table 6.7 Level of life satisfaction in European countries (country ranking), ESS 2010

Country ranking	*Population as a whole*	*Categories based on self-assessments of financial wellbeing*			
		Able to live without difficulties	*Current income is generally sufficient*	*Difficult to live on their income*	*Very difficult to live on their income*
1	Denmark	Denmark	Finland	Denmark	Norway
2	Switzerland	Switzerland	Switzerland	Switzerland	Israel
3	Finland	Finland	Denmark	Norway	Denmark
4	Norway	Poland	Norway	Israel	Finland
5	Sweden	Sweden	The Netherlands	Sweden	Spain
6	The Netherlands	Israel	Israel	Finland	Cyprus
7	Belgium	Norway	Belgium	The Netherlands	Sweden
8	Israel	The Netherlands	Cyprus	Spain	Belgium
9	Spain	Germany	Sweden	Belgium	Switzerland
10	Germany	Belgium	Spain	Cyprus	The Netherlands
11	UK	Estonia	Poland	Poland	Ireland
12	Cyprus	UK	Germany	Slovenia	Slovakia
13	Poland	Cyprus	UK	Ireland	UK
14	Slovenia	Hungary	Estonia	UK	Czech Republic
15	Ireland	Slovakia	Slovakia	Czech Republic	Greece
16	Slovakia	Spain	Slovenia	Slovakia	Portugal
17	Estonia	Slovenia	Czech Republic	Greece	Germany
18	Czech Republic	France	Ireland	Germany	**Russia**
19	France	Croatia	Croatia	Portugal	Slovenia
20	Croatia	Ireland	Hungary	**Russia**	Croatia
21	Portugal	Czech Republic	Greece	Estonia	Estonia
22	Hungary	Ukraine	Portugal	Hungary	Poland
23	Greece	Bulgaria	Bulgaria	Croatia	Hungary
24	**Russia**	**Russia**	France	Bulgaria	Ukraine
25	Bulgaria	Greece	**Russia**	Ukraine	Bulgaria
26	Ukraine	Portugal	Ukraine	France	France

Source: Gorshkov and Tikhonova (eds), *Bednost i bednye v sovremennoi Rossii*, pp. 189–190.

Note: The table presents country rankings based on mean scores. First place in the rankings corresponds to the highest mean score for a country compared with other countries (most favourable conditions).

Slovenia, Slovakia, Estonia and the Czech Republic have middling rankings. They have traversed a comparable path and are similar to Russia in many indices, and yet their citizens report leading better lives. As is known, people's socio-psychological state is a product of both the circumstances of their private lives and various external factors that always accompany a society in transition. An analysis of data characterizing Russians' everyday emotional and psychological state reveals that over a half of the Russian Federation's population (52%) feels at ease emotionally, while another 6% feel elation. At the same time, there are quite a few people whose everyday emotional state is rather negative (42%), with some feeling apathetic (11%), others feeling anxious about their lives and family (15%), and still others irritated with the people in their lives (13%) or even feeling exasperated and aggressive (3%).

Returning to the ESS, which puts the situation in Russia in an international context, the country again fares modestly in terms of intensity of emotion. For example, Russia ranks 22nd in frequency of cheerful moods, 23rd in energy and vitality, and 23rd for feelings of loneliness. Russians fare somewhat better on feelings of peace and tranquility, coming in 19th place. The post-1995 data confirms the trend towards less negativity and an improved socio-psychological state among Russians. In 1999, there was a surge of negative feelings, but it quickly began to subside. An important positive sign is the decline in the number of people identifying with the statement 'one can't go on living like this', which covers a wide range of negative emotions. The intensity of this indicator is at its lowest point in over a decade. Currently just 18% of people claim to feel this way often, compared with 65% in the critical year 1999 (Figure 6.7) and 29% in 2011.

At the same time, a characteristic feature of the post-reform years is a pervasive, growing sense of unease. At the end of the second decade of reforms, Russians were most of all worried by the crisis in the housing and utilities sector and associated cost increases. But if we look at how Russians' concerns have changed over time, the biggest problems are corruption and bureaucracy. Moreover, the most important objective factor influencing whether a person shares these concerns is not so much the social group they belong to as the region where they live, which is further evidence of Russia's profound regional heterogeneity. A mere quarter or so of Russians believe that their life is normal. The problems viewed as making life difficult are low living standards and lack of social guarantees in case of ill health, old age, unemployment or disability (Table 6.8).

The twentieth anniversary of the radical reforms highlighted one of the key characteristics of Russian society – the high level of socioeconomic inequality, as captured by the dramatic growth of the decile income differentiation ratio (the income gap between the richest 10% and the poorest 10%). During just the first stage of reforms, this coefficient increased by 4.5 times (from 3 in 1980 to 13.5 in 1995). The situation was aggravated by the unrelenting pace of radical liberal reforms conducted under the influence of dubious strains of Western economic thought. Within a mere 20 years, this resulted in massive social differentiation, with social inequality reaching unprecedented levels. The results of the study 'Russians in the Mirror of Consumption', released in September 2010, forced

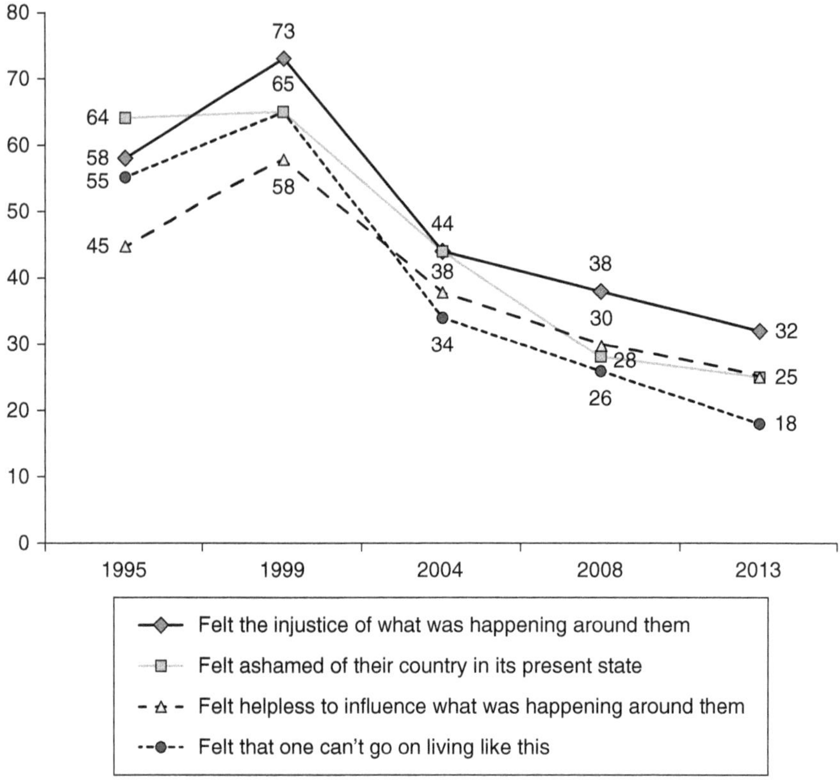

Figure 6.7 Negative feelings in Russia (1995–2013, %).

Source: Gorshkov and Tikhonova (eds), *Bednost i bednye v sovremennoi Rossii*, p. 199.

Note: The figure shows the share of respondents who reported feeling that way often.

the Federal State Statistics Service to acknowledge that despite the fact that the population had become slightly richer and Russia had turned into a middle-income country, wealth differentiation had increased dramatically.[7]

In fact, the parallel growth of real wages and the ranks of the super-rich observed in Russia since the early 2000s did nothing to promote the overall well-being of Russian society. And the income gap continued to grow, occasionally reaching critical proportions. In the years leading up to the 2008–2009 crisis, economic growth primarily benefitted the rich. According to the Federal State Statistics Service, for example, income inequality between the richest and poorest 10% increased from 13.9 to 16.7 times between 2000 and 2007. During the 2008–2010 crisis, the decile income ratio paradoxically stabilized at 16.6 and even declined to 16.4 towards the end of 2012 (Table 6.9).[8]

In comparison, this coefficient is between 3 and 4 in the Nordic countries (Denmark, Finland and Sweden) and varies between 5 and 7 in Germany, Austria

Table 6.8 Problems causing dissatisfaction with life, 2001/2011 (%)

Reason	*2001*	*2011*
Financial problems	**44**	38
Lack of social guarantees in the case of ill health, old age, unemployment or disability	23	**31**
Health problems (personal or in the family)	22	20
Employment problems	16	20
Unable to spend free time as they want	18	19
Housing problems	19	19
Vulnerability to violence	13	**18**
Family problems	17	15
Lack of time for everyday chores	12	11
Problems related to changes in social status in recent years	8	8
Bad habits (alcoholism, drug addiction etc.) in a family member	6	7
Loneliness	6	5
No chance to socialize with family and friends	4	4
Poor diet	8	4
Lack of attention from other people	3	4
Inadequate clothing or footwear	–	3
Regard their life as normal and free from any particular problems	24	26

Source: Gorshkov et al. (eds), *Dvatsat let reform glazami rossiyan*, p. 85.

Notes: Several answers were allowed; arranged in descending order. Bold font denotes changes of five or more percentage points over the last 10 years.

and France. At its current level, the danger for Russia is not so much social upheaval and revolution like in the early twentieth century, when the coefficient exceeded 25, but rather a kind of social apathy that makes more and more people feel like outsiders. Economists believe that the optimal level is between 5 and 7. And there is every reason to believe that the conditions for social unrest ripen in a society as the decile ratio approaches 10. The only exception to this rule is

Table 6.9 Income inequality decile ratio, 1995–2012

Year	*Decile coefficient*
1995	13.5
1998	13.8
2001	13.9
2003	14.5
2005	15.2
2006	15.9
2007	16.7
2008–2010	16.6
2011	16.2
2012	16.4

the United States, where it is between 10 and 12. But in the USA this is seen as normal because of the ingrained belief in American society that the poor alone are to blame for their condition.

At the same time, we should not exaggerate the problem. According to official statistics, the poverty level in Russia declined to 11.2% in 2013 (compared to 33.5% in 1992). But the fact remains that the poorest Russians have not seen any meaningful improvement in their lives. A study of world wealth distribution released by Credit Suisse in October 2012 showed that 30% of the Russian Federation's wealth is controlled by the one hundred richest Russians, while 10% of the poorest Russians account for less than 2% – far worse than all other major world economies.[9] Social inequality is measured through the Gini coefficient, a quantitative statistical indicator that expresses income differentiation as the degree of deviation of the actual income distribution from an absolutely even distribution. Essentially, this coefficient reflects the extent of social differentiation in a country or region with regard to this or that feature being studied. The Federal Service for State Statistics reports that the Gini coefficient stood at 0.42 in 2012 (with 1.0 indicating total inequality).

It is important to remember, however, that in Russia, unlike advanced Western countries, the income gap varies greatly by region. Moreover, modern Russia has one of the highest levels of regional inequality: people in a wealthy region may be 25 times richer than their compatriots in the poorest one.[10] A general answer to the question of how the reforms affected individual lives can be found in the extent to which people believe they personally gained or lost as a result of the wholesale transformation of the country over the last two decades. The share of self-identified winners is a mere 10%, or 2.5 times less than the share of self-identified losers (25%). Another one-third of the population broke even, neither benefitting nor losing out. This reflects Russians' verdict on the last 20 years of the country's social history.

Research shows that there have been positive trends in social mobility in the past 20 years. However, the rapid growth of social aspirations brought about by growing social differentiation and inequality tends to cancel out recent achievements, because for the majority of Russians the gulf between their real and desired status continues to grow or at best remains the same. Russians' self-assessments of their achievements in various spheres of life are evidence that there is relatively more opportunity for success at the micro-level of family, friends and free time. However, respondents acknowledge that some things are still out of reach in their private lives. Many are dissatisfied with the lack of time and opportunities for hobbies and leisure. They are even more downbeat on macro-social opportunities, where getting a good education is the only recorded mass achievement (45% of respondents). All other achievements (a prestigious job, career advancement, owning a business etc.) are accessible only to a small part of Russian society, even though their importance in the national system of values continues to grow.

Yet another significant sociological fact is that the deterioration of social wellbeing for many Russians was largely due to the narrowing of opportunities for social mobility, including horizontal mobility. Today there are practically no opportunities for improving social status by moving to another place of residence. A few exceptions are urbanites moving to a rural location or residents of big cities moving to smaller towns. However, the vector of internal migration in Russia is the reverse, with the majority of migrants heading for larger populated areas. Geographic mobility is seen in different generations of Russians to varying degrees. Migrants are generally under 30 years of age. Yet today's young people, though demonstrating high mobility (13% of those who moved to their current place of residence in the last decade are under 30), are not as mobile as the 40+ age group were in their younger years. This suggests that the mobility potential of young Russians has yet to be fully tapped and argues against the idea of importing labour en masse, given the country's enormous capacity for redistributing the available workforce.

The emigration potential is very high in Russia and has grown even higher in the first decade of the new century. Currently, nearly a half of the population would like to leave Russia for various reasons, and this proportion is even higher for Russians under 30: 13%, or twice as many as in the early 2000s, would like to leave for good, and another 35% would like to leave temporarily for work. That more than one-third of employed Russians are willing to become guest workers is a clear sign of trouble in the Russian labour market and helps us better understand the widespread discontent with the situation in the country.

Patience and work

It would be remiss not to mention the substantial changes wrought by the reforms on the national labour market, which took shape under extremely difficult circumstances after decades of a centrally planned and managed economic system. Even today, 20 years on, the state and development of the labour market are influenced not only by the factors involved in transitioning to a fundamentally different economic system (privatization, new forms of economic activity, Russia's integration into the international market, economic liberalization etc.), but also by the specific features of its development in the past, primarily the strict administrative oversight and state regulation that characterized the Soviet Union.[11] The transition to a market economy weakened Soviet-era economic incentives to accumulate labour surpluses. Tighter budget constraints, businesses' newfound freedom to decide the number and composition of their staff, and the end of guaranteed employment inevitably led to undisguised unemployment – something that hadn't been seen in the country until the radical economic reforms that began in 1992.

In the early 1990s, Russian society was consumed by fear that the country was heading for massive unemployment. But reality exceeded these grim expectations. The unemployment trend line was fairly flat, without any dramatic spikes in either direction. It was only when the market reforms were in their sixth year that total unemployment (which in Russia had never spiked like in other post-socialist economies undergoing reforms) exceeded 10%, while the highest level (14.6%) came in the first quarter of 1999. But as soon as the Russian economy began to recover, total unemployment rapidly declined.

Obviously, the 2008–2009 economic crisis had an impact on the labour market. Among other things, its influence was evident in the growing share of unemployed Russians who lost their jobs as a result of layoffs, dismissals, company closures, declining real wages and the rapid rise of underemployment, and so on. At the same time, labour market experts unanimously acknowledge that Russia's unemployment level during the crisis and in the years immediately after proved much lower than had been forecast and lower than in similar economies (in September 2013, for example, unemployment stood at 5.3%).[12] By international standards, the official statistics on the number of job seekers in Russia have always been extremely low, fluctuating between 1.4% and 3.5% of the total labour force throughout the post-reform period. Russia was the absolute leader in this regard, as no other post-socialist country could boast a consistently low registered unemployment rate.[13]

Nevertheless, the fear of job loss remained strong despite the actual unemployment situation. For all the irrationality of this fear in light of the notable economic growth and workforce shortages in certain economic sectors, it was and still is motivated by wholly objective and important factors, such as the lack of social protection, an inadequate unemployment insurance system, and extremely low wages. The fear of unemployment observed during the period of reforms and aggravated by the economic crisis partially explains why the share of Russians satisfied with their work situation plummeted from 65% in 2007 to 51% in 2013. At the same time, the shares of respondents answering 'good' or 'bad' have remained practically unchanged for years (Figure 6.8). Thus, the research confirms the general absence of qualitative changes in the socio-professional sphere in modern Russia: the labour market situation only seems stable and there is a strategic need

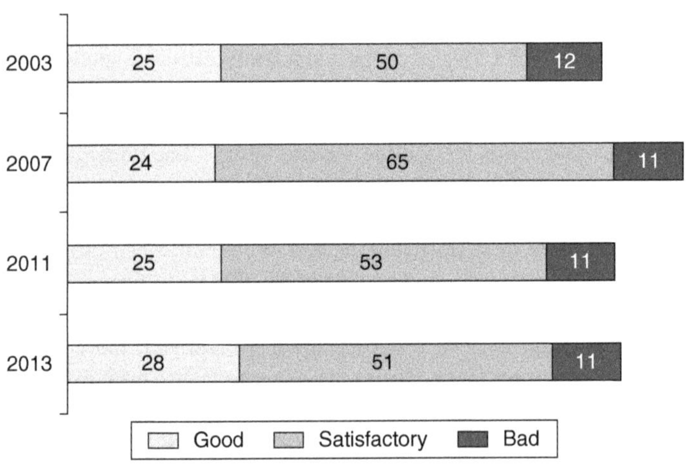

Figure 6.8 How Russians rate their work situation (2003–2013, %).

Note: The figure does not represent those who answered 'don't know/not sure', meaning the sum total for each year may be less than 100%.

to create good, high-paying jobs for highly skilled workers and devise adequate remuneration policies.

The transformation of Russia has significantly altered the composition of industries in which Russians are employed, reducing the proportion of those working in manufacturing, scientific research and related industries, and agriculture, and increasing the number of people employed in trade, transportation, communications, housing and utilities, healthcare, credit and financial services, and administrative agencies (i.e. mostly in the service sector). A clear imbalance in labour resources has emerged as a consequence of the failure of households to adequately invest in education due to lack of information. This resulted in a dearth of certain categories of workers and a surplus of others. As economic instability resulted in waves of layoffs, many Russians were forced to change not only jobs but also professions and industries (45%). Moreover, a fifth of them had to do this several times. The most frequently cited reasons for changing profession are desire for higher income (29%), dissatisfaction with working conditions (13%) and layoffs caused by the crisis in the labour market (10%).

Periods of economic trouble make many workers more cautious about the mere possibility of dramatic life changes. Yet the number of those willing to move in order to find an interesting, well-paid job consistently exceeds that of people who seek to avoid change. Moreover, this number has been trending upward (25% in 1994, 34% in 2001, 43% in 2011). Studies of the 'Putin period' of reforms have shown that despite economic crisis and the corresponding uncertainty in the future, the majority of employed Russians today are mostly focused on finding an interesting job that is fulfilling and makes use of their skills and abilities. This can be seen, for example, in what Russians say about what makes a job good (Figure 6.9).

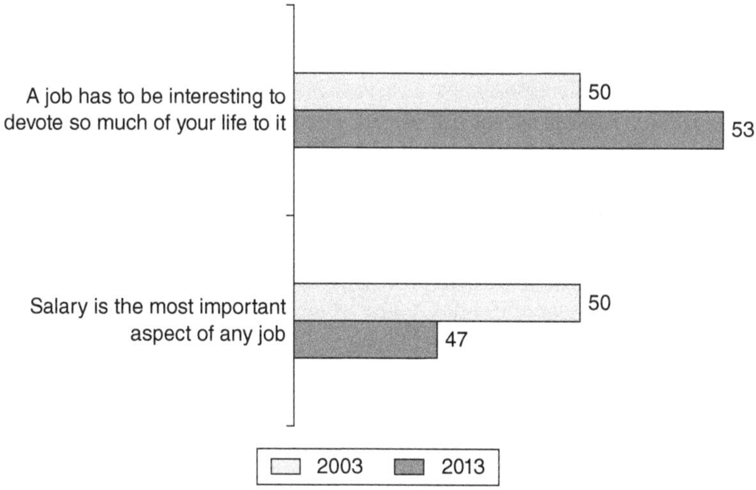

Figure 6.9 Russians' changing attitudes to work (2003/2013, % of employed respondents).

Source: Gorshkov et al. (eds), *Dvadsat let reform glazami rossiyan*, p. 93.

The fact that the overwhelming majority of Russians prefer interesting work to simple career advancement, despite all the socioeconomic and psychological trauma inflicted by the reforms, bodes well for the further modernization of Russian society. The question, however, is how people's aspirations compare to the opportunities available. Research has shown that Russians are ambivalent but mildly positive in how they see the prospects for success in different spheres of life (better personal finances, opportunities for professional fulfilment and career advancement, business pursuits). According to sociological data for the last decade, Russians have become more positive in how they perceive opportunities for career and professional advancement. For example, while 14% saw such opportunities as expanding in the 1990s, that figure reached 24% (almost a quarter of working age Russians) in the 2000s. The share of people claiming that the reform years limited opportunities for professional and career advancement for the majority of Russians shrunk by 10% by 2013 (from 25% in the 1990s to 15% in the 2000s).

At the same time, a quarter of Russians believe that their opportunities for professional and career advancement essentially remained the same in the 1990s and 2000s. More than a third of respondents (36% in 1990s and 38% in the 2000s) said that 'there were more opportunities, but only for a small group of people'. No wonder that under these circumstances many Russians do not regard career as a priority, nor do they see any real opportunities on this front, as was mentioned above. Thus, the minor positive shifts in perceptions of opportunities for career and life success are no reason for equanimity. On the contrary, the existing situation is evidence of incipient stagnation in the labour market and calls for measures to increase socio-professional mobility.

An identical conclusion is suggested by an analysis of how perceptions of business opportunities have changed over time. As is known, the reform years radically changed workforce distribution by industry and sector. Businesses were privatized, new private companies were founded, and self-employment was promoted. This resulted in the emergence of a vast private sector and new market segments based on private property and private ownership and self-employment. The 1990s were understandably associated with new business opportunities. That period saw the emergence and rapid growth of a new entrepreneurial class, the offspring of the privatization programmes. Some of its members, however, were 'reluctant businessmen' who had to enter a new field because they could not provide for their families in their former profession or had no other employment options. And as was the case with other kinds of opportunities, Russians tend to believe that in the period under review business opportunities were not available to all or even many Russians (34%), but to a limited group of people (45%).

Growth problems and the cost of progress

Among the factors that changed impressions of the 1990s were economic consolidation and the corresponding increase in competition, economic crises that seriously damaged or destroyed small and medium-sized businesses, obstacles to upward mobility, and the nature of the relationship between business and government. In the 2000s, this translated into a 6% reduction in the number of respondents who, using the same criteria, said that there were now more business opportunities, at least for a limited group of people. Not surprisingly, 49% of Russians do not regard starting a business as a priority, while another one-third would like to but doubt that it is possible. Notably, the latter group grew by 6% in the first decade of the twenty-first century (from 23% in 2001 to 29% in 2011).

Shifting socioeconomic conditions led to considerable changes in the worldview of Russians. Soviet-era ideological homogeneity dissolved with the USSR, and was replaced by a chaotic mixture of views instead of the kind of pluralism predicted by theory. Different social and socio-demographic groups, as well as territorial entities (even the smallest among them) started pursuing their specific, local interests and adopted their own mini-ideologies. However, the 2000s reinvigorated certain generally accepted ideas from the 1990s, such as the cohesion of Russia's peoples as a means of restoring the country as a great power, strengthening the rule of law, and working with all nations to address global problems facing mankind. A notable data point is the rise in the number of respondents expressing support for socialist ideals (Table 6.10), which indicates that the spread of socialist convictions among Russians has less to do with the legacy of the Soviet experience than the negative aspects of life in modern Russia and the accumulation of life experience in general.

Table 6.10 Changing opinions on ideas capable of uniting Russian society, 1995–2011 (%)

Ideas	*1995*	*2001*	*2011*
Cohesion of Russia's peoples to reclaim great-power status	41	48	42
Strengthening rule of law in Russia	30	47	38
Unification of nations to address global problems facing mankind	24	24	26
Rapprochement with the West, Russia as part of the common European home	12	15	7
Returning to socialist ideals and values	10	15	21
Unification of all Slav peoples	9	15	13
National uniqueness, the special historical mission of the Russian people	7	8	9
Individual freedom, the primacy of personal interests over those of the state	6	10	8
Purifying society with the Orthodox faith	6	8	9
Confrontation with the West, self-reliance	2	13	12
Some other idea	1	2	1
Don't know	7	6	18

Source: Gorshkov et al. (eds), *Dvadsat let reform glazami rossiyan*, p. 146.

Note: The sum of figures in the columns can exceed 100% because respondents could choose up to three replies.

The Russian attitude to democratic values and institutions can be described as 'sympathetic scepticism' – in other words, sympathetic to the idea of democracy itself as the optimal form of societal organization, but extremely sceptical or at times dismissive of the majority of democratic institutions (elections, parliamentarianism, a multi-party system, freedom of speech etc.), hence the rather lukewarm interest in politics displayed by the majority of Russians. But periodically there are signs of renewed civic engagement, mostly at the local level. We can see this indirectly in the markedly higher engagement with the tools of democracy (direct action like rallies, processions, strikes, legal action, media campaigns etc.) towards the end of the second decade of reforms than earlier in the decade.

Extensive, periodic surveys permit us to say that the 'Putin period' of reforms has been marked by a powerful surge of patriotism, particularly during Crimea's reunification with Russia, which was approved by 95% of Russians. Moreover, the patriotic groundswell in society helped Russians rediscover their country as a unique nation with its own place and role in the world. It was security considerations rather than emotionally tinged ideological motives that guided the public in the early 1990s and informed the 'average' Russian citizen's attitude to international politics and different countries of the world. Respondents (as well as expert groups) name international terrorism and the global economic crisis as the main threats to modern-day Russia. The cooling in Russian attitudes to the USA and the majority of West European countries during the August 2008 war with Georgia quickly dissipated for the most part. But these emotions surged even higher in response to Western countries' policy towards Russia during the escalation of hostilities in Ukraine in 2014 and their economic sanctions against Russia.

Any accounting of this most recent period in the social history of Russia must include the fact that Russians' value orientations, unlike worldview, are sufficiently *stable* and encompass freedom, work, patriotism, fairness and social equality understood as equality of opportunity. To be sure, the new images and ideas promoted by the reformers in the media have influenced the popular consciousness, particularly among young people. But this influence was only expressed in certain fluctuations of the 'values cardiogram', incapable of changing the hierarchy of values and distribution of value preferences in society. Even though there is a 'value consensus' between different generations (despite certain age-related differences, in particular the optimism and ambitiousness characteristic of youth), young people in post-reform Russian society are significantly less conformist. This is why they have a more positive view of the last 20 years of reforms than the rest of the population. The main advantage, as they see it, consists of greater opportunities for self-fulfilment and career growth.

The social component of reforms inevitably comes to the fore when attempting to apply a socio-historical approach to the question of whether it is possible to create the necessary conditions to build a modern democratic society and market economy in Russia. The most important issue in this regard is whether reforms are supported 'from below' by the majority of people. If they are not, any attempt at progressive change is doomed to failure, as Russia's experience has borne out. Our many years of surveys show that for Russians the crucial aspect of reforms is whether government institutions are involved in tackling social problems. Russians believe that the state will always play a key role not only in the economy but also in the social sphere, and for this reason evince little support for either liberal models of social policy, under which government interference in the social sphere is minimal, or the free market economy, where everything depends on private actors. The optimal model identified by majorities in recent years is where the state guarantees a certain minimum to all and lets everyone achieve whatever they can on top.

The optimal model for the country, in the majorities' view, is one based on a mixed economy with the public sector in the lead. In other words, the majority of Russians are in favour of all strategic branches of the economy being controlled by the state, with private management of certain companies to be complemented by state oversight. While Russians' perceptions of the role of the state in the social and economic spheres vary somewhat by age, education level, where they live and other factors, the demand for a leading role for the state in all these spheres predominates in practically every population group. Where they differ is largely on the question of how the state should perform this role (Table 6.11).

The 20 years of reforms have been a serious test for the moral foundations of society. After the state effectively renounced the role of moral 'mentor', and other public institutions were unable or unwilling to assume it, Russians found themselves face-to-face with free choice in their moral reference points, with many deciding to shed the excessive 'moral burden'. In a number of cases, ignoring traditional moral precepts was economically and socially profitable. Naturally, this was a source of significant concern for many people. One in every three citizens in Russia identified the worsening moral climate in society as one of the most negative consequences of the two decades. Despite this critical view of the state of public morals, the majority of people have continued to uphold traditional values

Table 6.11 What type of relationship between government and economy is most in Russia's interests? 1994–2011 (%)

Types of state	*1994*	*2001*	*2011*
A state that fully restores centralized regulation of the economy and price control	16	18	28
A state that reduces economic interference to a minimum and provides maximum freedom for private initiative	13	8	9
A state that revives the public sector, while expanding private economic and political opportunities	40	37	41
The type of state is unimportant; the country needs a leader who will assume full responsibility for the situation in Russia and take decisive action	21	23	22
Don't know	10	14	0

Source: Gorshkov et al. (eds), *Dvadsat let reform glazami rossiyan*, p. 169.

and standards of everyday behaviour. Russians express commitment to traditional attitudes toward most actions and phenomena perceived as immoral or at least unethical (including drug use, homosexuality, exploiting sexuality for personal gain, tax evasion, bribery etc.). Moreover, today the majority of moral norms are valued much higher than in the 1990s.

At the same time, surveys conducted by the Institute of Sociology of the Russian Academy of Sciences reveal respondents' relativism toward certain questions regulated by public morality alone (for example, deceiving people for personal gain). The surveys also register the emergence of *multimorality*, a comparatively new phenomenon for Russia, implying that people, while living within their own moral framework, recognize other people's right to live by their own code. Nevertheless, many Russians express concern over the current moral climate in society and feel keenly the 'loss of traditional morality'. Whether such a loss objectively occurred, there was certainly a pervasive sense in society of the need for moral imperatives and norms.

Leisure is one of the few spheres of life where one really feels how much progress has been achieved during the reform decades. Although many Russians report lacking free time, the polls reveal that they lead eventful and varied personal lives. Increasingly, leisure for Russians consists of diverse activities outside the home – socializing, entertainment or self-improvement. The majority of Russians (51%), however, continue to engage in traditional forms of leisure at home or spend time with an inner circle of relatives and friends outside the home. However, there are many (39%) who lead more active lifestyles that involve elements of self-improvement, entertainment, culture, recreation and civic engagement. The main factors determining quality of leisure and, accordingly, quality of life in general are financial security, social status and place of residence. People who report high financial security, hold top positions in the social hierarchy and reside in big cities are particularly interested in how they spend their free time and in leading an active lifestyle, which includes taking advantage of cultural and self-improvement opportunities, entertainment and sports. Conversely, people with low financial security who live in small communities, particularly rural villages, have less interest in how they spend their free time, as well as fewer and less diverting leisure opportunities.

Computers and the Internet are emerging as one possible factor capable of increasing the richness and variety of leisure opportunities for Russians. Data show that computer-savvy Russians spend their free time more productively than others, and are more likely to take advantage of cultural and self-improvement opportunities.

Russia's future: the faith and hopes of its citizens

It is natural for the Russians who lived and suffered through the reform years to wonder about Russia's future prospects. The data clearly points to mixed and even contradictory attitudes to the recent past, the present and the future of the country. On the one hand, the majority of respondents (60%) believe that the development path chosen after the collapse of communism is generally correct and the country will sooner or later settle onto a trajectory of stable economic and political development. On the other hand, there are many Russians (40%) who are certain that the country's current track leads to a dead-end. In this context, 54% think that the country and its economy have become less dynamic, making it hard to bridge the gap between Russia and the leading world powers.

Today only 18% of respondents believe that Russia will join the group of leading economies and become an advanced democracy within the next five to 10 years, which explains the modest rise in the number of Russians supporting change and more decisive measures to modernize the economy, the political system and the social sphere, even though supporters of stability continue to prevail, albeit not by an overwhelming margin (57% vs. 42%). And yet the support of young people for the idea of achieving a modernization breakthrough is rather pronounced. As we know from history, once the demand for change penetrates the minds of the people, particularly young and active minds, it is unstoppable.

In conclusion, it is logical to ask some questions. For example: what is the best way to understand the 20 years of uniquely Russian reforms? Can they be regarded as a linear and consistent process – a well-conceived, wholesale transformation of society, where each next step is the logical continuation of previous ones? The answer is clearly no. As convincingly shown by representative national sociological surveys, these difficult two decades of reforms were not the result of a coherent and coordinated process. So, what has been the result? There were two fairly distinct reform periods: the 1990s and the 2000s, roughly divided into the Yeltsin decade and the Putin period. The most important, and possibly fairest, verdict will be passed on them by the popular majority as represented by the country's various socio-professional and demographic groups. The first decade was widely viewed as a failure, a time of dashed hopes and a string of ill-conceived, uncoordinated and radical measures in different spheres of life, which eventually led to the impoverishment of a great many people and set the country's development back by many years. The so-called young reformers, who were particularly zealous in their pursuit of radical transformation, put themselves in charge of privatization, doling out public property to their cronies in exchange for privatization vouchers worth less than the paper they were printed on.

According to public opinion, the second period – associated primarily with the name of Vladimir Putin – marked a decisive shift in politics towards society, accompanied by the restoration of constitutional order, the country's emergence from acute crisis and onto a trajectory of sustained and stable development, and the recovery of its status as an influential world power. The country inherited from the 1990s such basic economic institutions as privatization, private property, price liberalization and so on, while the Putin team managed to bring the state back to the social sphere, considerably reduce the ranks of the poorest Russians, strengthen the army and bolster the country's international standing. And yet, the legacy of the 1990s – grave problems that are unlikely to be solved within

10 or even 15 years – is still with us in the form of pervasive corruption, profound social inequality and huge income and quality-of-life disparities between the rich and the poor, which dampen public perceptions of the authorities' efforts.

Notes

1 For more detail on the socio-political and psychological aspects of the civil confrontation in 1991, see Mikhail Gorshkov and Valeria Zhuravlyova (eds), *Krasnoye ili beloye? Drama avgusta-91: fakty, gipotezy, stolknoveniye mneniy* (*Red or White? The August 1991 Drama: Facts, Hypotheses, Clashes of Opinion*) (Moscow: Terra Publishers, 1992).

2 For more detail, see Natalya Tikhonova, *Faktory sotsialnoi stratifikatsii v usloviyakh perekhoda k rynochnoi ekonomike* (*Social Stratification Factors in Market Transition*) (Moscow: Rosspen, 1999).

3 For more detail, see Mikhail Gorshkov and Valeria Zhuravlyova (eds), *Gorbachev-Yeltsin: 1500 dnei politicheskogo protivostoyaniya* (*Gorbachev-Yeltsin: 1500 Days of Political Confrontation*) (Moscow: Terra Publishers, 1992).

4 According to a VTsIOM poll, 46% of Russians were in a negative mood in fall 1996. Only 6.4% of respondents called the political situation in the country calm or favorable, while 84.2% said it was tense, critical or even explosive. President Boris Yeltsin had the full support of just 6.6% of people and another one-third supported only some of his actions. Almost a half of the population (45.2%) believed that he should resign. At the same time, 36.3% wanted the economic reforms to continue, while 24.4% wanted them to end (the rest were unsure). See *Ekonomicheskiye i sotsialnye peremeny: monitoring obshchestvennogo mneniya* (*Economic and Social Changes: Monitoring Public Opinion*), No. 6, 1996, pp. 53–55.

5 For more detail, see *Obshchestvennoye mneniye-1999* (*Public Opinion-1999*) (Moscow, 2000), p. 99. To compare, Yevgeny Primakov's resignation as prime minister in May 1999 was met with regret and anger by 65% of Russians and with approval and relief by 4%.

6 See Mikhail Gorshkov, Reinhard Krumm and Vladimir Petukhov (eds), *Dvatsat let reform glazami rossiyan: opyt mnogoletnikh sotsiologicheskikh zamerov* (*Twenty Years of Reforms Through the Eyes of Russians: Results of Long-Range Sociological Measurements*) (Moscow: Ves Mir Publishers, 2011).

7 Ilya Zinenko and Irina Vlasova, 'Sotsialnoye neravenstvo v Rossiyi stavit novye rekordy' ('New Records of Social Inequality in Russia'), http://newsland.com/news/detail/id/563868. [Accessed on: 17 June 2015].

8 'Raspredeleniye obshchego obyoma denezhnykh dokhodov i kharakteristiki differentsiatsii denezhnykh dokhodov naseleniya' ('Distribution of the General Amount of Monetary Incomes and Characteristics of the Differentiation of the Population's Monetary Incomes'), Website of the Federal Service for State Statistics, http://www.gks.ru/free_doc/new_site/population/bednost/tabl/1-2-2.htm. [Accessed on: 17 June 2015]. Along with the official statistics, there are unofficial data that are mostly obtained through public opinion polls. According to these data, the actual decile ratio was 28–30 in 2013. Moreover, the figures in Moscow are absolutely exorbitant: in some years the average rich earned 40–50 times more than the average poor.

9 'Analitiki: razryv v dokhodakh rossiyan obyektiven' ('Analysts: There is an Objective Gap in the Income of Russians'), http://www.vesti.ru/doc.html?id=356705. [Accessed on: 17 June 2015].

10 Yakov Grabar, 'Bogach – bednyak: mir okazalsya nespravedliv' ('Rich Man – Poor Man: The World Proved Unfair'), http://top.rbc.ru/economics/17/07/2013/866357.shtml. [Accessed on: 17 June 2015]. According to some data, this indicator exceeds 40.

11 For more detail on Soviet labour market specifics, see, for example, Rostislav Kapelyushnikov, *Konets rossiyskoi modeli rynka truda?* (*The End of the Russian Labour Market Model?*) (Moscow: Liberal Mission Foundation, 2009); Rostislav Kapelyushnikov and Vladimir Gimpelson (eds), *Nestandartnaya zanyatost v rossiyskoi ekonomike* (*Unconventional Employment in the Russian Economy*) (Moscow: GU-VSE Publishers, 2006).

12 'Zanyatost i bezrabotitsa v Rossiyskoi Federatsii v sentyabre 2013 goda: po itogam obsledovaniy naseleniya po problemam zanyatosty)' ('Employment and Unemployment in the Russian Federation in September 2013: Results of Polls on Employment Problems'), Official Website of the Federal Service for State Statistics, http://www.gks.ru/bgd/free/b04_03/IssWWW.exe/Stg/d02/219.htm. [Accessed on: 17 June 2015].

13 Kapelyushnikov, 'Konets rossiyskoi modeli rynka truda?'.

7 The Russian roller coaster

Changes in social structure in the post-communist period

Natalya Tikhonova

The reform years following the collapse of the Soviet Union brought about serious changes both in the economic and social life of the country. The structure of Russian society and the social status of the majority of its members changed dramatically in a mere quarter century. During these years of wholesale transformation, tens of millions of people became the subjects of an experiment that demonstrated both the role of the individual activities of citizens and the structural restrictions dictated by social relations, which compelled people to act in a certain way in order to occupy a certain place in society. What was Russia's social structure like at the outset of these changes and what is it like today? More importantly, what can these changes tell us about Russian society?[1]

The beginning

The point of departure for the social structure of modern Russia is the late 1980s. Soviet society was built on the merger of power and property relations, and under those circumstances it was meaningless to divide society into classes, which implies the existence of owners independent of the state. The real foundation of the Soviet social structure was people's place in the process of non-commercial redistribution and their proximity to institutions that controlled the supply network for all resources. Society was divided into two main groups: (1) the 'managed', that is the majority of workers, who were essentially in the same position – a turner was employed by the state in much the same manner as a doctor or tractor driver; and (2) the 'managers' who performed various administrative and distributive functions.

This was not merely a classless society but a corporate-stratified structure where inequality was justified by ideology. The status of the 'managed', that is 'ordinary' people, was primarily determined by their positions in priority industries, which received much more resources than the rest. Their status also largely depended on region and place of residence. All these factors affected the social status of individuals and determined both their material wellbeing and professional prestige. Their position in a stratified society was primarily expressed in the privileges or non-monetary benefits they received, such as interesting and prestigious jobs, decent working conditions, better medical services, the ability to send children to a departmental kindergarten or pioneer camp, better employee housing and a wider choice of goods in shops (sometimes located at enterprises).[2] While the kinds of privileges available varied significantly, they reflected the more important forms of social inequality in labour and consumption that existed among the 'managed' at the time, including the prestige of their jobs. Importantly, along with the 'official' hierarchy of privileges that was frequently codified in statutory acts or delegated legislation and instructions, the twilight Soviet years also witnessed 'unofficial' privileges that were based on different levels of access to the channels of redistribution, particularly in retail trade and services.

Soviet society consisted of dozens of groups, which, broadly speaking, included: (1) a relatively small upper-middle stratum – managers of small enterprises, skilled professionals (primarily the creative and intellectual class, scientists and defense industry employees), as well as those involved in the informal system of wealth redistribution; (2) workers, collective farmers and the mass intelligentsia that justifiably regarded themselves as the middle strata. They formed the fairly homogeneous majority of society. Moreover, their living standards were perceived as 'typical' for society in general. The poorest among them were still able to lead a comparable lifestyle to the rest of the population and did not form a distinct social group, although their incomes were lower (generally by virtue of their family status); (3) lumpen (the bottom of society), who were relatively few in number; (4) the 'managers', that is the notorious *nomenklatura* that stood in marked contrast to all others. In the late 1980s these four groups were joined by small business owners.[3]

This was the social structure with which Russia entered the period of transformation that later came to be known as 'the economic reforms of the 1990s'. The key feature of this essentially classless structure was that *forms of monetary inequality played a relatively minor role,* primarily because the gap between groups in these terms was relatively small at that time. Even in 1992, five years after the adoption of laws that de facto allowed private ownership of the means of production and legalized entrepreneurship, incomes of the top 10% were still only 8 times higher than the bottom 10% (decile ratio).[4] As shown in Table 7.1, incomes of the top 20% were a mere 3.4 times higher than the bottom 20% (quintile ratio) by the start of perestroika. But money had little value in the USSR given the severe, chronic shortages of goods and services, making non-monetary forms of inequality much more important.

The situation changed completely with the start of the market reforms in the 1990s. At that time, Russia was undergoing several simultaneous processes that drastically changed the nature of social stratification in the country – both its foundation and components. First among these processes was the emergence and gradual saturation of the free market of goods and services. Once the link between one's profession and many of the non-monetary forms of inequality was severed, the role of money in inequality rapidly rose. This fact was all the more important because at that time the use of money as the universal equivalent was foreign to the Russian mind. Second, economic reforms led to the development of a powerful private sector that now employs the bulk of the workforce. Third, the social

Table 7.1 Income distribution and differentiation, 1980–2013

Year	*Population quintiles*					*Decile ratio*	*Gini index*
	first (lowest incomes)	*second*	*third*	*fourth*	*fifth (highest incomes)*		
1980	10.1	14.8	18.6	23.1	33.4	...	...
1985	10.0	14.6	18.3	23.1	34.0	...	...
1990	9.8	14.9	18.8	23.8	32.7	...	...
1995	6.1	10.8	15.2	21.6	46.3	13.5	0.387
2000	5.9	10.4	15.1	21.9	46.7	13.9	0.395
2005	5.4	10.1	15.1	22.7	46.7	15.2	0.409
2010	5.2	9.8	14.8	22.5	47.7	16.6	0.421
2013	5.2	9.9	14.9	22.5	47.5	16.2	0.418

Notes: FSSS data based on a random study of household budgets and the macroeconomic index of monetary incomes and Russian Statistical Yearbook, 2003. Data for 2013 is preliminary.

prestige of education and qualifications became more important for professionals in the private sector, and began to play a bigger role in shaping social status and the associated economic benefits. Fourth, the social structures of large territorial entities became more diverse. Fifth, the relative importance of the different components of social status underwent a significant change. While the stratification of Soviet society was based primarily on profession and position in the administrative apparatus, by the mid-1990s property and income gained the upper hand.[5] Sixth, social differentiation increased enormously and the number of people at the bottom of the social ladder rose sharply. According to Rosstat (Federal State Statistics Service), the share of people with average per capita incomes below the subsistence level (SL) went from 2.8% in 1989 to 19.1% by the mid-1990s. At the same time, the share of relatively well-to-do individuals plummeted, and social inequality continued to grow over time.[6] Thus, the Gini index increased from 0.39 in 1995 to 0.42 in 2013. The decile ratio also rose from 13.5 to 16.4 over the same years.[7]

Finally, seventh, the steady restructuring of the economy in the 1990s weakened some industries (the defence industry, for one) in terms of job prestige and other criteria, and led to the rapid growth of others (for instance, the financial sector). As for job opportunities, the restructuring of the economy dramatically reduced overall employment from 73.8 million in 1991 to 67.7 million in 2011. The following sectors were the hardest hit: science (employment fell 200%); manufacturing (more than 100%), construction (1.6 times) and agriculture (1.5 times). All in all, these sectors lost over 12 million jobs. However, this drastic decline in the sectors that were traditional for Russia as an industrial nation was not offset by a comparable increase in the number of jobs in the tertiary and quaternary industries, although jobs in management and professional services (real estate, finance, legal services etc.) increased several times over during these years. But this increase constituted less than a third of the jobs lost elsewhere. Retail and public services accounted for the biggest rise in employment – from 5.6 million in 1991 to 12.2 million in 2011.[8]

All of these processes were completed for the most part by the mid-2000s. The main statistical indicators illustrating the distribution of inequality in Russian society in different industries and professions have remained practically unchanged since that time.[9] This suggests that by the latter half of the 2000s the new social structure of Russian society took on its final shape. Importantly, the transformation of Russia's social structure consisted of two fundamentally different stages during the period of reforms. During the first stage in the 1990s, it seemed that the changes underway in Russian society were so dramatic that they were eroding the very foundations of the former social structure – ever greater power and property for managers and access to privileges for the managed. This stage also witnessed rapid deterioration in the economic wellbeing of the population in general and skyrocketing social differentiation.

During the second stage that started in the 2000s, the pendulum swung back and these trends began to reverse. There was a sharp reduction in poverty and a substantial increase in consumption among almost all strata of the population. Although the scale of differentiation remained the same, income inequality stopped growing (Figure 7.1). However, these positive trends were accompanied by a significant reduction in the number of entrepreneurs, especially small business owners. Government and business were rapidly becoming intertwined, and government officials were becoming increasingly corrupt. In the 1990s, old structural positions were replaced en masse, making each individual the main factor in determining their place in the system of stratification. However, starting in the mid-2000s, structural restrictions began to play a decisive role in determining the overwhelming majority of people's place in society, while their personal efforts to improve their social status were limited to a very narrow window of opportunity.[10]

The dominant trends in both periods of transformation substantially changed the general configuration of the structural positions in ways that were typical not only for the Soviet era but also the 1990s. The most striking changes were as follows: (1) the formation of new social groups (business elites, small and medium business owners, farmers, etc.); (2) enormous social differentiation and the emergence of lower social strata on a mass scale; (3) further increase in the already large role of place of residence in social stratification; (4) changes in which industries were leading and which were secondary. These trends were responsible for the changing social positions of about half of all people in Russia even if they did not directly alter anything in their lives. At the micro-level, the direction of change varied, but the number of people who fell to the bottom of the social ladder was ten times higher than the number who received a chance to ascend to the kinds of top positions that didn't even exist in Soviet times. [11]

This dramatic change in the structure of Russian society led to unprecedented mobility of the population at the micro-level. Tens of millions of people participated in the continuous Brownian motion of society by changing jobs and professions, moving and starting their own businesses in order to improve their positions on the new social ladder and their lives. However, during this large-scale transformation, upward mobility was the exception in the low-resource groups that made up the bottom two-thirds of Soviet society. The private sector was the primary means of upward mobility, but those who succeeded in business usually ran small companies. Medium-sized businesses were out of the ordinary, while big businesses were the domain of the high-resource groups in Soviet society.

The destiny of the latter is no less interesting than that of low-resource groups, and outcomes were certainly more diverse. Some in the high-resource groups of the former Soviet population made active use of the broad range of opportunities that were opened by the transition to a market economy. They could start their own business, take part in privatization, or occupy lucrative top positions. Other options included self-employment or new occupations in the private sector (consulting, auditing, marketing, stock trading etc.). However, only about half of the high-resource groups managed to attain positions that led to prosperity. The rest continued working as specialists or held middle-management positions that were not especially well paid.[12]

Public opinion on the structure of Russian society

Are people in Russia happy about the results of their efforts? What do they think about the new structure of society? How is it viewed by average people? Typically sociologists use graphical tests to gauge how the public perceives social structure models in different societies. This is the most informative and at the same time emotionally neutral way to analyze such perceptions. The results of these tests in modern Russia show that people are convinced that the bulk of the population is concentrated at the bottom of the social hierarchy and consider this social model 'unfair' and 'unfit for Russia' (Figure 7.1).

As Figure 7.1 shows, Russian people believe that the real and the ideal social structure models are diametrically opposed. A mere 14% of the population believes that the ideal models reflect reality. The desirable models (Model 3 and Model 4) have large middle sections, representing the proverbial middle-class society. This choice does not mean that all Russians without exception favour a one-size-fits-all approach. While 40% prefer a society with a limited range in social status (Model 4), the remaining 60% would like to live in a society with a high level of inequality, albeit one with a large middle class rather than a large underclass, as is currently the case in Russia.

The majority of Russians (57%) believe that Russia's real social structure is a pyramid, while others (28%) think that most people are at the bottom of the social hierarchy, with only a narrow elite and sub-elite at the top. Many, especially relatively young Russians, believe that the elite is completely isolated from the rest of society. In other words, Russians understand that the upper echelons and society at large are alienated from each other. To sum up, as a result of the transformation of the social structure, the public believes that society is highly stratified, with the majority of people concentrated at the bottom of the social hierarchy and only the few 'elite' at the top.

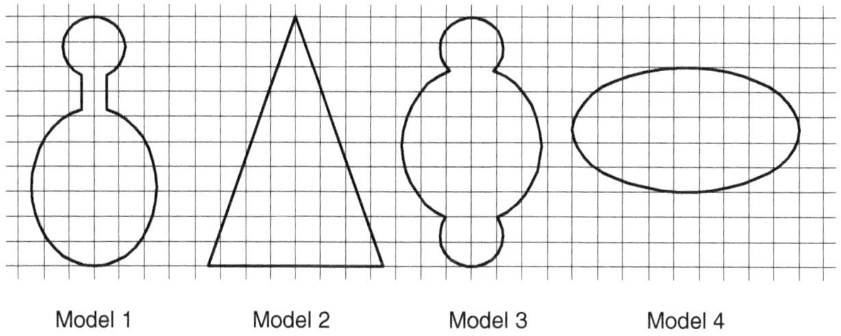

Real Model:	**28**	**57**	12	2
Desirable Model:	9	20	**31**	**40**
Difference:	–19	–37	+19	+38

Figure 7.1 Russian perceptions of which models best reflect the real and desirable social structure, 2012 (%).

Source: Data from Gorshkov and Tikhonova (eds), 'O chyom mechtayut rossiyane?' (2012).

To what extent does this view reflect the real state of Russian society? To answer this question let's look at the so-called subjective stratification model based on people's perceptions of their own place in society. One widely used method for this purpose is a graphical test with a vertical 10-point social status scale (social ladder) on which the respondent indicates his/her place in society. Figure 7.2 shows this subjective model of the structure of Russian society as it entered the active phase of social transformation.

At that time, a bottom-heavy model, similar to the one depicted in Figure 7.2, was typical of all post-socialist countries covered by the ISSP-1992 study, with most respondents placing themselves on the sixth rung of the social ladder from the bottom. However, the subjective social structure model in Russia changed dramatically in the early post-reform years. Its main feature soon became apparent – the majority of people began to feel dejected about their social status, and this feeling has characterized the model for the past 20 years. The bulge that had been concentrated in the middle sank to the bottom (Figure 7.3) as people who had identified themselves as middle class came to see themselves at the bottom of the social hierarchy. The resulting shape reflects the aforementioned objective changes in the positions of Russians during that period, as well as changes in the number of different structural positions in Russian society.

The general situation in the country improved considerably in the beginning of the Putin era, and people became more optimistic about their social status. At first sight, it appears as if their self-rating produced an entirely different structure (Figure 7.4). However, the characteristic feature of the subjective social structure

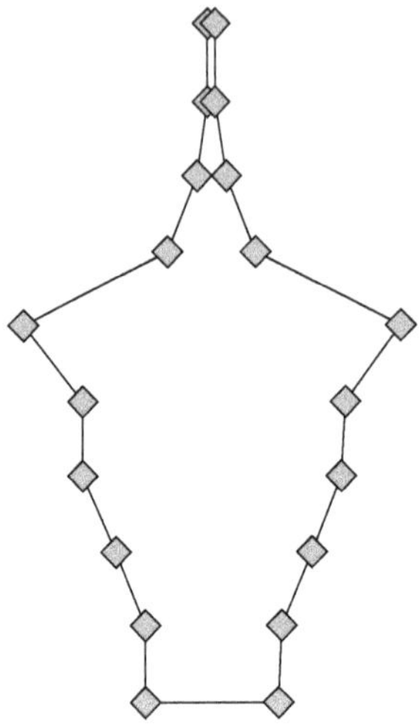

Figure 7.2 Russia's subjective social structure model based on respondents' self-rated social status, ISSP-1992.

Notes: International Social Survey Programme (ISSP) – an annual international programme of studies that cover issues that are important for the social sciences. Polls are conducted in dozens of European and American countries, including Russia. Topics of studies change every year but once every 5–8 years polls are held on issues of social structure (for more details on samples and methodology see: http://www.issp.org). Data from ISSP-1992 and ISSP-2009 were used in this chapter).

Methodologically, the model was built as follows: the percentage of respondents who chose their step on the social ladder are depicted on the vertical axis (since status is a vertical hierarchy); subsequently they were depicted as negative percentages to make the figure look symmetrical. To preserve the proportions, the model was constrained by 200% on the horizontal axis. The numerical values used to build the model were as follows:

1st (top) position – 0.4%	6th position – 17.6%
2nd position – 0.5%	7th position – 17.3%
3rd position – 1.9%	8th position – 13.1%
4th position – 5.9%	9th position – 9.2%
5th position – 25.3%	10th (bottom) position – 8.8%.

model that emerged in the mid-1990s remained the same (a narrow top with two-thirds of the population on the lower part of the social ladder). The result is that the share of those who consider themselves middle class in Russia is lower than in post-socialist countries of Central and Eastern Europe, not to mention West European states.

Therefore, despite dramatic changes in Russians' self-perception during the transformation of the 1990s and 2000s, the majority still placed themselves fairly low on the social ladder. Nevertheless, the underclass of the 1990s turned into the lower middle class, which is a substantial achievement of the Putin era. Where Russians place themselves on the social hierarchy is based primarily on their

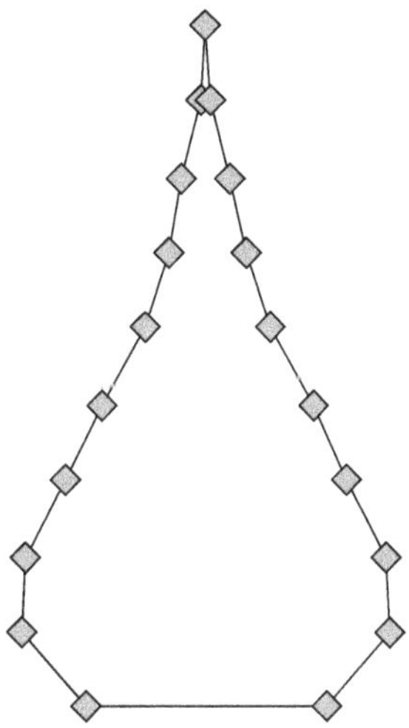

Figure 7.3 Russia's subjective social structure model based on respondents' self-rated social status, June 1998.

Source: Data from Gorshkov and Tikhanova (eds) (2000).

Note: Numerical values used for building the model:

1st (top) position – 0%	6th position – 12.4%
2nd position – 0.5%	7th position – 16.3%
3rd position – 2.8%	8th position – 20.9%
4th position – 4.3%	9th position – 21.4%
5th position – 7.3%	10th (bottom) position – 14.1%.

material wellbeing, so this positive change is largely a reflection of the marked improvement in living standards that occurred in the past 10 years.

Stratification of Russian society by living standards

So what does the stratification in Russian society look like today in terms of living standards? In other words, what is Russia's objective social structure? Social stratification can be analyzed using different variables, such as income, property and living standards. In the latter case, the cost-of-living index[13] (CLI[14]), is used to delineate the different strata of society. The stratification model of Russian society based on living standards exhibits the same features as the subjective model of its social structure – the distribution median is closer to the bottom. This is not surprising considering that Russians living in deprivation (those with more indicators of deprivation than prosperity) account for half of Russian society, including 16% who live in deep deprivation (five and more indicators of deprivation). This is a high figure but much smaller than in the early 2000s when over a quarter of Russian society were living in deep deprivation.

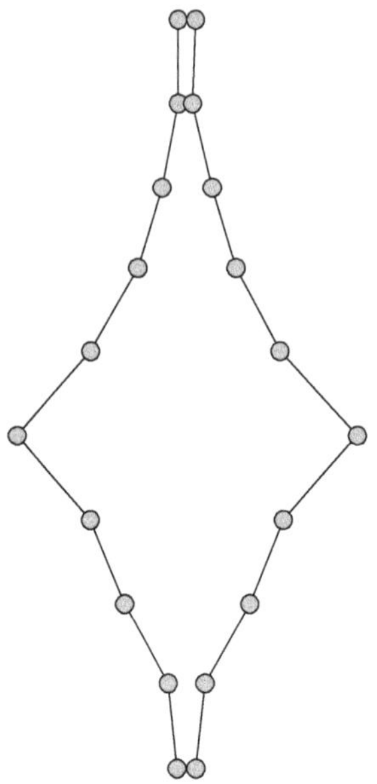

Figure 7.4 Russia's subjective social structure model based on respondents' self-rated social status, 2014.

Source: Data from Mikhail Gorshkov and Natalya Tikhonova (eds), 'Sredniy klass v sovremennoi Rossii' ('The Middle Class in Contemporary Russia'), *Obshchestvo i ekonomika*, No. 6, 2014, pp. 13–79.

Note: Numerical values used for building the model:

10th (top) position – 0.4%	5th position – 31.5%
9th position – 1.3%	4th position – 18%
8th position – 4.5%	3rd position – 11.4%
7th position – 9.2%	2nd position – 3.6%
6th position – 17.5%	1st (bottom) position – 1.6%.

What kind of life in today's Russia exhibits equal indicators of markers of prosperity and deprivation? The typical Russian family of three lives in a two-room apartment with a total area of 45–50 sq m and owns some other property – usually a summer house, a plot of land or a garage (in most cases people with these living standards already have a car – most often of domestic make, less often a used foreign car); they do not have any savings but they do not have debt, either; they express satisfaction with their level of material wellbeing, food, clothing and so on. At home they have everything they need for everyday life (a fridge, TV, mobile phone, vacuum cleaner, washing machine, computer and small kitchen appliances). However, they seldom have stylish or prestigious durable goods or digital devices of any kind. These typical living standards reflect the median for the population in Russia.

Based on the CLI, Russian society can be divided into five relatively homogenous strata:[15] the needy,[16] low-income, middle-income, high-income and the affluent[17] (Table 7.2). A considerable reduction in the share of needy was the most important change in the last few years. It was brought about by the completion of the restructuring of the economy, a substantial increase in pensions, and the end of the widespread practices of long unpaid vacations and delays in paying wages that sometimes lasted years. Not surprisingly, the low-income strata increased considerably in the early 2000s as people moved up from the ranks of the needy.

The *needy* include both those living in deep deprivation and those who are on the brink of poverty. The latter group may fall below the poverty line or rise a little above it, depending on circumstances. However, all of them typically endure multiple forms of deprivation. The *low-income* strata lead a very modest life that rules out conspicuous consumption of any kind. Practically all of them were poor in the past. They have very limited opportunities for improving their position. Incidentally, some of them, especially those living in poor regions or those who have improved their positions relatively recently, feel quite comfortable although they don't have any margin of safety. The *middle-income stratum* can be considered relatively well-to-do in Russian terms. Their material status is fairly stable and they can afford some minor degree of conspicuous consumption. *High-income* and *affluent* individuals make broad use of the opportunities that were opened up to consumers by the transition to a market economy. In addition, they usually have assets that yield – or at least have the potential to yield – meaningful revenue, such as a second residence, savings, securities or their own business. Importantly, the main thing that sets these strata apart is their ability to take action to improve their own lives (Table 7.3).

It is clear from Figure 7.3 that for several years running there has been no meaningful change for the better in the lives of the majority in the needy and low-income strata. Importantly, low-income people, representing half of Russia's population, are more similar to the needy than the middle-income stratum in this respect. The lives of middle-income people have seen the most positive change. As for high-income and affluent individuals, their circumstances are invariably positive. In recent years, the gap between well-off Russians and relatively disadvantaged or truly disadvantaged Russians that amount to half the population has continued to grow.

Table 7.2 Main social strata based on living standards, 2003/2014 (%)

Strata	*2003*	*2014*
Needy	36	22
Low-income	35	51
Middle-income	15	16
High-income	12	10
Affluent	2	1

Sources: Data from the studies 'Bogatiye i bedniye v sovremennoi Rossii' (2003) and 'Srednyi klass v sovremennoi Rossii' (2014). Data for 2014 are cited from the latter study.

Notes: Strata whose strength has changed the most are highlighted. The minor reduction in the number of high-income and affluent people is a result of declining participation rate in sociological polls.

Table 7.3 Achievements of different strata in the past three years, 2014 (%, rated by the gap (times) between the needy and the affluent)

Achievements	*Needy*	*Low-income*	*Middle-income*	*High-income*	*Affluent*	*Gap (times)*
Received a promotion or found a new, more desirable job	4	7	10	17	16	4
Improved housing conditions	5	10	20	25	37	7.4
Opened a business	1	1	3	5	9	9
Improved material wellbeing	5	16	35	44	**54**	10.8
Upgraded education or qualifications	2	7	17	18	27	13.5
Made expensive purchases	3	10	21	29	**61**	20.33
Visited a foreign country	1	7	22	44	**71**	71
Two or more achievements	***3***	***13***	***33***	***56***	***88***	***29.33***
Achieved none of the above	***86***	***58***	***25***	***14***	***0***	∞

Notes: Indicators surpassing half of the group are in bold and highlighted. Data are for the working members of the relevant strata. Both market (acquisition or construction of housing) and non-market (inheritance etc.) means of improving housing conditions are implied.

Table 7.4 shows in more detail the variety and scale of differences in the everyday lives of the five strata of Russian society. Representatives of different strata have extremely diverse views not only on those aspects of life related to differences in income and economic position in general but also on status-related issues, vacations, time with friends and family life. This means that there is a gap between different strata of Russian society not only in terms of living standards but also quality of life.

The different strata of Russian society are becoming increasingly divided by access to IT. The needy are essentially excluded from IT. The share of needy Russians that use a computer daily, even if just to play games, is less than one-third, while more than half never use a computer. Access to IT is the norm for low-income Russians, but the middle-income stratum is the first in which a majority uses a computer for work.

Factors that determine stratum by living standards

What are the reasons for the profound differences in living standards and way of life for the five main strata of Russian society? And what occupations are typical for each? The first factor that determines a person's stratum is *character of employment*. High-income and affluent people are not just white-collar workers; they also hold jobs that are traditionally considered middle-class. Needy and low-income Russians typically hold blue-collar jobs. Middle-income Russians holds a diverse range of jobs, but they are predominately white-collar (Table 7.5).

Table 7.4 Self-rating various aspects of life as positive, 2014 (%, rated by the middle-income strata)

Aspects of life	*Needy*	*Low-income*	*Middle-income*	*High-income*	*Affluent*
Family relations	39	**61**	**73**	**84**	**93**
Friendships	33	**53**	**69**	**80**	**81**
Food	13	42	**68**	**85**	**95**
Clothing	8	27	**57**	**76**	**88**
Housing	12	35	**56**	**71**	**83**
Leisure	12	32	**53**	**68**	**78**
Vacation	9	21	48	**65**	**81**
Health	17	30	48	**53**	**73**
Educational opportunities	6	24	42	**60**	**68**
Personal security	14	24	41	**46**	**54**
Life in general	***11***	***34***	***62***	***72***	***85***

Source: The answers 'satisfactory' and 'bad' were also options, although they are not represented in the table. The most popular positions chosen by respondents in the relevant strata are highlighted; the integral assessment of one's life by representatives of different strata is in bold and italics.

Table 7.5 Employment by different strata, 2014 (% of the total workforce)

Employment	*Needy*	*Low-income*	*Middle-income*	*High-income*	*Affluent*
Middle-class jobs:	**12**	**26**	**46**	**83**	**94**
Business owners with hired labour; family business, self-employment	0	2	4	18	12
Managers of different levels	3	4	10	18	48
Professionals, including commissioned officers	9	20	32	47	34
Blue-collar jobs:	**53**	**43**	**29**	**7**	**3**
Highly skilled	17	23	17	4	3
Semi-skilled	28	16	8	3	–
Unskilled	8	4	4	–	–
Other:	**35**	**31**	**25**	**10**	**3**
Semi-professionals, office personnel, technical personnel (including non-officers of security agencies)	15	17	18	6	–
Retail and domestic services	20	14	7	4	3
For reference: the share of non-working	41	30	28	25	24
Including pensioners	28	20	14	7	0

Note: The most common types of professions for each stratum are highlighted.

Unlike in the 1990s and even the 2000s, jobs in the public sector place people in the category of the well-to-do rather than the poor. Besides earning better wages, they enjoy other ancillary benefits, such as proper working conditions, job security, higher official salaries (ie not including wages earned off the books) and so on.

The second factor that influences and reflects the level of wellbeing in Russian society is the scale and composition of a person's resources. Economic resources primarily include income and property. According to public opinion polls, the median income of the affluent is several times higher than the needy (Table 7.6). As distinct from industrialized countries and even East European countries, in Russia source of income plays a minor role in differences in living standards. All large strata in Russia consist of wage-earners or pensioners. Few Russians own small businesses or securities.

Property is another important component of the economic resources of different strata. Even if not used to generate income, property is liquid enough to be sold for a sum comparable with several months' worth of income from employment or business ownership. This primarily applies to real estate. Table 7.7 shows that only middle- and high-income Russians and the affluent own property. This economic resource is relatively large and ensures some freedom of action for the upper two strata.

The trend lines in property ownership in Russia have been negative. A decade ago, representatives of all strata except the needy owned some property that they could sell to improve their financial situation. Now the picture is dramatically different. First, the amount of privately owned real estate has declined (not counting primary residences): in 2014 more than half of all rural residents did not own any land, not even a patch of land for farming. Second, a decade ago the types of real estate were distributed among the population more evenly. Now middle-income, high-income and affluent Russians usually own a summer house, a plot of land or a garage, whereas people with low incomes (not to mention the needy) have at most a plot of land without a house, the sale of which would not do much to improve the material wellbeing of its owner.

People from the different strata of Russian society differ substantially in terms of ownership of household appliances, computers, a stereo and other equipment. In 2014 the average household owned 8.6 out of 16 common durables, while the median household owned 9. The figure for the two bottom strata were lower (5.9 and 6 for the needy and 8.5 and 8 for low-income), while the figures for

Table 7.6 Monthly incomes of different strata, 2014 (rubles)

Income	*Needy*	*Low-income*	*Middle-income*	*High-income*	*Affluent*
Average per capita	11,236	12,840	15,548	20,607	31,790
Median	10,000	12,000	15,000	19,300	24,500
Mode	10,000	10,000	15,000	20,000	30,000

Note: Incomes are quoted in absolute terms, as they provided by poll respondents.

Table 7.7 Real estate owned by different strata, 2014 (%)

Types of real estate	*Needy*	*Low-income*	*Middle-income*	*High-income*	*Affluent*
Land	2	7	7	7	24
Parcel of land without a building	9	13	11	10	17
Second place of residence fit for year-round living	0	1	5	17	68
Garage or place in a parking lot	2	12	29	48	78
Plot of land with a summer house	7	24	37	54	63
For reference:					
None of the above	***82***	***52***	***34***	***17***	***0***
Two or more of the above	***2***	***9***	***20***	***45***	***88***

middle-income, high-income and affluent Russians were higher (from 10.38 and 10 for middle-income households to 13.6 and 14 for the affluent). Living standards, as defined by household goods, differ widely between strata (Table 7.8).

The middle-income stratum is the first in which a majority has savings. The relevant figure for the affluent is 96%. Only a quarter of people with low incomes have any savings. The data in the table suggests that only high-income or affluent Russians possess meaningful and growing economic resources. Most people with middle incomes have expanding economic resources, albeit fewer. They are able to balance the family budget and can afford limited displays of conspicuous consumption but lack a margin of safety. Their situation has not changed for the better in the past few years. Progress for people with low incomes has been mixed: a relative increase in consumption accompanied by rising indebtedness in the past decade and declining real estate holdings and savings. As for the needy, they have become increasingly marginalized as their resource base shrinks. This applies to savings, real estate and the number of durable goods in their households. But while the economic wellbeing of the needy has worsened in the past decade, their overall numbers have been on the decline. Apparently everyone who was capable of improving their standard of living did so in the sustained period of economic growth that followed the 1990s. However, the socioeconomic inequalities of the main strata of Russian society are not only based on their material resources. Social, human and cultural capital are equally if not more important, and there are huge variations in the quantity and quality of *social capital* among different strata (Table 7.9).

As we can see, people with middle and high incomes and especially the affluent have a much larger and more sophisticated network of social connections, and the peers in their social networks also have much greater opportunity.

Table 7.8 Ownership of durables by different strata, 2014 (%)

Durables	*Needy*	*Low-income*	*Middle-income*	*High-income*	*Affluent*
TV:	*96*	*99*	*99*	*98*	*100*
Ordinary colour TV,	83	77	67	62	58
LCD and plasma	29	61	85	91	95
Refrigerator	94	99	100	100	100
Cell phone	83	94	94	91	95
Vacuum cleaner	75	93	96	97	100
Washing machine	64	89	99	97	100
Computer, including notebook	48	72	89	94	100
Microwave, food processor, grill, toaster etc.	46	77	90	96	98
Car:	*21*	*55*	*75*	*90*	*97*
Foreign, foreign assembled in Russia,	5	26	52	77	90
Russian-made	16	32	31	28	26
Video or digital camera	19	46	73	85	88
iPhone, smartphone	12	22	47	63	83
Tablet, iPad	6	22	46	62	83
Satellite TV antenna	13	29	44	53	78
Air conditioner	3	13	26	41	81
Dishwasher	1	4	14	32	85

Notes: The presence of a particular durable in the household of over 50% of representative of the respective group is highlighted in grey. Some households have two TV sets. Therefore, the number of households with TVs is lower than the sum of those with two TV sets. Some households have both foreign and Russian cars, therefore the number of car owners is lower than the sum of those who have foreign and Russian cars.

As for *human capital*, its quality primarily depends on formal education (Figure 7.5). Again, there is enormous variation among the different strata in this regard.

The role of *cultural capital* in social mobility has been on the rise. It consists primarily of an individual's social background, which affects their socialization and hence marketable skills (Figure 7.6).

Considering the educational level of their parents, it is not surprising that wealthy and affluent people have higher-status backgrounds. People with middle incomes have middle-class backgrounds for the most part. Most had parents on the fifth or sixth step of the social ladder. Over one-third of people with low incomes have underclass backgrounds, while the rest had origins considered

Table 7.9 Social capital of different strata, 2013 and 2014 (%)

Social capital	*Needy*	*Low-income*	*Middle-income*	*High-income*	*Affluent*
Number of different types of social connections, 2013:					
1	33	17	13	18	12
2	26	26	28	23	6
3	20	32	31	26	25
4	13	18	20	20	29
5	2	3	5	9	21
6–7	0	1	3	3	6
Do not socialize with anyone except for family members	***6***	***3***	***0***	***0***	***0***
Social networking opportunities, 2014:					
Finding a good job	7	8	17	28	25
Attending a prestigious university	1	3	9	16	30
Career advancement	2	2	5	11	15
Placing children in decent school	3	7	12	20	15
Resolving housing issues	4	5	6	7	5
Access to good doctors or hospital	9	21	33	38	65
Able to borrow a large sum of money	22	33	40	42	40
Social networks cannot render these types of support	***61***	***40***	***22***	***14***	***10***

Source: Data for 2013 from the study 'Bednost and bedniye v sovremennoi Rossii' (2013).

Notes: Including interactions with neighbours, relatives, co-workers, old friends (since childhood or elementary school), acquaintances from clubs and recreation centres and people with the same religious or philosophical views – seven types of contacts all in all. The most typical type of contact for each stratum is highlighted.

lower middle-class. Finally, most of the needy (52%) come from the underclass in their own estimate. *Age* is another important factor affecting stratification. In the Soviet era, the older a person was, the more likely it was that they would be relatively comfortable financially. This situation reversed under the reforms of the 1990s, with young people finding themselves in a much better position. In the last few years, age has essentially ceased to be a factor in determining one's place in a particular stratum (except for pensioners).

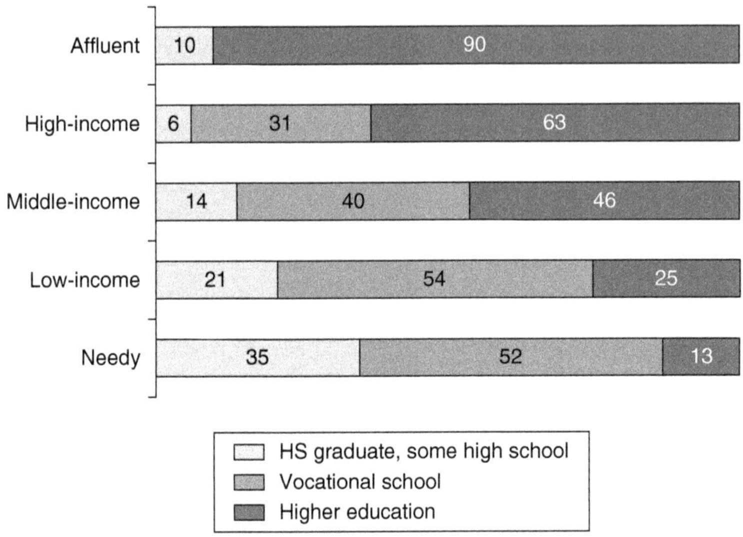

Figure 7.5 Educational attainment of different strata, 2014 (%).

Finally, there is *place of residence* (both the region and type of locality). Without addressing in detail the problem of regional inequality (which is considered in a later chapter) it is important to note that rural residents fare worst in terms of stratification. However, the issue is less about the share of the needy (which varies by a mere 1.5 times in different types of localities) than the share of high-income or affluent people. Even in random samples, the share of the wealthy is about a quarter of the total (in reality it is higher), whereas in rural areas it is several times less (a mere 6%). Incidentally, the living standards of rural residents were lower both in the Soviet era and the 1990s. However, it is important to point out that the chances of rural residents becoming prosperous have increased dramatically in the past decade, unlike residents of big cities where social mobility has stalled.

Conclusions

Social inequality in today's Russia is a logical consequence of the unequal resources held by different groups of Russian society, accumulated over generations in many cases, when the reforms began in the 1990s. In the planned economy of the Soviet Union, when these resources did not function as capital, differences in resource levels affected the living standards of various strata but could not lead to serious social differentiation. During the transition to a market economy, these resources were converted into capital or used to build up other intangible forms of capital. In post-Soviet Russia, the primitive accumulation of capital was characterized by the rapid conversion of different types of resources into one another. This process led to the emergence of new ruling classes from

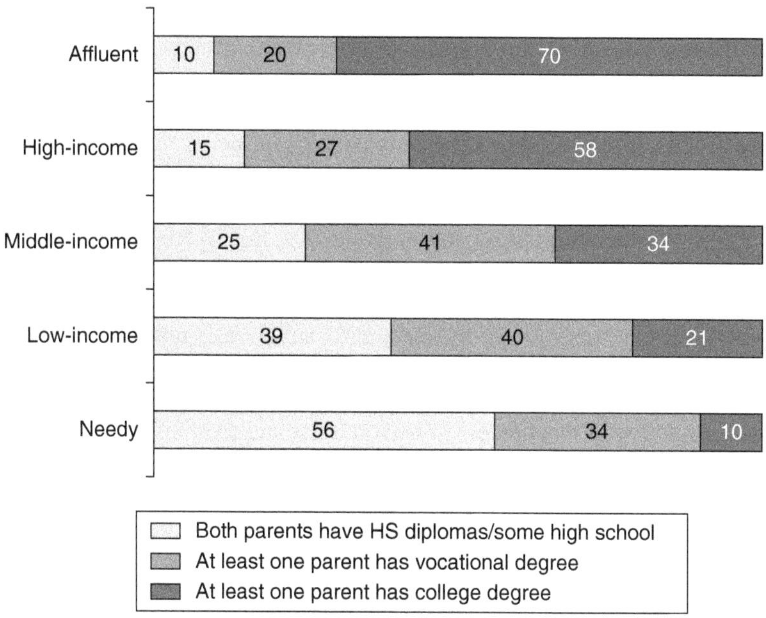

Figure 7.6 Educational attainment by *parents* of representatives of different strata, 2014 (%).

among the high-resource groups of Soviet society. Many of them managed to take advantage of the new opportunities afforded by the economic transformation owing to their social and cultural capital, which granted access to the most profitable economic and power resources.

Different types of capital are concentrated in the hands of one and the same group of 'new capitalists', albeit in various combinations. Today the 'new capitalists' include more than just entrepreneurs, because all types of resources can be successfully converted into economic resources in modern Russian society. This is why they come in all shapes and sizes. A person with sufficient resources can be categorized as a capitalist without being involved in any business. However, far from all descendants from high-resource groups of Soviet society became 'new capitalists' as a result of Russia's post-Soviet transformation. For a number of reasons, some of them did not climb any higher than 'specialists', and went on to form the backbone of Russia's middle class. This latter group occupied managerial positions of varying levels, which are not especially lucrative, and in this regard their position is very similar to that of the majority of 'specialists'. On the whole, both groups are relatively well-off compared to the rest of Russian society, although their place in society depends heavily on circumstances (types of resources, conditions in the regions and the job market for different industries).

Indicatively, the low living standards of a considerable part of the population in today's Russia are the result not simply of inadequate incomes but the almost total lack of resources that would allow them to boost their incomes. This lack of resources is perpetuated from one generation to the next, going back to the Soviet era. Thus, the lower two-thirds of Soviet society generally occupy the same place in today's Russia. However, deepening social differentiation has divided this previously homogenous group into a number of layers with large differences in status and prospects. One in ten Russians occupies a position in society that did not exist on a mass scale in the Soviet Union and as many have a precarious existence. About half of the population is low-income. Although the extent of their deprivation varies, they cannot afford conspicuous consumption. The rest of Russian society is relatively prosperous, although the extent of their wellbeing varies significantly.

Although resources are decisive in defining one's place in society, as is typical is class societies, the formation of Russia's class structure is not yet complete. But we can already see fairly clearly the outlines of a class stratification model in which social status is dependent upon one's position in the market. Several factors inhibit the completion of this process in Russia. First and foremost is the continued predominance of a state-centric development model based on the merger of power with property relations. Second are the imbalances in the development of different sectors, regions and types of localities inherited from Soviet times. They have become more pronounced in the new conditions and are increasing the role of non-class types of social inequality. Third, Russia still does not have a fully-fledged national labour market. Fourth, the formation of the class structure of Russian society is being impeded by the preservation of the powerful public sector, which employs a substantial part (about 30%) of the total workforce.

The factors affecting stratification have changed repeatedly in Russia over the past 20 years. In the late 1990s the main factor was whether a person was employed in the public or private sector. All other factors boiled down to whether they led to a greater chance of employment in the private sector. Now, 15 years later, family background plays a greater role in determining a person's status. In other words, drivers of social mobility are stalling. The competition for favourable structural positions is becoming tougher and involves more and more frequent use of non-market mechanisms. While this does not mean that education and other forms of human capital are altogether unimportant in modern Russian society, they have become much more dependent on one's background than they were 15 years ago. In the late 1990s anyone who could get a job in the private sector owing to personal qualities immediately benefited, whereas now access to good jobs in any sector is reserved for high-profile and educated families. Over the past 15 years, the role of structural restrictions resulting from economic restructuring has increased the importance of stratification factors that ensure the social reproduction of classes and decreased the influence of factors related to individual initiative. This type of class reproduction underscores the fairly closed social structure of today's Russia. Moreover, the growing role of social capital and family background as stratification factors and the current mechanisms of social mobility are increasingly alienating Russia from the meritocratic ideal of an equal opportunity society, which the overwhelming majority of Russians choose as the ideal social model.

Despite their higher tolerance for social inequality, Russians are growing increasingly dissatisfied, though many are still content with the greater prosperity they began to enjoy in the 2000s. Throughout the reform years, Russians have recognized that despite the rising prosperity in the country, most of the population fall below the middle of the social ladder. They are now coming to realize that the top of society is isolated from the majority of the population and that the two stand in opposition to each other.

Notes

1 This chapter uses data from polls conducted by the Russian Academy of Sciences (RAS) Institute of Comprehensive Social Studies (1998–2003) and the RAS Institute of Sociology (2008–2014) by the same team of scholars under the leadership of Mikhail Gorshkov. The polls used one-type samplings that divided the country's population by region of residence, and within each region by gender, age and type of settlement. The following studies were cited: Mikhai Gorshkov and Natalya Tikhonova (eds), *Rossiya na rubezhe vekov* (*Russia at the Turn of the Century*) (Moscow: Rosspen, 2000); Mikhail Gorshkov and Natalya Tikhonova (eds), *Rossiya – novaya sotsialnaya realnost: bogatyye, bednyye, srednyi klass* (*Russia – New Social Reality: Wealthy, Poor, Middle Class*) (Moscow: Nauka, 2004). For more details on sampling and the results of these studies, see Mikhail Gorshkov and Natalya Tikhonova (eds), *O chyom mechtayut rossiyane*? (*What are Russians Dreaming About?* (Moscow: Ves mir, 2013); and Mikhail Gorshkov and Natalya Tikhonova (eds), *Bednost i bednyye v sovremennoi Rossii* (*Poverty and the Poor in Modern Russia*) (Moscow: Ves mir, 2014).

2 The term 'social structure' is used interchangeably in the chapter with 'social stratification', 'stratification system', and so on.

3 For more details about the social structure of the late Soviet era see Vadim Radayev, and Ovsei Shkaratan, *Sotsialnaya stratifikatsiya* (*Social Stratification*) (Moscow: Aspekt Press, 1996); Natalya Tikhonova, *Faktory sotsialnoi stratifikatsii v usloviyakh perekhoda k rynochnoi ekonomike* (*Stratification Factors During the Transition to a Market Economy*) (Moscow: Rosspen, 1999); Ovsei Shkaratan and Vladimir Ilyin, *Sotsialnaya stratifikatsiya Rossii i Vostochnoi Yevropy: sravnitelnyi analiz* (*Social Stratification in Russia and Eastern Europe: Comparative Analysis*) (Moscow: Higher School of Economics, 2006); Ovsei Shkaratan, *Sotsiologiya neravenstva. Teoriya i realnost* (*Sociology of Inequality: Theory and Reality*) (Moscow: Higher School of Economics, 2012).

4 *Rossiya v tsifrah* (*Russia in figures*), FSGS RF (Federal State Statistics Service), 2014, available at http://www.gks.ru/bgd/regl/b14_11/IssWWW.exe/Stg/d01/07-01.htm. [Accessed on: 17 June 2015].

5 Tatyana Zaslavskaya, 'Transformatsiya sotsialnoi struktury rossiyskogo obshchestva' ('The Transformation of the Social Structure of Russian Society'), *Kuda idyot Rossiya? Sotsialnaya transformatsiya postsovetskogo prostranstva* (*Where Is Russia Headed? The Social Transformation of the Post-Soviet Space*), 3rd edn (Moscow, 1996), p. 18.

6 See *SSSR v tsifrakh v 1989 godu (USSR in Figures in 1989) (Moscow: Finansy i statistika, 1990), p. 79, and Informatsiya o sotsialno-ekonomicheskom polozhenii Rossii. Yanvar-avgust 1997 g. (Information on Russia's Socio-Economic Status. January–August 1997)* (Moscow: Goskomitet RF po statistike, 1997), p. 69.

7 *Raspredelenie obschego ob'ema denezhnih dokhodov po 20-protsentnym gruppam naselenia i osnovnye pokazateli sotsialno-ekonomicheskoi differentsiatsii. Dinamicheskie ryady*. (*Distribution of Total Income Per Quintile and Main Indicators of Socioeconomic Differentiation. Dynamic Rows*). FSGS RF (Federal State Statistics Service). Official site. Updated on 5 June 2014. Available at http://www.gks.ru/wps/wcm/connect/rosstat_main/rosstat/ru/statistics/population/level/#. [Accessed on: 17 June 2015].

8 Calculated by Rossyiskyi statisticheskyi yezhegodnik, 2000 g. (Statistical Yearbook of Russia, 2000) (Moscow: Goskomitet, 2000); Rossyiskyi statisticheskyi yezhegodnik, 2003 (Statistical Yearbook of Russia, 2003), available at http://www.gks.ru/bgd/regl/b03_13/IssWWW.exe/Stg/d010/i011440r.htm/ [Accessed on: 17 June 2015]; Rossyiskyi statisticheskyi yezhegodnik (Statistical Yearbook of Russia, 2012), available at http://www.gks.ru/bgd/regl/b12_13/IssWWW.exe/Stg/d1/05-05.htm [Accessed on: 17 June 2015].

9 Income distribution in deciles and quintiles of the population, the Gini index, R/P 10% ratio, the ratio between the urban and rural population, and so on.

10 Natalya Tikhonova, 'Faktory stratifikatsii v sovremennoi Rossii: dinamika sravnitelnoi znachimosti'(Stratification Factors in Modern Russia: Dynamics of Relative Importance), *Sotsiologicheskiye issledovaniya* (*Sociological Research*), No. 10, 2014.

11 Considering those who attempted to change their status, the transformation of the stratification model covered practically the entire Russian population in some form or other.

12 Natalya Tikhonova, *Sotsialnaya struktura Rossii: teorii i realnost* (*Russia's Social Structure: Theories and Reality*) (Moscow: Novyi Khronograf (Institute of Sociology at the Russian Academy of Sciences), 2014).

13 Based on the idea that any analysis of real living standards should include not only a measure of wellbeing but also deprivation, that is, privations and restrictions in the standard package of consumer amenities. Put together, privations and luxuries paint an accurate picture of one's wellbeing because social differentiation is defined not only by what a family has but also what it does not have. Markers of prosperity indicators should include not only property but also services because some people use their resources primarily to purchase products whereas others prefer to spend them on services, social life and recreation.

14 In calculating the Satisfaction with Life Index (SLI) sociologists ask respondents to rate their material wellbeing in terms of food, clothing, the number of durable goods in households and the number of durables purchased in the past seven years, housing conditions, ownership of real estate, savings, payment for services and forms of recreation, major achievements in the past three years, and indebtedness. There are 14 indicators on the deprivation scale and 12 on the prosperity scale.

15 Without counting the upper layers and the underclass (homeless, etc.).

16 It should be emphasized that this group does not coincide with the poor. Although their incomes are fairly low (which will be discussed further in a later chapter), they are often above the subsistence level in the respective region. Therefore, three-quarters of the needy are not classified as poor by income. But while their incomes are above subsistence level, they live in fairly deep deprivation – its median level is at the fifth position. Their SLI is at the fourth position. In other words, they have almost no indicators of prosperity.

17 Representatives of the affluent are almost completely missed by public opinion polls. People in the top 2 or 3% of the upper crust are totally absent from this classification. They are never included in poll samples.

8 New Russia

The evolution of Russian public opinion, 1989–2014

Valery Fyodorov

Any effort to record modern Russian history can and must incorporate economic, social, political, cultural and other data and a variety of methods. Ultimately, history is written by onlookers, in this case social scientists. But in my opinion, the picture will remain incomplete and lopsided unless we give the object of our research – the people of Russia – an opportunity to express their opinions. Fortunately, their voice, or rather voices, could be heard in the past 25 years, even if faintly, thanks to consistent public opinion research conducted by pollsters (not sociologists, as we're somewhat inaccurately referred to). In this article, we listen to the voices of ordinary Russians to understand how they experienced and processed the dramatic events and changes that have roiled the country since the late 1980s.

Public opinion in the late and post-Soviet periods

Public opinion is an elusive, variable quantity that can be subjected to a range of sometimes contradictory interpretations, but it is nonetheless vital for understanding how society changes in any marginally democratic state. Public opinion emerged as a political factor in Russia in the late 1980s, when the decline of the Soviet Union gave rise to new social, political and economic patterns. While limited public opinion studies had been held in the Soviet Union since the late 1950s, they never dealt with hot-button political issues, because the Communist Party fiercely protected its monopoly on information. Only the Party could speak for the people, and it did not tolerate competition in this fundamentally important sphere.

How has public opinion taken root in modern Russia, which may not seem like the most fertile soil, as one of the country's most important social institutions? To begin with, the information and communication revolution has brought politics from behind the closed doors of government offices right into TV viewers' homes. This dramatically weakened politicians' prestige and status and strengthened the relative importance and self-esteem of the population. At the same time, the democratization of the political system made elections, which are invariably accompanied by opinion polls, the source of officials' legitimacy. Changes in some spheres of society paved the way for changes in others. For example, the emergence of political pluralism, democratization and media liberalization prevented public opinion as a social institution from disappearing as quickly as it appeared in the late 1980s.

In this chapter, we will consider the phenomenon of public opinion in the late and post-Soviet periods in Russian history (1989–2014). The main goal is to determine how changes in public opinion are related to broader trends in social stratification, economy, culture, information, the institutional design of the Russian political system and Russia's geopolitical standing. This should shed light on why similar events – economic crises, political decisions and foreign policy challenges – produced different responses in Russian society depending on what stage of evolution it was in.

Contemporary Russian history has not yet been divided into generally accepted periods, and so we will use a formula that is based on the inherent value of public opinion and can be used to characterize public opinion in terms of structural function or content. Since we will not study public opinion as a social institution but rather its evolution at different stages in the late and post-Soviet periods, we will focus on content. We will divide periods based on major, obvious shifts in people's attitudes to certain key issues and topics. Did demand for radical change dominate society in a given period, or was stability and normalization the priority? Was public opinion intensified, politicized and active, or was it depoliticized, demobilized and passive? Was it critical and demanding of politicians and government authorities, or resigned to cede to them the right to lead the country wherever they chose? Did it gravitate to a single policy or move in a single direction, or was it split into rival trends, coalitions and sides?

Using this approach, the past 25 years in Russian history can be divided into six roughly equal periods, each of them characterized by a different state of public opinion. These periods are separated, albeit somewhat loosely, by landmark political, economic or geopolitical events that dramatically altered public opinion, its trajectory and the dominant public attitudes to the main issues and topics. Public opinion might respond to changes by moving from an active and consolidated state to a passive and disjointed one, or vice versa. There were other combinations, too: active but split and pluralistic, or passive but consolidated.

The collapse of the Soviet system and the rise of a new government (1989–1993)

The collapse of the Soviet Union as a multinational country, an authoritarian state and a unique social system is the most dramatic and even tragic period in modern Russian history. The Soviet Union gave way to a much smaller and more ethnically homogenous country, with a more complicated, modern social system and greater liberties, but one that was also less balanced due to internal contradictions. The transition was marked by serious civil conflicts that escalated to the point of violence and deployment of the army to solve internal political disputes, as well as rising tensions between various social groups. The old development paradigm had been exhausted and needed to be replaced quickly and completely.

Society was engaged in a painful search for a new social model that could be adopted as soon as possible.

This period began in May 1989, when the First Congress of People's Deputies took over from the once omnipotent Communist Party, and ended with the first election to the State Duma in December 1993, when the institutional design and landscape of post-Soviet politics took its final shape. Politically, Russia evolved from a Soviet republic into a super-presidential republic, from a unitary into a federal state, and from a single party system into a pluralistic political system. That turbulent process of political transformation culminated in the military assault on the Russian White House (the government building) in October 1993 and the adoption of a new constitution in a referendum in December that year. This effectively eliminated any rival institutions to the presidency and limited political competition to the posts of head of state and head of government, the latter traditionally being seen as next in line for the presidency. Decentralization was legalized by the Federation Treaty of 1992 and a series of bilateral agreements signed between the federal centre and the regions in 1994–1998.

Economically, this period was marked by the collapse of the planned economic system and the rise of small-scale private property, the liberalization of trade and monetary transactions, and the creation of foundations for banking and the stock market. The majority of the population saw their economic wellbeing decline sharply, with high inflation giving way to hyperinflation and disguised unemployment turning to open unemployment. Wages were delayed or not paid, businesses were shuttered, and non-payment and bartering became facts of life. Budget shortfalls were covered by ballooning foreign debt. A shortage of goods amid an excess of money was replaced by an abundance of goods, a dire shortage of funds and

Table 8.1 Social stratification in Russia

Social groups		*Russia*		
		1985	*1990*	*1994*
1	Entrepreneurs, traders	0.4	1.4	3.2
2	Managers and civil servants	5.8	5.8	5.8
3	Mid-level managers	7.2	6.7	6.0
4	High-ranking professionals (with degrees)	1.6	1.8	1.3
5	Professionals with higher education	21.4	20.0	18.8
6	Professionals with specialized secondary education	9.9	10.2	10.1
7	Office personnel	3.4	3.1	3.6
8	Highly skilled blue-collar workers	2.8	3.5	2.4
9	Skilled blue-collar workers	34.3	32.3	29.4
10	Semi-skilled and unskilled workers	9.7	11.3	10.3
11	Housewives	3.1	3.4	3.9
12	Unemployed	0.4	0.5	5.2

Source: Vadim Radayev and Ovsei Shkaratan, *Sotsial'naya stratifikatsiya* (*Social Stratification*) (Moscow: Aspect Press, 1996).

a rapid devaluation of the rouble. The growing criminalization of the economy and society complicated economic activity and primitivized the economy. From a social standpoint, 1989–1993 marked the end of the Soviet stratification system and the division of social groups into intellectuals, engineering personnel, blue-collar workers and peasants, and the development of new classes such as small businessmen including 'suitcase' traders (*chelnoki*, shuttle traders personally importing cheap goods), public sector employees, criminals and so on.

The social structure became unbalanced, and social mobility was growing rapidly. The end of the egalitarian Soviet system rapidly accelerated property and social stratification, which came as a profound shock for a society that was brought up on ideas of egalitarian fairness.

During the same period, Russia moved from Mikhail Gorbachev's glasnost to freedom of speech. Journalists had unprecedented opportunities and became the heroes of the day, while people had newfound access to a huge amount of independent and contradictory information. There were no private media outlets yet, but the government could no longer directly control publically funded media. Geopolitically, the collapse of the Soviet Union and the loss of former allies and satellites to the US and NATO was a heavy blow to Russians' conception of their country as a great power. But the bitter loss was largely offset by hope for rapid improvement and Western assistance. The Commonwealth of Independent States (CIS) was seen as a milder version of the Soviet Union rather than a civilized divorce between the former Soviet republics. Russia's role in the conflicts in Transnistria, Abkhazia and South Ossetia showed its

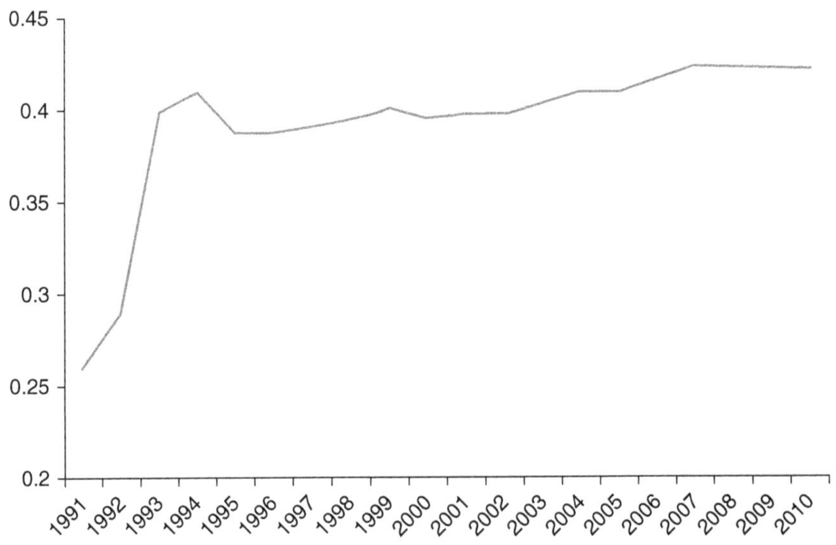

Figure 8.1 Gini index in Russia, 1991–2010.

Source: Federal State Statistics Service, Supplements to the yearbook *Russian Socioeconomic Indicators 1991–2010*.

citizens that the new national borders were malleable and could be changed as Moscow deemed necessary.

Pro-western liberal democratic progressivism was the most active and influential movement in that period. It advocated dismantling the autocratic state, transitioning to a market economy, immediate privatization of state property, and Russia's reintegration in the global community as a privileged partner and 'favourite disciple' of the West. The movement forced its agenda on the authorities, pushing back both its old rivals (Communists and Socialists, who tried to preserve at least parts of the disintegrating Soviet system) and new adversaries – patriotic nationalists who were seeking a viable alternative to the pro-western trend. Standing apart from them was a motley coalition of nationalists. Pro-western Liberals formed a coalition with external nationalist groups in order to explode the Soviet Union, and at the same time declared war on internal nationalists to preserve the territorial integrity of the Russian Federation.

Progressive pro-reform sentiments waned as economic reforms became more radical and life became increasingly harder for the majority of population. First,

Table 8.2 Life is made up of good and bad moments. But are you happy, in general? (closed question, one answer)

	1991	*1992*
Yes	60	42
No	29	36
Don't know	12	23
Happiness Index	31	6

Notes: The Happiness Index tracks national happiness in Russia. The higher the index, the happier Russians are. The index is calculated on the basis of answers to the question, 'Life is made up of good and bad moments. But are you happy, in general?' as a difference between the sum total of positive answers ('Definitely yes' and 'Mostly yes') and negative answers ('Definitely no' and 'Mostly no'). The index is measured in points ranging from -100 to 100.

Table 8.3 Is the worst behind us, still to come or right now? (closed question, one answer)

	1991	*1992*	*1994*
Right now	23	23	22
Behind us	3	3	4
Still to come	66	67	60
Don't know	9	7	15
Index	–86	–87	–78

Source: National representative survey conducted by VTsIOM.

Notes: The index measures optimism about Russia's future. It is calculated as the difference between the answer 'Behind us' and the sum total of answers 'Right now' and 'Still to come' and can range from −100 to +100. The higher the figure, the more optimistic Russians are about their country's future. Zero indicates an equal share of optimistic and pessimistic answers.

Table 8.4 What is Russia's current priority? (closed question, one answer)

	1994
To complete the economic reforms even if this entails abandoning some democratic elements (elections, the constitution)	25
To continue to honour democratic principles even if this would slow or stop reforms	23
Both democracy and reforms can be abandoned if this helps revive Russia as a great power within Soviet borders	26
Don't know	26

Source: VTsIOM, http://wciom.ru/zh/print_q.php?s_id=483&q_id=36138&date=10.03.1994.

the 'better tomorrow' promised by pro-democracy politicians did not materialize, and there was strong evidence of a deepening economic crisis and imminent social catastrophe rather than rising prosperity and democracy.

Second, the liberal democratic doctrine did not envision the dissolution of the Soviet Union, which came as a shock to the people and encouraged a considerable part of moderate pro-reformers to denounce the reforms as 'anti-Russian' because they weakened rather than strengthened the country.

Third, wage arrears and hyperinflation greatly reduced the income of a large part of engineering professionals and academic intelligentsia, who are the main driving force of democracy. They had to take second or even third jobs and were too busy trying to find a place in the chaotic new pseudo-market economy to spend any time on political activity. The heroes of that tumultuous period came from widely different backgrounds: coal miners (considered part of the blue-collar aristocracy in the Soviet Union), who first went on strike in support of Yeltsin and radical reforms, and then camped at the government building to protest against wage arrears and the closure of unprofitable mines; disoriented engineers, who resigned when their research institutes lost state contracts and turned to selling gum and beer in the kiosks that lined the streets in Russian cities; highly politicized journalists, who told people the truth about the horrors of the Stalin era and the good life in that ideal democracy, the United States; the new rich, many of them former members of cooperatives or owners of an underground workshop or factory in the late Soviet period, who demonstrated their high standing by wearing flashy and tasteless clothes and massive gold jewellery; and the former Komsomol (Young Communist) leaders, who quickly adjusted to the new conditions, accumulated wealth by importing computers and then invested it in a bank or an exchange on their way to the real prize – an oil or metals company.

Fluctuating stability of the new Russian government (1994–1997)

The dramatic events of the autumn of 1993 put an end to Russia's political disintegration, while Yeltsin's victory in the 1996 presidential election gave his regime several more years in power.[1] Taken together, these created conditions for a new system of ownership and new economic rules in 1994–1997, which included commodities sector privatization, financial stabilization and control of hyperinflation. However, these goals were not achieved on the back of an improving economy, but rather loans from international financial organizations that increased Russia's sovereign debt. After seven years of continued decline, when GDP fell by 40% and the industrial production index by 50%, Russia recorded minor economic growth and declining inflation in 1997.

This was a time of 'oligarchic empires', which combined huge metal and oil companies with Soviet roots and mini banks, including Menatep (Mikhail Khodorkovsky), Alpha Bank (Mikhail Fridman), Incombank (Vladimir Vinogradov), Bank Stolichny, later known as SBS-Agro (Alexander Smolensky), and other banks, that flourished by lending the government and industry money back to them at sky-high interest rates.[2] Federal agencies were too weak and corrupt to provide an effective counterweight, but regional heads could. They strengthened their positions by winning direct elections and signing agreements on the division of power between the federal centre and the regions. Governors who proved their loyalty to Yeltsin and had no secessionist aspirations redoubled efforts to create closed regional political systems that would keep them in power for as long as they wanted and protect them from encroachment by national oligarchs.

The oligarchs who assumed control of the federal media strengthened their own influence and also that of Yeltsin's corrupt team. Political pluralism was reduced to meaningless debate in a feeble State Duma, while practical politics was usurped by two oligarchic television networks, NTV and ORT (currently Channel One), which waged information warfare against each other. The pluralism and independence of the media were lost, and newspaper readership fell in step with rising poverty in the country and the dislocation of the intellectual class, which was the main consumer of news.

Relative political stability at a time when the country was burning through the remaining reserves of the Soviet economy led to the appearance of a group that can be loosely described as a post-Soviet middle class[3] – a mixture of small businessmen, freelancers, the white collar workers of the rapidly growing service sector, suitcase traders and semi-criminal characters who happened to be in the right place at the right time during the often illegal privatization of the 'national wealth'. While it had vague political views, this class clearly benefited from the post-Soviet economic and social transformation and linked its hopes to Russia's progress on the course charted by the 'young reformers'.

But a crisis in the defence sector, the implosion of the domestic market and the consumer goods industry, as well as the collapse of agriculture had dramatic social consequences. The vast majority of Russians, from engineers and intellectuals to workers and peasants, failed to adjust to a new reality and ever-changing rules. They had to drastically curtail their consumer aspirations, and in some cases were left without a stable source of income. This majority quickly became disenchanted with the reforms, the market economy and democracy, and turned to communists or populists, or most often, came to mistrust all politicians and focused instead on physical survival.

Table 8.5 What are the main results of the reforms begun in April 1985? (closed question, any number of answers)

	1995
Increasing chaos and disorder in state governance	62
Increasing economic insecurity	51
Ethnic tensions	38
A deepening economic crisis	37
Weaker national defence	31
More political rights and freedoms	12
People are more politically and economically active	11
Nascent economic renewal	9
Improved international standing	8
Cultural revival in different ethnic groups	8
Other	2

Source: VTsIOM representative survey 1995, http://wciom.ru/zh/print_q.php?s_id=429&q_id=34561&date=20.02.1995.

In geopolitical terms, 1994–1997 saw the slow but steady erosion of Russia's sphere of influence. The country was also denied the ability to integrate into Euro-Atlantic structures. Russian membership in the G7, IMF loans and the creation of the Gore–Chernomyrdin Commission on economic and technological cooperation were balanced by the admission of the Visegrád Group – the Czech Republic, Hungary, Poland and Slovakia – into NATO, Russia's military withdrawal from the Baltic states, the Dayton Peace Agreement in the former Yugoslavia and other events that the majority of Russians interpreted as evidence of Russia's waning status in the world. The appointment of an anti-Western politician, Yevgeny Primakov, as foreign minister in January 1996 signalled Russia's desire to pursue a more independent and multipolar foreign policy. But that goal remained out of reach due to Russia's growing internal weakness and the United States' unassailable domination on the international stage. Likewise, the Union State of Russia and Belarus, which

Table 8.6 How interested are you in politics? (closed question, one answer)

	1990	*1991*	*1992*	*1997*
Very	21	16	15	11
Somewhat	44	40	33	36
A little or not at all	35	36	52	49
Don't know	<1	8	<1	4
Political Awareness Index	30	20	–4	-2

Source: VTsIOM representative surveys 1990–1997.

Note: The Political Awareness Index gauges Russians' interest in politics. It is calculated as the difference between the sum total of answers 'Very' and 'Somewhat' and the answer 'A little or not at all' and is measured in points from –100 to +100. The higher the index, the higher the level of Russians' political awareness.

Yeltsin and president Alexander Lukashenko announced as their goal in April 1996, was only an election promise. Public opinion was apathetic, impotent, fragmented and passive, while the authorities were tough and consolidated.

Public support for the government plunged to a historical low (the party in power only won 10% of the vote at the 1995 parliamentary election), which did not affect the government's resolve to continue the planned reforms. Relying on media control, political manipulation and, when necessary, undisguised threats of force, the government managed to head off public disappointment and protests. Pro-reform sentiments in society dwindled almost to zero (Yegor Gaidar's liberal bloc Democratic Choice of Russia did not win any seats in parliament in 1995), but the opposition was split into retrograde communist (Communist Party) and populist-nationalist wings (Liberal Democratic Party). They were kept apart by the deft political manoeuvring of Yeltsin's team. It became clear that there would be no returning to the Soviet past, and that the public's nostalgia and resentment, which the resurfacing Communist Party was trying to exploit, was not strong enough to make the government change its course.

The two sides eventually reached an unspoken 'historic compromise': the opposition stopped trying to pry power away from Yeltsin in return for privileged positions in parliament and political control of several regions. The State Duma did its best to torpedo the government's pro-reform aspirations. But even the accommodating stand of the opposition could not last forever as a weak government continued to lose legitimacy at home and abroad. The most glaring example of the country's degradation was the First Chechen War, which Yeltsin began in December 1994 hoping to quickly overthrow the separatist government. But the war only ended in August 1996 with the controversial Khasavyurt Peace Agreement, in which Russia recognized Chechnya's de facto independence. The legalization of that seat of separatism, terrorism and Islamic extremism in the North Caucasus drastically undermined Russia's government, international standing and internal support. The Chechen war also led to Yeltsin's break with the pro-western liberal reformers, problems in relations with the western and Islamic countries, declining confidence in the army, law enforcement and security agencies, and growing separatist sentiment in other Russian regions.

Among the shady and/or criminal types that were so common in the post-reform period were organizers of pyramid schemes who took money from gullible

Table 8.7 What should the relationship between the state and the people look like? (closed question, one answer)

	1990	*1997*
People should make sacrifices for the benefit of the state	7	6
The state should take better care of the people	57	68
People should show initiative and take care of themselves	25	18
Don't know	11	8

Source: VTsIOM representative survey 1990–1997.

Table 8.8 Did the MMM fraudulent investment scheme influence your attitude to market reforms in Russia? (closed question, one answer)

	1994
I've always had a negative view of the market reforms	29
This has only reinforced my negative view of the market reforms	15
I've always had a positive view of the market reforms	22
This has undermined my positive view of the market reforms	5
Don't care	21
Unfamiliar with this scandal	7

Source: Public Opinion Foundation, http://bd.fom.ru/report/map/of19942203

Table 8.9 Do you think privatization was carried out according to or in violation of law? (closed question, one answer)

	1998
According to the law	6
Both	16
In violation of the law	63
Don't know	15

Source: Public Opinion Foundation, http://bd.fom.ru/report/map/t8036403.

people with the promise of unrealistic returns; people who bought up privatization vouchers to take over whole plants cheaply; the 'red directors' who paid their workers meagre wages while requesting subsidies from the regional government or Moscow to produce goods which no one needed; and lastly, high-flying financiers who used soft corruption tactics on federal ministers to gain access to privatization auctions of energy enterprises.

There were also all kinds of bandits recruited from former athletes and veterans of the Afghan war; low-class prostitutes from small towns and villages who filled the streets of Moscow, St. Petersburg and other large cities; workers from idling plants who were hired as office and shopping centre security staff; engineers from research institutions who planted potatoes in the countryside or accepted seasonal and sporadic jobs; retired women who received their meagre pensions every half-year and had to sell their belongings to buy food or ask for handouts; and suitcase traders who brought goods from Poland and China to sell in a huge unregulated outdoor market that popped up in a former stadium.

System-wide crisis (1998–2000)

The brief window of tenuous stability that opened in Russia was slammed shut by a system-wide crisis that tested absolutely all Russian institutions for a second time in a decade. The crisis also shifted the basic paradigm of public opinion and discredited many values and goals of the 1990s, which were replaced by new or forgotten ones. Many public institutions were transformed, the political system was reset, and social change was given new momentum.

The crisis began in March 1998, when Yeltsin dismissed the government of Viktor Chernomyrdin, whom he suspected of seeking to usurp power. Over the next six months, the country was hit by a default, a six-fold devaluation of the rouble, an economic crisis and another replacement of the government. Oligarchic empires collapsed, and the nascent middle class lost all its savings, sources of income and optimism. Months-long wage and pension arrears became routine for many other groups of the population hovering near the official poverty line. To keep his post, Yeltsin in September 1998 had to approve a coalition government led by Primakov, who quickly managed to calm the opposition, come to terms with the IMF, and restart money circulation and economic growth. The period of his premiership between September 1998 and May 1999 was actually a period of dual power, when open battle between the opposition-minded State Duma and the president was prevented by the mediation of a prime minister who was an obvious candidate for president. The truce was disturbed by the Duma, which decided to impeach the president, and ended by Yeltsin, who dismissed Primakov in May 1999 for gaining too much influence.

The internal economic and political crisis was greatly compounded by external events: the USA and NATO launched a war against Yugoslavia, dispelling Russians' illusions about their ability to lead the world to a new, just international peace. Chechen separatists invaded Dagestan, seeking to carve out an Islamic state from both territories, and carried out several high-profile terrorist attacks across Russia. These events accelerated the centrifugal forces at work in the country. Regional leaders began interfering with foodstuff transfers to the federal centre citing the needs of their own people, and some of them formed a political bloc led by Primakov allied with Moscow mayor Yury Luzhkov. The disintegration of the Russian Federation was fast becoming a distinct possibility.

The crisis was ebbing when Yeltsin found a successor, FSB director and Russian Security Council secretary Vladimir Putin, who bet everything on a successful outcome to the Chechen conflict. The Chechen incursion into Dagestan of August 1999 was repelled, and Russian troops started winning Chechen territory back from separatists, and the information war against the opposition was won thanks to an alliance with oligarchic media outlets. The hastily formed pro-Putin

Table 8.10 What is most important for Russia now? (closed question, one answer)

	1998	*1999*	*2000*
Order, even if democratic principles and personal freedoms are violated	69	74	75
Democracy, even if destructive elements are empowered in the process	15	11	13
Don't know	15	14	13

Source: VTsIOM representative surveys, http://wciom.ru/index.php?id=459&uid=114767.

Table 8.11 How possible is it that Russia could disintegrate into provinces as a result of the current financial crisis or measures taken in response? (closed question, one answer)

	August 1998
Quite possible	15
Rather possible	26
Unlikely	41
Absolutely impossible	19

Source: VTsIOM representative survey, http://wciom.ru/zh/print_q.php?s_id=398&q_id=32224&date=15.08.1998.

Table 8.12 Is it possible that Russia could split into several independent states? (closed question, one answer)

	June 1998
Yes	43
No	35
Don't know	22

Source: Public Opinion Foundation, http://bd.fom.ru/report/map/t8036820.

Unity bloc won as many votes in the December 1999 parliamentary election as the Communist Party and nearly twice as many as the bloc led by Yevgeny Primakov. Yeltsin's retirement soon after cleared the way for Putin's victory in the March 2000 presidential election.

Although the 1998–2000 crisis was relatively short-lived, it marked a turning point in the post-Soviet evolution of public opinion. It laid to rest the main ideological underpinnings and stereotypes that had formed in the outgoing period of perestroika and had shaped social trends in the 1990s. The war in Yugoslavia eroded Russians' trust in the West, which they came to see as a potential enemy rather than a senior partner. The second Chechen war revived Russians' confidence and belief that military force is central to Russia's survival in a harsh and dangerous world. Putin's leading role in overcoming the crisis and the 'succession and inheritance' model of power transfer between him and Yeltsin, bypassing elections, made the opposition, the Russian parliamentary system and the value of political competition irrelevant. The monarchist and personalistic strains in Russian political thinking quickly reasserted themselves, while the imported elements of pluralist democracy were reconsidered and cast out as alien and useless, or changed beyond recognition.

The post-Soviet economic collapse turned oligarchs into the targets of public ire and delivered them into the hands of the state, which alone could save them from financial destruction and public persecution. The default completely discredited the model of 'a free market with the state acting as night watchman'.

Everyone again looked to a strong and fair state as the best hope for both the rich and the poor. There was widespread public demand for a new role for the state, which cannot be described as fully liberal, patriarchal or communist. The public wanted conciliation, tranquility, stability, dignity, sovereignty and an end to painful reforms and experiments, as well as to the idea of alliance with the discredited West. It was a non-partisan, 'mainstream' request, as Leonty Byzov put it, that was directed at one leader, Vladimir Putin, giving him a mandate to restore order and reset the country's political and economic system provided he could avoid new shocks, divisions or revolutions in the country.

The 1998–2000 crisis affected absolutely everyone: successful small importers, who lost their business to the rouble's devaluation and the bankruptcy of banks, and were forced to turn the cars they bought with credit shortly before the crisis into taxis; civil servants who saved for decades to buy an apartment; people who fled from single-industry cities in Siberia or the Urals to Moscow. There were also the Dagestanis who took up arms to protect their republic from an invasion by terrorists who wanted to turn their land into an Islamic caliphate; pension-age Soviet politicians who had to look for work to survive crises brought about by

Table 8.13 Read the following list carefully and choose which proposals would best unite Russians (closed question, any number of answers)

	1998
Unconditional compliance with the law	39
Respect for justice and human rights	35
Focus on internal affairs, abandon rivalries with other countries	34
Create a strong government capable of maintaining order in the country	32
Create a coherent nation uniting all of Russia's ethnic groups	29
Make Russia a high-tech country	27
Create a democratic society that respects the rights and freedoms of every individual	22
Regain a leading position on the international stage	21
Bring up a generation capable of succeeding in the modern world	21
Strive for spiritual rather than material enrichment	20
Revive and protect Russia's identity	20
Create conditions for the development of all Russian ethnic groups	16
Revive the communist idea and free it from distortions	11
Make Russia a bridge for West and East, the world at large and the CIS countries	9
Restore the country within its former borders	9
Strengthen the role of traditional religious values in society	7
Accept the Western social and economic model of development	4
Unite with Islamic countries	1
Restore the monarchy	1
Don't know	7

Source: VTsIOM representative surveys, http://wciom.ru/zh/print_q.php?s_id=401&q_id=32401&date=30.10.1998.

Table 8.14 Is the worst behind us, still to come, or right now? (closed question, one answer)

	1991	*1992*	*1994*	*1995*	*1996*	*1997*	*1998*
Right now	23	23	22	22	22	23	28
Behind us	3	3	4	6	10	7	11
Still to come	66	67	60	52	46	52	49
Don't know	9	7	15	20	21	18	11
Index	–86	–87	–78	–68	–58	–68	–66

Source: VTsIOM representative surveys 1991–1998.

Note: The index measures optimism about Russia's future. It is calculated as the difference between the answer 'Behind us' and the sum total of answers 'Right now' and 'Still to come' and can range from −100 to +100. The higher the figure, the more optimistic Russians are about their country's future. Zero indicates an equal share of optimistic and pessimistic answers.

young reformers; and generals who created the world's most effective emergencies ministry but became politicians to 'save the country from national catastrophe'.

Standing between these two groups were a set of Mephistophelian characters who both provoked the crisis and benefited from it. They included law enforcement and security officials who played both ends against the middle, hunting down bandits and terrorists while also supplying them with weapons and targets in order to distinguish themselves and make a career; young ministers, protégés of the half-dead president, who were completely useless in a crisis but were always in good standing with any government; Western favourites and big-time negotiators who brought billion-dollar loans from the IMF that were immediately lost to devaluation or plundered by bankers with close ties to the government; and oligarchs with media assets – sophisticated, worldly men who believed that 'only the weak repay loans' and stiffed their own creditors.

Post-crisis consolidation and stabilization (2000–2008)

The 'golden decade' of the 2000s was the longest and so far the most successful period in Russia's post-Soviet history. It began with Vladimir Putin's first presidential term and lasted until the global economic crisis. Eight years of economic growth helped Russia balance the budget, repay the bulk of its huge foreign debt that accumulated under Mikhail Gorbachev and Boris Yeltsin, streamline the tax system, deal with internal arrears, and increase payments to pensioners and public sector workers several times over. Growth was driven by the export of commodities – a sector that was now largely back under government control. State-owned companies, corporations and banks formed a new foundation for the Russian economy in the most capital-intensive sectors. Import substitution in the private sector helped revive the domestic market, with additional support coming from people's rising purchasing power. The consumer revolution, which began in Russia's relatively small middle class in the 1990s, finally reached the majority of Russians in the 2000s.

Russia's social transformation in the 2000s included improvements in social infrastructure, higher living standards and quality of life, and declining poverty. The Russian middle class, though different from its West European and North American counterparts, grew from about 5 to 20% of the population, with another 30% of the population forming the pre-middle class, which matched the middle class in terms of education and skills but earned less money. Putin's focused policy lifted the bulk of pensioners and public sector workers out of poverty. The number of businesspeople stabilized as the cost of market entry increased. The economy was purged of a significant amount of criminality, and the responsibility to provide protection and settle conflicts was rightfully assumed by the courts, law enforcement and security services. Street crime plummeted, and many criminals either legitimized their operations or departed.

The ranks of the rich expanded considerably, with elite enclaves appearing in all regional centres. In cities with populations exceeding one million, large job markets emerged for skilled professionals, including foreign ones. Incomes rose dramatically for the upper class, which expanded to include highly placed civil servants, senior officials of law enforcement and security services, and administrators of healthcare and educational institutions. A rising group of state managers – heads of state-owned companies and corporations – had more influence and better reputations than the oligarchs of the 1990s.

The oligarchic domination of the media was rooted out swiftly and mercilessly, with the state taking direct or indirect control of all key media outlets. Information wars were replaced with a common information space controlled by a single centre. The depoliticized media outlets almost never reported controversial issues and events, and the consumer revolution generated an entertainment revolution which made media and related industries incredibly profitable. Mass culture was dominated by the vapid allure of glamour, beautiful people and luxury. Political disputes came to focus on the burgeoning Internet, which turned politics itself into an exotic form of entertainment for the growing audience of mostly young web users rather than a means to express one's priorities. Print media became marginalized and lost nearly all of their political relevance, while electronic media became the main proponent of the values of 'stability and order', which the new president promised and delivered to the people.

The political sphere was restructured in 2000–2009 to lock in the dominance of Putin's team and to prevent any chance of the opposition gaining power. New election and party laws had the effect of limiting the number of parties to seven and the number of parliamentary parties to four. The Kremlin took control of the political parties' sources of funding after oligarch Mikhail Khodorkovsky attempted to influence parliamentary elections. This served as a warning to all other oligarchs: stay out of politics, and you will be free to grow your businesses around the world. The independence of governors was curtailed in 2000, when they were removed from the upper house of parliament, and again in 2004, when the president decided that governors should be appointed rather than elected. Within several years, the Chechen war turned into a police operation and then ended completely with the creation of a regional authoritarian regime led by

Akhmad Kadyrov (and later his son Ramzan Kadyrov). The fight against terror continued, with each new terrorist act only increasing the power of the president and the security services and further eroding pluralism in politics and the media.

The regional political elite integrated into the party of power, which took control of parliament in 2001 and further strengthened its grip in the 2003 and 2007 elections. Nearly all governors soon joined United Russia. The only candidates who could win in local elections either had the support of the ruling party or promised to join it after the election. Many of the president's cronies from the security services and his St. Petersburg days were appointed governor, including General Vladimir Shamanov, who pacified Chechnya, and later became governor of the Ulyanovsk Region. Governorships were also doled out to major businessmen with close ties to oligarchic empires: Alexander Khloponin from Norilsk Nickel became governor of the Krasnoyarsk Territory and Roman Abramovich took over in the Chukotka Autonomous Area. The posts of presidential envoys, created to oversee the regions on behalf of the president, were awarded to army, Interior Ministry (MVD) and security service generals.

At the federal level, other parties in parliament accepted their status as the sanctioned opposition, which means that they did not question the primacy of the president or his party. The unsanctioned opposition was blocked from the media and from running in elections thanks, in part, to a draconian new law on extremism. The ideological image of the new regime was fleshed out with the 'sovereign democracy' doctrine created in 2006, which asserted the right of countries to choose a form of government consistent with their national character, contrary to the 'international standards of democracy' advocated in the West.

Russia's geopolitical status climbed rapidly in the 2000s. It pursued a variety of political initiatives, from strategic partnership with China to the launch of Eurasian integration out of the ruins of the CIS. Growing financial capabilities, revived commodity exports and an expanding internal market made Russia an attractive trade partner. Russia's growing role in the global economy gave rise to the concept of Russia as an 'energy superpower'. The war on terror, declared by the USA in 2001, further strengthened Russia's value as an important US partner. Moscow and St. Petersburg hosted numerous meetings of the global elite, including G8 summit meetings in 2006 and 2013. Despite lingering bad feelings over the Chechen war, the International Olympic Committee awarded the 2014 Winter Olympics to Sochi.

But this rosy chapter in Russia's relationship with the West ended when the US focus shifted from the war on terror to intervention in Iraq. Western-backed 'colour revolutions' ousted governments in Georgia and Ukraine. Since then, Russia has been fighting the USA and the EU in an increasingly pitched battle for influence in the former Soviet republics, denouncing US 'punitive operations' in 'disloyal' countries, stifling US missile defence plans, and forming alliances with anti-American governments in Asia and Latin America. The focal point of Putin's pro-sovereignty rhetoric was his speech at the Munich security conference in February 2007, which was translated into practice in the Caucasus war of August 2008. Despite US and NATO stonewalling, Russia burnished its prestige in the Caucasus and many other countries by taking an independent stance and by consistently defending its positions by any means possible.

August and September 2008 were the pinnacle of Putin's and his team's popularity in the 2000s. Popular support for the president was based on recognition of the economic achievements under his presidency (GDP grew by more than 8% in 2007), impressive gains in wages and foreign policy success. Russia's ability to stand up to the USA and its allies soothed, if not erased, Russians' inferiority complex, which resulted from the collapse of the Soviet Union and the dramatic changes of the 1990s, often referred to as the 'troubled 1990s'. The new social ideology was rooted largely in the contrasting images of the crisis, general decline and national humiliation under Gorbachev and Yeltsin, and the national ascendency, prosperity and growing strength under Putin. Other contrasts forming the basis of this ideology were crisis versus economic growth, impoverishment versus a flourishing consumer society, crime versus order, state disintegration versus state revival, centrifugal versus centripetal forces, and the failed Chechen war versus the victorious war with Georgia.

Putin's numerous supporters believe that he helped Russia rise from its knees and regain international standing and self-respect. Putin managed to meet the expectations of a diverse coalition: he gave liberals impressive market growth and integration into the global economy, restored Russia's imperial might for

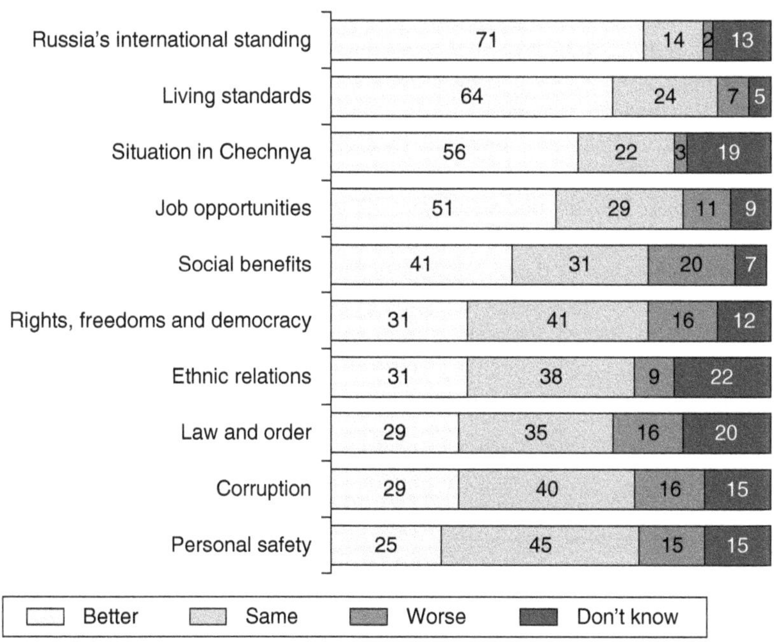

Figure 8.2 Did things get better or worse during Vladimir Putin's presidency in the following areas? (closed question, one answer for each line, January 2008).

Source: VTsIOM representative survey http://wciom.ru/index.php?id=459&uid=13384.

patriots and nationalists, and curried favour with Communists by showing respect for Soviet-era historical and cultural symbols. The pro-Putin majority stood above ideological divides, and the president's United Russia party drew significant support from young people, women and pensioners. Putin chose the most respectable representatives from every ideology and interest group and incorporated them in his political system, including marginal groups, in order to sideline them from politics.

Putin's ideology, although amorphous and not clearly articulated, saturated society, pushing aside pro-Western liberals and retrograde Stalinists. Public opinion consolidated under the banner of stability and the general belief that Putin can handle anything. The president managed to unite the most contradictory currents in Russian society thanks to his flexibility, sagacity and phenomenal luck. The term 'national leader', which was invented for him after he ceded the post of president to Medvedev, adequately characterized his new status as a figure above politics, society and nation, who, while unopposed at home, faces external competitors and enemies.

The eclectic Russia of the 2000s included the youthful Gazprom 'general' who invested big kick-backs in a rental business officially owned by his current model wife; the extravagant new-wave businessman whose talent and luck helped him rise from a modest outdoor market trader all the way to the owner of a nationwide cell phone retailer but who continues to speak almost exclusively in expletives; the glamorous socialite from the Moscow/St. Petersburg jet set who hosts a TV show for young provincials dreaming of an apartment in the capital city; the dishonest but lucky cop or KGB/FSB officer who knows how to get things done, has the right connections and provides criminal protection to a bank or a small industrial company; and the super-energetic governor/mayor who is developing the territory assigned by the president like a feudal estate, levying tribute on all businesses, big and small, and taking over the ones he likes best 'for the good of the region'.

The most interesting of these types is the governor/mayor – a pillar of the community who embodied authority in his or her locale. In the 1990s, mayors and governors were elected. They were responsive to voters, and so they tried to run their region or city as best as they could. Everything changed in the 2000s, when elections were replaced by appointments (whether direct or hidden).

Table 8.15 Do you think that Vladimir Putin's political and economic policies should continue after the 2008 presidential election? (closed question, one answer)

	2006	*2007*	*2008*
Yes	27	42	42
Yes, but with some changes	47	39	40
No	18	10	10
Don't know	8	9	8

Source: VTsIOM representative surveys, http://wciom.ru/index.php?id=268&uid=9817.

This reduced the risk of officials losing their posts due to public discontent but increased the risk of being fired by the Kremlin. Many heavyweight local leaders of the Yeltsin era were replaced with technocrats from the business world or generals who knew how to carry out orders from the central government. However, regional leadership in Russia has always offered opportunities for personal enrichment, a temptation to which almost all newly appointed regional leaders eventually succumb. The Kremlin oversees politics, but cannot root out corruption. The new governors, who owed their office entirely to the central government, could steal to their heart's content as long as they never forgot to send tribute to their federal patrons.

Alongside the mix of business, bureaucracy, law enforcement and security officials and glamorous socialites, there existed a world of ordinary Russians who received some breathing room and no longer had to fight so hard for survival. The state resumed payments of pensions and wages to public sector workers, the enterprises that survived reopened, new employers (agricultural holding companies) were reviving the countryside, and growing wages and the expansion of credit allowed people to buy new household appliances or take vacations in Crimea or Egypt. Young people again enrolled at universities with dreams of becoming bankers or lawyers or, at the least, a civil servant – not a worker, engineer or academic, as in the old days. The federal healthcare and education systems continued to deteriorate, but teachers and doctors supplemented their meagre salaries by soliciting bribes from students and their parents and from patients. Of course, this portrait gallery of Russian society in the 2000s would be incomplete without low-paid, low-skilled immigrant workers from Kyrgyzstan, Tajikistan or Moldova, who lived in shacks or dilapidated hostels and had no rights, but were at least able to send money to their families back home.

Global crisis and political destabilization (2009–2012)

The golden age of the 2000s under Putin came to an abrupt end in the autumn of 2008 with the global economic crisis. The confusion it unleashed, which knocked Russia off balance and set in motion efforts to chart a new course for the country, lasted until 2012. However, the direct effects of the crisis were relatively mild and even obscured by the country's accumulated financial reserves and Putin's leverage over the political system. It did not result in a dramatic shakeup of the government or the country's development paradigm.

Economically, the crisis was not as deep or systemic as those of 1989–1993 or 1998–2000. However, it began just a few months after the country's economic development and political confidence peaked. The crisis highlighted all the hidden drawbacks and weaknesses of the golden 2000s and revealed that the old model of economic growth and political stability had exhausted its potential. It forced the government to seek out new development strategies, which had the effect of weakening the regime and undermining the prestige of its leader, dividing Putin's coalition, and eroding government support among many social groups. Russia's GDP contracted and unemployment rose for less than a year, and the majority of large companies and banks survived thanks to the government's lavish financial support. But the recovery was not as rapid as expected and did not spread to all sectors. Instead of rising, economic growth rates fell, despite the high prices of Russia's traditional commodity exports. And the government had to raise taxes to finance more generous social commitments, an expensive 2011 rearmament programme and the 2014 Winter Olympics, which had an extremely detrimental effect on business, slowing the pace of economic development and souring the mood in the business community and society as a whole. Seeking to jumpstart growth, the new president, Dmitry Medvedev, announced a new focus on innovation and modernization, but these initiatives had a vanishingly small effect on Russians' lives and the national economy.

The US and Russian presidents elected in 2008 embarked on a new détente, which came to be known as the 'reset'. Russia gained access to innovative technology and expanded research and industrial cooperation with the USA in the interests of economic modernization, but the rapprochement abruptly ended when the protests collectively referred to as the Arab Spring swept through North Africa in 2011. With the overthrow of Muammar Gaddafi in Libya in late 2011 and the civil war in Syria, supported by the USA and the EU, the reset was replaced by a new round of confrontation between Russia and the West.

Russia's social structure changed during the crisis. The wellbeing of the poorest groups (primarily pensioners and public sector workers) improved thanks to increased government spending. Reforms of the army and police returned soldiers and police officials to the middle class. Salaried employees and businesspeople were hit harder by the crisis, but demographic decline kept unemployment relatively low and prevented wages from plummeting. Especially hard hit was the middle class, including small business owners and freelancers, whose incomes stagnated and became unstable. Given the general mood of the so-called 'creative class' concentrated in Moscow, anti-government sentiment swelled in the capital. The government's inability to deal with the 2010 summer wildfires

Table 8.16 Some think that people should actively contribute to their own safety and help fight the wildfires, while others believe this is the job of the authorities. Which statement do you agree with? (closed question, one answer)

	September 2010
People should be involved in ensuring their own safety and fighting wildfires. The government has limited capabilities and cannot deal with the problem without volunteers.	54
Public safety and fighting wildfires are primarily the responsibility of the government. Fighting wildfires is a dangerous enterprise that should be dealt with by specially trained professionals rather than volunteers, who would only be putting their lives at risk.	42
Don't know	4

Source: A VTsIOM representative poll, http://wciom.ru/zh/print_q.php?s_id=686&q_id=49717&date=04.09.2010.

in the Moscow Region spurred the capital's politically engaged but previously disorganized middle class into action.

Emigration was another response to the crisis: well-off Moscow intellectuals 'downshifted' to Goa in India or Thailand, while many businesspeople and officials moved their families to London, Geneva or Miami.

Immigrants from Central Asia and the Caucasus posed another challenge. Xenophobia increased in Russia even during the golden decade, but it was during the crisis that nationalist rallies became alarmingly regular, primarily in Moscow. Elements of the opposition without representation in parliament launched a campaign in Moscow under the slogan, 'Stop feeding the Caucasus', which played on Muscovites' dislike of people from Chechnya and Dagestan and the criticism heard in many Russian regions of excessive budget transfers to the North Caucasus. The nationalists' march to Moscow's Manezh Square in December 2010 created a surge in political organizing, leading ultimately to the demonstrations on Bolotnaya Square a year later. Russia's political stability was undermined not only by the economic crisis but also by infighting in the Putin–Medvedev team, billed as the 'tandem' in 2008. The question was whether the tandem's creator would become a Russian Deng Xiaoping or return to power as soon as the constitution permitted. Uncertainty about the future greatly undermined the Kremlin's effectiveness and had a destructive impact on the regime's social foundation. President Medvedev opted for rapprochement with the West; technological modernization in Russian industries; reforms of the army, police and education; fighting corruption; and modest political liberalization. None of his reforms, with the exception of the military reform, achieved their goals, largely because of resistance mounted by the former president's protégés who remained in key government posts. The unfinished and ineffective reforms further weakened popular support for the government, and the fight against corruption was turned against the authorities through the efforts of Alexei Navalny, a new leader of the informal opposition and the self-proclaimed 'president of the Internet', whose blog was phenomenally popular in the political segment of the Internet despite his banishment from television.

The pro-Western liberals initially supported Medvedev, hoping that he would eventually break with his political mentor. But they openly sided with the opposition when Medvedev refused to run for a second term against Putin in September 2011 and announced that he would head United Russia, a party whose

Table 8.17 Would you be willing to move abroad permanently? (closed question, one answer, June 2011)

	All respondents	*High-income respondents*	*Middle-income respondents*	*Low-income respondents*
Yes	22	26	22	19
No	75	71	75	78
Don't know	3	3	3	3

Source: A VTsIOM representative poll, http://wciom.ru/index.php?id=459&uid=111681.

monopoly on power he had previously tried to limit. Putin's popularity suffered, and the standing of his ruling party was critically weakened by political missteps and the unification of the opposition against United Russia, who came together under the slogan of Navalny's political campaign, 'Vote for Anyone Except the Party of Crooks and Thieves'. In the parliamentary election in December 2011, United Russia won only 49% of the vote (compared to 64% in 2007), but even that result was contested by a diverse coalition of nationalist, liberal and leftwing groups, who held a rally on Bolotnaya Square to demand a recount or the nullification of what they saw as a fraudulent election. But while the mass protests shook Russians out of their decade-long slumber, they remained largely confined to Moscow.

Putin powerfully undercut the protesters three months later by handily winning the March 2012 presidential election in the first round. He easily rallied the conservative majority, which was frightened by the spectre of chaos and the return of the dark days of the 1990s. Respected but underpaid professions – doctors and teachers – were promised a big raise. Large-scale counter-protests of 'ordinary Russians' – working people and public sector employees – were organized all across Russia, in contrast to localized opposition protests. The rallies on Bolotnaya Square and Sakharov Prospekt were countered with patriotic demonstrations at Poklonnaya Hill and Luzhniki Stadium that called on Russians to defend the country's sovereignty from pro-American agents and the progress of the 2000s from the return of the oligarchs and their political servants.

The authorities reacted to allegations of vote rigging by launching an unprecedented and extremely expensive election transparency initiative, robbing the united opposition of the only slogan that was supported by a large number of voters. It was left with demands that were of concern only to the small creative class, and even those demands were largely rendered moot by a series of sweeping gestures by the government. In December 2011 Medvedev announced a political reform that included the freedom to form parties and reinstated gubernatorial elections, and also partly liberalized the editorial policy of state-owned television networks. Taken together, this satisfied moderate protesters. Radical protestors were deprived of their leaders, some of whom were arrested and others charged following a clash with the police, which may or not have been provoked, at the 6 May 2012 rally in Moscow.

The protest movement withered. Putin regained control over the situation but was no longer a truly national leader, having lost the support of the young, the college educated and Muscovites (he won less than 50% of the vote in Moscow). Putin won the 2012 presidential election not by consolidating the people, as he had done before, but by polarizing the electorate on pseudo-ideological grounds: the people versus intellectuals, patriots versus pro-Westerners, and hardliners versus democrats. The pro-Putin majority fell apart and the new coalition that emerged needed clearer and deeper unifying principles beyond a single leader. The informal opposition was demoralized and retreated to social media, emigration or charitable and non-political civil activities. But the call for new faces in politics, while not a serious threat to the Kremlin, did not abate, as evidenced by Alexei Navalny's second-place finish in the Moscow mayoral election and by Yevgeny Roizman's election as mayor of Yekaterinburg in September 2013.

The crisis was accompanied by a limited renaissance of political pluralism in the media. Dmitry Medvedev's team promoted the liberal opposition online television channel Dozhd (Rain) and several other web projects. The rapid spread of Internet access allowed the opposition to move their political agitation online, pushing aside Kremlin proponents in cyberspace. The political landscape was divided into the pro-government 'television party' and the opposition 'Internet party', on the basis of media habits. Russian public opinion from 2009–2012 became dramatically more divided and politicized than in the stable 2000s. It was once again characterized by demands that the government swiftly correct course. For all the diversity of public opinion, it could be divided broadly into two distinct camps. The smaller one, whose dominance in Moscow gave it outsized influence, included college educated Russians and the upper middle class. They criticized the authorities for corruption, inefficiency and an inability to keep up with the times, and demanded a government and society along European lines, an end to the policy of subsidizing the Caucasus, and the removal of the president and his team from power.

The other much larger camp represented the majority in provincial, industrial and agricultural Russia, as well as in the Caucasus. It demanded that the government adopt more socially and ethnically focused policies, stop emulating Europe, abandon pro-Western reforms and increase social equality without disrupting stability. The Putin–Medvedev tandem failed to keep the support of both groups and opted for the paternalist majority. Having made his choice, Putin then needed to find a way to maintain that group's loyalty in the longer term and to jumpstart the Russian economy, because hopes for an automatic post-crisis recovery were not realized and the modernization and innovation policy had failed. Russian society at the time of the global economic crisis was extremely diverse and divided. To one side were flamboyantly dressed, independent-minded 'hipsters'; volunteers who took up shovels and buckets to help fight the terrible wildfires in 2010; copywriters who spent their days in the French style café Jean-Jacques, thought of themselves as 'creative' and regularly posted anti-Putin demotivational messages on Facebook; unprofessional but ideologically committed Dozhd journalists who flaunted their contempt for the government; and enthusiastic innovators from Russia's Internet startup scene.

On the other side, there were the Uralvagonzavod workers from Nizhny Tagil who made tanks and tractors; the OMON police whose job was to break up unsanctioned demonstrations; members of the pro-Putin Young Guard of the United Russia party who wanted a good career and dreamed about a job at Gazprom; an aging and nearly forgotten writer from the Pochvennichestvo (Soil-based) school, which sought to bridge the divide between educated Russians and the people, who saw his work get a new lease on life; and provincial pensioners, more likely Communists than Putin supporters, who fear a Russia 'tormented by yids and Chechens' and demand that the government restore order 'like under Stalin'.

Conservative consolidation and mobilization (from 2012)

Vladimir Putin's victory in 2012 presidential election marked the beginning of a period of conservative political consolidation. In the face of an economic slowdown and worsening relations with the West, the government took a series of measures that has strengthened its support among the conservative-paternalist majority, demoralized the liberal minority and deepened divisions between these two groups.

The issue of political power was settled for the time being, and public discussions moved from a pragmatic-political to a moral-ideological plane that focused on morals, religion, sexual conduct, the treatment of children and orphans, the use of profanity in literature and movies, sex education in schools, and so on. The addition of 'moral' aspects to politics only strengthened the sides' mutual hostility and irreconcilability. Due to the complete domination of Putin's team in government bodies, conservative initiatives were quickly signed into law, whereas their opponents' room for manoeuvre was rapidly diminishing. The Pussy Riot scandal, the Dima Yakovlev law banning Americans from adopting Russian orphans, the gay propaganda law, and the law on foreign agents, as NGOs that receive foreign

Table 8.18 How would you describe your life (your family's life)? (closed question, one answer)

	1994	*1998*	*2002*	*2005*	*2008*	*2009*	*2010*	*2011*	*2012*	*2013*	*Q2 2014*
Intolerable	32	61	20	21	14	12	11	11	9	10	6
Difficult but tolerable	47	30	51	52	54	63	55	56	55	53	46
Good. I know I can deal with problems if they arise (things are not all that bad, life is bearable)	12	3	22	22	27	22	31	30	35	36	46
Don't know	9	6	8	6	5	3	3	2	2	1	2
Index	38	24	55	48	53	53	57	56	60	60	65

Source: National representative surveys conducted by VTsIOM http://wciom.ru/index.php?id=459&uid=114876.

Notes: The index measures Russians' perceptions of their life and the life of their families. It is calculated as the sum total of answers multiplied by the relevant coefficient. The answer 'Intolerable' has a coefficient of 0.1, 'Difficult but tolerable' is 0.5, and the answer 'Good. I know I can deal with problems if they arise' is 0.9. The index can vary between 10 and 90 points. The higher the index, the better is the respondent's life.

Table 8.19 Are you satisfied with your life? (closed question, one answer)

	2005	*2006*	*2007*	*2008*	*2009*	*2010*	*2011*	*2012*	*2013*	*Q4 2014*
Quite satisfied, mostly satisfied	25	27	27	28	27	30	28	37	40	46
Somewhat satisfied	39	43	43	48	45	44	43	41	40	39
Completely dissatisfied, mostly dissatisfied	36	29	29	25	26	24	28	21	20	13
Don't know	1	1	1	2	2	2	1	1	1	3
Satisfaction with Life Index	28	41	41	51	47	50	43	58	60	72

Source: National representative surveys conducted by VTsIOM, http://wciom.ru/index.php?id=459&uid=114891.

Note: The Satisfaction with Life Index records the degree of Russians' satisfaction with their lives. It is calculated as the difference between positive/average assessments and negative assessments. The higher the index, the higher the respondents' satisfaction with their lives. The index can vary between −100 and +100. A positive value indicates more positive answers than negative ones, and zero indicates a balance of positive and negative answers.

funding have been termed, are some of the better known conservative victories on a long list that has shifted the agenda from the struggle against corrupt authorities to the fight for public morals and the protection of society from the 'corrupt foreign influence'. Unable to stop the cascade of new prohibitions, liberal intellectuals labelled the State Duma a 'mad printer' and urged all reasonable people to emigrate from this 'land of slaves and masters'.

Even the banner of fighting corruption, which Navalny took up and unfurled so cleverly, lost its power as an anti-government weapon after Putin fired the man who proposed the military reform, Anatoly Serdyukov. Strangely, corruption cases in the army have helped instead of hurt the regime, especially after the discredited defence minister was replaced by the phenomenally popular Sergei Shoigu. It allowed the authorities to initiate lawsuits and criminal investigations against the most promising opposition leaders to remove them from the political stage. The remaining opposition leaders were unable to create an influential political movement and were defeated in a series of local elections. The pinnacle of the opposition's success was the 28% of the vote won by Alexei Navalny in the Moscow mayoral election in September 2013, even though turnout was very low (about 32%) and the city authorities created favourable conditions for Navalny.

In short, limited political liberalization did not unsettle the regime but rather created additional opportunities for manoeuvre. The weakened brand of United Russia as the ruling party was handed over to Medvedev, while the post-partisan Russian Popular Front was given the central role in structuring the political foundation of the regime. Chaired by the president himself, the Russian Popular Front rallied his supporters among teachers, doctors, journalists and businesspeople.

A vital element of Putin's new ideology is patriotism, which includes respect for one's roots and ancestors, and traditional values and institutions ('spiritual bonds')

Table 8.20 What is Russia's biggest problem? (closed question, up to seven answers, the most popular four are given below)

	2008	*2009*	*2010*	*2011*	*2012*	*2013*	*Q1 2014*	*Q4 2014*
Inflation, rising prices	67	61	52	53	49	49	53	59
The housing and utility sector and related services	44	24	35	50	55	57	56	54
Low living standards	20	32	44	50	50	47	45	45
Corruption and red tape	30	41	41	44	46	44	47	44

Source: http://wciom.ru/index.php?id=459&uid=114712.

such as the homeland, the family, history, school, the army, the Russian language and the Orthodox Church. It has become fashionable to contemplate Russian ethnic and national identity, and debates on the nature of Russian conservatism have entered a new round. Patriotism, which the president views as the only acceptable state ideology, is contrasted not only with cosmopolitism but also more recent liberal inventions such as multiculturalism, same-sex marriage, juvenile justice and contemporary art. Russia is presented as the guardian of Christian morals that the corrupt West has betrayed. The highest value is to serve the homeland, which is defined as a global power locked in battle with Western imperialist, cultural and ideological expansion.

Russia's place in the world and conspicuous signs of its greatness and international recognition are issues of special concern for the president. It is at his initiative that the Eurasian Economic Union (EEU) is being built on the ruins of the CIS, creating a common market for Russian industry and science that would not only rival North American and Western European markets one day, but also offer the world (or at least Eurasia) a new geopolitical and cultural-civilizational model. Putin's Russia is attempting to answer a question that has been nagging the country for centuries (is Russia a European or an Asian country?) through the EEU, its own version of Europe with vast territory and people with a unique moral and cultural identity, strong and independent of Atlantic influence.

This idea is only just taking shape. In the meantime, Russia implemented many expensive projects in 2012–2014, such as the APEC summit in Vladivostok, the Universiade in Kazan and the February 2014 Winter Olympics in Sochi. Launched long ago to improve Russia's image and to boost Russians' self-esteem, these projects were a huge success, silencing the chorus of foreign and domestic critics. Russia won the medal count at the Sochi Olympics, which no one in Russia or anywhere else expected. Russia has been entrusted to host the 2018 FIFA World Cup. Success in sports, as an attribute of a strong and healthy nation, affirms Putin's ideas about reviving Russia as a great nation.

The new conservative ideology borrows heavily from the Soviet era. For example, Putin has revived the Soviet-era system of promoting physical fitness and the health of the nation, GTO (Ready to Work and Defend the USSR) and the title Hero of Labour (Hero of Socialist Labour in the Soviet Union). He reintroduced some old names such as DOSAAF (Volunteer Society for Assistance to the Army,

Table 8.21 Life is made up of good and bad moments. But are you happy, in general? (closed question, one answer)

	1990	*1991*	*1992*	*1998*	*2009*	*2010*	*2011*	*2012*	*2014*
Definitely yes	5	8	2	19	19	17	17	22	25
Mostly yes	39	52	40	50	52	54	50	55	53
Mostly no	22	24	31	16	17	17	21	15	12
Definitely no	5	5	5	5	5	3	5	3	2
Don't know	29	12	23	12	9	10	9	5	8
Happiness Index	17	31	6	49	50	52	42	59	64

Source: http://wciom.ru/index.php?id=459&uid=114812.

the Air Force and the Navy) and Moscow's largest exhibition centre VDNKh (National Exhibition of Economic Achievements). At the same time, he increased pressure on the excessively globalized bureaucratic and business elite, prohibiting elected officials from owning property abroad, capping salaries and severance packages ('golden parachutes') and ordering them to declare their income and property. He also launched a vigorous campaign against dual citizenship for politicians and state officials, which is designed to 'nationalize' the elite and to encourage a considerable part of the creative class and its sympathizers in government to choose between abandoning their political ambitions and keeping their property, business interests or residency permits in western countries as 'insurance'.

Massive projects are even more expensive during periods of economic stagnation, and so the government raised taxes on businesses. It also reviewed the pension reform, adding to the frustrations of the middle class and business. The number of small businesses is decreasing, with some companies receding into the shadows. The federal budget is strained by the need to simultaneously support the banking system, industry and the social sector. The budget deficit is rapidly increasing in the regions, which bear the brunt of the responsibility for fulfilling Putin's social commitments. In May 2012, Putin signed executive orders to sharply increase the salaries of doctors and teachers to lift them into the middle class. However, the middle class is growing very slowly, because the regions have no funds for this noble goal and small businesses are struggling to weather the crisis.

Table 8.22 How do you understand conservatism? (based on VTsIOM polls, closed question, one answer)

	2003	*2014*
Conservatism is preserving customs, traditions and the social system, and moving forward without sudden change or shocks	44	56
Conservatism prevents society from moving forward	27	31
Don't know	29	13

Source: http://wciom.ru/index.php?id=459&uid=114768.

Table 8.23 Do you sympathize with the ideas of conservatism? (based on VTsIOM polls, closed question, one answer)

	2003	*2014*
Definitely yes	9	11
Mostly yes	28	37
Mostly no	24	27
Definitely no	9	8
Don't know	30	17

Source: http://wciom.ru/index.php?id=459&uid=114768.

The demoralized liberal minority has been offered several options: financial support in exchange for political loyalty, or integration into the political system through lowly and politically powerless positions. State grants have been provided to NGOs that previously received funding from the USA or the EU. A draft law on volunteers would legalize volunteer movements, provided they accept the supervision of state agencies and only take part in official patriotic projects such as the Universiade or the Olympic Games. Moscow, the main residence of the creative class, is being improved to meet western standards. The Moscow mayor appointed in October 2010, Sergei Sobyanin, is creating new parks and upgrading old ones, and is building bicycle lanes, theatres and sports grounds. The Kremlin strongly encourages the opposition to limit their activity to the local level and blocks attempts to enter regional or federal politics. A number of opposition leaders, including Yevgeny Roizman (elected mayor of Yekaterinburg in September 2013) and Anatoly Lokot (elected mayor of Novosibirsk in April 2014), have done as asked. While this clearly benefits the Kremlin, the same can hardly be said for the opposition.

To ensure the success of the Sochi Games, in December 2013 Putin paroled Mikhail Khodorkovsky and Pussy Riot. This ratcheted down Russia's confrontation with the United States for a while, especially after Putin helped President Obama out of the political trap of his own making in Syria. The uproar over Edward Snowden, the NSA whistleblower who was given asylum in Russia in mid-2013, harmed the United States' international image but did not damage US–Russian relations. A more formidable threat has come from Ukraine, where President Viktor Yanukovych was overthrown in February 2014 with the encouragement of the USA and EU. A month later, Putin approved Crimea's reunification with Russia at the request of local Russian speakers who feared persecution by the new ultranationalist regime. This turned him into a towering historical figure for Russians, but provoked the worst crisis in relations with the West since 2008. Putin's approval rating soared to 85%. The only part of society that did not join the post-Crimean majority that rallied around Putin was the 'fifth column', as the president called them. The social polarization of 2010–2012 gave way to a nationwide patriotic groundswell. Putin advanced a doctrine of defending the 'Russian world', which includes all ethnic Russians and Russian speakers of the former Soviet Union whom Russia must protect and support. The parliament approved a simplified procedure for granting Russian citizenship to members of this 'Russian world'.

The civil war in Ukraine's Donbass region became the key issue on the Russian agenda, with discussions focused on a single question: should Russia send troops there or not. Emotions were running high, and the political role of state television expanded dramatically, going from a Kremlin-controlled asset to an independent creator of political reality. The Russian public believes that power in Ukraine has been seized by Nazis and followers of Ukrainian nationalist icon Stepan Bandera, vacillating between a desire to help their 'Russian brothers' in Donbass and fear of starting a war with the West with unpredictable consequences. Volunteers are encouraged to fight in Donbass, and opposition parties are advancing increasingly radical nationalist initiatives.

Who are the 'heroes' of the conservative wave of 2012–2014? There are the student volunteers at the Winter Olympics and the Universiade; athletes, not necessarily Russian by birth, who won international competitions for Russia; the believers with small children who stood in line all night to see the miracle-working holy relics brought from Mount Athos in Greece; patriotic oligarchs who invested in St Petersburg and Yamal instead of Europe and America; the 'polite' paratroopers who aided Crimea's peaceful reunification with Russia; and volunteers from Siberia or Rostov, who were just getting used to civilian life after serving in the army, when they left for Donbass to defend their 'brothers' from Nazis and Bandera followers.

There has been little evolution of the social structure in post-crisis Russia: economic growth is not robust enough, and it takes increasingly more time and effort to increase GDP. On the other hand, there has been no social catastrophe

Table 8.24 Do you agree that the country is moving in the right direction? (closed question, one answer)

	2005	*2006*	*2007*	*2008*	*2009*	*2010*	*2011*	*2012*	*2013*	*Q4 2014*
Completely agree, mostly agree	19	26	28	31	23	25	22	31	30	47
Maybe	39	44	43	44	44	47	46	44	43	39
Completely disagree, mostly disagree	36	24	22	20	26	23	28	22	24	12
Don't know	6	6	6	6	6	6	4	4	3	2
Index	22	45	49	54	41	48	39	52	49	74

Source: National representative surveys conducted by VTsIOM, http://wciom.ru/index.php?id=459&uid=114891.

Note: The index gauges Russians' assessment of the country's course and is calculated as the difference between positive/average and negative assessments answers. The higher the index, the more people approve of the country's development trajectory. The index can vary between -100 and +100. A positive value indicates more positive answers than negative ones, and zero indicates a balance of positive and negative answers.

either. All processes are proceeding slowly due to the paternalist social policy of the state, which has been trying to satisfy its core supporters – pensioners, the police and servicemen – without infringing too much on the interests of businesspeople and the intellectual class. The most painful processes are underway in education, science and healthcare, where a generational shift is making it difficult to implement the rather disorganized and ineffective reforms despite increased government funding. The army and police reforms, which got off to a rocky start, eventually yielded results, while growing chaos in healthcare and education has become one of the biggest public concerns.

Public opinion and political decisions

Mikhail Gorbachev established the National Public Opinion Research Centre (VTsIOM) in late 1987 not so much to provide a scientific basis for the country's new trajectory, as to enhance its legitimacy amid the increasingly heated debates between perestroika's leader and his conservative and radical progressive opponents. Under the direction of Tatyana Zaslavskaya, VTsIOM published its first surveys in 1989, but what they showed was that people were losing track of the twists and turns of Gorbachev's policies, that support for the last General Secretary of the Soviet Communist Party was waning, and that the once monolithic Soviet people were becoming increasingly polarized. This data could not be used to prop up Gorbachev's policies, which means that VTsIOM failed in its political mission.[4] On the other hand, for the first time in decades Soviet society had an opportunity to learn what it thought about itself, the government and its decisions. Opinion polls regularly conducted by VTsIOM since 1991 gauged where the public stood on a variety of issues and also introduced public opinion as a political factor in Russia. From then on, political decisions were made with due regard for and sometimes under the direct influence of public opinion, as captured by VTsIOM.

The power to measure, interpret and present public opinion, which had been the prerogative of the Communist Party, was turned over to an independent agency. This helped establish public opinion as an institution that does not depend on the will of the ruling party and sometimes contradicts it. The demise of the Communist Party, the subsequent collapse of the Soviet Union, the reform of the Russian system of government, and the transition to free elections of members of parliament, the president, mayors and governors made public opinion a force to be reckoned with. The authorities had to at least take into account, if not heed, the will of the people, which meant they had to analyze it. You cannot control what you cannot measure. VTsIOM and the competitors it spawned learnt to accurately gauge public opinion in a matter of a few years, with invaluable assistance from American and Western European pollsters.

Many politicians believe that public opinion has become too influential, as evidenced by the media wars launched against sociologists who allegedly falsify their data to mislead the people. But no matter how hard some tried to smear pollsters, public opinion remained in the focus of politicians, the media and business leaders.

The political elite's interest in public opinion did not wane even when it was silent or inactive. The first recorded case of a poll directly influencing decision making came from Yegor Gaidar, who explained on multiple occasions how his cabinet's resolve not to deviate from its course in early 1992 was informed by a VTsIOM report. The legendary reformer said he was shocked by the huge number of respondents in the survey who, when asked when the economic situation in the country would improve, responded 'Never'. He concluded from this that fears that people would not understand why his reformist government had to take such radical measures were ungrounded.[5]

The role of public opinion at another crucial moment of modern Russian history – the 1996 presidential election – was relayed by Alexander Oslon, who worked in Boris Yeltsin's campaign headquarters. Before polling revealed that Yeltsin was still clinging to the support of a small segment of the electorate, his campaign team acted as if the Communist leader Gennady Zyuganov's victory was all but assured. By incorporating polling into Yeltsin's political decision making, they helped him eke out a win at the last moment without resorting to military force or massive fraud. Since then, the Presidential Administration (executive office), which guides policy making in the country, has always kept its finger on the pulse of public opinion in order to calibrate the president's policies.[6]

There are many examples of poll results being ignored, but they consistently illustrate how neglecting public opinion is not only unwise, but is suicidal for even the most respected and influential politicians. A good example is the transition from benefits in kind to cash payments proposed in 2005 by Minister of Labour and Social Development Mikhail Zurabov, an economic technocrat who cared nothing for public opinion. It led to Vladimir Putin's first serious political crisis. The reform ended up costing many times more than planned because of the need to appease outraged benefit recipients. Zurabov's decision nearly destroyed the president's political support among beneficiaries and larger social groups, including students and pensioners.

Disregard for public opinion provoked another political crisis in September 2011, when the role reversal between Putin and Medvedev was announced and the public learnt that the agreement between the two leaders to switch jobs allegedly dated back to 2007. The decision to govern as a 'tandem' was based 'on a mistaken assumption that managed democracy can handle any burden and that the only danger comes from the street', as Gleb Pavlovsky put it.[7] This disrespect for democratic norms led to a full-blown political crisis several months later with the demonstrations on Bolotnaya Square. To remain in power, the Putin–Medvedev team had to make significant policy changes and also adopt limited political reforms. In other words, disregard for the preconceptions, expectations and mood of the Russian people can cost the political elite dearly. Unfortunately, they never learn these lessons because of Russia's completely archaic political structure. The authorities believe they can keep getting away with ignoring public opinion, because they interpret public silence as apathy and passivity as weakness. But if their decisions factor in the public mood, they are almost always successful, provided success is measured in the degree of public support.

The pitfalls of public opinion research

Why do political decisions seldom coincide with the needs and expectations of the majority of population, even when they are carefully calculated to achieve the desired effect? To begin with, public opinion is reactive rather than proactive, and so politicians have to take the lead and cannot always correctly predict the public response to their actions. Politicians have to take risks, which can either bring them enormous popularity or lead to misunderstanding or even public outrage.

In the autumn of 1999, Putin made several tough decisions (the riskiest of which was sending troops to Chechnya) that increased his public support many times over. Conversely, some of his political stunts in the second half of 2011 received a very good press but did not impress the public, like flying alongside cranes to reintroduce them into the wild or diving in the Black Sea and miraculously finding ancient Greek vases. These specific failures could be pinned on the government services whose task is to explain the authorities' intentions to the public. And certainly, failures are more likely to occur when political strategists disregard the opinion of public relations experts and only call them in to put out fires caused by political miscalculations.

On the other hand, sometimes politicians deliberately make unpopular decisions for what they see as higher goals and interests. This is the logic of so-called kamikaze governments, which are willing to sacrifice their short-term reputation to make the difficult but necessary decisions whether out of conscience or concern for their place in history, or to comply with IMF terms. Examples of this kind of messianic reformer from recent Russian history include Yegor Gaidar, Mikhail Zurabov and Dmitry Livanov. Less egotistical and more pragmatic politicians usually try to maintain public support even when making tough calls, unless their actions are guided by narrow interest groups or entrenched coalitions whose goal is to protect their privileged position from larger groups of society. In 1995, the Yeltsin–Chernomyrdin government authorized loans-for-shares auctions to privatize the most valuable state-owned oil and mining companies, even though it was an unfair and unpopular decision.

This authorization was not made for ideological reasons, but to create a coalition of business leaders who would have a stake in Yeltsin's reelection and finance a winning campaign. The short-term goal was achieved, but this unfair division of public property among 'insiders' generated a huge public backlash and discredited big business as an institution. In fact, big business became the hostage of the government, which alone could protect it from public outrage over the unseemly origin of its wealth. Public opinion and government policies also diverge when politicians try to play to public sentiment in order to increase their popularity. But they often seriously miscalculate what the public wants, overestimate what they can achieve and underestimate the scale of the problems standing in the way. As a result, instead of winning public support, they breed public discontent and protest. A case in point is the 'splendid little war' Yeltsin launched in Chechnya in late 1994 to boost his chances of winning re-election. It is not always politicians who are to blame. Pollsters often undermine the influence of public opinion in politics by failing to recognize shifts in public opinion, or recognizing them too late. In the first elections to the State Duma in December 1993, none of the polling centres forecast the triumph of Vladimir Zhirinovsky's Liberal Democratic Party, with nearly all of them predicting a win by the party in power.

The science of election forecasting has made huge strides since then, but mistakes can happen. Recent examples include the 2011 State Duma elections, when the ruling party did worse and the opposition did better than pollsters predicted, and the mayoral election in Moscow in September 2013, when opposition leader Alexei Navalny won twice as many votes as expected. No opinion surveys saw the mass protests coming in December 2011. These shortcomings have eroded trust in sociologists and pollsters, and so politicians often improvise, with mixed results. Mistrust of sociologists creates situations when politicians act contrary to public expectations, launching bold initiatives because 'fortune smiles upon the brave'. They completely disregard public opinion, claiming that it does not exist and that sociologists falsify the data. The opposition often resorts to this tactic to make its electoral chances seem better. Denouncing sociologists as pseudo-scientists in the service of the Kremlin was a requirement of the past few election cycles. The last time this charge was heard was in the winter of 2011–2012, when the opposition accused the regime of falsifying parliamentary election results and slandered all pollsters by association, including the Levada Centre. The most persistent critic of sociologists is Alexei Navalny, who created his own polling team.

Another common misperception about public opinion has to do with the media. The power of the media over the electorate is a widespread myth of the industrial age that has continued into the information age. Public opinion is presented not as a subject but an object that is easy to manipulate, and major media outlets, primarily television, are seen as a shortcut to power. Politicians who dismiss polls and trust television think that their popularity will soar if they gain control of television. The conspicuous failure of the Bolotnaya Square opposition, whose leaders finally gained access to television in the first half of 2012, showed that the power of the 'boob tube' over hearts and minds is greatly overstated, and political manipulation can only do so much. However, the myth lives on, with more politicians shrugging off public opinion in the belief that they can mould opinion through television.

These are just some of the conflicts that occur at the intersection of politics and public opinion that lead politicians to ignore, underestimate or misinterpret the intensity of the public mood or the direction in which it is moving. On a deeper level, politicians are suspicious of public opinion because it is fickle and fluid by nature, with similar decisions sometimes producing opposite results. For example, the public sharply criticized the first Chechen war (1994–1996) but approved the second Chechen war (1999–2002), boosting the presidents' ratings. It is not enough to divide collisions between politicians and public opinion into types and categories, because public opinion is a highly complex and evolving phenomenon. What explains its complexity and fluidity? Does it swing regularly like a pendulum, or does it follow some other, more complex cycle? Is it directed evolution, meaning we should regard the history of public opinion as steady movement towards a deterministic result? Is it an internal determinism based on the laws governing public opinion itself (the conceptual instability of the public mood and its inherent fluidity)? Or is it an external determinism informed by changes in the economic, social, cultural and political environment? What are the basic evolutionary mechanisms that connect the external environment to internal changes in public opinion? What are the main landmarks and stages of the evolution of public opinion? And lastly, how is the institution of public opinion changing, including its structure, functions, political role and interaction with the political system and the media?

Analysts and chroniclers of public opinions should focus on these extremely important and relevant questions in the years to come, in order to understand the recent history of the Russian nation with greater depth and clarity. The silent majority has acquired a voice. Politicians and experts can hear it, but they do not yet have the necessary tools to fully understand the people, their grievances and their needs. It is our task to create them.

Notes

1 This concerns an internal leadership conflict that began in 1992. The once united team of democratic reformers split. Boris Yeltsin and Yegor Gaidar insisted on rapid, radical reforms and power centralization as the only way to implement them, while Alexander Rutskoi, Ruslan Khasbulatov and others advocated evolutionary development and the division of power between the president and the parliament. The battle lasted over 18 months and ended in a military coup in October 1993. This marked the start of Russia's modern political history. For details, see Vladimir Sogrin, *Politicheskaya istoriya sovremennoi Rossii. 1985–2001: Ot Gorbacheva do Putina* (*Political History of Modern Russia 1985–2001: From Gorbachev to Putin*) (Moscow: 2001).

2 For details, see Yakov Pappe, *Oligarkhi: ekonomicheskaya khronika 1992–2000* (*Oligarchs: Economic Chronicle 1992–2000*) (Moscow: HSE, 2000).

3 For details, see Tatyana Maleva (ed.), *Sredniye klassy v Rossii: ekonomicheskiye i sotsialnye strategii* (*Middle Classes in Russia: Economic and Social Strategies*) (Moscow: Gendalf, 2003).

4 See Alexei Levinson, 'Mne vypala rol vestovogo, kotoryi bukvalno donyos mneniye naroda do vlastei' (I was a messenger who made people's opinion known to the authorities), *Kommersant-Weekend*, 23 May 2014.

5 See Yegor Gaidar, *Gibel imperii* (*Collapse of an Empire*) (Moscow, 2006).

6 See Alexander Oslon, 'Kak v 1996 g. analiticheskaya gruppa sdelala oprosy sotsialnym faktom' ('How the Analytical Group Made Opinion Polls a Fact of Social Life in 1996'), *Sotsial'naya real'nost*, No. 6, 2006.

7 Gleb Pavlovsky, 'Vlasti, emotsii i protesty v Rossii' ('Authorities, Emotions and Protest in Russia'), Gefter.ru, 2014.

9 Images of authority in a time of change

The psychological transformation of society in post-Soviet Russia

Elena Shestopal

This chapter will focus on the images, perceptions and values that developed and disappeared in Russian society after the Soviet Union's disintegration. The image of authority is especially important in this context, because the post-Soviet psychological drama revolves around the authorities and people's relationship and attitude to them. The developments of the last 25 years in Russia have been dramatic. It is not surprising that Vladimir Putin in 2005 described the processes that took place after 1991 as one of the greatest humanitarian catastrophes of the twentieth century. Russian sociologist Boris Grushin coined the term 'social quakes' to describe the tectonic shift that dislocated the very foundations of life in the country and swept away old standards and values, with new ones struggling to develop in their place. Many people have lost not only their money and jobs, but also their country. Fortunately, the changes that began in 1991 are not a revolution, even though they are comparable to the tragic events of 1917 in duration and social impact.

Framing the issue

When you first try to take stock of the path Russia has travelled in the nearly 25 years since the Soviet Union's collapse, it seems as if everything has changed – the country, the government, people's way of thinking and system of values, and even their consciousness. But then you realize that this cannot be, and that something must have remained as it was. What appears to be entirely new, upon closer examination, bears traces of traditional modes of behaviour and persistent thought patterns. Therefore, when speaking about psychological transformations in post-Soviet Russia, we should not only record changes in mentality and behaviour, but also try to understand what has remained unchanged.

In this chapter I will describe the broad contours of the transformation that has occurred in the psychological conceptions of how the country has changed. I will provide facts and figures about wages and GDP, the level of personal freedom and the democratic standards of the Russian constitution, but mostly I will address this central issue from the point of view of emotion, motive and sentiment. The human or psychological dimension is seldom taken into account by historians, political scientists, sociologists or economists, who are more interested in broader institutional changes in the political system and the actions of a country's leaders, than in the sentiments and feelings of people during times of change. But the psychological context is very important for the people experiencing the effects of this transformation. It influences people's mood and the motives behind their actions, as well as their trust or mistrust for the authorities and the state and their support or rejection of reforms. Moreover, this psychological factor influences demography. The chapter in this volume on the economic and social development of Russia discusses the shocking statistics on the rise in the country's mortality rate after the collapse of the Soviet Union. Vladimir Popov and Piotr Dutkiewicz write that apart from external reasons, 'the main cause of the rising mortality rate was cardiovascular diseases in 40–50-year-old males, who could not deal with the shock of the instantaneous transition to a market economy'.[1] In other words, a psychological factor like stress can explain the spike in the mortality rate.

Without understanding the psychological state of society, any conclusions regarding the success or failure of reforms and Russia's democratic transition will be incomplete and incorrect. Until recently, researchers did not focus on the human or psychological dimension in history and politics. The term 'human dimension' itself was only coined a few years ago. In the 1950s and 1960s, discussions of the human dimension in politics were mostly confined to the influence of individual leaders. Later the focus shifted to mass forms of political behaviour.[2] Karl Deutsch, the outstanding US political scientist and president of the International Political Science Association (IPSA), attributed the fundamental changes that occurred in political science in the second half of the twentieth century to the studies of political behaviour (primarily electoral behaviour) conducted by sociologists and psychologists.[3] The so-called behavioural revolution encouraged political scientists to look beyond political institutions and consider the people involved in politics. However, until recently the term 'human dimension' was applied mechanistically because of the positivist approaches favoured by the majority of scholars. The situation has started to change in the past decade.

First, *Homo politicus* and the context in which it acts are changing rapidly. Irina Semenenko and Vladimir Lapkin explain the new role of individuals in politics in terms of the challenges of what they call *infomodernity* amid growing globalization.[4] Human behaviour and consciousness are becoming more important in new forms of politics and political communication. Not only leaders but also ordinary uninformed people have become active participants in the political process. The role of leaders is even declining in many respects. Yves Cohen writes in his study of leadership, *Le siècle des chefs*, that leaders are not a necessary part of the globalizing post-industrial world.[5] The industrial societies of the twentieth century needed leaders, but politics are now the province of individuals and even the 'masses', as evidenced by the Arab Spring and the sit-ins in Istanbul, Turkey. Cohen writes about democracies in which leaders will have to coexist with leaderless crowds, which he explains by the appearance of fundamentally new forms of social groups on the political stage and different forms of communication between these groups and the authorities. The idea of the death of leadership has become very popular. Barbara Kellerman writes about the growing role of followers and the waning role of leaders in her book, *Followership: How Followers Are Creating Change and Changing Leaders*.[6]

Second, fundamentally new forms of political activity are emerging as a result of changing mechanisms of political socialization.[7] Studying the characteristics of socialization reveals the distinguishing features of different generational models of political behaviour, with a population group's political views depending on when it entered politics. Third, ordinary people now have more opportunities to influence political events not only as part of the crowd but also individually. There are many different ways to engage in politics interactively, such as flash mobs and online activism. Political scientists are talking more and more about electronic democracy (e-democracy), which actually harkens back to old debates about whether direct democracy can exist alongside representative democracy. An analysis of the generational effect is vital for understanding recent Russian politics.[8]

Given the metaphorical nature of the term 'human dimension', we will not venture a strict definition. A narrower, psychological interpretation of what is meant by the 'political dimension of political transformations in post-Soviet society' need not include absolutely all psychological phenomena at the social and individual level. We will only describe changes in such vital psychological phenomena as images, perceptions and values of the collective consciousness.

Methodology and theory

We have been studying the image of authority in Russia, which has both qualitative and quantitative aspects, for more than 20 years, since 1993, in annual and sometimes semi-annual surveys. Every time we have chosen different sample groups that were not representative of the country as a whole, but were balanced in terms of gender, age and education, as is necessary for doing quality research. We tried to accumulate as much data as possible to ensure quality results, and published the main findings of the first stages of this project in articles and books.[9] We conducted surveys in different regions. It was impossible to survey the same regions at different stages, but the regional data have revealed regional variations in perceptions.

Our methods evolved from one stage of the project to the next. In the mid-1990s we combined questionnaires that had many open-ended questions asked during in-depth interviews with the respondents, which explains the relatively small number of respondents initially. In 2001 we could not include all the previous questions and did not conduct in-depth interviews, but a large number of respondents participated, over 1,400. Beginning in 2005, we started using a projective test, A Sketch of Authority, in the survey. We have accumulated a large collection of these 'sketches', which we use to analyse the unconscious aspects of political perceptions. In 2010–2011, we polled more than 680 respondents not only in Moscow but also in Chelyabinsk, Saratov, Smolensk, Vladikavkaz, Novosibirsk and St. Petersburg. In 2013–2014, we polled 898 people in eight regions: the Moscow metropolitan area, as well as the Moscow, Saratov, Chelyabinsk, Voronezh and Tomsk regions, and the Republic of Bashkortostan and the Krasnodar Territory. The sample groups were not representative of the country as a whole, but they were balanced and proportional for each region. Thus, all stages of this project followed a single logic and produced comparable results for quantitative and qualitative analysis.[10]

Studying the psychological aspects of the political transformation in Russian society has confirmed our conviction that these non-institutional aspects offer a better understanding of the nature of the ongoing changes. Moreover, psychological changes not only provide the background for political changes, but help drive them. In order to understand the nature of the government and the results of political transformations, it is essential to understand the relationship between the people and the authorities, the mechanisms of public perceptions of the authorities, and public expectations and concepts of the authorities.

Our previous studies (listed in footnote 9) have shown that, first, the image of authority has a complicated psychological structure that includes both rational and unconscious levels. *Perceptions* (of democracy, power and politics) are predominantly cognitive structures, while *images* are broader, 'stereoscopic' psychological characteristics that are significantly influenced by emotions that typically reside in the realm of the unconscious. We considered both perceptions and images in our studies. In addition to these two categories, we also studied political values as a psychological phenomenon. Values hold one of the highest positions in the personality structure, because they are involved in the creation of meaning, in particular political meaning. Moreover, the changes that occur in perceptions, images and values as the system undergoes transformation signify changes in both the *essence* of images, how representatives of authority are evaluated and the *optics* that shape perception.[11] We present below a selection of results from our studies, with a focus on changing perceptions, images and values in the course of the country's political transformation. We will only discuss public perceptions, images and values as they relate to the authorities.

Changing perceptions of democracy, politics and authority

Numerous studies point to continuing changes in public perceptions of political and social realities in Russia that start in the 1990s.[12] One of the core concepts in post-Soviet political discourse has been the perception of democracy. Transformation processes were discussed only in the context of democracy and democratization. The concept of democracy became the cornerstone of the official ideology and its critics. Research conducted in the 1990s showed that the majority of respondents had extremely negative feelings for the *concept of democracy*, because to them it was connected with political practices that worsened economic conditions for people. It is therefore surprising that in 2000–2010 people became accustomed, at least at a rhetorical level, to democracy as the official goal of political development. They accepted it as a conventional political standard and even a goal to strive for.

This is demonstrated by the fact that 76% of respondents described the existing political system as undemocratic in 2011, revealing a stark divide between the existing political system in Russia and the system people want. Moreover, 49% said they expected Russia to become more democratic, compared to 51% who did not. Of course, 49% is not insignificant, especially compared to the 1990s and the 2000s. In fact, respondents who were asked to describe the ideal form of government listed *democratic* as the top characteristic. Of course, some respondents expressed support for authoritarian rule, but they were not as numerous as is generally believed (only 13%).

More importantly, in the past few years respondents have increasingly explained their perception of democracy using clichés such as government by the people, freedom of speech and equality before the law. In cognitive terms, perceptions have become more generic over time. In the 1990s, the descriptions respondents offered were not precise but were definitely more striking and colourful: 'Democracy is something nice that helps you wake up smiling', or 'Democracy is when everyone is equal and has a Mercedes and three slaves' (from a 1993 interview).

It is telling that negative perceptions of democracy were expressed by a relatively small share of respondents, only 14.2%. Some claimed not to believe in democracy, especially in Russia, which they described in words suggesting it is illusory or mythical: 'empty rhetoric', 'windbaggery', 'deception', 'meaningless words', 'delusion', 'nonsense', 'unlikely in Russia', 'something distant and unclear' and 'anarchy'. Note that these definitions are impersonal, so it is unclear who is guilty of the deception or whose nonsense respondents speak of. Another group of respondents with negative attitudes to democracy is clearly focused on the enemies who brought democracy to Russia. They include the West ('it came from the West', 'the US regime', 'it's what America is forcing on everyone') and also internal enemies, namely proponents of the West, thieves, the rich, the elite or the government, which are described using terms like 'Western henchmen', 'the rule of the rich', 'the rule of money', 'the rule of thieves', 'the rule of the elite' and 'capitalism'.

The types of attitudes to democracy likewise differ, and not only for socio-demographic factors such as gender, age, education, region of residence and the like, but also purely political views that developed in the post-Soviet period. In the 1990s, types could not be identified because the respondents' answers differed immensely and cluster analysis was not possible. In the 2000s, perceptions could already be divided into rough types, which became clearer in the 2010s. Answers to the question, 'Democracy for me is . . . ', could be divided into distinct categories based on political and ideological preferences, namely liberal-individualistic, authoritarian-communitarian and mixed types. A liberal conception of democracy includes various ideals of freedom, such as 'freedom of speech and opinion', 'freedom of choice' including political choice, and 'respect for human rights and liberties'. Authoritarian-communitarian perceptions of democracy emphasize power, subordination, discipline, demands to restore order and appeals to law and moral norms. Power relations are viewed as a confrontation between the abstract 'authorities', 'the state' and 'the government' and 'people', 'the people' or 'ordinary people' (Figure 9.1).

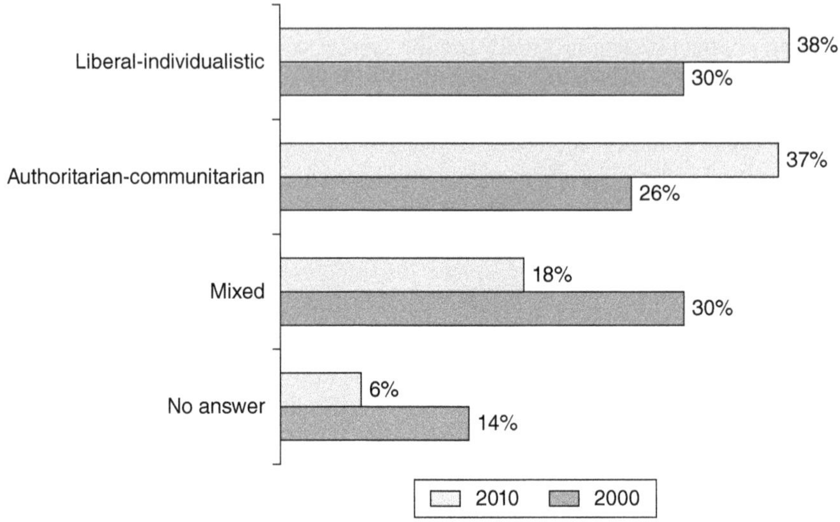

Figure 9.1 Perceptions of democracy by type.

Over the past decade, people's perceptions have become more solid, as evidenced by the declining share of people with mixed perceptions of democracy and those who were unable to answer. At the same time, the number of 'liberals' and 'authoritarians' has evened out. Furthermore, the weight of the liberal component in liberal-individualistic perceptions has decreased, whereas individualism has clearly become more pronounced. As for the conservative, or rather authoritarian-communitarian, model of democracy, it has crystallized in the past years in terms of attitudes to justice, equality and responsibility. It is notable that respect for law, which used to feature prominently, has taken a plunge, while activism, which is more commonly associated with liberal values, has gained weight since 2010 and now is considered the dominant value.

In addition to values, which can be used to divide perceptions of democracy into three groups, one should also take into account political identification, which can be gleaned from answers to the following question: 'How would you define your political preferences?' (Table 9.1).[13] The number of the respondents who defined themselves as liberal grew especially rapidly in 2010–2013. In fact, the figure has reached a historical high (20.4%) relative to past surveys. While self-identified democrats declined slightly, they are still the largest category (30.4%). The number of socialists has declined, but conservatives and communists remain at roughly the same level (10.2% and 7.2%, respectively).

Perceptions are closely connected to the basic *needs* (especially unfulfilled) that inform political demands. The hierarchy of needs proposed by American psychologist Abraham Maslow includes physiological needs, safety needs, love and belonging, self-esteem, and self-actualization. Unlike people's perceptions of the

Table 9.1 How would you define your political preferences? (%)

	1993	*2000*	*2010*	*2013*
Liberal	4.2	13.4	17	20.4
Socialist	0	8.4	10	9.7
Anarchist	0	2.5	3	1.4
Democrat	33.3	27.6	33	30.4
Patriot	0	0	0	0
Nationalist	0	0	0	0
Radical	4.2	2.5	3	1.3
Conservative	20.8	12.1	10	10.2
Communist	25	7.1	7	7.2
Apolitical	8.3	19.2	16	14.8
Other	4.2	4.2	2	5.7

current authorities, where the dominant need is safety, perceptions of democracy are based primarily on higher-order, social needs such as self-esteem and self-actualization.[14] This may mean that democracy is not considered a basic need in everyday life. The exceptional moral characteristics attributed to democracy are lacking in everyday political life (Figure 9.2).

An assessment of changes in political perceptions in the post-Soviet period should take into account two basic aspects: the first is a conceptual aspect that concerns the essence of perceptions, and the second deals with 'political optics', or the nature of political mentality. The conceptual aspect has changed radically.

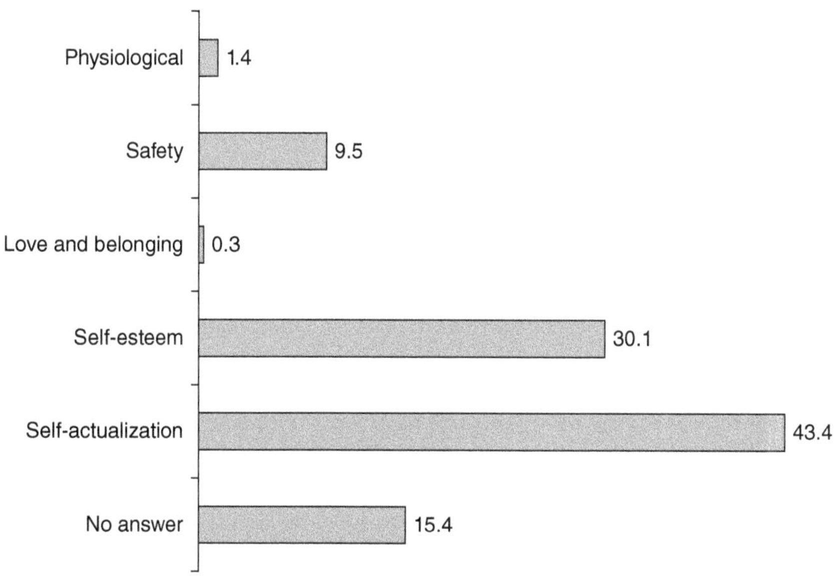

Figure 9.2 Needs that determine perceptions of democracy, 2011.

People use the democratic norms espoused by officials as the standard against which to measure their actions, and demands for more effective government and political actors have only increased.

Political optics is a somewhat different matter. First, cognitive processes change relatively slowly. And second, during times of instability, the rational structures of political mentality do not play the key role in decision making, in particular electoral decisions. Rather, it is emotional processes that most often take the lead. At any rate, it should be noted that Soviet-era perceptions were still dominant in the immediate post-Soviet period of the 1990s. For example, such protest tactics as strikes and demonstrations were rejected as 'improper'. For the most part, people adopted conventional perceptions of the various forms of political participation. Marked by cognitive simplicity and poverty, such perceptions are abstract and generalized. This demonstrates that politics is not a central element in the lives of ordinary people, but rather something apart from them.

In the 2000s, as the vertical power structure was being built in Russia, society was growing accustomed to a new political vocabulary. For the first time, relatively coherent systems of perceptions began to emerge in the public consciousness. Political perceptions began to consolidate in the early 2010s, and are already clearly distinguishable, even if they have yet to take their final shape.

Images of authority in historical perspective[15]

For two decades now, we have been studying people's perceptions, views and image of authority in Russia in an effort to understand their origins. Like any other image, the image of authority reflects the existing properties of the object of perception (percept), in this case, political authority. These properties can be described as the percept's components, which largely determine the political content of the image.

On the other hand, image is a projection of the expectations of the perceiver, that is, the people. The image of political power reflects the needs, motivations, knowledge, perceptions, opinions, judgments, stereotypes, expectations, emotions and demands of the authorities in the public consciousness. The image components can be described as subjective. Political images change alongside changes in the psychology of the public consciousness. Moreover, the nature of images changes depending on such characteristics as the perceiver's gender, age, education, region of residence and so on. An image is a more stereoscopic psychological substance that includes not only conscious (cognitive) perceptions, but also emotional and behavioural components, which often remain at the level of the unconscious. We asked respondents to describe power in Russia at different stages in its history – the Soviet era, under Yeltsin, Putin's first two terms as president and his current term.[16]

This survey differed from ordinary sociological polls in that it included many open-ended questions, which were interpreted using a scaling method. We mostly used qualitative methods such as analysis of open-ended questions, in-depth interviews and projective tests. Below are comparisons of images of power from different historical periods as our respondents described them throughout this project.

The image of Soviet power in 2013–2014 differs from 2000 or 2003, primarily in terms of emotional response (Table 9.2). In 2000, there were more negative than positive responses. The situation reversed in 2003 and 2013, and now the number of positive responses has reached a historical high of 43.8%. In other words, the public perception of Soviet power is gradually improving, and not only in older age groups where there is typically more Soviet nostalgia, but also among young people. The table below shows that Russian society is almost evenly divided in their attitude to the Soviet period. There were almost no neutral answers. The share of respondents who have a neutral attitude to the Soviet past has plummeted to 4%.

Cognitive properties of the image of Soviet power. It is notable that in only 7% of cases were perceptions tied to a *subject* of power, which means that people have a depersonalized view of power. Russian society does not connect Soviet power with the Soviet Communist Party, for example, despite official disapproval of the latter in today's Russia. We gauged the behavioural component by considering *needs*. The predominance of *self-esteem and self-actualization* shows that the respondents highly value newfound opportunities for personal growth and freedom, the lack of which is grounds for most of the criticism of Soviet power. Positive perceptions mostly focus on the need for *safety*, which many respondents believe was assured during Soviet rule. The conceptual components of the image of Soviet power include primarily *rigidity* (totalitarian rule), *efficiency* (while this word can be ambiguous, it was used with positive connotations twice as often as negative) and *strength* (Table 9.3). Respondents were adamant in their judgment. Positive views were expressed in maximalist terms: 'the best power', 'the best period' and so on. And the same was true of negative views: 'hate', 'dictatorship' and 'collapse'. In other words, society is still divided over the Soviet period. 'Stability' and 'law and order' are very important characteristics of Soviet power, cited by 8.4% and 6.5% of respondents, respectively.

Power under Yeltsin. Emotional characteristics. The image of power in a given historical period does not refer to the image of the leader that personifies state power at the time. Although Boris Yeltsin's personal image and the image of power under his leadership are, of course, connected, in this study we seek to analyse power in the abstract. Most respondents had a negative view of Yeltsin's rule: 74% were strongly negative, with only 5% positive. Predominantly negative views of

Table 9.2 Emotional response to the image of Soviet power (%)

	2000	*2003*	*2013*
Positive	30.1	40.6	43.8
Negative	34.3	27.2	31
Neutral	27.6	13.9	3.9
Ambivalent	–	–	11

Table 9.3 Conceptual components of the image of Soviet power (%)

No answer	11.5
Totalitarian rule	21.3
Stagnation	4
Inefficient	9.7
Efficient	18.2
Restricted personal rights, no opportunities for self-actualization	3
Stability	8.4
Equality	6.2
Strength	10.9
Law and order	6.5

Yeltsin's rule were observed in all of our surveys, peaking in 2010. At the same time, the share of neutral views has declined (Table 9.4). This is not surprising, as the majority of Russians suffered major hardships during Yeltsin's rule, primarily financial and safety-related. Respondents with memories of what life was like in the Soviet period had an even more negative view of Yeltsin's rule.

Cognitive characteristics. The number of generalized and even simplistic assessments of power under Yeltsin such as 'arbitrariness', 'anarchy' and 'chaos' was more than twice the number of concrete assessments (62% to 25%). The image of power during Yeltsin's rule is more cognitively poor and simple (61%) than cognitively rich and complex (27%). The explanation is most likely that people blame the chaos of the 1990s on the authorities and not on an objective 'situation'. The problems appeared so complex and the authorities' efforts so ineffective that the people concluded that the authorities had no control of the situation.

Behavioural characteristics. The main needs people mentioned when speaking about the image of power during Yeltsin's presidency were *self-actualization* (41%) and *safety* (29%). The need for *safety* is understandable, considering what life was like in this period in Russia's history. As for *self-actualization*, for all the drawbacks people cite, Yeltsin's presidency represented the beginnings of democracy and is often associated with freedom. It is notable that when respondents are asked to assess power in the Yeltsin era in terms of strength and weakness, most of them (14% as opposed to 1% against) describe it as 'weak, fading, and dependent'. What this means is public sentiment about the hardships of that era (difficult/dark/scary, the turbulent 1990s) outweighs positive memories of individual actors.

Table 9.4 Emotional response (%)

Positive	4.8
Negative	73.6
Neutral	1.4
Ambivalent	8.1
No answer	8.6

A survey of the content characteristics of the image of power during Yeltsin's presidency showed that the most popular descriptions were collapse, demise of the system, disintegration of the country, chaos, shaky (power), disorder and so on. Respondents tend to see the authorities at that time as inefficient, unable to control the situation, irresponsible and isolated from the people ('ungrateful' was the most frequently used term in this context) (Table 9.5). As for the general image of power under Yeltsin, throughout this project respondents have held consistently negative views of that period, seeing it as a leaderless era despite the presence of a charismatic leader. In the public consciousness, the Yeltsin era is associated with danger and instability, but also greater opportunities for self-actualization.

The image of power during Vladimir Putin's first and second terms as president (2000–2008). The Putin era began in 2000. The new president inherited an economic crisis, dangerous instability in the North Caucasus and other security issues that required immediate attention. In the six years since the end of Putin's second term, attitudes to that period have gone through several changes, first during the presidency of Dmitry Medvedev, and then following the powerful protests of 2011–2012, which influenced current attitudes to Putin's first two terms. The *emotional response* to the image of power in that period can be described as ambivalent. On the one hand, people view it positively due to the restoration of stability ('Putin revived Russia after what Yeltsin did', 'the authorities have ensured stability'). At the same time, the authorities under Putin are still seen as corrupt and oligarchic ('arbitrariness and corruption flourished', 'the country has been plundered') (Table 9.6).

Cognitive characteristics. The respondents' answers are marked by extreme *cognitive simplicity* (89.7%): 'strong', 'revival' and 'stable'. Only 3.7% of respondents used cognitively complex images such as 'stability, steady development, crisis' and 'the excessive role of the law enforcement and security agencies'. As many as 84.3% of the respondents described these images as vague, abstract and depersonalized (Table 9.7). *Self-esteem* is the main unfulfilled need (47.2%) shaping the image of power in 2000–2008. The respondents' answers

Table 9.5 Content characteristics (%)

Corruption	1.6
Alcoholism	2.2
Oligarchy	1.3
Difficult, dark time, the turbulent 1990s	3.1
Chaos, disintegration, disorder, outrage	20.5
Efficient	0.6
Inefficient	13.5
Transition to democracy, the dawn of democracy	4.2
Democracy, freedom, liberalism	2.8
Other	30.4
No answer	7.8

Table 9.6 Emotional response (%)

Positive	43.1
Negative	35.1
Neutral	6.6
Ambivalent	4.5

presented this need in both a positive and negative light. The next most important requirement was *love and belonging* (19.2%), which can be interpreted as a desire to see the authorities show more concern for the people. It is notable that respondents did not mention this need in previous surveys. The need for safety (16.7%) was ranked third: 'strengthening the country's defences', 'restoring law and order', 'fighting terrorism as defined by the authorities' and 'life has become calmer and better'. As physiological needs (4.1%) came to occupy an insignificant place in respondents' lives, the need for self-actualization became the priority in this period.

Strength. Views on the strength of the authorities vary, and it is difficult to assess them out of context. Of the total number of respondents, 43% associate Putin's rule with strength ('a strong government has created stability', 'Russia as a strong power'), while 29.3% associate it with weakness ('frequent crises are due to the weakness of the government', 'dependence in domestic and foreign affairs'), and 26.8% have a neutral attitude ('the government tried to normalize the situation).

Conceptual characteristics. A qualitative analysis of respondents' answers in the 2013 survey sheds light on some of the conceptual categories that inform the image of power in the early days of Putin's rule (Table 9.8).

The 2013 surveys showed that a considerable share of respondents (28.5%) said the government pursued a policy of stabilization and sought to shore up the foundations of power and overcome Yeltsin's legacy. Answers like 'policy stabilization', 'strengthening the state' and 'harsh measures to save the country' indicate that in 2000–2008 the government was seeing as pursuing a conservative policy aimed at bolstering 'stability'. More detailed answers included explanations of the government's conservative measures – 'clamping down', 'restoring basic order', 'restoring sovereignty', 'stabilization in all spheres of society' and 'undemocratic measures to stabilize society'. At the same time, conservatism and attempts to undertake reforms are cited alongside the reforms frequently associated with

Table 9.7 Behavioural characteristics: needs (%)

Physiological	4.1
Safety	16.7
Love and belonging	19.2
Self-esteem	47.2
Self-actualization	0.3
No answer	8.4

Table 9.8 Conceptual characteristics (%)

Conservatism, stability, defensive inhibition	28.5
Negative appeal	14.8
Reform, development, transformation	14.4
Personal power, autocracy	8.5
Oligarchy, rule of the elites	2.2
Other/No answer	24.1

Putin. A considerable share of respondents (14.4%) said that the government was implementing positive reforms or attempting to 'move from stagnation to radical pro-development reforms'.

Negative perceptions of the authorities (14.8%) are tied to the expansion of corruption and bureaucratic rule. However, the number of answers that cited the power of the oligarchy, security agencies and criminal elements is much lower than in previous surveys (2.2%). The conclusion to be drawn from the above is that the fundamental perception of the authorities in that period is of a strong and centralized power that acted in an authoritarian manner, and that this was the price to pay for stability, safety and self-esteem.

The image of power during Vladimir Putin's third term as president (2012–2013). Emotional characteristics. Data show that over a half of respondents (52.3%) view the current authorities negatively: 'lack of concrete achievements', 'corruption and bureaucratic arbitrariness', 'empty promises', 'not confident in the future' and 'stagnation'.[17] Many respondents explain that their negative views are rooted in the authorities' passivity and in the lack of action taken to improve life in the country. A desire for change, though not as strong as during perestroika, can be gleaned from many answers: 'six of one and half a dozen of the other', 'currently not satisfied', 'change is needed', 'disappointment'. At the same time, a considerable share of respondents (21.7%) also sees *positive* aspects to the authorities. The majority of positive assessments concern the clear vertical system of power and policy ('high standards', 'a clear policy', 'substantiated', 'consistent forward progress' and 'a streamlined system of power') and the authorities' efficiency: 'reviving the economy', 'economic growth', 'restoration of at least a semblance of order' and 'solving problems'. The limited number of respondents expressing *neutral* and *ambivalent* views is striking. Views in society have become more pronounced (Table 9.9).

Emotional responses to the authorities show that people are wary of the current political situation despite the fact that there were no political or economic crises in that period. Rather, there are fears of an impending crisis: 'I expect a crisis', 'I'm hoping for the best, for promises to be kept', 'no confidence in the future', 'disorder bordering on lawlessness', 'chaos', 'reforms that would meet social needs are needed', 'gap between word and deed'. The largest group of people polled in 2013 (48.8%) characterized the authorities as weak: 'the authorities are breaking down', 'the leadership is not tackling vital issues' and 'the apparatus has created a power vertical it cannot handle'.

Table 9.9 Emotional response (%)

Positive	21.7
Negative	52.3
Neutral	9.6
Ambivalent	5.1
No answer	6.8

Cognitive characteristics. The image of power is cognitively impoverished (76.6%), with respondents using several simple words or phrases to describe the authorities. There were few substantive responses (12.7%). However, despite the cognitive simplicity of the image of power conveyed by respondents, they have a relatively clear perception of the authorities and can easily explain their views (69.8%). Only 19% had difficulty describing their views, which is considerably less than in the Soviet period, under Yeltsin or during Putin's first two terms. It is worth noting that respondents tend to associate the current authorities with Putin's rule and hence do not distinguish between his first two terms and his current term: 'this is the Putin era', 'the Putin era goes on', 'Putin's rule continues', 'like it was under Putin', 'Putin is in charge' (Table 9.10).

The dominant need in today's Russia is for *self-esteem* (38.5%). According to the results of the survey, the need for self-esteem is related to the lack of action and positive change on the part of the authorities. The need for *safety* ranks second (32.7%). It is important to note that the last survey was completed before events in Ukraine, so the importance given to safety reflects an anticipation of crisis. Russians no longer expect the authorities to care for them, which explains the decline in the need for love and belonging. *Physiological needs* ranked last with only 3%, which indicates that material problems have become less acute compared to previous surveys.

There are conflicting views on whether the authorities' image is one of strength or weakness, though the latter view prevails (strong – 30.8%, weak – 48.8%). The most prominent feature of the current authorities is inefficiency (19.8%), although some respondents think otherwise (11.2%). This is the first time in the project's history that the majority of respondents described the authorities as inefficient, which points to an important trend. For the first time in the post-Soviet period, efficiency has become a key metric for evaluating the authorities, which means that people's attitudes to government have become more rational.

Table 9.10 Behavioural characteristics: needs (%)

Physiological	3
Safety	32.7
Love and belonging	0.7
Self-esteem	38.5
Self-actualization	11.7
No answer	8.7

Table 9.11 Content characteristics of the image of power (%)

Corruption	9.8
Authoritarianism	2.2
Oligarchy	11.7
Democracy	2.1
Oligarchy, power held by a single group	2.8
Arbitrariness, chaos	6.9
Efficient, positive	11.2
Inefficient	19.8
Stagnation	4.5
Stability	6.6
Other	20

A large group of respondents highlighted *corruption*, which they often mention together with words like oligarchy, bureaucracy, red tape and bribery: 'corruption and red tape everywhere', 'pervasive corruption', 'corrupt officials', 'corrupt, greedy authorities that ignore people's needs', 'the rule of bureaucracy'. Another group used words associated with confusion and chaos: 'disorder', 'bordering on disorder', 'arbitrariness', 'collapse', 'total disorder', 'disorder bordering on lawlessness'. For the first time since the Yeltsin era, respondents' answers showed intensity on the issues of instability and disorder in global politics, as evidenced by the growing prominence of the need for safety.

To sum up the image of authority as it stands today, people are above all dissatisfied because they hoped for more from the government, which is seen as marking time and not making progress or working to effect positive change. The word 'stability' features prominently in respondents' answers, but its tenor has changed. Two years ago, stability was seen as the main achievement of the Putin era and a prerequisite for development, whereas now respondents perceive stability as an obstacle to development. The aforementioned results of the survey prompt the following conclusions:

1 Our initial hypothesis that the image of power in the distant past would be more positive than in the recent past due to nostalgia was partially confirmed. There is no relationship between emotional responses to the image of power and distance from the present. The image of the current authorities is worse than the image of power in past periods of the Putin era or the Soviet period. However, the Yeltsin era is viewed more negatively than any other period in Russia's history. Therefore, simple nostalgia for the past cannot explain everything. Society is becoming increasingly aware of the severity of the catastrophe that followed the Soviet Union's collapse, and increasingly believes that the reformers threw out the baby with the bath water and destroyed the nation's standing as a great power. The respondents' answers point to a desire to create an image of modern Russia as it should be.
2 As for the emotional components if the image of power, the data show that society is almost evenly split in assessment of earlier periods in post-Soviet

history, with the exception of the Yeltsin era, about which respondents were almost uniformly negative.

3 The survey partially confirmed our hypothesis that cognitive clarity in perceptions of power would decline as we go back further in history. In other words, respondents would have a clearer image of the current authorities than of the Yeltsin or Soviet eras. However, all cognitive characteristics of the image of power (both existing and imaginary/ideal) are remarkably underdeveloped and ill-defined. People have a poor understanding of government, which they view as opaque. For example, they cannot identify the people or institutions that exercise power and found it difficult to name political leaders, past and present, other than Putin and Stalin.

4 The behavioural aspects of the image of power were analysed through the needs that informed respondents' answers. For example, *safety* was identified as the most important element of an ideal system of government. However, the top needs change from one historical period to another. The predominant feature of perceptions of the Soviet period was the belief that the government cared for the people (*love and belonging*), while the main achievement of the Yeltsin era was freedom. Putin's first two presidential terms were evaluated in terms of the *self-esteem* it fostered, but this measure has declined during his current term. Remarkably, over one-third of the respondents feel a greater need for *safety* in today's Russia than during the troubled Yeltsin era, which cannot be explained on the basis of objective economic or political conditions. However, the events of 2014 showed that respondents' expectations of a crisis were prescient.

5 Each period was assessed through a specific matrix of content parameters. For example, *moral standards* are the main parameter in people's views of an ideal system of power, followed by a *better system of government*. As for the present system, respondents stressed different things. Efficiency factored into assessments for the first time, and monarchy emerged as a new theme.

In conclusion, we can say that the current psychological state of society is characterized by anxiety, weariness of stagnation, demand for change, and expectations of crisis. These feelings create the background for the images of past and present systems of power.

A changing hierarchy of values

Of the three variables we analysed, values underwent the most complex and dramatic changes within the broader psychological transformation of post-Soviet Russia. The core political and moral values that people born in the Soviet Union grew up on were destroyed by the reforms initiated in 1991, and the speed of the change caught ordinary people by surprise. The old social values were swept away, but no new values took their place other than the norms and values of unbridled capitalism, which is more like 'the war of all against all' described by Thomas Hobbes, in which morality has been discarded.

The memoirs and speeches of Mikhail Gorbachev, Yegor Gaidar, Boris Yeltsin and other leading figures in these events clearly show that neither perestroika nor the subsequent post-Soviet reforms under Yeltsin were carefully conceived. It appears that the Russian political elite launched the reforms before even formulating goals and values for themselves or the people. In the late 1980s and the early 1990s, society was reeling. Everything people believed (or pretended to believe) during the Soviet era was destroyed and no new ideals were offered in their place. In the interregnum that followed the collapse of the Soviet Union, not only regimes and leaders, but also values changed

The Soviet system of values, which was dominated by equality, justice, internationalism and collectivism, was already losing ground by the end of the 1980s – a period defined by political cynicism and doublethink. But the dawning of a new political era did not completely erase these values from the public consciousness. People still held on to some of them, such as justice, which Yeltsin invoked to rally public support. But the values of collectivism, equality and internationalism were replaced by the values of individualism and the free market, and the property and social stratification the market entails. The ruling post-Soviet elites officially proclaimed the end of the Soviet system of power and socialist values and the start of democratization, but had no clear conception of where they were taking the country or why. The imitative nature of early democratic reforms was obvious to everyone. The authorities did not fully understand how to use the tools of democracy in order to catch up with Western democracies, and, more importantly, the drive for democratization lacked clear goals, which led to the chaotic adoption of laws and executive orders and to conflicts between different branches of government and between the central and regional governments.

Elites have never been able to clearly explain to the public the new system of 'democratic' values – the product of a chaotic process begun in the early 1990s. The official system of values was poorly articulated and fragmented, which led to dramatic polarization between advocates of liberal Western democracy ('Democrats') and of the Soviet system of values ('Communists') in the 1990s. In fact, the real polarization of values was between statists and anti-statists. Regardless of the exact ideological grounds on which the battle was fought, the polarization of values in the early 1990s led to increasing moral and political relativism with regard to core values.[18] That divide narrowed when Vladimir Putin came to power in 2000. However, the consolidation of society that marked the 2000s was not built on a consensus on values. Rather, support for the president was the only thing that united segments of the population that otherwise had different values. No political force – not from the left, the right or the ruling elite – offered a clear and coherent ideology that could work as a national strategy. This only began to be addressed early in Putin's third term (see the articles he penned during the campaign).

Many surveys show that, starting in the early 1990s, 'the old monolithic and ideology driven system started changing into a pluralistic ideology divided into more than a dozen elementary value positions'.[19] Regular sampling in the 1990s confirmed that the system of political values was differentiated, and revealed growing fragmentation in society's values.[20] Researchers emphasize the generational divides in political values in Russia.[21] This fragmentation of values has begun to decline in the 15 years since 2000, giving way to a trend of consolidation. A growing consensus on values filled the vacuum of the 1990s. Even the subset of political values changed radically in the post-Soviet period in both number and configuration. We focused on eight key values and asked respondents to rank them in order of importance. All of the terms listed in the table below were offered by respondents, though in different combinations. Many of these values form the core of social perceptions of power and democracy. They were frequently mentioned and linked to other descriptors.[22] Our focus was to track how value rankings changed over time (Table 9.12). As the table shows, political values have been in considerable flux in the post-Soviet period. However, the transformation has not been linear. Changes in the past decade were much more pronounced than could be expected based on the preceding periods. Activism underwent the most dramatic change, ascending to the top spot for the very first time in 2010. Meanwhile, human rights have plummeted to the bottom of the ranking.

The 'strong state' value has special significance. In the literature on authoritarianism, this value is often treated as an indicator of authoritarian rule. But our survey results make the picture more complex. As the table below shows, values associated with a strong state occupy a central place in democratic values in Russia, possibly due to Russia's state-centric political culture. The survey conducted in 2013 provided a clear picture of values in society (Table 9.13).[23] It is understandable that the four most important values are safety, discipline, law and order, and peace, just as in the early post-Soviet years, because crime, corruption and instability remain causes for concern today. One of our surveys highlighted an interesting fact: though people's need for safety and stability were seemingly met in the 2000s, safety again became one of the top five needs this year. Human rights, ranked third currently, hasn't held the top spot since 1993, with the exception of a brief period in the 1990s.[24]

The bottom three values are nationalism, collectivism and traditionalism.[25] Surprisingly, over 25% of the respondents defined traditionalism as a negative,

Table 9.12 In my opinion, democracy means . . . (rank in order of importance)

Values	*1993*	*1995*	*1996*	*1997*	*2000*	*2006*	*2010*
Freedom	4	4	3	1	2	2	6
Equality	2	1	8	8	8	8	4
Human rights	5	4	1	3	2	2	8
Individual autonomy	1	2	4	7	6	7	3
Responsibility	3	3	6	3	3	6	5
Respect for law	5	4	5	4	3	3	7
Actively participating in the political process	2	2	7	8	7	5	1
Strong state	3	2	2	5	4	4	2

Table 9.13 Rate the importance of the following values (%)

	Negative	*No value*	*Somewhat important*	*Rather important*	*Very important*	*Rank*
Equality	4.8	15.1	20.8	31.8	27.5	9
Democracy	3.7	17.1	22.3	32.5	24.4	10
Private property	3.5	13.4	20.5	31.7	30.9	7
Nationalism	25.9	27.5	20.3	16.3	10.0	14
Traditionalism	3.8	25.7	26.0	26.0	18.5	12
Stability	1.0	8.7	10.5	28.2	51.6	5
Solidarity	2.8	21.2	26.3	29.0	20.7	11
Tolerance	7.3	20.5	22.9	25.2	24.1	11
Peace	0.7	6.4	5.9	15.5	71.5	2
Discipline	0.7	5.4	5.5	22.7	65.7	1
Freedom	0.6	6.9	8.9	25.5	58.0	4
Law and order	0.5	6.1	6.0	20.3	67.1	2
Patriotism	1.4	10.9	16.7	28.6	42.4	6
Safety	0.4	5.9	5.6	18.3	69.9	1
Justice	0.6	7.7	8.2	21.7	61.7	4
Collectivism	11.5	27.9	24.4	22.2	14.1	13
Individual initiative	1.9	16.1	23.7	33.6	24.8	8
Human rights	0.5	5.8	6.3	21.6	65.9	3

although 10% consider it a very important value and 16.3% a fairly important value. Respondents broadly disapproved of nationalism, but their real views, whether concealed or subconscious, may differ from the opinions they expressed in the survey. Collectivism is associated with the Soviet past and is not an officially approved value. Post-Soviet social policy encouraged extreme individualism rather than collectivism or solidarity. As for traditionalism, respondents see it as an archaic value.

The above data show that Russians still have rather contradictory value systems: liberal respondents prioritize freedom and human rights, as well as safety, justice and law and order, while authoritarian-communitarians recognize private property, human rights and democracy. This divide was especially stark in the 1990s, but there was some convergence of values in the 2000s. The need for discipline and justice dominated in absolutely all prominent social groups that were polled, alternating between first and second place. The government's priorities of building a strong state and market economy have become the only option.[26]

Conclusions

The collapse of the Soviet model and the ensuing transformation of Russian society have had the biggest impact on the spiritual, moral and psychological dimensions of life in Russia. Old value systems have been destroyed, while new ones are still developing. Russian society now lacks more than ever the high-minded values and goals that go beyond the enrichment of some and the impoverishment of others, which can only lead to spiritual lassitude and loss of direction. The psychological crisis in post-Soviet Russia led not only to the lack of high-minded values but also to the dominance of consumerism. We are witnessing *ideological and spiritual differentiation.* Unlike the monolithic Soviet past, we now see a plurality of political, religious and cultural values: conservative, radical, liberal, socialist, pro-Western, patriotic. Attempts to simplify this heterogeneity run up against the very values of pluralism. Therefore, the authorities should respect the diverse views and values of the people.

Political parties have a big role to play given this plurality of values, because they can help consolidate society while also reflecting specific group interests. In this respect, a strategic goal should be *government support for the party system*, where the authorities act as the arbiter of competition between parties and ensure equal opportunities for different political forces. Social harmony is only possible if there is confidence in the rules of political participation. There is a growing shift in the world from a focus on material prosperity to values such as sustainable development, healthy lifestyle, environmental protection, personal development and spiritual improvement. These values are completely in line with traditional priorities in Russian society: service to country, self-denial, solidarity and mutual assistance. A new moral climate cannot be created by executive order. It can only be achieved through upbringing and education. Hence, the government should invest in education, science and culture, and support Russia's main religions, which alone are capable of reviving the most noble of values. In working to attain this goal, the state should rely on one of the more highly ranked values at its disposal – *patriotism*.

As for the goals and values of internal political development, we can say with confidence that democratic values have taken root in Russian society, and the majority of people would reject any attempt to go back. However, Russians are wary of chaos and disorder, and expect the authorities to act more consistently to promote order and justice. The *creation of a strong government* is a vital condition for preserving democratic values and ensuring social stability in Russia. A strong government is above all one whose strength is derived from people's trust and support, as well as general respect for the law and human and civil rights. Russia's trajectory in the past few years and months has shown that certain values, images and perceptions are an organic part of our political and spiritual culture and not simply copied from others. Moreover, they can serve as a solid foundation for greater consolidation in Russian society.

Russia's entire post-Soviet transformation can be divided into three stages. The first stage began in the 1990s, when political perspectives were so unfocused that people could sympathize with one politician, trust another and vote for a third. This period of political astigmatism ended in 2000, and stabilization followed in the wake of Putin's political ascension. In the 2000s, views of the authorities, democracy, power and politics in society began to consolidate. At that time, people from different age groups, regions and professions increasingly held similar views. But that positive trend ended abruptly in 2010, approximately a year before the protest rallies of 2011. The current stage is marked by a return to the fragmentation of perceptions, views and values that characterized the 1990s, although the current situation is considerably milder. There are both nascent positive trends and dangers.

One reason for this psychological change was the appearance of millennials on the political scene. Millennials completed their political socialization during the turbulent 1990s, and so their world outlook was influenced by extreme chaos and instability. Their political views were shaped both by official pro-democracy rhetoric and the discrepancy between rhetoric and reality. The resulting cognitive dissonance encourages this generation to protest. A new generation of 'angry young people' aged 18–25, who are dissatisfied with everything, has unexpectedly emerged. They show some overlap with pre-retirement and retired people, who are dissatisfied with the moral degradation of Russian politics rather than the political model as such.

However, the defining psychological feature of this period is greater demand in Russian society for the traditional moral and political values of leftwing parties, such as social justice. This demand is common to all people regardless of ideology, who hold a dim view of the authorities from the standpoint of justice, honesty and integrity.[27]

Notes

1 See Vladimir Popov and Piotr Dutkiewicz in this volume, Chapter 3, p. 47.

2 Elena Shestopal, 'Vvedeniye v rubriku: Chelovecheskoye izmereniye politiki' ('Introduction to the Human Dimension in Politics'), *Polis*, No. 6, 2013, p. 8.

3 Karl Doitch (Deutsch), 'Osnovnye izmenenia v politologii (1952–1977)' ('Major Changes in Political Science'), *Politicheskiye Otnoshenia: Prognozirovaniye i Planirovaniye.Yezhegodnik* (*Political Relations: Forecasting and Planning Yearbook*) (Moscow, 1979).

4 Vladimir Lapkin and Ivan Semenenko, 'Chelovek politichesky' pered vyzovami "infomodernity" ('Homo Politicus' and the Challenge of "Infomodernity"'), *Polis*, No. 6, 2013, pp. 64–82.

5 Yves *Cohen, Le siècle des chefs: Une histoire transnationale du commandement et de l'autorité (1890–1940)* (Paris: Éditions Amsterdam, 2013), p. 871.

6 Barbara Kellerman, *Iduschie za liderom* (*Followership*) (Moscow: Akvamarinovaya Kniga, 2009).

7 Orit Ichilov, 'To Be or Not to Be: Political Socialization in a Changing world', in Elena Shestopal (ed.), *Citizens and Leaders in a Comparative Perspective: What can Political Psychology Tell Us About Recent Trends and Events in Politics?*, conference proceedings (Moscow: MSU Publisher, 2013), pp. 11–25.

8 Elena Shestopal (ed.), *Politicheskaya sotsializatsiya rossiyskikh grazhdan v period transformatsii* (*Political Socialization of Russians in the Period of Transformation*) (Moscow: Novy Khronograf, 2008).

9 Elena Shestopal, *Obrazy vlasti v postsovetskoi Rossii* (*Images of Power in Post-Soviet Russia*) (Moscow: Aletheia Publishers, 2004); Elena Shestopal, *Obrazy rossiyskoi vlasti: Ot Yeltsina do Putina* (*Images of Power in Russia: From Yeltsin to Putin*) (Moscow: Rosspen, 2008); Elena Shestopal (ed.), *Psikhologiya politicheskogo*

vospriyatiya v sovremennoi Rossii (*The Psychology of Political Perception in Contemporary Russia*) (Moscow: Rosspen, 2012).

10 Survey findings were processed with the use of standard cluster and factor methods of analysis using SPSS. The questionnaire included many open-ended questions, which were processed using the scaling method. The qualitative measurement was mostly used for in-depth interviews and projective tests.

11 Due to the complex psychological structure of images and perceptions mentioned above, in-depth interviews, fixed association methods, projective tests and other refined psychological techniques, rather than standard sociological methods with close-ended questions, were used to reveal deeper levels of perception.

12 Iosif Diskin, 'Rossiyskaya model sotsialnoi transformatsii' ('A Russian Model of Social Transformation'), *Pro et Contra*, No. 3, 1999, p. 34; Nikolai Lapin, 'Kak chuvstvuyut sebya, k chemu stremyatsya grazhdane Rossii' ('What Russians Feel and Want'), *Sotsis*, No. 6, 2003, p. 83; Valery Fyodorov *(ed.), Ot Yeltsina do Putina: Tri epokhi v istoricheskom soznanii rossiyan* (*From Yeltsin to Putin: Three Periods of Russians' Historical Thinking*) (Moscow: VTsIOM, 2007).

13 It should be remembered that the respondents interpret these terms (liberal, socialist etc.) differently from each other, but this is a form of self-identification.

14 The respondents had different aspects of safety in mind, but in recent years the term has come to indicate not so much road safety or freedom from crime, but broader notions such as economic, international, military and other types of security.

15 Materials for this part of the survey were collected, processed and analysed with the assistance of the faculty and post-graduate students of the Chair of Political Sociology and Psychology at the MSU Faculty of Political Science: Svetlana Nesterova, Svetlana Akhmatnurova, Ignat Bogdan, S. Davydov, V. Markov, Ye. Muzyka, Gajibala Ramaldanov, Natalya Smulkina, Anastasia Trushchyova and Angela Cherdantseva.

16 In a 2013 survey, we asked the respondents to answer open-ended questions about the real authorities: 'How would you describe political authority?' (Soviet, under Yeltsin, in Putin's first two terms and current term as president) and an ideal system of political authority ('What kind of government could help the country overcome the crisis?'). As a result, we mostly focused on the real authorities.

17 When analysing the image of power in modern Russia and other periods, we came across a remarkable psychological phenomenon: The image of power during Putin's third term is negative, while his personal image as president and an individual is positive. There is, of course, the old trope about the tsar being good but the boyars being bad, but this is definitely a more complex phenomenon connected with the psychology of the perceivers of power and the nature of power itself. Moreover, we believe that the public images of power reflect rather clearly and correctly the nature of power as a generalized image of state governance.

18 Nikolai Lapin, 'Funktsionalno-orientiruyushchiye klastery bazovykh tsennostei naseleniya Rossii i eyo regionov' ('Functionally Orienting Clusters of Basic Values of the Population of Russia and its Regions'), *Sotsiologicheskiye issledovaniya* (*Sociological Research*), No. 1, 2010, pp. 28–36; Vladimir Magun and Maxim Rudnev, 'Tsennostnyi portret rossiyan na yevropeiskom fone: Rossiya v zerkale yevropeiskogo sotsialnogo issledovaniya' ('Russian Values against a European Backdrop: Russia in the Mirror of European Social Research'), *Demoskop Weekly* (*Demoscope Weekly*), Nos 503–504, 2012, http://demoscope.ru/weekly/2012/0503/tema01.php [Accessed on: 17 June 2015]; Valentin Nemirovsky, 'Tsennostnye i sotsialno-soslovnye prepyatstviya na puti sotsiokulturnoi modernizatsii Rossii i eyo regionov' ('Value, Social and Class Obstacles

to the Sociocultural Modernization of Russia and its Regions'), *Monitoring obshchestvennogo mneniya* (*Public Opinion Monitoring*), No. 4 (116), 2013, pp. 57–71.

19 Nikolai Lapin, 'Modernizatsiya bazovykh tsennostei rossiyan' ('Modernization of Russians' Basic Values'), *Sotsis*, No. 5, 1996, p. 9.

20 Nikolai Lapin, 'Tsennosti kak komponenty sotsiokulturnoi evolyutsii sovremennoi Rossii' ('Values as Components of Sociocultural Evolution in Contemporary Russia'), *Sotsiologicheskiye issledovaniya* (*Sociological Research*), No. 5, 1994; Nikolai Lapin, 'Modernizatsiya bazovykh tsennostei rossiyan' (Modernization of Russians' Basic Values), *Sotsis*, No. 5, 1996; Nikolai Lapin 'Izmeneniye tsennostei i novye sotsiokulturnye struktury' in Tatyana Zaslavskaya (ed.), *Kuda idyot Rossiya: Transformatsiya sotsialnoi sfery i sotsialnaya politika* (*Where is Russia Headed? Changing Values and New Sociocultural Structures*) (Moscow: Delo, 1998); Svetlana Nesterova, 'Nekotorye osobennosti politicheskoi kultury v sovremennoi Rossii (psykhologichesky aspekt) ('Some Features of Political Culture in Contemporary Russia (The Psychological Aspect)'), in Elena Shestopal (ed.) *Grazhdanskaya Kultura v Sovremennoi Rossii* (*Civil Culture in Contemporary Russia*) (Moscow: Moscow Public Science Foundation, 1999).

21 Elena Shestopal, *Psikhologichesky profil rossiyskoi politki 1990-kh. Teoreticheskiye i prikladnye problemy politicheskoi psykhologii* (*A Psychological Profile of Russian Politics in the 1990s. Theoretical and Applied Issues of Political Psychology*) (Moscow: Rosspen, 2000); Ludmila Belyayeva, 'Vozrastnye kogorty v period institutsionalnykh izmeneniy v Rossii' ('Age Cohorts during Institutional Changes in Russia'), in Tatyana Zaslavskaya (ed.), *Kuda idyot Rossiya? Formalnye instituty i realnye praktiki* (*Where is Russia Headed? Formal Institutions and Practice*) (Moscow: Moscow School of Social and Economic Sciences, 2002); Ludmila Belyayeva, 'Sotsialny portret vozrastnykh kogort v postsovetskoi Rossii ('A social portrait of age cohorts in post-Soviet Russia'), Sotsis, No. 10, 2004; Irina Busygina, 'Kakiye tsennosti v tsene?' ('Which Values are in Demand?'), *Polis*, No. 1, 2004; Vera Gavrilyuk and Trikoz, Natalia, 'Dinamika tsennostnykh orientatsiy v period sotsialnoi transformatsii (pokolenny podkhod)' ('Changes in the Value Systems during Social Transformations: A Generational Approach'), *Sotsis*, No. 1, 2002; Vladimir Goryainov, 'Empiricheskiye klassifikatsii zhiznennykh tsennostei rossiyan v postsovetskiy period' ('Empirical Classifications of Russians' Life Values in the Post-Soviet Period'), *Polis*, No. 4, 1996; Lev Gudkov and Boris Dubin, 'Konets 90-kh godov: zatukhaniye obraztsov' ('The Late 1990s: Waning Ideals'), *Monitoring obshchestvennogo mneniya* (*Public Opinion Monitoring*), No. 1, 2001; I.A. Demidov, 'Tsennostnye izmereniya vlasti' ('The Value Dimension of Political Authority'), *Polis*, No. 3, 1996; Vladimir Lapkin and Vladimir Pantin, 'Vospriyatiye zapadnykh institutov i tsennostei v postsovetskom prostranstve: opyt Ukrainy i Rossii' ('The Perception of Western Institutions and Values in the Post-Soviet Space: The Experience of Ukraine and Russia'), *Polis*, No. 1, 2004; Yury Levada, 'Koordinaty cheloveka: K itogam izucheniya "cheloveka sovetskogo"' ('Human Coordinates: Results of a Study of Homo Sovieticus'), *Monitoring obshchestvennogo mneniya* (*Public Opinion Monitoring*), No.1, 2001; Viktoria Semyonova, 'Zhiznenny put' i sotsialnoye samochuvstviye v kogorte 30-letnikh: Ot eiforii k razocharovaniyu' ('The Trajectory of Life and Social Health in the Cohort of 30-year Olds: From Euphoria to Disillusionment'), *Monitoring obshchestvennogo mneniya* (*Public Opinion Monitoring*), No.5, 2002.

22 The table includes a ranking of values. This method offers more information than numerical values alone, because samples collected in different years differed from each other in numerical value.

23 The survey included residents of 42 regions of the Central, Southern, North Caucasus, Siberian and Volga federal districts, including Moscow and the Moscow Region, St. Petersburg and the Leningrad Region, Kursk Region, Belgorod Region, Lipetsk Region, Vladimir Region, Bryansk Region, Ivanovo Region, Stavropol Territory, Krasnoyarsk Territory, Samara Region, Udmurtia, Bashkortostan, Perm Territory, Krasnodar Territory, Volgograd Region, Dagestan, Volgograd Region, Novosibirsk Region and other Russian regions.

24 Elena Shestopal, 'Politicheskaya povestka dnya rossiyskoi vlasti i eyo vospriyatiye grazhdanami' ('The Russian Authorities' Political Agenda and its Perception by the People'), *Polis*, No. 2, 2011, pp. 7–25.

25 Respondents were not prompted with the researchers' interpretation of 'nationalism' and other terms. The respondents used them in the sense in which they are generally used in society, which in Russian differs from the English or French meaning. Unlike patriotism, nationalism is interpreted exclusively negatively, as chauvinism, in Russia.

26 Leonty Byzov, 'Izbiratelny tsikl 2011–2012 cherez prizmu tsennostnykh i ideinykh protivorechiy obshchestva (chast I)' ('The 2011–2012 Election Cycle through the Prism of Value and Ideological Contradictions in Society. Part I'), *Monitoring obshchestvennogo mneniya* (*Public Opinion Monitoring*), No. 2 (114), *2013*.

27 Elena Shestopal, 'Politicheskaya povestka dnya rossiyskoi vlasti i eyo vospriyatiye grazhdanami' ('The Russian Authorities' Political Agenda and its Perception by the People'), *Polis*, No. 2, 2011.

10 Ethnic and religious relations in Russia since the 1980s

Galina Gribanova

As we try to understand the road that our country has gone down over the last three decades, and to figure out which way we are going and what chance we have to preserve its unity and integrity, we cannot avoid considering a range of issues that stem from the cultural diversity that is unique to Russian society. The key factors of Russia's cultural diversity are Russians' varied ethnic and religious backgrounds. It appears that these aspects of self-identification have undergone the most substantive change over the period in question. It was a time of transition from the monolithic (at least in words) 'Soviet people' and belligerent atheism to a heterogeneous society with a range of ethnic and religious groups, each with its own social particularities, protecting the interests of its members, which are not necessarily congruent with the national ones. On the other hand, national interests will be clearly identified later. However, they can only be identified after we adequately assess the influence of ethnic and religious relations on the country's social life. In this chapter we will try to outline our vision of the issue.

National identity and ethnic group dynamics in modern Russia

For the last Soviet census in 1989, respondents were asked to name their *nationality*, as was done throughout the Soviet period. Parents were asked to give their children's nationality. At the same time, Soviet passports also contained the bearer's nationality, which could not be changed at the owner's wish (and therefore had nothing to do with self-identification); it was taken from the person's birth certificate, which contained the nationalities of his or her mother and father, and if those were different, either one could be chosen. In other words, a Soviet citizen's ethnicity was identified on the 'blood principle'. It was only natural that, when asked by census takers, most people cited their 'nationality' as it was indicated in their passports. In this respect, the post-Soviet censuses of 2002 and 2010 were very different, because by then the 'nationality' box had been removed from passports. We will discuss the controversy over that move and its consequences later, but for now we will look at some statistics to see how Russia's ethnic composition changed over time.

The 1989 census showed no significant change compared with the previous one (in 1979), as some 30 major ethnic groups accounted for roughly the same percentage.

However, the situation changed sharply after that. First of all, intensive emigration significantly reduced the number of Germans and Jews. The percentage of Ukrainians and Belarusians decreased due to assimilation, which became especially obvious between 2002 and 2010. At the same time, the share of the non-Slavic population gradually increased due to their high birth rate.

It should be noted that, according to the 2010 census results, the number of Kazakhs, Dargins and Mari exceeded the number of Belarusians, placing Kazakhs among the 10 largest ethnic groups in Russia. The share of peoples of the Caucasus and groups that for our purposes can be referred to as Muslims is gradually increasing. These are dry statistics. Still, it is clear that figures do not cause problems; problems arise from relations established between various ethnic groups. Therefore, it appears necessary to outline and evaluate the ethnic policy of the Soviet government, which certainly influenced the nature of ethnic relations in Russia for the later period as well.

One of the most persistent myths in the study of modern forms of nationalism in the post-Soviet states is the theory that nations, which had been suppressed by the communist regime, awoke when it collapsed and rushed into war and devastation. We, however, agree with Czech historian and political theorist Miroslav Hroch's statement that 'the conventional view that current turmoil is the result of the release of irrational forces that were long suppressed – "deeply frozen" as it were – under communism and now are in full revival after a lapse of fifty years, is

Table 10.1 National composition of Russia, 1979 and 1989 censuses

Ethnic group	*1979* %	*1989* %
Russians	82.6	81.5
Tatars	3.6	3.7
Ukrainians	2.7	3.0
Chuvash	1.2	1.2
Bashkirs	0.9	0.9
Mordovians	0.8	0.7
Belarusians	0.8	0.8
Germans	0.6	0.6
Chechens	0.5	0.6
Jews	0.5	0.4

Sources: *Vsesoyuznaya perepis naseleniya 1979 goda. Natsionalny sostav naseleniya po regionam Rossii, RSFSR* (*1979 Soviet National Census. Ethnic Structure of Russia's Regions. RSFSR*), http://demoscope.ru/weekly/ssp/rus_nac_79.php.

Vsesoyuznaya perepis naseleniya 1989 goda. Natsionalny sostav naseleniya po regionam Rossii. RSFSR (*1989 Soviet National Census. Ethnic Structure of Russia's Regions. RSFSR*), http://demoscope.ru/weekly/ssp/rus_nac_89.php.

Table 10.2 National composition of Russia, 2002 and 2010

Ethnic group	*2002* %	*2010* %
Russians	79.8	80.9
Tatars	3.8	3.9
Ukrainians	2.0	1.4
Bashkirs	1.1	1.2
Chuvash	1.1	1.0
Chechens	0.9	1.0
Armenians	0.8	0.9
Avars	0.6	0.7
Mordovians	0.6	0.5
Belarusians	0.6	0.4

Sources: *Vsesoyuznaya perepis naseleniya 2002 goda* (*2002 National census*), http://www.perepis2002.ru/index.html?id=17.

Federalnaya sluzhba gosudarstvennoi statistiki (Rosstat). Informatsionnye materialy ob okonchatelnykh itogakh Vserossiyskoi perepisi naseleniya 2010 goda (*Federal State Statistics Service (Rosstat). Report on the Final Results of the 2010 Census*), http://www.gks.ru/free_doc/new_site/perepis2010/perepis_itogi1612.htm.

evidently superficial'.[1] This is because the 'level of institutionalization of nationalities was very high in Soviet-type regimes, and nationality became one of the fundamental categories of social stratification'.[2]

Indeed the idea of a nation as a state-forming factor (where 'nation' is defined in terms of ethnicity, not as 'civil nation') was not destroyed, but was moved down to the subnational level, and used as a basis for Russia's territorial division into hierarchically arranged ethnic entities, from Soviet republics to autonomous republics to autonomous regions and areas.[3] Having announced the right of nations to self-determination, the Bolsheviks not only formed administrative territories in accordance with this principle, but also in many cases advanced the formation of large nations. In other words, despite the attempts to create 'a new historical entity: the Soviet people' at the national level, ethnic identification remained, in no small part due to the government's ethnic policy. Moreover, the declared equality of all nations and peoples in reality was often replaced by ethnic discrimination.

Ethnicity is generally defined as a complex blend of mentality and culture, which not only characterizes the people, but unites it and makes it different from other communities. The specificity of ethnicity includes three components: the need for ethnic affiliation, the need for positive ethnic identity and the need for ethnic security. The need for psychological affinity with a group is known in psychology as affiliative motivation. Individuals seek membership in one or more groups for social security, stability and the possibility of engaging in certain activities, to satisfy their need for social, economic and psychological association. It follows that one's ethnic affiliation serves as a means of adaptation, for better orientation and achieving certain social goals in the complex modern world.[4]

All of the longstanding communist dogmas and Soviet public-conscience stereotypes collapsed in the system-wide crisis that plagued the country in the late 1980s, eventually leading to the Soviet Union's disintegration. People began losing their familiar social cues and were forced to revise their values and priorities. This situation often led to confusion for people over their position in the social structure. The identity crisis was aggravated by the fact that the attempts to achieve dominance of class consciousness of the Soviet people had failed. Class-based solidarity had been gradually losing its role as a guideline with the development of Soviet society, and was to a large extent replaced by ethnic self-identification. Therefore, loyalty to one's social class gave way to a different loyalty: to one's nation. In other words, the liberalization of the Soviet political system during perestroika led to the 'politicization of ethnic solidarity', a term coined by Charles Foster.[5]

It needs to be emphasized that an obvious ethnic revival, which began in the Soviet Union in the mid-1980s, while not an ethnic conflict, still had powerful conflict-creating potential. The border that separates ethnic patriotism from nationalism is vague and unstable. A small shift of emphasis often tips us over the edge, where there is a favourable intellectual and cultural environment for emerging conflict. This is what happened in the Soviet Union, leading to ethnic and political conflicts in such places as Nagorny Karabakh and the Osh Valley, which catalysed the collapse of Soviet post-totalitarianism and the country's disintegration.

However, the Soviet Union's disintegration has not resolved ethnic confrontations; in fact, it only generated new ethnic-political conflicts, circumstantially provoked by a number of other factors:

- the economic crisis, which caused frustration among the bulk of the population, forcing people to search for someone to blame ('a scapegoat') for the disastrous situation;
- a sharp weakening of the political regime, which lost control of Russia;
- a tangled historical heritage of ethnic relations in many regions of post-Soviet states;
- an underdeveloped culture of ethnic relations, and a shortage of tolerance and willingness to compromise; and
- activists vying for leadership within political elites and making use of the ethnic factor to achieve dominance.

The last point needs to be emphasized here. Ethnicity, as one of the strongest social characteristics of an individual, has become extremely politicized in the modern world, and unfortunately it has become a widely used instrument of mobilization within society. Therefore, ethnicity becomes less a reflection of real problems in intergroup relations than an instrument of political mobilization.

We must bear in mind that the use of negative bias against other ethnic groups, and declaring that they are to blame for the current economic troubles, sometimes brings a certain amount of psychological comfort to ordinary people having a rough time and suffering from economic uncertainty, in the hope that getting rid of 'those to blame' can improve their social and economic prospects. As a result, political elites are often tempted to shift the responsibility to someone else, and other ethnic groups are the most obvious targets.

This kind of propaganda is usually most effective on young people: those who cannot expect significant improvements to their social or economic status due to being part of the lower social strata or to their lack of the skills or will required for success. When people have nothing to be particularly proud of, they often try to boost their self-esteem based on their ethnic identity. These people are most easily recruited to all sorts of extremist nationalist groups. 'Comrade! You were born in the *great Russian land*! You are lucky because *you are Russian*' is a slogan used by the National Bolshevik Party (NBP), one of the best known radical organizations in modern Russia. This suggests that the very fact of being born Russian makes one above everybody else – a perfect slogan in fact, well-tested on several occasions in human history, and which has led to innumerable disasters – and gives one the right to impose their will on others.

At the first stage, the 'politicization of ethnicity' flourished among the non-Russian ethnic groups in the Russian Federation.[6] In the course of socialization – with self-identification being an integral part of the process – a person develops a dominating feeling of belonging to a specific ethnic group or nation as co-citizenship. In cases where an individual belongs to the titular ethnic group, as a rule the two identities do not come into conflict. However, if one belongs to an ethnic minority, the issue of self-identification becomes extremely sensitive. This is what happened in the 'new' and 'independent' Russia, which had not formed as a civil nation. The general protest against over-centralized government transformed into regional separatism in 'Russian' regions, and swelled into ethnic-political conflict in 'non-Russian' ones, which interpreted the dictatorship of the 'centre' as an attempt to restore the empire and downgrade them to the status of colonies. As a result, nationalist movements emerged as ethnic-regional groups and associations. This tendency became especially prominent in places where an ethnic identity overlapped with a regional one.

Therefore, it was not surprising that the predominantly Muslim regions of Tatarstan and the North Caucasus (primarily Chechnya) and Tyva (where the dominant religion is Buddhism) caused the Russian leadership the most trouble at the turn of the 1980s–1990s. Nationalist sentiments were also characteristic of part of the ethnic-Russian population, which came as a defence reaction to the Soviet Union's collapse, the worst social and economic crisis ever and the loss of their Soviet identity. However, neither of the many new Russian nationalist organizations actually succeeded in rallying any serious electoral support. Yet the activity of these groups – Pamyat, Chernaya Sotnya, Russian National Unity, Narodny Sobor, Eduard Limonov's National Bolshevik Party and many others, as well as the skinhead movement, which had not formed into an actual organization but was nevertheless quite widespread – suggested the potential threat of Russian nationalism becoming quite radical.

On the whole the ethnic-political situation in the 1990s was a combination of several trends and conflict between:

- each ethnic group's striving for self-identification and self-assertion – and intrinsic integration processes in society;
- the growing independence of Russian regions – and the indispensability of strengthening Russia's statehood in the interest of all peoples living in it; and
- the desire for ethnic and cultural distinctiveness – and historical cultural commonality.

Problems were further aggravated by other negative factors, which have led to mounting interethnic tensions and conflicts in some of the Russian regions. Among these factors are:

- significant gaps between various regions' social and economic development levels;
- human rights abuses, especially failure to apply the same standards of social and economic welfare across the board;
- growing unemployment, especially in regions with excessive labour resources;
- underdeveloped legal framework for land relations;
- mutual territorial claims remaining between Russian regions, especially in the North Caucasus;
- weak legal regulation of interethnic relations; and
- the consequences of the Chechen war.

Interethnic tensions peaked:

- directly along the borders with countries where civil or interethnic conflicts broke out;
- where substantial numbers of refugees and forced migrants were concentrated;
- in areas home to ethnic groups split by the new state borders following the Soviet Union's disintegration;
- in regions plagued by unfavourable environmental situations that threatened the respective populations' ecosystems;
- in areas (big cities) with high crime rates and where crime is often ethnically-motivated; and
- in areas home to small native peoples of the North.

Deni Teps, evaluating the ethnic-political situation in the 1990s, wrote that the continuing 'expansion of ethnic conflicts, the national elites' ambitions to redistribute land and gain greater sovereignty, and their vying for power pose a threat to the country's territorial integrity and statehood. The following developments pose a direct threat to ethnic relations: attempts to form ethnic enclaves; the growing socio-economic inequality of various peoples or ethnic groups; growing ethnic migration, such as refugees and forced migrants; and massive abuse of civil rights and freedoms in specific regions of Russia.'[7] Even though ethnic-regional separatism was largely dealt with after Vladimir Putin

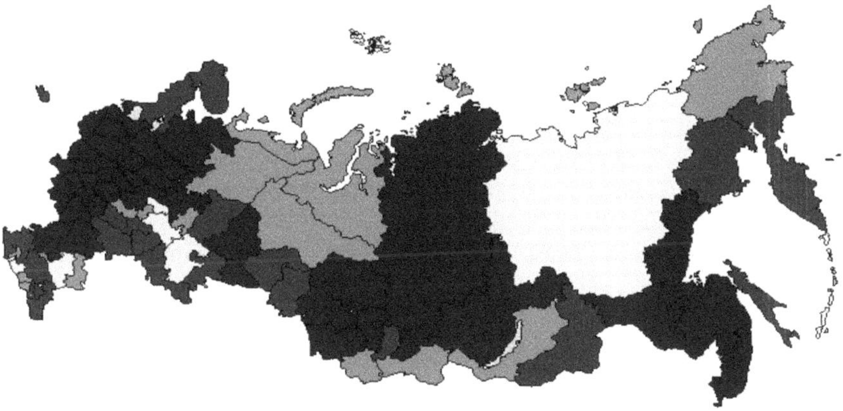

Figure 10.1 Territorial concentration of ethnic groups.

was elected president, it is still too early to say that the ethnic component of modern Russia's life has stabilized. Moreover, a series of alarming trends have been observed over the past few years.

First, I would like to note that various demographic factors have a very different influence on ethnic processes. On the one hand, as the 2010 census results show, ethnic Russians account for 80.9% of the country's population. At the same time, the Russian language has become more widespread compared with prior reports. In 2010, the share of Russian speakers rose to 99.4% from 98.2% during the previous census.[8] In other words, among the world's largest countries, Russia has one of the highest concentrations of ethnic majority members. Yet, according to the final census documents, 'The results of this census have confirmed that Russia is one of the leaders among multi-ethnic countries'. However, the picture of an 'ethnically fragmented' Russia, as portrayed by certain experts, is questionable.

As is known, the United Nations uses a typology of ethnic structures that distinguishes countries according to their levels of ethnic polarization. Countries are therefore classified into four types. First are those in which one ethnicity is overwhelmingly dominant (referred to as unipolar); second, those in which there are only two main groups, or where two roughly equal groups account for over 60% in a multiethnic setting (bipolar); and third, those in which there are only three groups, or three large groups in a multiethnic setting (tripolar). Other countries have multipolar structures. Russia's ethnic structure is unipolar according to this typology, as there is only one predominant group, Russians, and this certainly plays a role in securing ethnic-political stability. On the other hand, the territorial concentration of ethnic groups is on the rise.

Distribution of ethnic Russians across Russia[9]

As we can see, ethnic Russians are concentrated in Russia's territories, regions and autonomous areas, but their numbers are lower in most republics. The largest titular ethnicities of the Russian Federation's constituent republics have grown in numbers and significance in their traditional areas of living, while reducing their presence in most other regions. This trend is unlikely to change soon. Even economic growth (which is nowhere to be seen at this stage), which must lead to greater territorial mobility, is unlikely to cause significant changes in ethnic structures apart from the few seats of growth. So far this trend can only be witnessed in Moscow and St Petersburg.

At the same time, protracted ethnic-territorial concentration can proceed in some regions, unless regulated by the government. State regulation is especially important in cases where this trend results from the outflow of Russians and other ethnic groups from constituent republics, which leads to brain drain and the flight of qualified workforce, as well as the fading influence of the secular multi-ethnic culture as opposed to ethnic and religious extremism. It should be noted, however, that I am referring to mild and mainly economic regulatory measures. However, while this problem has been around for a long time and is not leading to any serious aggravation of the ethnic situation in Russia, there are other, much more sensitive issues.

One of them is persistent ethnic and religious separatism. Whereas the number of armed separatists in Chechnya has been reduced, and the republic (at least its lowlands) has largely stabilized, the neighbouring regions of Dagestan and Ingushetia are witnessing an escalation of violence. Another problem is the very authoritarian policies that have effectively stabilized some of the ethnic republics and Russia as a whole. The leaders of the most risk-prone republics are essentially given carte blanche to carry out any measures, including those that violate civil rights and freedoms guaranteed by the Russian Constitution, in exchange for their loyalty to the federal government. The most vivid example of this is the Chechen Republic and its leader Ramzan Kadyrov.

The third issue is that constituent republics in Russia have long served the self-determination of the titular ethnic group. However, the boundaries of areas populated by these groups are not the same as the administrative borders; only one-third of ethnic groups that lend their name to that of the republic actually live in 'their' republic. In most cases, the 'titular' ethnic group accounts for less than half of the population. This kind of forced ethnization, which naturally affects the distribution of authority, employment and personnel policies, often leads to ethnic or clan-based solidarity and provokes ethnic tensions. Ethnic-based rationalization of a desired form of government is often highly emotional and may sound irrational. However, on a closer look, it is possible to discern the poorly disguised interests of the respective ethnic elites, who seek absolute control over their republics' material resources. They need power as a tool for redistributing property in their own favour. This is the reason why regional elites chose ethnic-based models of legitimizing their power in 'ethnic' republics.

The ongoing debate over how wise it was to eliminate the ethnicity status from internal passports in the 1990s confirms that the ethnic-political situation in Russia is indeed complex and controversial. The move seemed logical from the perspective of building a pan-Russian civil nation, but provoked a negative response, mainly in certain republics where it was seen as an attempt to eliminate their ethnic identity and change the ethnic-based nature of some of the constituent regions. As a result, special inserts were introduced for passports to specify the bearer's ethnicity if they wished. These inserts were introduced in ethnic regions. It would be only fair to add that most Russian chauvinist groups were not happy about the move either, taking it as an encroachment on the pre-eminence of the state-forming ethnic group. The new right to determine their own ethnicity curiously led many people to identify themselves, during the 2002 census, as peoples whose status as separate ethnic groups is disputed, such as the Cossacks, Pomors or Scythians. Some chose to use fantastical races such as hobbit, elf and so on.[10]

Finally, Rosstat on 27 January 2010 issued Order No. 74 approving an alphabetical list of possible responses for the 2010 census (ethnicity came under No. 7 on the form).[11] The extended list was nevertheless limited to 1,840 ethnic groups, including very strange options such as 'Cross Breed', 'Soviet', 'Citizen of the Earth', 'Citizen of the World', 'Foreigner', 'Internationalist', 'Citizen of the Universe', as well as several slang or derogatory terms. It appears, however, that the problem is far greater than the presence or absence of one's official ethnicity status on their passport, and should be considered in the larger context of ethnic tensions. For example, in March 2007, the Moscow legislature considered draft amendments to the federal law on the mass media. The lawmakers wanted to stop the media from mentioning criminals' and their victims' ethnicity in their crime reports. They believed this policy would help uphold ethnic tolerance.[12] However, the initiative was not supported, while the debate about ethnic crime and the way it is covered in the media is continuing.

The Russian question: a real problem or political speculation?

Although a whole range of ethnic-regional issues remain unresolved, it is the so-called Russian question that has moved into the spotlight. It is manifested in a general deterioration of psychological wellbeing among Russians, a weakening of their traditional ethnic tolerance and an increased frequency of xenophobic outbreaks. The problem is that there is a growing danger of these sentiments possibly being used by extreme nationalist groups.[13] The results of surveys are fairly clear on this. Let us look at the dynamics of responses to the idea of *Russia for Russians*.[14]

According to a nationwide study conducted by the Levada Center in October 2013 (after the Biryulyovo 'race riot'),[15] 66% of people supported the Russia for Russians slogan, the biggest share in 11 years. The appeal to stop 'feeding the Caucasus' was popular with 71% of respondents (up from 62% in 2011). More than half of respondents said people from the Caucasus should be allowed only a limited stay in Russia (54%), 45% each supported the same idea with regard to

Table 10.3 Russia for Russians

	1998	*2000*	*2001*	*2002*	*2003*	*2004*	*2005*	*2006*	*2007*	*2008*	*2009*	*2009*	*2010*	*2011*	*2012*
Strongly support, high time we adopt it	13	15	16	16	21	16	16	15	14	15	19	18	19	15	19
Probably a good idea, but within reasonable limits	30	34	42	38	32	37	37	35	41	42	35	36	35	43	40
Strongly against, it's Nazism	30	27	20	26	18	25	23	26	27	25	27	32	21	24	23
No opinion	14	12	11	9	7	12	12	12	11	12	11	9	16	13	11
Difficult to answer	7	6	5	3	8	4	5	4	7	7	8	5	9	5	7

Chinese and Central Asian nationals, and 32% each with regard to Vietnamese nationals and Gypsies. The negative sentiment about Central Asian immigrants showed the most dramatic growth of 50% in three or four years. This kind of sentiment stems directly from migration, which not only brings together people from different ethnic groups, but also leads to contact between people representing significantly different cultures and values. Two important points have to be emphasized here.

First, ordinary Russians rarely bother to note the difference between migrants from the North Caucasus, who are legitimate Russian citizens, and nationals of other countries. In other words, it is not a matter of co-citizenship, but rather of cultural compatibility. Overall, the North Caucasus is seen as a source of danger, terrorism, ethnic crime and corruption. The key problem of modern Russian identity, VTsIOM head Valery Fyodorov suggest, is the clear demarcation line that separates residents of big Russian cities and central Russia in general from people from the North Caucasus Federal District.[16] 'If we manage to harmonize the relations and accept that residents of the Caucasus are as much Russian citizens as we are, and therefore enjoy the same rights and opportunities, and if at least some of these people begin to behave in big cities in a way that is acceptable for a big city, maybe both sides will try to meet each other halfway and we will realize that it is more important to be a good person than a member of a certain ethnic group.' At this stage, however, almost 50% of Russians see Ukrainians and Belarusians living in Russia as 'Russian', while only 7% would say the same about Chechens or Dagestanis, he said, citing the survey *Modern Russian Identity: Measurements and Challenges*.

Second, significant changes have occurred in Russians' perception of immigrants from other post-Soviet states. In the 1990s, few Russians saw them as 'aliens', because their ideas about the Soviet people as a 'new multiethnic entity' were still fresh. At this point, however, we can witness more and more often a clear delineation between locals and immigrants, between 'us' and 'them' in the public consciousness. Not least of all, this change has to do with the different 'quality' of modern immigrants, their lower levels of education and professional qualifications. They mostly come from villages and small towns back home. Most of them are closer to the poorer end of the social spectrum. These new immigrants are less fluent in Russian, not only because of a lack of education, but also because of a generational shift. While in the 1990s, the bulk of these people were still graduates of Soviet schools, where Russian was mandatory and therefore a major part of the curriculum, today we have to deal with the products of new national education systems from countries whose political elite are focused on building statehood based on the titular nation, using nationalism as a powerful tool of ethnic mobilization and deliberately ousting the Russian language from education, science and culture. As a result, surveys say that around 15–20% of immigrants working in Russia communicate in their native language, which significantly complicates their integration. Only about 50% of labour migrants are able to fill out official forms without assistance.[17]

It is these qualitative changes in the structure of immigration that we believe have actually influenced the Russians' attitude toward immigrants. This is partly confirmed by the results of the surveys the VTsIOM national pollster presented in August 2013.[18] Most Russians mainly point to the negative consequences of massive immigration from the post-Soviet states: above all, growing crime and corruption rates (65% of respondents said immigration exacerbates these problems) and higher competition on the employment market (56%). At the same time, 47% said immigrants actually compensate for the shortage of a low-skilled and low-pay workforce. A relative majority of respondents do not believe immigration can help resolve the country's demographic problems (53%, up from 46% in 2005) and enrich its culture (45%). And the influence on the economy is more often seen as negative (40%).

At the same time, most Russians support the ideas of repatriating ethnic Russians and Russian-speakers while limiting entrance for representatives of other ethnic groups (58%, down from 69% in 2005), and attracting young and educated immigrants while restricting the inflow of immigrants who are uneducated or unable to work (53%). Overall in 2008–2013, a highly negative trend was revealed in inter-ethnic relations in Russia, as reflected in the respective VTsIOM surveys.[19]

Thus the conclusion can be drawn that the government's recent attempts to wrest the initiative from nationalists who accuse internal and external enemies of genocide of Russians have not been particularly successful. However, the previously predominant trend in Russia's public sentiment began changing after the Ukrainian crisis, which showed that ethnic conflicts are a threat not only to stability but also to the existence of the state. This change was evidenced by more VTsIOM surveys in April to May 2014.[20]

It appears, in these conditions, that the future of ethnic relations in Russia will depend on the progress the regime and civil society institutions will be able to make in the following areas:

- Shaping an ideology for the prevalence of individual rights over those of any superpersonal social structures, and for the prevalence of the rights of civil society over those of the state.
- Further development of a new element in public consciousness, which would combine a Russian civil mentality with a national-ethnic mentality; a unity of patriotism and internationalism, free from social-class content and filled with the ideals and values of civil society.

Table 10.4 Dynamics of interethnic relations

How would you say interethnic relations have changed over the last year (close-ended question, one answer)

	2006	*2008*	*2010*	*2011*	*2013*
Became more tense, less tolerant	36	24	32	39	49
Remained as before	40	40	44	40	39
Became more tolerant	17	27	16	11	9
Difficult to answer	7	9	8	10	3

Table 10.5 What Russia should be like

There is a variety of views of what Russia should be like. Please pick the statement below that you most strongly agree with. (closed question, choose one answer)

	2003	*2004*	*2005*	*2006*	*2009*	*2011*	*July 2013*	*Nov 2013*	*Apr–May 2014*
Russia is a common home for many peoples. All ethnic groups living in Russia should enjoy equal rights, and none of them should have any advantages over the others	49	49	53	61	44	46	44	37	57
Russia is a multiethnic country, but Russians, as the majority, should have more rights than others	31	34	27	26	38	39	37	38	26
Russia should be a country for ethnic Russians	17	11	16	9	14	10	18	23	10
Russia is a multiethnic country, but ethnic minorities need to be supported, and more rights should be given to them*	–	–	–	–	–	–	–	–	6
Difficult to answer	4	6	4	4	4	5	1	3	1

** this option was not offered before 2014*

- Development and expansion of the territorial foundations for federalism combined with the development of a system of national-cultural autonomies as a means of ethnic-minorities' self-determination in a multi-ethnic country, a way for them to identify and express their original traditions, to preserve their language, education and culture. According to Valery Tishkov, the director of the Russian Academy of Sciences' Institute of Ethnography, 'national cultural-autonomy is the most important format of self-determination for the peoples living in Russia, and should be combined with national-state structures rather than replace them.'[21]
- Reaching accord on the foundation for Russia's ethnic policy through recognition of the priority need to build a 'Russian' civil nation and develop a unifying sentiment, which Jurgen Habermas termed *constitutional patriotism.*[22]

Further development of ethnic relations in Russia will also largely depend on the extent to which we will achieve harmony between various religious groups, especially those that are considered 'traditional' for Russia. Therefore, it should be noted that Russia embarked on a 'religious renaissance' alongside its ethnic one in the mid-1980s. Although mainly parallel, the two trends at times were in opposition, and at other times overlapped with each other.

The religious factor in Russians' lives: religion, church, culture

The most obvious sign of the Soviet leadership's departure from official atheism was the 1988 celebration of the millennium of Christianity in Russia, the first time the Russian Orthodox Church, along with other faiths, was granted relative liberty in Russia since 1917. It was also the first recognition of the influence of Orthodox Christianity on Russian culture and history. As Leonid Parfyonov noted in his commentary on the initial phase of the Nagorny Karabakh conflict, 'we had only just been told that we were Orthodox Christians'.[23] People's interest in churchgoing began growing amid utter disappointment in the political, social, economic, cultural and ideological institutions of the Soviet era, so the Church began to be seen as the only institution that had not lost the confidence of the people. Head of the Levada Center Lev Gudkov noted that the church was destined to 'become the custodian of good, of morality and conscience after the Soviet ideology was forgotten, in a situation where society was demoralized and in need of a moral authority'.[24]

As a result, the number of people who think of themselves as religious has been on the rise since the second half of 1980s. At the same time, it does not seem possible to cite any specific figures as Russia has no official statistics on membership in religious organizations, because Russian laws do not allow asking people to report their religion. Therefore, the number of believers and their religious self-identification can only be evaluated through surveys. The results are rather confusing. For example, representatives of the Russian Orthodox Church claimed in a 2007 survey they have some 120 million followers in Russia, while local Islamic leaders said there were 13 to 49 million Muslims in Russia. Given that the total population was estimated at 144 million that year, it seems one of the churches, at least, overstated its popularity.[25]

A November 2012 Levada Center survey[26] suggested that 77% of Russians thought of themselves as religious. Of them, 68% identified themselves as Orthodox Christians, their number growing by 12 percentage points over a decade (from 56% of respondents in 2002). As before, Islam appeared to be Russia's second most popular religion, with 7% of respondents identifying themselves as Muslim, or twice as many as at the turn of the century (4% in 2002). Western Christian churches – Catholic and Protestant – appeared to have 1% of followers each, and Judaism had 1% too. At the same time, 19% of respondents claimed to be atheists, down from 32% in 2002.

On the other hand, it would probably be wrong to describe Russians as deeply religious, as many tend to see Christianity (or Islam, for that matter) as more of an ethnic and cultural factor than a purely religious one. While the number of people identifying themselves with a certain religious group has certainly grown, the number of active believers remains rather small. Only 14% of respondents admitted going to church at least once a month. In fact, religious enthusiasm has somewhat faded over the past few years, down from 20% of fairly active churchgoers in 2007. Most believers attend church once a year (16%) or a few times a year (17%). Another 13% said they attend a church service once every few years, while 35% never go to church. Still fewer people actually take part in religious rites: 62% of Orthodox Christians and Catholics never take the sacrament, while 22% do so once a year or less, and 14% do so more often. This 'puts the number of Russians who actually *are* religious, rather than simply identifying themselves with a certain church based on their cultural identity without really going to church, at 14%', said Alexei Grazhdankin, deputy head of the Levada Center. 'The concept of spiritual and religious identity is far broader than having stable and specific religious beliefs. Even this number may be overstated: no more than 5–6% of people out there actually participate in the life of their religious community, maintain regular contact with other believers and are guided in their actions by religious rules.'

There are several explanations for this,[27] which can be generalized into two prevailing viewpoints. The first attributes this kind of attitude towards religion to several decades of official atheism imposed by the regime, and suggests that the number of committed churchgoers should grow as the influence of the past fades and the church enjoys greater government support. But this is not happening. The statistics on the newly introduced introductory courses in Religious Cultures and Secular Ethics in schools are very indicative in this respect. According to Education Ministry data of 1 September 2012, the parents of fourth-graders across Russia chose the following options for their children for the 2012–2013 school year:

- Secular Ethics – 42.7%
- Orthodox Christian Culture – 31.7%
- Global religious Cultures – 21.2%
- Islamic Culture – 4%
- Buddhist Culture – 0.4%
- Judaist Culture – 0.1%

In Moscow, 47.4% of parents chose Secular Ethics, while 27.7% preferred Global Religious Cultures; in St. Petersburg and Bashkortostan, the distribution is even more telling: in St. Petersburg, 52.6% and 37.7%, and in Bashkortostan, 67% and 25%, respectively.[28] In other words, an overwhelming majority of Russians want their children to study culture rather than religion.

In my opinion, this actually supports the second viewpoint, which suggests this situation is normal for secular society in the early twenty-first century, where the majority of people identifying themselves as Orthodox Christians, Muslims and so on do so in terms of cultural, ethnic or linguistic identification. They hardy have

Table 10.6 Relations between state/society and the church

How do you see the ideal relationship between the state/society and church?(closed question, choose one answer)	*2009*	*2012*	*2013*
The Church should address issues of religion and faith without interfering in the life of society or the state	27	31	30
The Church should influence the moral and spiritual life of society but should not interfere in politics or government	43	44	50
The Church should be actively involved in discussing and addressing all problems of modern society and the state	16	17	15
Difficult to answer	14	7	5

any need for any religious life or active involvement in their religious communities. This suggests that the cultural component of Orthodox Christianity is what attracts people, rather than the purely religious one. As many as 42% of atheists who do not believe in the Resurrection also celebrate Easter, making Easter cakes, painting eggs and so on.[29] How Russians see the relationship between the church and the state also, in our opinion, confirms this latter point. The majority of Russians believe that the church should influence the moral life of society without interfering in politics or government in any way. This idea is adopted by more people every year.

This suggests that only 15% of Russians want the church to be actively involved in discussing and addressing all problems of modern society and the state.[30] Lev Gudkov also cited Levada Center data to suggest a certain recent decline in people's attitude toward the church due to its political activity and various scandals involving priests. At the same time, most Russians distinguish between Christianity and the Church, believing that criticizing the Patriarch does not mean criticizing the Russian Orthodox Church as an institution.[31]

Conclusion

An analysis of trends in ethnic and religious relations in Russia since the mid-1980s and how they have influenced Russians' social life has enabled us to draw the following conclusions. First, we can see that the collapse of communist ideas in Russia – just as in the other post-Soviet states – created a vacuum, which was quickly filled by various forms of nationalism or chauvinism based (or not) on one of the religions. Even if this vacuum was expected to be taken up by democracy and liberal ideas and civil society values, this never actually happened. The reason behind this is probably that religion and nationalism involved the sort of collective emotional drive that attracts people's hearts and souls. It seems the democratic idea did not fulfil this role well enough. Most people tend to take democracy for granted, as a condition for normal life; in other words, this sentiment is dominated by reason, not emotion. Furthermore, the very idea of democracy immediately became linked in people's minds with economic and social shock reforms, which drove down most people's living standards. In addition, many so-called democratic politicians largely discredited the idea with their behaviour. At the same time it should be stressed that the possibility of building a social life along democratic lines depends not only on economic and political factors but also on the emotional forces dominating society. In this sense, the various types of nationalism that emerged and began conflicting in all post-communist states pose a serious threat to democracy and the development of civil society.

Second, contemporary Russian statehood has never been properly defined. Is the country a nation state or an empire? If it is a nation state, which nation is it based on: an ethnic nation or a civil nation? Is it a secular state or is Orthodox Christianity the official religion? This uncertainty leaves people disoriented and leads to what is described as 'schizophrenia' of the Russian public consciousness, something that, according to Gudkov, reliably reflects the stance of the liberal part of Russia's political spectrum.[32]

Third, the image of Russia as a fortress surrounded by enemies that many Russians developed under the influence of the Ukrainian events from late 2013 can be used to consolidate society, to overcome its ethnic and religious disunity, given a balanced and flexible government policy. However, this path has many pitfalls, such as a potential sliding into radical nationalism, which could lead to self-isolation from the rest of the world, on the one hand (which, in a global world, means stagnation in all areas of life), and to a temptation to explain all Russia's problems by malicious schemes of its external and internal enemies, on the other. Totalitarian trends could also escalate, which, in turn, may lead to further shrinking of the field of public policy and, ultimately, to a possible escalation of violence against individuals or social groups, including ethnic and religious communities.

Notes

1 Miroslav Hroch, 'From National Movement to the Fully-Formed Nation: The Nation-Building Process in Europe', in Gopal Balakrishnan (ed.), *Mapping the Nation* (New York and London: Verso, 1996), p. 89.

2 Sergei Glebov, 'Chitaya R. Brubeikera' ('Reading Rogers Brubaker'), *Ab Imperio*, No. 1, 2000, p. 148.

3 For more information see Ramazan Abdulatipov, *Rossiyskaya natsia: Etnonatsionalnaya i grazhdanskaya identichnost rossiyan v sovremennykh usloviyakh (Russian Nation. Russians' Ethnic and Civil Identity in the Modern World)* (Moscow: Nauchnaya Kniga, 2005); Veljko Vujacic and Victor Zaslavsky, 'SSSR i Yugoslaviya: prichiny raspada' ('The Causes of Disintegration in the USSR and Yugoslavia'), *Etnograficheskoye Obozreniye* (*Ethnographic Review*), No. 1, 1993, pp. 37–56; Grigory Sevastyanov (ed.), 'Tragediya velikoi derzhavy: Natsionalny vopros i raspad Sovetskogo Soyuza' ('The Tragedy of a Great Power: Ethnic Issues and the Soviet Union's Disintegration') (Moscow: Mysl, 2005); Valery Tishkov, *Etnologiya i politika* (*Ethnology and Politics*) (Moscow: Nauka, 2001).

4 Valentina Levkovich and Irina Andrushchak, 'Etnotsentrizm kak sotsialno-psikholo gicheskiy fenomen' ('Ethnocentrism as a Socio-Psychological Phenomenon'), *Dinamika*

sotsialno-psikhologicheskikh yavleny v izmenyayushchemsya obshchestve (*Dynamics of Socio-Psychological Phenomena in Changing Society*) (Moscow: Institute of Psychology, Russian Academy of Sciences, 1996).

5 Charles R. Foster, 'Political Culture and Regional Ethnic Minorities', *The Journal of Politics*, Vol. 44, No. 2, May, 1982, pp. 560–568.

6 For more information, see Leokadia Drobizheva, Airat Aklayev, Viktoria Koroteyeva and Galina Soldatova (eds), *Demokratizatsia i obrazy natsionalizma v Rossiyskoi Federatsii 90-kh godov* (*Democratization and Images of Nationalism in the Russian Federation in the 1990s*) (Moscow: Mysl, 1996); Emil Pain, *Etnopolitichesky mayatnik: Dinamika i mekhanizmy etnopoliticheskikh protsessov v postsovetskoi Rossii (The Ethno-Political Pendulum: The Dynamics of the Relationship Between Ethnic Minorities and Majorities in Post-Soviet Russia*) (Moscow: Institute of Anthropology and Ethnography, Russian Academy of Sciences, 2004); Vasily Filippov, 'Reformirovanie rossiyskoi gosudarstvennosti: politizatsia etnichnosti ili deetnizatsia politiki?' ('Reforming Russian Statehood: Politicized Ethnicity or De-Ethnicized Politics?'), 2002, http://www.kazanfed.ru/publications/kazanfederalist/n1/stat3/; Valery Tishkov (ed.), *Etnichnost i vlast v polietnichnykh gosudarstvakh (Ethnicity and Power in Multiethnic States*), Notes of International Conference, 25–27 January 1993, (Moscow: Nauka, 1994).

7 Deni Teps, *Kontseptualnye osnovy federalizma* (*Conceptual Basis for Federalism*) (Moscow: Yuridichesky Tsentr Press, 2002), p. 115.

8 Federalnaya sluzhba gosudarstvennoi statistiki (Rosstat) (Federal State Statistics Service), *Informatsionnye materialy ob okonchatelnykh itogakh Vserossiyskoi perepisi naseleniya 2010 goda (Report on the Final Results of the 2010 Census*), http://www.gks.ru/free_doc/new_site/perepis2010/perepis_itogi1612.htm. [Accessed on: 17 June 2015].

9 'Russkoye Naselenie v Rossii' ('Distribution of Ethnic Russians in Russia'), http://www.skyscrapercity.com/showthread.php?t=211076&page=284. [Accessed on: 17 June 2015].

10 'Perepis vyavila v Rossii khobbitov, elfov i skifov' ('Population Census: Russia has Hobbits, Elves and Scythians'), available at http://riw.ru/russia4165.html. [Accessed on: 17 June 2015].

11 'Alfavitny perechen vozmozhnykh variantov otvetov naselenia dlya kodirovania otvetov na voprosy razdela 9 perepisnogo lista formy L Vserossiyskoi perepisi naseleniya 2010 goda' ('Alphabetical List of Possible Responses for Coding Section 9 on the Ballot To Be Used for the 2010 Census'), http://www.gks.ru/free_doc/new_site/perepis2010/croc/perepis_itogi1612.htm. [Accessed on: 17 June 2015].

12 '"Pyataya grafa" pod zapretom' ('"Point Five" Cancelled'), *Vzglyad*, 7 March 2007, http://www.vz.ru/politics/2007/3/7/71406.html. [Accessed on: 17 June 2015].

13 See, for example, Alexei Chelnokov and Konstantin Poltoranin, Etnicheskaya katastrofa: Rossiya bez Russkikh? (Ethnic Catastrophe: Russia Without Russians) (Moscow: Yauza, 2014).

14 'Kak vy otnosites k idee Rossiya dlya Russkikh?' ('What is Your Attitude Toward the "Russia for Russians" idea?'), http://www.levada.ru/archive/mezhetnicheskie-otnosheniya/kak-vy-otnosites-k-idee-rossiya-dlya-russkikh. [Accessed on: 17 June 2015].

15 'Interviu na porokhovoi bochke' ('Interview While Seated on a Powder Keg'), 2 December 2013, http://www.levada.ru/02-12-2013/intervyu-na-porokhovoi-bochke. [Accessed on: 17 June 2015].

16 'VTsIOM nazval glavnuyu problemu sovremennoi rossiyskoi identichnosti' ('VTsIOM Names the Main Problem of Modern Russian Identity'), 12 September 2013, http://wciom.ru/index.php?id=266&uid=114472. [Accessed on: 17 June 2015].

17 Yelena Tyuryukanova, 'Diskussiya o tom, nuzhny li inostrannye rabotniki, zakonchena' ('The Discussion of Whether Russia Needs Foreign Workers Is Over'), *Nezavisimaya Gazeta*, 23 November 2010, http://www.ng.ru/scenario/2010-11-23/13_migraciya.html. [Accessed on: 17 June 2015].

18 'Immigratsiya v Rossiyu: blago ili vred dlya strany? ('Immigration into Russia: Good Thing or Bad Thing?'), Press release No. 2360, http://wciom.ru/index.php?id=459&uid=114322. [Accessed on: 17 June 2015].

19 'Mezhnatsionalnye otnosheniya v Rossii: monitoring' ('Ethnic Relations in Russia: Monitoring'), weekly survey by Omnibus VTsIOM, http://wciom.ru/index.php?id=459&uid=114690. [Accessed on: 17 June 2015].

20 'Sobytiya na Ukraine i 'Russkaya vesna' usilili negativnoye otnosheniye bolshinstva Rossiyan k lyubyn vidam natsionalizma' ('Ukrainian Developments and "Russian Spring" Intensify Many of Russia's Negative Perception of any Kinds of Nationalism'), weekly survey by Omnibus VTsIOM, http://wciom.ru/index.php?id=459&uid=114874. [Accessed on: 17 June 2015].

21 Valery Tishkov, *Stanovleniye novoi rossiyskoi gosudarstvennosti: realnost i perspektivy* (*Development of Russian Statehood: Reality and Prospects*), (Moscow: Strategy Humanitarian and Policy Center (Strategia), URSS Publishers, 1996), p. 79.

22 For more information, see Galina Gribanova and Anatoly Sidorenko, *Federalism i dostizheniye etnopoliticheskogo konsensusa v transformiruyushchikhsya obshhestvakh* (*Federalism and Reaching Ethnopolitical Consensus in a Transforming Society*) (Syktyvkar: KRAGSiU, 2008), pp. 117–136.

23 Leonid Parfyonov, *Namedni. Nasha era: 1980–1990 gody* (*Our Era: 1980–1990*) (Moscow: Kolibri, 2010), p. 210.

24 'S tochki zreniya ratsionalnogo cheloveka, eto shezofreniya' ('This is Schizophrenia, from a Rational Point of View'), 29 November 2013, http://www.levada.ru/29-11-2013/s-tochki-zreniya-ratsionalnogo-cheloveka-eto-shizofreniya. [Accessed on: 17 June 2015].

25 'Religiya v tsifrakh i faktakh' ('Religion in Figures and Facts'), Statistika.ru, 5 December 2007, http://statistika.ru/naselen/2007/12/05/naselen_9686.html. [Accessed on: 17 June 2015].

26 'Rossiyane schitayut sebya veruyushchimi, no v tserkov ne khodyat' ('Russians Think of Themselves as Believers, Only Don't Go to Church'), 14 December 2013, http://www.levada.ru/24-12-2013/rossiyane-schitayut-sebya-veruyushchimi-no-v-tserkov-ne-khodyat. [Accessed on: 17 June 2015].

27 See, for example, Michael Bourdeaux (ed.), *Sovremennaya religioznaya zhizn Rossii: Opyt sistematicheskogo opisaniya (Religious Life in Russia Today: a Systematic Study*), Vols. I–III, Moscow: Logos; 2004–2005); Sergei Firsov, *Na vesakh very: Ot kommunisticheskoi religii k novym "svyatym" postkommunisticheskoi Rossii* (*On the Scale of Faith: From the Communist Religion to New "Saints" of Post-Communist Russia*) (St. Petersburg: Vita Nova, 2012); Anatoly Krasikov and Roman Lunkin, *Religiya i grazhdanskoye obshchestvo v Rossii. Preodoleniye stereotipov i sotsialnoye sluzhenie* (*Religion and Civil Society in Russia: Overcoming Stereotypes and Serving Society*) (Moscow: Yurisprudentsiya, 2012); Sergei Filatov, *Religiya i obshchestvo: Ocherki religioznoi zhizni sovremennoi Rossii* (*Sketches of Modern Religious Life in Russia*) (Moscow: Sad, 2002); Konstantin Yerofeyev and Yury Ryzhov, *Religiya i obshchestvo v sovremennoi Rossii: sotsiokulturnye i pravovye aspekty (Religion and Society in Modern Russia: Sociocultural and Legal Aspects*) (Moscow: Drevo Zhizni, 2009).

28 'Nichego krome tsifr' ('Nothing but Figures'), http://www.echo.msk.ru/blog/aav/930092-echo/ [Accessed on: 17 June 2015]; 'V Bashkirii 67% roditelei predpochli,

chtoby deti izuchali osnovy svetskoi etiki' ('Over 67% of Parents in Bashkortostan Want Their Children to Study Secular Ethics Rather Than Religion'), http://www.bashinform.ru/news/487475-v-bashkirii-bolee-67-roditeley-predpochli-chtoby-deti-izuchali-osnovy-svetskoy-etiki/. [Accessed on: 17 June 2015].

29 'Pochti polovina ateistov budet prazdnovat paskhu' ('Almost Half of Russian Atheists Going to Celebrate Easter'), 6 May 2013, http://wciom.ru/index.php?id=269&uid=114039. [Accessed on: 17 June 2015].

30 'Pravoslaviye v Rossii: proshloye i nastoyashcheye' ('Orthodox Christianity in Russia: Past and Present'), Press Release No. 2451 of 12 November 2013, http://wciom.ru/index.php?id=459&uid=114598. [Accessed on: 17 June 2015].

31 'Rossiyane otdelyayut patriarkha ot tserkvi'('Russians Distinguish Between Patriarch and Church'), 3 February 2014, http://www.levada.ru/03-02-2014/rossiyane-otdelyayut-patriarkha-ot-tserkvi.

32 'S tochki zreniya ratsionalnogo cheloveka, eto shezofreniya' ('This is Schizophrenia, from a Rational Point of View'), 29 November 2013, http://www.levada.ru/29-11-2013/s-tochki-zreniya-ratsionalnogo-cheloveka-eto-shizofreniya. [Accessed on: 17 June 2015].

11 Post-Soviet society and elites in the Russian regions

Natalya Zubarevich

Over two decades have passed since the dissolution of the Soviet Union, during which period Russia's regions have gone through major and heterogeneous economic and social transformations that had a serious influence on the regional elites and ordinary people from various social groups. Three of these transformations had the greatest impact: (1) growing territorial inequality in terms of economic development and household income (on the national and regional level); (2) increased differences between territories in terms of values and lifestyle: deterioration on the periphery (rural areas, small cities) and accelerated modernization of major cities in the 2000s; and (3) the emergence of a new, more complex social stratification of Russian society compared to the Soviet period.[1]

Four social strata clearly stand out. First, a small stratum of extremely wealthy people concentrated in the country's largest cities. Second, social groups pertaining to the middle class by such factors as income, social and professional status and identification. According to research by the Independent Institute for Social Policy (IISP), these groups account for almost 20% of the population. This proportion varies not from region to region, but depending on the size of the community. In Moscow, the middle class accounts for 40% of the population. In other major cities, this group comprises up to 30%. It accounts for 20% in smaller cities and up to 11% in rural areas.[2] The structure of the middle class is constantly evolving: in early 2000s it was dominated by entrepreneurs and highly skilled professionals, but by 2011 public sector employees (working for government bodies and law enforcement agencies) and their families constituted almost half of this group.[3] Third is the largest group (up to 60% of the population, according to IISP estimates) and the most amorphous between the lower social stratum and the middle class, with 10% of this group potentially aspiring to join the middle class and 15–20% poised to head down the social ladder into the lower stratum. Finally, the lower stratum is represented by the poor (up to 20% of the population), more widely represented on the periphery.

Transformations typically start with the centre and trickle down to the periphery (from major cities to medium-sized cities and further down to small cities and rural areas). The scale and speed of change were to a large extent influenced by regional specifics. What do they consist of? Some factors underpinning the development of Russian regions and cities are rooted in their past (what is called 'path dependence' in the theory of institutions) or the 'track effect'.[4] In this sense, what matters is the history of a region or a city, its key economic activities inherited from the Soviet past, varying characteristics in terms of demographics, occupational mix, education level, specifics of cultural and ethnical backgrounds, and so on. The path dependence phenomenon can be schematized by a vector scheme proposed by Andrei Treyvish.[5]

The centre-periphery divide is the central differentiating factor for Russia, especially when it comes to intraregional differentiation (major regional centre vs. peripheral rural areas and small cities). However, the same is not true when comparing regions, as the geographical factor does not apply. In fact, it is not true that regions tend to become increasingly peripheral the further you travel from Moscow. Federal centres, chiefly Moscow, are at the centre, and the periphery is represented by the least developed Russian republics and economically depressed regions regardless of their distance from the capital. Most of the Russian regions fall into the semi-peripheral category, which covers the whole country from Kaliningrad to Vladivostok.

The North–South divide highlights the differences between mostly industrialized and agricultural regions, and therefore reflects diverging income levels, lifestyles and strategies to adapt to post-Soviet transformations. *The East–West* divide is about the differences between the developed regions in European Russia, dominated by processing industries, and less developed regions of Siberia and the Far East where extraction industries prevail, the population density is low, cities are few, infrastructure scarce and living conditions are harsh. In addition, regions in the East of Russia have a more pronounced macro-regional identity (Siberians, Far East residents and Urals residents have also a strong regional identity) and are more independent from the state (the frontier effect).[6]

The divide between *regions dominated by ethnic Russians* and *republics with a different ethnic structure* is also an important factor, although it mostly affects values, lifestyles and modernization potential and the emergence of local elites rather than the level of economic development, since there are both developed and underdeveloped regions of that kind. All poorly developed regions are still run by clans, which are based on family ties, ethnic affiliation or the place of origin (bringing together people from one village or district). Clans are important in other Russian regions as well, but they are not usually structured along family or ethnicity lines.

Of course, the proposed scheme can hardly reflect the actual diversity. Many Russian regions are in a transitional position with respect to all of the abovementioned factors, and their combination produces an even more complex and blurry picture. It is for that reason that a commonly accepted classification of Russian regions in terms of social and economic development has yet to be developed. Furthermore, Russian regional studies and social geography have yet to come up with a method for analysing transformations in the post-Soviet period that would schematize and integrate huge amounts of data and various trends. In this research, we will focus on *two groups of actors*: regional elites and local residents, which will be analysed in terms of their transformation in the post-Soviet period.

Since the *elites* wield political and economic resources, the analysis examines the issues in the following order:

- political transformations in the relations between the centre and the regions during the post-Soviet period, which have influenced regional elites;
- level and dynamics of regional economic development affecting resources controlled by the elite;
- control over budget resource allocation as the main governance tool for the regional authorities; and
- specifics of regional elite transformation: common traits and individual features.

The analysis of how the *population* adapted to the transformations of the post-Soviet period and its behavioural models covers all important areas of life:

- transformation of regional labour markets and employment strategies, including labour mobility;
- regional differences in terms of household income levels and differentiation, the availability of the social safety net;
- changes in territorial mobility (migrations) during the post-Soviet period;
- regional education and healthcare; and
- regional lifestyles and their transformation: from modernization to marginalization.

The analysis of all these factors is expected to enable us to produce a typology of regions that would reflect regional differences.

Factors in the transformation of regional elites

Political changes in relations between the centre and the regions

In this area, development trends reversed from decentralization to excessive centralization. The decentralization of the 1990s resulted from the federal government's weakening and an economic crisis, which led to a 'sovereignty parade'.[7] The authorities of such Russian republics as Tatarstan, Bashkortostan, Komi, Karelia and Yakutia were the most active in claiming political and economic privileges in order to be able to manage their resources independently. Lacking such resources, poorly developed republics focused on gaining some sort of special status for their territory such as a special customs zone in Ingushetia, a special economic zone in Kalmykia and an environment and economic zone in the Republic of Altai, to attract companies from across Russia to move their headquarters to their regions. Obtaining a special status provided additional revenue, both for the budget and off-the-books. In some regions, including the Sverdlovsk and Vologda regions and Primorsk Territory, the authorities made attempts in 1992–1993 to transform their respective constituent entities into republics to secure the same tax and budget privileges and control of resources as the most developed republics within Russia. It was only in the Chechen Republic that a pronounced separatist movement emerged. The decentralization movement picked up steam during the First Chechen War of 1994–1995, although the Russian regions benefited from considerable political independence from the federal centre throughout Boris Yeltsin's presidency.

The accession of Vladimir Putin to power and the Second Chechen War (1999) reversed the decentralization trend. Russians viewed the victory in Chechnya, which came at the cost of using harsh military force, as a restoration of order and strengthening of the federal government. The creation of the so-called 'power vertical' was started in 2000 by creating federal districts and appointing presidential plenipotentiary envoys to these entities (with most of such appointees coming from enforcement agencies). It took two years to harmonize regional and federal laws. Regions lost much of their control over the Federation Council, the upper house of the Russian Parliament, which was no longer formed by regional governors and heads of regional-level legislative bodies, but by candidates endorsed by the federal government. In the 2000s, the Federation Council was dominated by major businessmen, retired public servants and other people whom the Kremlin could rely on.

The overly centralized nature of the Russian governance system was finalized during Putin's second presidential term. In 2005, gubernatorial elections were cancelled, and the appointment of new governors was now contingent upon them displaying total loyalty toward the Kremlin and relying on lobbying groups within the federal government. By the mid-2000s, Russia shifted to what was called a 'managed democracy' with respect to federal and local elections and the regime of electoral authoritarianism. During Medvedev's presidency, almost all heavyweights among governors, who until then had managed to hold on to their positions and had high approval ratings, were removed from office. Regional leaders were changed much more frequently and many appointments were hard to explain. All in all, the ranks of the governors counted few prominent figures.

The 2011 State Duma elections and the succession from Putin to Medvedev led to mass protests in many major cities. This protest wave resulted in the restoration of direct gubernatorial elections in 2012, which, however, did not mean that the country reversed to decentralization. The election process is full of strict restrictions such as electoral filters introduced to prevent undesirable candidates from running for office, making a farce out of the elections. The Kremlin also took precautions in the run-up to gubernatorial elections by replacing unpopular governors with new faces who could win more easily. The 2012–2014 gubernatorial elections saw few competitive races, with the incumbents securing victories by a wide margin due to the lack of strong rivals. Candidates from the parliamentary opposition were allowed by the Kremlin to run for governor and actually won in just two regions: the Smolensk Region (Liberal Democratic Party of Russia) and the Trans-Baikal Territory (Just Russia).

Regional authorities were thus fully integrated into the power vertical and unable to challenge even the most unfavourable decisions of the federal government.

For instance, although the presidential executive order to increase salaries to social workers destabilized regional budgets, governors had to implement it, since their efforts in this respect were regarded as the main efficiency criteria. Governors are now forced to operate in a very harsh environment: they may report success in public while in private beg the federal centre for assistance. Any other forms of interaction are inadmissible. Regional governance has also become overly centralized, which is attributable to the concentration of powers and budget resources. In 2014, a new law was adopted that allowed governors to oversee mayoral and municipal elections. This highly centralized governance system encompassed all levels of power and pushed the limits of inefficiency even further. Political transformations did not fail to affect regional elites, as will be shown in the next sections.

Regional economic development levels and trends

The regions specializing in uncompetitive processing industries were the hardest hit by the crisis of the 1990s, which has also led to the deindustrialization of underdeveloped republics. The industrial decline was less pronounced in regions involved in the extraction and export of such raw materials as oil, gas and diamonds. Moscow's economy recovered quicker than in any other region, transforming into a postindustrial economy despite the 1998 financial crisis. In the new market environment, competitiveness factors changed, which considerably increased economic inequality among Russian regions.

The decade of robust economic growth from 1999 to 2008 brought about economic revival not only in commodities-driven regions and federal cities, but also in regions dominated by processing industries and agricultural regions with favourable climate conditions (the Black Earth belt, southern regions). However, development in underdeveloped republics and regions of the Far East was mainly driven by allocations from the federal budget, which surged on the back of booming oil prices. Highly industrialized regions suffered the hardest blow during the next crisis of 2008–2009, while regions receiving major subsidies, those underdeveloped republics and regions of the Far East, were practically unaffected. The economy has been stagnating since 2013, which had a varying impact on the regions depending on their core economic activities.

Severe regional economic disparity emerged in the 1990s and to a large extent remained in place despite the shift in macroeconomic trends. Only Moscow and two oil producing regions, the Tyumen Region and, since the late 2000s, the Sakhalin Region, post a high gross regional product adjusted for regional prices.[8] A dozen other regions, including St. Petersburg, are above average. Most regions, about two thirds of the total, fall into the median category and are quite similar in terms of economic development. About 15 constituent entities are outsiders with economic performance indicators two to four times below average – these are the least developed republics and depressed regions. That said, the line that separates them from the median group is quite blurred. What matters for this study is the social differentiation among territories with different development levels. In fact,

11% of Russians live in economically developed regions, 17% live in regions that are relatively developed, regions with average development levels are home to two thirds of the population, and 10% live in poorly developed regions. This ratio has been quite stable throughout the 2000s.

The question could be restated in the following terms: who are the winners and losers from post-Soviet changes?

- Federal cities, above all Moscow, benefitted most from post-Soviet changes. St. Petersburg came close in mid-2000s when it was granted preferential treatment after its natives came to power and reshaped the country's political elite.
- The major oil and gas extracting regions, primarily the autonomous districts of the Tyumen Region, maintained their edge, and were joined in the mid-2000s by the Nenets Autonomous Area and the Sakhalin Region, where new oil deposits were put into operation, some with the help of foreign investors.
- The inflow of investments promoted recovery and development in regions of the 'new industrialization age', which benefitted from their proximity to markets and West-bound trade routes (Kaluga, Belgorod, Leningrad and Kaliningrad regions).
- Some regions benefited from major projects, such as the Olympics or the Universiade, and were able to attract investments, including from the federal budget (Tatarstan Republic, Krasnodar Territory).

A large proportion of Russian regions did not benefit from the changes and were unable to reach Soviet-era growth rates:

- underdeveloped North Caucasus republics and southern Siberia (Republic of Altai, Republic of Tuva), which depend on federal subsidies to make ends meet;
- semi-depressed regions of European Russia and Urals, specializing in uncompetitive machine building and textiles (Bryansk, Ivanovo, Smolensk, Pskov, Kirov, Penza, Kurgan regions, Republic of Mari El, Republic of Mordovia and Udmurtia);
- Trans-Baikal regions (Republic of Buryatia and the Trans-Baikal Territory), as well as most of Russia's Far East, especially its northern part (Magadan Region, Kamchatka Territory and Chukotka Autonomous Area).

Budget resources

Changes in these areas are important for this research for a number of reasons. First, these changes are indicative of the changes in financial resources available to regional authorities, since budget funds are the main governance tool. Second, analysing these changes will enable us to compare regions in terms of the availability of social services, since in most regions such services, including education, healthcare, culture and social security, account for 60–70% of budget spending.

Following changes in intergovernmental fiscal relations is important for understanding what economic resources are available to regional authorities. In the first half of the 1990s, there were no rules in this respect, and tax revenues were scarce. For this reason, regional governments strived to minimize by various means tax proceeds they had to pay to the federal budget. For instance, Tatarstan did not pay anything into the Russian budget until the late 1990s, and many regions tried to negotiate special terms and benefits. Fiscal federalism policies started to take shape from the mid-1990s with efforts aimed at ensuring equal fiscal capacity using simple and transparent formula. In the second half of the 2000s, the administration of the mineral tax (the so-called 'oil rent') was fully centralized and channelled into the federal budget. The purpose of the new fiscal system in Russia was to centralize and redistribute the oil rent. By 2013, the ratio of revenues paid to the federal budget to those left in regional consolidated budgets stood at 61% to 39%, while in the early 2000s revenues were split evenly between the two.

Allocations from the federal budget increased on the back of higher oil revenues, accounting for an increasingly large portion of regional budgets. However, regional differences persisted, with transfers from the federal budget accounting for 70–90% of regional budgets in underdeveloped republics and less than 5% in such 'prosperous' places as Moscow and the Khanty-Mansi Autonomous Area. This system of intergovernmental transfers became less transparent as it grew increasingly complex. The so-called 'equalization transfer', calculated under a transparent formula, declined in the 2000s from one-half to one-quarter of all transfers, while non-transparent criteria were used by federal agencies regarding other allocations (other grants, over a hundred various subsidies, numerous subventions). In order to secure as much funding as possible, governors and their teams began to lobby their interests in various federal ministries, which translated into higher levels of corruption. Federal funds secured by all ways and means provide much more benefits to regional leaders than improving governance within their regions. The Republic of Tatarstan, the Chechen Republic, the Krasnodar Territory and St. Petersburg had the most success in securing transfers from such nontransparent sources.

The increase in budget transfers was accompanied by the tightening of control over regional budget spending by the prosecutor's office and the Accounts Chamber, substantially restricting the independence of regional executive bodies, while failing to improve the efficiency of budget spending. A similar system was developed in the relations between regional and municipal authorities as budget revenue and spending powers shifted to regional bodies. Consequently, not only politics, but also budget spending were marked by excessive centralization.

So how does the current budget system affect regions and their population? An increase in budget transfers narrowed the gap in terms of per capita budget spending across the country, although Moscow and the oil producing autonomous areas maintained a considerable edge. There is less difference in terms of budget capacity between other regions (does not exceed 100%). In most constituent entities of Russia, 60% to 70% of budget spending goes towards social purposes (education, healthcare, culture and social security), which means that transfer equalization policies did help reduce regional differences in terms of social spending.

Perspectives on the transformation of regional elites

The configuration of regional elites is determined by a combination of factors. Although the significance and interrelation of these factors changed in the past two decades, they are still worth highlighting to understand what regional elites are. Here are the most important of these factors.

1 *Development level and regional economic structure*, which underpins the diversity of major business groups and the resources they command. Regions with competing elites (the Sverdlovsk, Irkutsk, Samara regions and the Krasnoyarsk Territory) are usually well-developed, have a diversified economy with a substantial bias towards export sectors. In regions with single-commodity export economies the impact of major businesses on regional authorities is usually higher (Vologda and Sakhalin regions), although sometimes conflicts occur (Lipetsk Region). Oil producing regions (Khanty-Mansi Autonomous Area, Nenets Autonomous Area, Yamal-Nenets Autonomous Area) are a different story since they are dominated by the largest Russian companies. Such major oil and gas companies are controlled by the state in one way or the other, which often makes them reluctant to get involved in regional affairs, since all the issues they are concerned with are settled on the national level.

   In regions with limited economic resources and where big business does not call the shots, elite groups mostly rely on medium-sized businesses (local oligarchs, regional-level manufacturers, retail chain operators and real estate developers), and are thus eclectic and isolated. It is on the municipal level that we see the most pronounced coalescence between local authorities and businesses. Economic factors also matter for poorly developed republics, where elite groups seek to win control over budget resources and various sectors of the economy, including the informal economy (Dagestan, for example), although clan and ethnic affiliation still prevail. Chechnya stands out in this respect, since a single clan was able to subdue regional elites in the aftermath of the Chechen war supported by the federal government leveraging violence and the control over redistribution of major budget allocations that were channeled into the region.

2 *The size of the main city.* The bigger the regional capital, the stronger the regional elites, as they derive much of their economic clout from trade and real estate development, which tend to be concentrated in large urban areas. Big cities can also entail conflicts between regional governors and mayors of the regional capitals (Nizhny Novgorod, Samara, Volgograd, Sverdlovsk, Omsk regions etc.). Most Russian regions have only one major city. The existence of a second one (usually a big industrial hub) makes competition between regional elites even more intense due to the diversity of economic resources

(Chelyabinsk and Yaroslavl regions). The governor may use such rivalry within the elite to stay in power, or may opt for supporting one of the factions.

3 *The governor's political weight.* Political heavyweights, especially those who have been at the helm of their regions for a long time, are usually able to shape governance hierarchies and to keep regional elites under control (Moscow during the Luzhkov era, Republic of Tatarstan, Kemerovo, Belgorod, Tyumen regions, the Krasnodar Territory and to a lesser extent the Kaluga Region). Political regimes in such regions tend to be authoritarian. For instance, Yury Luzhkov as the Mayor of Moscow was the first to use the city's vast economic resources to create a municipal bureaucratic mechanism which provided him with full control over municipal bodies and ensured victories in mayoral and legislative elections by a comfortable margin. Conflicts among regional elites are more pronounced in regions with weak governors (Sverdlovsk, Irkutsk, Ryazan regions, Stavropol Territory etc. in certain periods of their history), as such leaders are unable to act as arbitrators or dominate the political landscape. When gubernatorial elections were cancelled in 2005, some governors were appointed from the outside, and most of them failed in establishing ties with regional elites. In some regions, regional elites even forgot about their conflicts for some time and joined efforts to oust the outsider. Such developments occurred in Kaliningrad, Tver, Amur, Volgograd regions and the Altai Territory. Some outside appointees came from the Federal Security Service and the army (Ulyanovsk, Ryazan, Voronezh regions and the Krasnodar Territory): their term in office usually yielded disastrous results and led to conflicts within the elite.

The transformations of regional elites could be analysed from different perspectives. The first and most important factor for Russian elites is probably the relations between power and property. During the decentralization years in the second half of the 1990s, a system of 'government-controlled entrepreneurship' emerged in which regional authorities not only controlled regional administrations, but actually coalesced with businesses to get a share in their profits. On the regional, municipal and federal levels, having close relatives appointed to high-ranking posts in private entities dependent on government contracts has become and still is a norm. The only difference is how it is being done.

In Moscow, Luzhkov contributed to the success of the real estate development business operate by his wife, Yelena Baturina. In the Republic of Bashkortostan, the key assets of the oil and chemical industry were illegally privatized by the son of the region's head, Murtaza Rakhimov. In the Republic of Tatarstan, regional authorities still control the main assets, including oil extraction, forming opaque holdings such as Tatinvestneftekhim and TAIF. In the Krasnodar Territory, agricultural land and agricultural holdings in two districts are owned by the family of governor Alexander Tkachyov. Regions where such practices are less pronounced are hard to single out: they may not be visible on the regional level, but on the municipal level the coalescence between the authorities and business can be found almost anywhere.

In the 2000s a new phenomenon emerged, when law enforcement agencies (the Federal Security Service, police, prosecutor's offices, customs authorities) brought regional and local businesses under their control. This is a national phenomenon, but it is especially pronounced in Moscow, where descendants of the Federal Security Service gained considerable influence over the banking sector, foreign trade and so on, and in some regions of Russia's Far East, such as Kamchatka and Sakhalin, where customs and border control agencies cemented control over the fishing industry. This 'enforcer entrepreneurship' did not come out of nowhere. It came on the heels of the 'robber capitalism' of the 1990s, which until recently was prevalent in regions specializing in trade and cross-border operations (Kaliningrad Region, Primorsk Territory). In the Kemerovo Region, criminal groups controlled coal sales until major corporations took hold of this segment. In the Kaliningrad Region, things started to change only in 2006 when a special economic zone was created there, while Primorsk Territory was put on the right track only recently, after the gubernatorial elections in the early 2010s.

The second perspective is to examine relations between regional elites and *big Russian businesses*. In the 1990s, major corporate players sought to amass industrial assets across the country, which involved working with regional authorities by either purchasing what they needed or pressuring local officials during electoral campaigns. By the early 2000s, major companies had expanded their regional political and economic power in some regions in the East of Russia (Chukotka, Taimyr, Evenki autonomous areas, Krasnoyarsk Territory) to such an extent that their representatives even ran for governor. The goal was lowering costs for such corporations through regional tax benefits and shielding new extraction sites from competition.

In fact, big businesses succeeded in capturing the state in some regions, although they still had to channel part of local revenue into development and corporate managers contributed to modernizing regional governance practices, of which the Chukotka Autonomous Area is a spectacular example. However, the federal government's initiatives to cap regional tax benefits and centralize mineral extraction licensing made businesses less eager to engage in regional politics. The next step was to cancel gubernatorial elections. Nevertheless, major companies still have a powerful lobby in key regions and are able to have their representatives appointed to executive and legislative bodies, as well as the Federation Council, the upper chamber of the Russian parliament. Since the late 1990s, regional legislatures have morphed into a bargaining platform where regional authorities and major corporations could harmonize their interests.

By the late 2000s, the state cemented control over a considerable part of big companies and shifted to de facto colonial practices. State-owned companies obtain major benefits and breaks from the federal centre, including lower regional taxes (with the regions left without say) and are consequently able to move profits out from the regions (Krasnoyarsk Territory, Yakutia). The pay-off for the regions is that state-owned companies, having secured the benefits they needed, provide funding for inexpensive social projects in an effort to bolster their corporate image.

The third perspective is the *commitment of regional elites to modernization*, and liberal and democratic institutional reforms. This aspect is the hardest to analyse, since there are no formal criteria, so all that is left is to consider the political regime and the behaviour of the elite. Moreover, regional elites and authorities may not be on the same page in terms of modernization. For instance, elites in St. Petersburg are much more modern than the current city government. For these reasons, the analysis of regional elites is limited to the review of the most characteristic cases.

Few regions in Russia were controlled for a protracted period by democratic and liberal groups committed to market reforms. These few include the Perm Territory before Governor Oleg Chirkunov resigned in 2012, the Yaroslavl Region and St. Petersburg in the 1990s to early 2000s, and to some extent the Sverdlovsk Region, where democratic governance was supported by competition between elite groups until the resignation of Governor Eduard Rossel. Eastern regions, and especially the Tomsk regions and the Krasnoyarsk Territory (until the late 2000s), and partly the Novosibirsk and Irkutsk regions, are above average in terms of their commitment to democracy and modernization. In the Irkutsk Region, frequent changes of weak governors served as a barrier to authoritarian rule. The Republic of Karelia and the Kaliningrad Region could be added to this list, since their local elites maintain close contacts with European countries, while their regional governments are weak. Unfortunately, other examples of relatively democratic regions with modern elite are hard to find. Being 'advanced' or 'free thinking' has become dangerous.

On the other side of the spectrum are regions under authoritarian rule, which varied immensely in the 2000s. In Chechnya, it seems that the course of history has reversed with the restoration of a patriarchal society in which elites receiving budget allocations are expected to display full loyalty to the government. In the Kemerovo Region, a quasi-Soviet regime is still up and running, controlling businesses and social redistribution functions. In the Belgorod Region, the authoritarian regime seeks to introduce Orthodox Christianity in all areas, while successfully developing its market economy. The economy of the Krasnodar Territory is developing despite the authoritarian rule of its governor and traditionalist-minded elite. In the Republic of Tatarstan, a power vertical has been created, with elites split into clans, which does not impede economic modernization or the inflow of investors. The regional government of the Kaluga Region is not democratic, but it is committed to economic modernization and attracts investors. The Ulyanovsk Region is similar in this respect, although the results so far have been modest.

Peripheral regions with limited economic resources often have traditionally minded elites. This is the case in the most depressed Russian constituent entities. The elites in underdeveloped republics (Dagestan, North Ossetia, Tuva etc.) also fall behind in terms of modernization, although their governments are much less authoritarian than in Chechnya, while competition among the elite runs high.

The specifics of regional elites and political regimes affect ordinary people. Regions with weak governors often have weak social policy. People are unhappy, and confidence ratings in regional governments are low. In regions with strong governors and united elites social policy may be different, ranging from populist Soviet-style initiatives in the Kemerovo Region, where the governor forces big and medium-sized businesses to finance regional programmes, to paternalist policies aimed at cementing and reinforcing traditional values. In Chechnya, the redistribution of large transfers from the federal budget into social benefits ensured massive popular support, but at the same time traditional values in gender relations are restored and the rights of women are limited. Only Tatarstan seems to be able to combine modernization policies aimed at developing human capital with efforts to provide social security.

Changes in the labour market and employment strategies

We will now examine how ordinary people live and how they have adapted to post-Soviet changes. A key factor is the Russian labour market, which is special in a number of ways. First, the unemployment rate as measured by ILO standards remains relatively low even during crises. In the turmoil of the 1990s, while there were no mass layoffs, many people were underemployed and wages were delayed. During economic growth periods unemployment declined in most regions, except for the underdeveloped republics of Chechnya, Ingushetia and Tuva. The government responded to the downturn of 2009 by opposing industrial layoffs and went as far as financing public works to ease tensions on the labour market. In 2013, the unemployment rate in Russia and across almost all regions was at historic lows in all the post-Soviet period, which is attributable, among other things, to the shrinking of the working-age population.

The second distinctive feature of the Russian labour market is widespread informal employment and the decline in the number of those holding legal jobs. The number of people employed by big and medium-sized businesses and organizations dropped in the 2000s from over 40 million to 35 million, 20 million of whom are public sector employees, while according to Russia's State Statistics Services some 15 to 20 million work off the books. Informal employment is especially high in underdeveloped republics, depressed regions and peripheral municipalities in Russia, where very few new jobs are being created. Accordingly, the low unemployment rate is also attributable to an increase in informal employment.

Third, the small business sector is underdeveloped in Russia, employing just 16 million people, self-employed entrepreneurs included. Employment by small businesses is on the decline due to an unfavourable institutional environment and the obstacles these companies face. The share of people employed by small businesses approaches the 30% threshold only in the largest cities with higher purchasing power.

The fourth feature is that regions differ significantly in terms of the employment structure: in industrial regions of the Central, Northwestern, Volga and Urals federal districts 20–30% of the population are employed by various manufacturing enterprises; employment in agriculture is high in southern regions and the Black

Earth Region, reaching 20–25%. Moscow has the largest share (75%) of people employed in the service sector, both market and non-market. In underdeveloped republics, 35% to 40% of the workforce is public sector employees, which is attributable to the lack of other employment opportunities.

The fifth distinctive feature of the Russian labour market is gender-related. There are no visible gender differences in terms of unemployment rates, as women often take up less prestigious and worse paying jobs. But there is a wide pay gap, as wages earned by women are in Russia two-thirds lower, on average, than those for men. This is attributable to differences in the sectors in which women and men work, as well as in social status: more women work in the social services sector, where wages are lower. The share of women in high-profile jobs is still low. Although regions differ little in this respect, there are two 'poles' of gender equality. The rich city of Moscow offers many highly paid jobs in the service sector, tops the country in terms of the education level of its workforce, and people have a modern mindset in general. In fact, the gender pay gap has been narrowing in Moscow since the 2000s as gender roles evolved. Meanwhile, in underdeveloped republics in Siberia, such as the republics of Tuva and Altai, or northern regions inhabited by indigenous people, men and women are equally poor. Women mostly work as public sector employees with low wages, while many men are self-employed and receive low incomes, and the unemployment rate is high.

The structural specifics of regional and local labour markets affect the strategies people use to get a job and earn an income. In this respect, a lot depends on the geographical location of the region. In most regions, the workforce in peripheral municipalities consists of public sector employees, low paid agricultural workers, and the self-employed. The self-employed tend to work off the books. Their type of activity depends on geographical location. In the taiga, a popular occupation is gathering wild plants (berries, mushrooms and nuts) and selling them to resellers. In Siberia and the Far East, people earn a living by poaching and selling premium fish. This foraging economy is big in size. In agricultural regions with a favourable climate, people produce agricultural products on their private land plots (fruit and vegetables), as well as milk and meat. This produce is then sold on the market, and even more frequently to retailers. Informal employment is also widespread in the transportation sector (haulage on personal trucks), especially in the Russian south and the republics of the Volga Federal District.

Villages and small cities suffer from a decline in labour activity. Part of their population does not have regular jobs and is becoming increasingly marginalized; alcohol abuse is rampant in such places. Marginalization is especially relevant for regions in the European part of Russia outside the Black Earth Region, the Urals and the eastern regions. In small- and medium-sized cities, people hold public sector jobs, work at the remaining manufacturing businesses (which are also on the decline) and in small businesses, mostly retail. Seasonal employment increased in the 1990s, as people started to leave for big cities to build dacha country houses, renovate apartments (informal employment), and seek formal employment at construction and transport companies. Major cities recruit a seasonal workforce from rural areas as well, although to a lesser extent, since the rural population is shrinking, aging and marginalizing. Working on a rotation basis in Russia's northern or eastern regions (oil and gas extraction, construction) is another form of labour migration that affects small- and medium-sized cities. Oil and gas companies or intermediaries make transportation arrangements. Workforces are being moved from old oil producing regions in European Russia (republics of Bashkortostan, Tatarstan and other regions of the Volga Federal District) to new oil production facilities.

Modern labour markets of million-plus cities are still far behind Moscow and St. Petersburg in terms of wages and diversity of employment opportunities. Major cities have a higher employment rate in the market-related service sector (including modern jobs and traditional trade occupations). In many major cities, especially in the south and east of Russia, consumer goods markets still employ thousands of people. The markets are officially registered, but revenue generated by retailers often goes unreported. In Moscow and St. Petersburg local markets are being replaced by modern shopping centres, but in other cities with lower income residents this process is being delayed.

Since the 1990s, the Moscow metropolitan area has attracted labour migrants not only from the Moscow region, but also from the neighbouring regions of the Central Federal District. People living as far as 300 kilometres from Moscow are ready to cover this distance as part of their weekly labour migration routine. Moscow and, since the mid-2000s, St. Petersburg, attract labour migrants from across the country, employing young workers with varying levels of education and skills. In addition, major cities are witnessing an inflow of migrants from the CIS, who tend to work in construction, utilities and housing sectors, and retail trade. So far, there are no ethnic ghettos, while migrants rent apartments in the cheapest peripheral districts of Moscow and the Moscow Region.

Household income trends and differentiation

Household incomes went through a number of stages during the post-Soviet period: incomes more than halved in the first half of the 1990s, and declined by almost one third in the aftermath of the 1998 economic crisis that led to the depreciation of the ruble. In the decade that followed household incomes surged 2.6-fold amid increasing income inequality. The 2009 downturn had little impact on income levels, as the government used the country's oil and gas revenues to support the economy. In 2010–2013, household income growth lost momentum. Regional differences in this respect became increasingly pronounced in the 1990s and the income gap did not start to narrow until the 2000s on the back of growing oil revenues and their redistribution (Figure 11.1). The reasons that helped narrow this gap were, first, the increase of wages earned by public sector employees (benefiting underdeveloped regions where there are more public sector employees), and, second, higher retirement pensions, which improved the standing of regions in central and northwestern Russia, which have the highest share of seniors in their age structure.

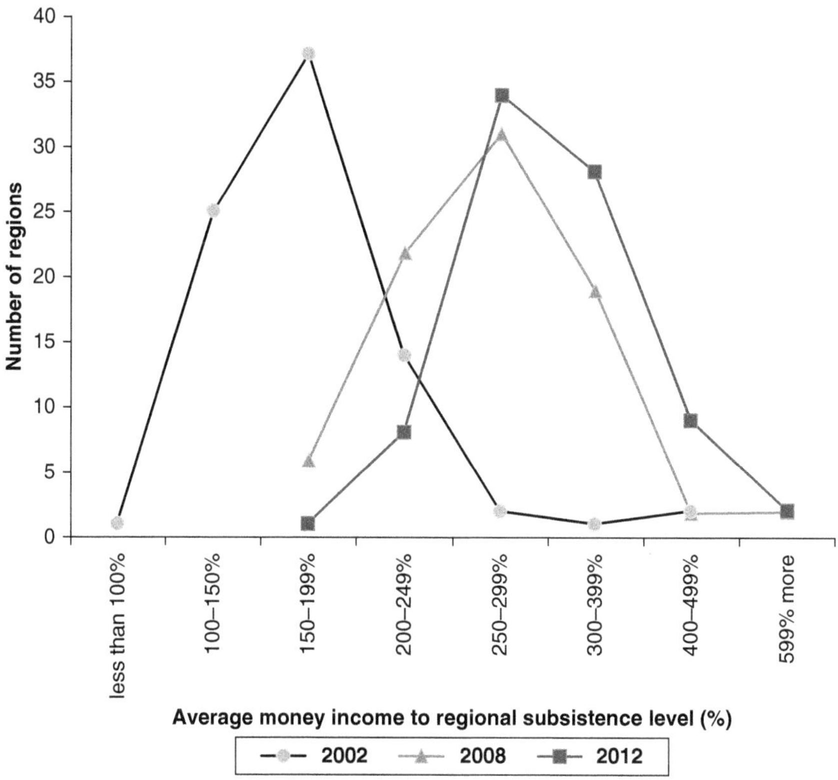

Figure 11.1 Breakdown of the Russian regions in terms of average per capita incomes to the subsistence level.

Source: Calculations by the author based on data from Russia's State Statistics Service.

There are established areas of wealth and poverty in Russia. Although regional-level statistics on household incomes are not always complete, especially in the regions where the informal economy plays an important role (republics of North Caucuses) or those with a substantial inflow of labour migrants (Moscow metropolitan area), such data still reflect the basic differences between the regions. Average per capita income in Moscow is 5–6 times higher than the subsistence level, 4–5 times higher in oil and gas producing regions, and only 2–2.5 times above the subsistence level in underdeveloped republics and the depressed regions. Although the gap between the regions has slightly narrowed in the 2000s, there are no fundamental changes.

Economic growth accentuated income inequality within regions, since the most affluent were the first to benefit from the surging oil revenues and their redistribution. The downturn of 2009 curbed the growth of inequality. The wealthiest regions have the highest income inequality. In Moscow, the average income of the richest 10% exceeds that of the poorest 10% 26 times, and the same ratio stands at 19–20 in the Tyumen Region, St. Petersburg and the Samara Region, with a national average of 16. Given such inequality it can be argued that data on average per capita income in Russian regions is of little use.

Significant inequality reproduces poverty. In Russia it is measured as a ratio of per capita income to the subsistence wage, which differs greatly depending on the region. In terms of geographical distribution, the underdeveloped republics and the depressed regions in the east of Russia, where the cost of living is higher, have the highest portion of people earning less than the subsistence wage at 17% in Ingushetia, 28% in Tuva, 30% in Kalmykia, as well as the Trans-Baikal, Altai and Kamchatka territories, and the Republic of Buryatia at 18–20%. Regions with a lower cost of living (Belgorod, Kaluga and Lipetsk regions, and the Republic of Tatarstan), the wealthy oil and gas producing regions with lavish social safety nets (Yamal-Nenets Autonomous Area, Khanty-Mansi Autonomous Area and Nenets Autonomous Area) and metropolitan areas of the federal cities with higher wages (Moscow, St. Petersburg and the Moscow Region) have the lowest level of poverty at 6–10%.

These statistics fail to reflect what people do to increase their income. In major cities, people tend to do some extra work (secondary employment) and delay retirement (over 50% of people beyond the retirement age in major cities continue to work to earn a salary and the retirement pensions – the same goes for the northern regions). In medium-sized and small cities there are fewer opportunities to get an extra job, which leads people to seek employment opportunities in other regions or work on rotating shift in remote areas. Rural areas are dominated by more traditional methods of generating additional income: people grow fruit and vegetables, breed cattle and gather mushrooms and wild berries for personal consumption and for sale.

How does the federal government support people with low incomes? As much as two-thirds of the total social benefits go towards paying retirement pensions. Other benefits have little to do with sustaining the poor, as 75% go towards certain categories of beneficiaries,[9] regardless of their income (handicapped, large families, single-parent families etc.), and only the remaining 25% are used to assist low income households.[10] Regional policies differ depending on two factors: the availability of funding from the regional budget and the priorities of the local government. In a wealthy city like Moscow, the municipal authorities have been supplementing federal pensions and wages of public sector employees ever since Luzhkov's tenure. In fact, as much as 10% of the capital's huge budget was used to this effect in the late 2000s. Rich oil and gas producing regions also run ambitious social programmes that benefit a broad spectrum of the population. However, in some developed regions (Belgorod and Tyumen regions, St. Petersburg and to a lesser extent Tatarstan) local governments do not view social protection as a priority, preferring instead to channel 20–30% of their spending into developing their economies and infrastructure. Average and underdeveloped regions have limited social protection budgets with no major differences in terms of per capita spending to this effect.[11] In some Russian regions social benefits fail to reach all recipients. In the North Caucasus, kickbacks are paid not only by businessmen, but also by ordinary people to those who pay salaries, pensions or other allowances.

Mobility and migration trends

With the collapse of the Soviet Union, as many as 4.5 million ethnic Russians and Russian speakers chose to leave the former republics of the USSR and resettle in Russia in the 1990s. The majority moved to the southern and central parts of the country that were close to the areas in which they used to live and that offered cheap housing. Over a million people opted for rural areas. This return migration ended by the late 1990s. The economic growth of the 2000s made Russia attractive for labour migrants from the CIS, with most of them heading to major cities and economically developed regions. The number of foreign migrants in Russia is estimated at 6–8 million. This mass labour migration and the difficulties such migrants faced in the new environment has led to a rise in xenophobia, especially in the largest Russian cities. Internal migration flows in Russia during the post-Soviet period almost halved, and their geography changed. Since the 1990s, people were leaving northern regions and Russia's Far East, since the incomes they earned could no longer compensate for higher living costs, poor infrastructure and an unfavourable climate. The population of the Chukotka Autonomous Area shrank threefold, and the population of Kamchatka and the Magadan Region almost halved. The migration outflow from the northern regions and the Far East continues to this day.

Once the forced migration flows from the CIS countries came to an end, economic factors came into play. People tend to leave underdeveloped republics of North Caucasus and the depressed and poorly developed regions, that is the periphery. Migrants are attracted by the federal cities and adjacent territories, as well as the southern regions (Krasnodar Territory), regions of central Russia surrounding the capital and the Belgorod region, which has been seeking to attract and support migrants since the 1990s, as well as the Kaliningrad Region. In Siberia, only the Tomsk and Novosibirsk regions still attract migrants as their regional centres are home to major universities. Mobility in the underdeveloped republics of southern Siberia is low.

Migration flows from the republics of the North Caucasus to neighbouring regions underpinned by demographical and economic factors stand out as a separate category. The share of people of Caucasian origin in the south of the Stavropol territory is rapidly expanding, while ethnic Russians are moving to the centre.[12] Border areas are increasingly involved in ethnic conflicts caused by economic factors: people from the Caucasus own dozens of cattle, which use cereal crop lands as pastures. The crop lands are the main source of income for local farmers, who are mostly ethnic Russians.

Education strategies

In the post-Soviet era, the strategies employed by Russian families to educate their children changed twice. In 1991–1995, when the country was going through economic hardships, having a university degree became less attractive, and the number of students enrolled in higher education institutions declined accordingly. However, this downward trend reversed in 1995 as the demand for higher education started to recover. In just 15 years, the number of institutions offering higher education programmes more than doubled, and the number of students surged 2.6 times, along with the increase in the share of fee-based education. In fact, more than half of university students pay for their education.

Having children receive a higher educational degree has become the norm for most Russian families, which was not the case in Soviet times. The demand created supply, and new higher education institutions emerged across the country, supplementing the established educational centres (federal cities, Rostov-on-Don, Voronezh, Samara, Novosibirsk, Tomsk, Khabarovsk etc.). The Magadan and Kursk regions, as well as the Stavropol Territory have reached high results in terms of the number of students per 1,000 residents, including by facilitating the establishment of local branches by universities from other regions. Some wealthy regions in eastern Russia (Khanty-Mansi Autonomous Area, Yakutia) focused on establishing universities by providing funding from the regional budget. Russians came to terms with the fact that higher education was becoming increasingly fee-based, which was due in part to the difference in tuition fees: studying at a peripheral branch of a regional university is usually dozens of times cheaper than attending one of the top Moscow schools. The price a family from a rural area or a small city has to pay for one semester in a provincial university is commensurate with the price of two suckling pigs or a calf. For families in federal cities sending an offspring to a top school may cost up to one half of the yearly income earned by one of the parents.

That said, the quality of education, especially in newly established centres, is low. However, neither the students nor their parents have any claims, and are willing to pay to receive a degree no matter what. Russia has become a country with mass, increasingly fee-based and low-quality higher education. Demand for higher education started to decline only in the late 2000s due to the specifics of Russia's age pyramid (the decrease of the population aged 17–23). The federal government is also seeking to bring down the number of higher education institutions, although they have yet to come up with credible criteria for selecting the best and the worst colleges. As a result, the interests of most Russian families (cheap and mass higher education) and the state (improving the quality of education) do not coincide.

Vocational training remains relevant in certain industrialized regions of the Urals, Volga Federal District and Siberia, as well as regions with fewer higher education institutions. The number of students enrolled in first-level vocational training programmes to master a blue-collar profession dropped threefold in the post-Soviet period across the country. In secondary education, the main trend consists of the enlargement and reduction of the number of schools, especially in small cities and rural areas. In 2000–2010, the number of schools dropped by 26% as schools with less than the required number of students were closed, and families with schoolchildren moved to bigger cities. In the cities, schools were often merged and enlarged. This effort to streamline budget spending made schools less accessible in certain regions.

The structure of the adult population in terms of education has also changed in the post-Soviet era, especially in urban areas. Federal cities and their metropolitan areas, and regions with major educational centres, which used to dominate this category, were joined by underdeveloped republics. This is due to two factors: a younger age structure of these republics, and a significant increase in the accessibility of higher education (with a lower quality). In industrial cities, especially in depressed regions, most people have vocational training, which reduces their mobility and their capacity to adapt to changes, and generally makes it harder to adopt a more modern lifestyle.

Access to healthcare

Comparing regions in terms of access to healthcare is more challenging. Statistical data on the number of doctors, medical staff and the availability of places in hospitals do not reflect the overall picture regarding the accessibility and quality of medical services. Two main trends stand out in this respect.

The first trend is that people are finding it increasingly hard to avoid paying for healthcare services. A research project carried out by the Independent Institute for Social Policy in the mid-2000s has shown that people had to pay for up to 50% of medical services, in most cases by paying doctors or medical staff under the table.[13] In addition, a growing number of medical services are now legally offered on a paid basis. The second trend is that the network of healthcare institutions is shrinking and becoming less dense. In 2000–2010, the number of places in Russian hospitals contracted by 20%, with the most notable drop of 30–40% in villages and small cities outside the Black Earth Region. The number of local outpatient clinics providing primary medical care and small local hospitals diminished throughout the 2000s. Specialized doctors are being replaced by general practitioners, but the healthcare modernization has so far failed to pick up steam. Modern medical centres have been established in major regional centres, while the availability of medical services in small cities is declining. Patients have to travel to regional centres if they need specialized care. The effort to reform the healthcare system established in the Soviet times caused major problems for the population.

That said, public health does not boil down to the healthcare system and is also contingent upon lifestyle. This factor has a major impact on life expectancy, which varies greatly across the country (from 61 to 76, with a national average of 70 in 2012). Federal cities rank high in this respect (76 years in Moscow), which is attributable to higher levels of education and income, as well as the fact that people pay more attention to their health. The North Caucasus republics are also high on the list due to a favourable climate and a lower drinking index, although data coming from these regions are not fully reliable due to the poor reporting of child mortality. Living in the more clement climate of the Russian south is also important in terms of life expectancy.

Regions with the lowest life expectancy can be split into three groups, although marginalization and alcohol abuse are relevant for all of them: regions dominated by ethnic minorities with alcohol abuse problems: Republic of Tuva, Chukotka Autonomous Area (61 years); constituent entities of the Baikal region and the Far East where there are many depressed villages and small cities, and availability of medical services is poor (63–66 years); regions outside the Black Earth Region with an aged population, depressed rural areas and small cities: Pskov, Novgorod, Tver regions and the Perm Territory (66–67 years).

Changing regional lifestyles: from modernization to marginalization

The rise of territorial inequality in the post-Soviet era has made the place of residence a much more important factor than it used to be. It determines what employment strategies people are likely to use and how they can earn their income, access healthcare and social protection services, and educate their children, as well as the efficiency of government and civil society institutions. It could be argued that the place of residence determines one's destiny to a great extent. The Russian social realm can be categorized using geographical, economic and social factors and conditions. The best way to produce a typology of various living conditions and lifestyles is to highlight several core types of territories, while bearing in mind that the frontier between territories of different types is often quite blurred. In fact, there are many in-between regions where the traits of various core types can be found.

The highly developed *federal cities and Moscow's metropolitan area* is the first core type, representing the leading regions of the postindustrial age where people live modern lifestyles. Moscow is far ahead of St. Petersburg in terms of household income, but income inequality is also much stronger. The labour markets in Moscow and St. Petersburg offer the most diverse opportunities and high-paid jobs, while unemployment is practically nonexistent. People in these two cities benefit from high levels of income and education people and live the most modern lifestyles. More people are employed by small businesses or are self-employed (27–30% of the total workforce), which makes them more independent. However, the population of federal cities is aging, with 24–25% of their population (31–32% for women) beyond retirement age. This means that a substantial share of senior voters, as well public-sector employees, are dependent on the pension increments paid by municipal authorities and other social safety net mechanisms. Just like in St. Petersburg, the Moscow Region began to develop more rapidly only in the 2000s on the back of a growing investment inflow and the creation of new jobs. A large proportion of people living in the Moscow region work in Moscow.

Gravitational zones (periphery) of the major metropolitan areas. These are areas of the Central Federal District surrounding Moscow, which went through a steep economic decline in the post-Soviet era as many enterprises closed. One of the ways in which people adapted to this unfavourable environment was to move to the capital in search of jobs. However, in the 2000s, these regions started to benefit from their proximity to the Moscow metropolitan area: investments picked up, and new manufacturing and service jobs, albeit less well paid than in the capital, were being created in regional centres. The Kaluga Region succeeded the most in this respect, which is attributable to the efforts by the regional authorities to attract investments. Small cities and rural areas in these regions have the oldest population; agriculture and manufacturing have long ceased to be major employers, while alternative employment opportunities are scarce. All in all, this led to a pronounced social marginalization. The St. Petersburg metropolitan area and regions of Russia's northwest followed a similar pattern.

The 'wealthy' oil and gas producing autonomous areas offer high per capita income and strong income inequality. These regions generate large revenues and can thus afford to offer their residents generous social security programmes and accessible and high-quality healthcare, and to fund education. The population of these regions was shaped by the migration flows of the 1970s–1980s, and is relatively young and mobile, and more apt to adapt to changing economic conditions. During the crises years of the 1990s, these regions attracted migrants seeking higher wages. However, things have changed. Extraction industries are becoming less labour intensive, so few new jobs are being created, which has given rise to a migration outflow in recent years. Young people tend to leave for major cities in other regions to get a university degree, and rarely come back. Since most families are not willing to spend their whole lives in the north, they invest their savings in buying real estate in other regions with a more favourable living environment.

The relatively developed industrial regions of the Volga Federal District, Urals and southern Siberia with major cities. These regions have supplemented the remaining industrial potential with the nascent service economy that has recently flourished in the largest cities of these regions. Although the million plus cities here are far less attractive than Moscow and St. Petersburg, they still attract young migrants from the periphery, who come to study or work. The cities of Yekaterinburg, Kazan and Novosibirsk are witnessing the most rapid changes. They offer the largest variety of job opportunities, and higher per capita incomes. That said, inequality is strong on the regional level. The periphery follows a downward trend, its population is aging and people living in former industrial centres stick to Soviet-era values. Only residents of the largest cities are inclined to adopt modern values and lifestyles.

Semi-depressive industrial regions have suffered the steepest economic and industrial slump and recovered very slowly in the 2000s. These regions are economically uncompetitive. Their regional centres fail to produce beneficial effects similar to those of the previous cases, which is due to the fact that their population is relatively small and household incomes low. People there are less educated and mobile. In these depressive economies, people are forced to concentrate on survival strategies instead of adopting a modern lifestyle. As the periphery sinks deeper into depression, its population is becoming increasingly marginalized.

The Far East and the Far North are inhabited by migrants from European Russia. Back in the Soviet times wages there were higher than elsewhere in Russia, but incomes fell sharply in the 1990s. The contraction of the labour market has led to a massive migration outflow, which continues to this day. Only a few cities that produce and export commodities (Norilsk, Mirny) offer decent wages. People living in Far East, Russia's eastern frontier, are more mobile and capable of adapting to changes, and have a distinct macro-regional identity. In addition, their elites have been criminalized like nowhere else in Russia. In fact, since the 1990s, businesses and people employed various strategies to generate profits, most of which were informal, if not illegal: shuttle trade with China (for the southern regions of Russia's Far East), importing and reselling cheap used Japanese cars (up to 100,000 people are employed in this shady segment in the Far East), and illegal fishing of premium fish varieties (Sakhalin, Kamchatka). In the second half of the 2000s, the federal government started to invest more in the Far East for geopolitical reasons. Major cities began to develop, especially Vladivostok. People in this coastal city are more open to outside contacts, which facilitates modernization. At the same time, people living in rural areas and small cities of the Far East are marginalized (alcohol abuse, high unemployment, poverty).

The 'Russian' south covers part of the North Caucasus (Krasnodar and Stavropol territories and the Rostov Region) and the Black Earth Region. These regions are dominated by ethnic Russians mostly living in rural areas. In the 1990s, the majority voted for the communists, before their political preferences shifted to the ruling party. After the breakdown of the Soviet Union, it was here that most of ethnic Russians from the CIS moved, which was among the key factors in the economic boom of the Belgorod Region. Wages are low in the Russian south, but almost all locals supplement their income by selling agricultural produce (Nefyodova, 2003). During the economic downturn of the 1990s many workers were made redundant and wages fell. Nevertheless, a large part of the population is still employed in the agricultural sector, since rural areas do not offer any other employment opportunities. The South has a favourable climate for agricultural activities. In the 1990s the number of private farms increased, only to decline later on. By the late 1990s, companies started buying agricultural lands, making the local workforce redundant. Investment increased. As the population of the Black Earth belt ages, companies are finding it increasingly difficult to find skilled workers for new agribusiness enterprises, and even the offer of higher wages is often insufficient to make local residents work more. While across Russia people in rural areas do not need much, in the South people have more opportunities to supplement their incomes by selling privately grown agricultural products. Major regional centres differ in terms of lifestyle modernization. In the Soviet times, Rostov-on-Don and Voronezh were the most developed industrial and educational centres, but in the post-Soviet period their leadership faded, outpaced by Krasnodar and Sochi, which benefited from an inflow of investment and higher household incomes. That said, higher incomes do not always lead to a more modern lifestyle, which is especially true in Russia's southern regions.

The North Caucasus republics are going through a transition from a traditional society dominated by clan structures, a prevailing rural population and a high birth rate, to a more urban lifestyle. A steady inflow of people to cities from rural areas slows down the modernization of the urban population. The economy is dominated by informal activity (trade, growing vegetables, shoe manufacturing etc.), with most of the legitimate jobs concentrated in the public sector. Investment is low and consequently new jobs are hard to find. For this reason labour migrants from the North Caucasus frequently go to other Russian regions. The transition to a more modern lifestyle is happening against a backdrop of extremely corrupt governance, which is resented by the population, especially the young. Religious norms are becoming increasingly widespread, including marginal Islamic movements. The need for modernization in a region where people are becoming more religious and view religion as an ideology may lead to a social explosion.

Conclusion

This analysis of the transformations the elites and ordinary people in the Russian regions are going through has demonstrated once again how different those regions are. The regional specifics of regional elites are attributable to the fact that they rely on different economic resources, although political, ethnic and other factors are also important. The ways in which people adapt to the changing environment are contingent upon the region's level of development, its geographical location, urbanization level and population structure. Differences between the centre and the periphery within regions are equally important. It is difficult to merge all the diverse characteristics and trends into a single typology of Russian regions. The proposed classification (Table 11.1) highlights the key differences, which are *the economic development level and the standard of living.* Such additional factors as the geographical location, urbanization and regional economic structure are taken into account to divide the abovementioned categories into subcategories. This detailed typology could help with choosing key regions for further research.

Table 11.1 Categories and subcategories in terms of economic development, economic structure, urbanization and geographical location

1 Most developed regions with high household incomes	
Federal cities and their metropolitan areas	*'Wealthy' oil and gas producing regions with population formed by migrants*
Moscow	Khanty-Mansi Autonomous Area
St. Petersburg	Yamal-Nenets Autonomous Area
Moscow Region	Nenets Autonomous Area
Leningrad Region	*Sakhalin Region*
2 Relatively developed regions	
Industrial regions of the Volga Federal District and Urals with million plus cities	*Regions in Siberia and the north of European Russia specialized in extraction and exports of commodities*
Samara Region	Tyumen Region
Nizhny Novgorod Region	Tomsk Region
Perm Territory	Kemerovo Region
Sverdlovsk Region	Krasnoyarsk Territory
Chelyabinsk Region	Irkutsk Region
Republic of Tatarstan	Republic of Sakha (Yakutia)
Republic of Bashkortostan	Komi Republic
Novosibirsk Region	
Lipetsk Region	
Belgorod Region	
3 Average regions in terms of development and incomes	
Urbanized regions surrounding metropolitan areas of federal cities	*Other urbanized industrial regions in the developed areas*
Kaluga Region	Vologda Region
Yaroslavl Region	Kaliningrad Region
Tula Region	Udmurtian Republic
Tver Region	Orenburg Region
Vladimir Region	Ulyanovsk Region
Ryazan Region	Astrakhan Region
Smolensk Region	Volgograd Region
Novgorod Region	Omsk Region
	Chuvash Republic
	Republic of Mordovia
Agrarian regions in the South of Russia and the Black Earth belt dominated by ethnic Russians and with a low urbanization rate	*Northern and eastern regions with commodity economies*
Krasnodar Territory	Arkhangelsk Region
Rostov Region	Murmansk Region

Stavropol Territory	Republic of Karelia
Kursk Region	Republic of Khakassia
Saratov Region	Khabarovsk Territory
Orel Region	Primorsk Territory
Voronezh Region	Magadan Region
Tambov Region	Chukotka Autonomous Area
Penza Region	Kamchatka Territory
Altai Territory	Amur Region
	Jewish Autonomous Region
4 Semi depressive industrial regions with small regional centres and low household incomes	
Republic of Buryatia	Pskov Region
Trans-Baikal Territory	Bryansk Region
Kurgan Region	Ivanovo Region
Republic of Mari El	Kostroma Region
	Kirov Region
5 Underdeveloped republics where the demographic transition has yet to be completed and the population still lives a traditional lifestyle	
Southern regions with high population density	*Regions with unfavourable living conditions and low population density*
Republic of Adygea	Republic of Kalmykia
Republic of North Ossetia-Alania	Republic of Altai
Karachayevo-Circassian Republic	Republic of Tuva
Kabardino-Balkarian Republic	
Republic of Dagestan	
Republic of Ingushetia	
Chechen Republic	

Note: Regions in transition (blending characteristics from various categories) are in italic.

Notes

1 For a full-scale study, see Natalya Zubarevich, *Regiony Rossii: neravenstvo, krizis, modernizatsiya* (*Russian Regions: Inequality, Crisis, Modernization*) (Moscow: Nezavisimy institut sotsialnoi politiki, 2010).

2 Tatyana Maleva and Lidiya Ovcharova, *Rossiiskiye sredniye klassy nakanune i na pike ekonomicheskogo rosta* (*The Russian Middle Class Before and at the Height of the Economic Growth Period*) (Moscow: Ekon-Inform, 2008).

3 Data from a study on the middle class by the Independent Institute for Social Policy (2004–2011)

4 Alexander Auzan, *Ekonomika vsego. Kak instituty opredelyauyt nashu zhizn* (*Economy Everywhere: How Institutions Determine our Life*) (Moscow: Mann, Ivanov and Farber, 2014).

5 Andrei Treyvish, *Gorod, rayon, strana i mir: razvitie Rossii glazami stranoveda* (*City, Region, Country and the World: Development of Russia from a Country Expert's Perspective*) (Moscow: Novy khronograph, 2009).

6 Remote Eastern regions were colonized by people migrating from the European part of Russia over three centuries. In regions with major migration inflows people are always much more able to adapt and less dependent on government support.

7 In 1992–1993, many republics adopted their own constitutions, securing broad powers and autonomy from the federal centre, which went as far as proclaiming sovereignty (Republic of Tatarstan).

8 Moscow's per capita GRP (purchasing power parity) in 2011 was equal to $47,000, which is comparable to that of developed countries.

9 Some categories of the population (the disabled, large families, single-parent families etc.) benefit from state support regardless of their income.

10 Tatyana Maleva and Lidiya Ovcharova (eds), *Sotsialnaya podderzhka: uroki krizisov i vektory modernizatsii* (*Social Safety Net: Lessons of Crises and Patterns of Modernization*) (Moscow: Nezavisimy institut sotsialnoi politiki, 2010).

11 See *Monitoring razvitiya regionov Nezavisimogo instituta sotsialnoy politiki* (*Regional Development Monitoring by the Independent Institute for Social Policy*) http://www.socpol.ru/atlas/overviews/social_sphere/kris.shtml#no28. [Accessed on: 17 June 2015].

12 Tatyana Nefyodova, *Selskaya Rossiya na pereputie* (*Rural Russia at the Crossroads*) (Moscow: Novoye Izdatelstvo, 2003).

13 Sergei Shishkin (ed.), *Rossiyskoye zdravookhranenie: motivatsiya vrachei i obshchestvennay dostupnost* (*Healthcare in Russia: Doctor Motivation and Accessibility to the Public*) (Moscow: Nezavisimy institut sotsialnoi politiki, 2008).

12 Social investment

Lessons learnt over the past two decades

Andrei Margolin

The Human Development Index (HDI) is used by the UN as a key indicator for comparing literacy rates, average life expectancy and quality of life across the world. It was developed by Mahbub ul Haq and Amartya Sen back in 1990, and while the methods underpinning the index were changed more than once, it remains the best tool for evaluating human development and understanding whether the prerequisites for sustainable social and economic development are in place. Russia is progressively improving its standing in the HDI, having ranked 55th in 2013 out of 187 countries. However, this result does not match the country's potential. In practice, HDI rankings are determined to a large extent by the efficiency of social investment (SI). Accordingly, this chapter will focus on exploring such topical issues as social investment trends in today's Russia alongside their short- and medium-term prospects.

The theory of social investment

While social investment is broadly recognized as an important tool for improving living standards and the quality of life, academics have so far been unable to agree on a definition of this term and have long debated such issues as (a) whether the purpose of social investment should be about economic benefit; (b) determining social investment targets; and (c) whether any social spending can be viewed as social investment. For the purposes of this chapter, social investment is defined as non-recurrent investment of resources (financial, material or intellectual) in societal economic activity (education, healthcare, utilities, social and personal services) for achieving the investor's strategic social objectives.[1] The definition can be backed by these arguments:

a It is not uncommon for various authors to define social investment by focusing on its economic effects.[2] This financial bias could be explained by the fact the research on this subject mostly presents social investment as a developed form of corporate social responsibility. However, even for corporate players social investment does not boil down to pursuing economic effects. Another important aspect is that social investment is mostly budget-financed as part of priority government programmes, which by definition do not concern financial gain, while their outcomes are evaluated in terms of target indicators. For instance, the State Programme on Healthcare Development until 2020 is aimed at lowering the mortality rate for every cause of death to 11.4 per 1,000 people, increasing average life expectancy at birth to 74.3 years and so on.[3] With this in mind, the objective of social investment should be not so much about deriving economic (financial) gains, as it should be about improving living standards and the quality of life.

b There is also debate regarding identifying social investment targets. In this respect, the report questionably places fair consumer and business practices on a par with such key areas of social investment as HR development, public health and labour safety, environmental protection, and the efficient use of resources.[4] In fact, executing fair consumer and business practices pursues such concrete objectives as brand promotion and has little to do with social investment. The notion of an expanded social sphere as proposed by Vladislav Lavrov and Nikita Krichevsky is also hardly acceptable.[5] For them, social investment includes, apart from services in education, healthcare, culture, art and sports, such segments as wholesale and retail, restaurant and hotel businesses, transportation and agriculture, and various other areas where investment is merely business initiatives deprived of any social dimensions.

One way of devising a single approach to social investment could be to look at the Russian Classifier of Types of Economic Activity, which has separate categories for education, healthcare and other utilities, and social and personal services. In fact, social investment to a large extent is focused on these types of activity. While there is no doubt that education and healthcare are socially-oriented, the 'provision of other utilities, social and personal services' calls for clarification. According to the Russian Classifier of Types of Economic Activity, such services include sewage and waste disposal; activities of public associations; organizing leisure, entertainment, cultural and sports events; and providing personal services. What this proves is that investment in this segment is just as social as investment in education and healthcare.

c Whether any social programme implemented by state or private entities can be regarded as social investment is another issue. For instance, paying for an employee's cellphone, commute and lunch can be part of the social benefits offered to that employee without being a social investment. Such spending can be easily monetized and paid out to the employee in cash, leaving it to him or her to decide how to spend the money. This has more to do with reallocating operating costs than with investment. A better option would be to stick to economic theory basics by such classics as Paul Samuelson and John Maynard Keynes, who underscored the two intertwined aspects of investment, which are delayed consumption and focus on meeting future needs.

Social investment: a retrospective analysis

Returning to Russian contemporary history for a fully fledged retrospective analysis of social investment in its abovementioned definition presents certain challenges, since Russia's Federal State Statistics Service abandoned the industry-based approach in 2005 and started providing data on specific types of economic activity. Before that, what is now called the 'provision of other utilities, social and personal services' did not exist as a category, which makes it hard to compare data from before 2005. Data for education and healthcare is available for 1994–2013. Table 12.1 features overall and industry-specific fixed capital investment trends (compared to base year) compared to the preceding years.[6] Figure 12.1 presents the cumulative outcome.[7]

Table 12.1 Investment indices

Year	*Total*	*Social investment breakdown*		
		Healthcare and social services	*Education*	*Provision of other utilities, social and personal services*
1994	1.0	1.0	1.0	–
1995	0.899	0.897	0.758	–
1996	0.81	0.715	0.711	–
1997	0.95	1.089	0.952	–
1998	0.88	0.811	0.964	–
1999	1.053	1.061	0.948	–
2000	1.174	1.296	1.004	–
2001	1.10	1.089	1.245	–
2002	1.028	0.879	1.034	–
2003	1.125	1.201	1.103	–
2004	1.109	1.052	1.104	–
2005	1.102	1.214	1.193	1.185
2006	1.167	1.246	1.311	1.254
2007	1.227	1.204	1.256	1.152
2008	1.099	1.081	1.025	1.211
2009	0.838	0.813	0.766	0.832
2010	1.063	1.036	1.097	1.047
2011	1.108	1.044	1.134	1.129
2012	1.066	1.129	1.022	1.080
2013	0.998	0.75	0.988	1.034

Sources: *Osnovnye pokazateli investitsionnoi i stroitelnoi deyatelnosti v Rossiyskoi Federatsii-2014* (Key indicators on investment and construction in Russia, 2014). Moscow: Rosstat, available at: http://www.gks.ru/wps/wcm/connect/rosstat_main/rosstat/ru/statistics/publications/catalog/doc_1140096774766, and calculations by the author based on data from *Rossiya v tsifrakh* (Russia in Figures), editions from 2003 to 2014, available at: http://www.gks.ru/wps/wcm/connect/rosstat_main/rosstat/ru/statistics/publications/catalog/doc_1135075100641.

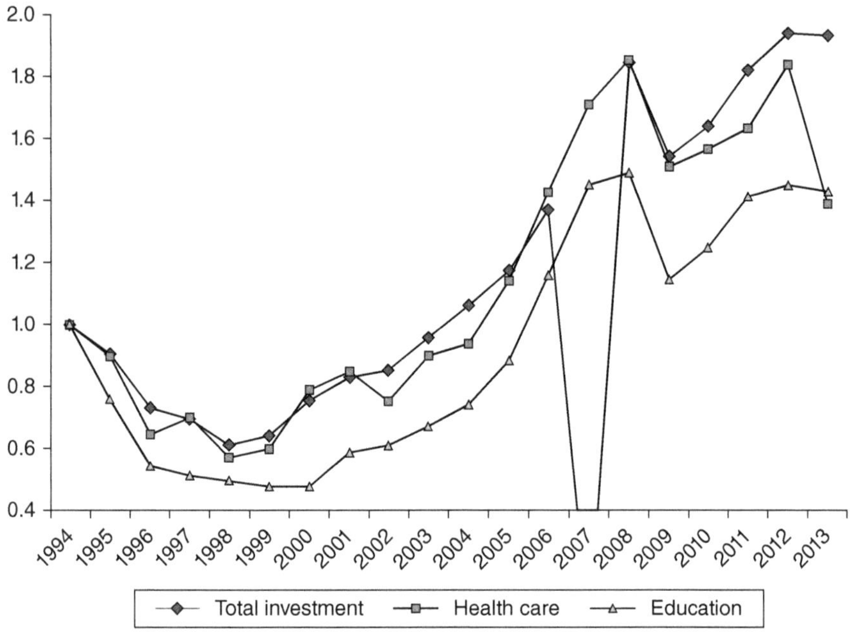

Figure 12.1 Total investment, healthcare and education investment in 1994–2013.

Source: Calculations by the author based on data from Table 12.1.

Analysis of the data in Table 12.1 and Figure 12.1 leads to the following conclusions:

- Investment activity decreased in the 1990s (reaching its low point in the crisis years of 1998 and 1999), but the trend reversed to move forward, exceeding the average level of the mid-1990s by the end of the period in question.
- Social investment (above all in education) grew at a much slower pace compared to investment in general. As for healthcare investment, it followed the same road as investment in general, but dropped in the aftermath of the 2008–2009 crisis, and especially in 2013. Ultimately, while the average annual investment almost doubled in this period, investment growth in social sectors such as education and healthcare was less than 150%.

At first glance, investment is picking up, which is a positive development, but the growth rate has so far been insufficient. This goes for investment in education and healthcare, as well as budget spending in these sectors in general. This is indirectly supported by data in Table 12.2, which features relevant comparisons with other countries.[8]

Table 12.2 Government spending on education and healthcare as percentage of GDP in G8 countries and the BRICS

Country	*Year*	*Education*	*Healthcare*
USA	2010 – Education 2011 – Healthcare	5.6	8.2
Canada	2010 – Education 2011 – Healthcare	5.5	7.9
Germany	2010	5.1	9.0
Great Britain	2010	6.3	8.1
France	2010	5.9	9.3
Italy	2010	4.5	7.4
Europe, average	2012	4.1	3.7
Japan	2010	3.8	7.8
India	2011	3.2	1.2
China	2010 – Education 2011 – Healthcare	1.9	2.9
Brazil	2010	5.8	4.1
South Africa	2010 – Education 2011 – Healthcare	6.0	4.1
Russia	2013	4.3	3.5

Sources: *Sotsialnoye polozhenie i uroven zhisni naseleniya Rossii–2013* (*Social status and living standards in Russia, 2013*). Moscow: Rosstat. Available at: http://www.gks.ru/bgd/regl/b13_44/Main.htm.

Rossiya v tsifrakh-2014 (*Russia in Figures, 2014*). Moscow: Rosstat. Available at: http://www.gks.ru/bgd/regl/b14_11/Main.htm.

Table 12.2 shows that Russia has reached the European average in terms of the share of GDP it spends on education and healthcare. What's more, Russia's results are quite good when compared to other BRICS countries (ahead of India and China, but trailing Brazil and South Africa). That said, Russia is still behind developed countries where spending on education and healthcare is regarded as a priority. While in terms of education spending the gap is not that wide (for instance, Russia is almost on a par with Italy), developed economies spend almost twice as much as Russia on healthcare. The insufficiency of social investment can also be demonstrated by analysing financing sources (Figure 12.2). The comparison of various aspects of investment in education and healthcare is rather telling.

The data featured in Figure 12.2 prove that there is some leeway for diverting resources toward social investment. In fact, both investment and government spending rose as a percentage of GDP (Figure 12.2a), although this failed to benefit education and healthcare (Figure 12.2b). What happened in these sectors between 2005 and 2013 could at best be described as stabilization of the key indicators. The only sector with an upward investment trend was the 'provision of other utilities, social and personal services'. This is largely attributable to investment in utilities and personal services, leaving the overall dynamic of

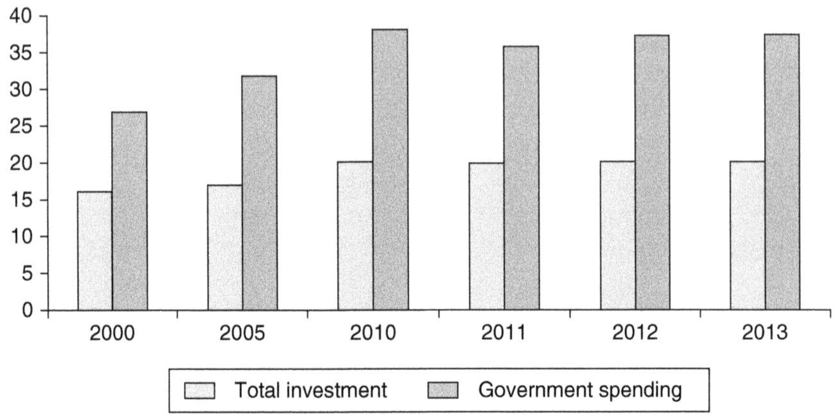

Figure 12.2a Overall fixed capital investment and government spending as percentage of GDP.

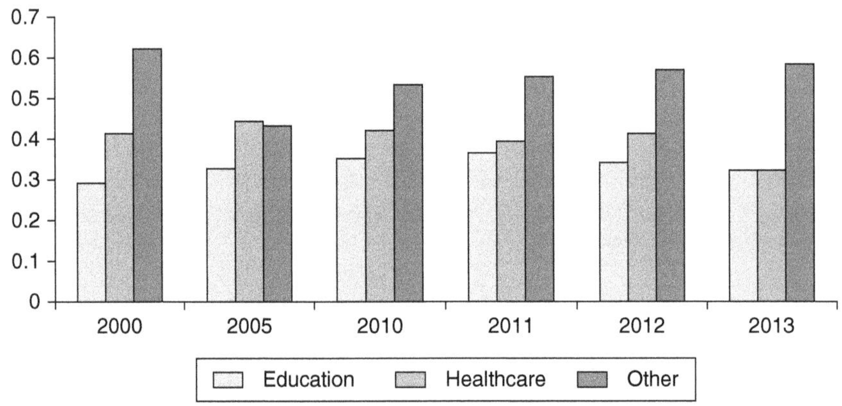

Figure 12.2b Fixed capital investment in social sectors as percentage of GDP.

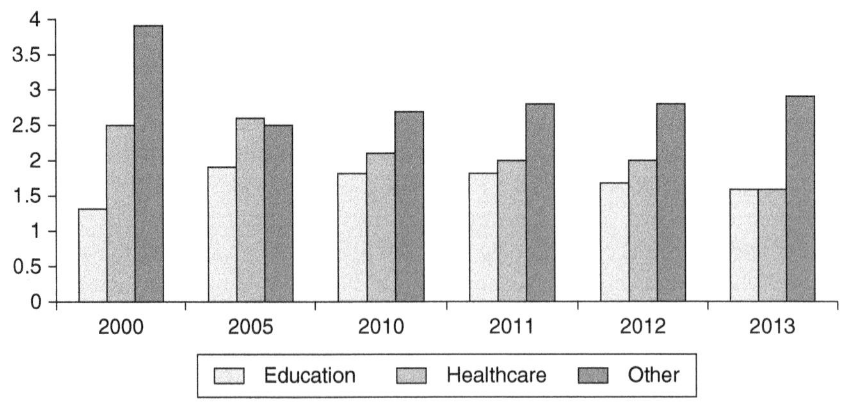

Figure 12.2c Fixed capital investment in social sectors as percentage of total fixed capital investment.

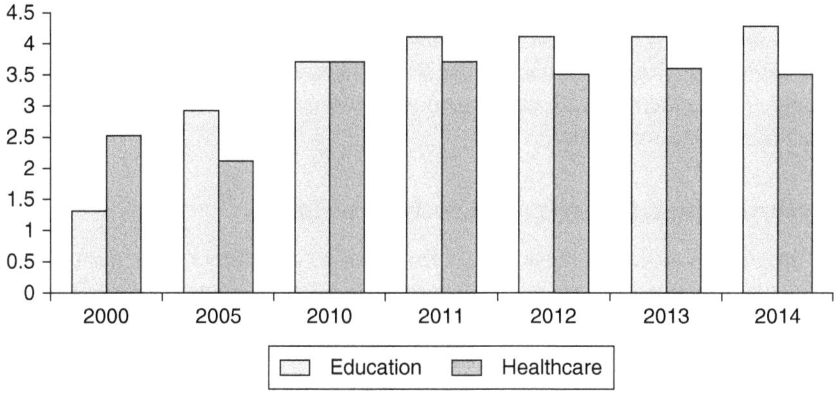

Figure 12.2d Government spending on education and healthcare as percentage of GDP.

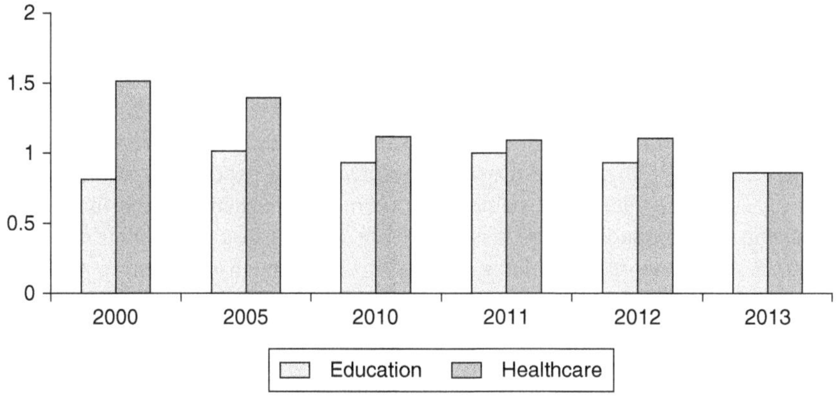

Figure 12.2e Share of investment in education and healthcare in total government spending.

Source: *Rossiya v tsifrakh-2014* (*Russia in Figures, 2014*) (Moscow: Rosstat, 2014). Available at: http://www.gks.ru/bgd/regl/b14_11/Main.htm.

social investment unaffected. Moreover, investment in education and healthcare declined compared to total investment (Figure 12.2c), as well as against government spending from the consolidated budget and extra budgetary funds (Figure 12.2e). The fact that the share of education and healthcare in government spending has remained quite stable is telling (Figure 12.2d). What this means is that priority is given to financing the daily activities of socially oriented economic sectors to ensure their smooth operation, while investment in developing these sectors is put on the back burner. That said, given that government spending as a percentage of GDP is on the rise, it can be argued that reviewing the priorities of social spending could free up resources to develop education and healthcare. Higher budget spending in these sectors could attract private investors, mainly through public–private partnerships.

This retrospective analysis of social investment shows that despite an increase in investment in absolute terms, the overall social investment is hardly sufficient. It could be expanded by reallocating resources within the consolidated budget and attracting private investment.

Measuring the actual return on social investment

The question of assessing the actual return on social investment is far from trivial and available approaches are few. One method consists of analysing data from the Russian Federal State Statistics Service on changes in living standards and economic activities related to social investment. Another option is to look at whether the relevant state programmes delivered on the indicators factored into them. These two approaches deliver the same results with the only difference that the target indicators of state programmes are more detailed compared to official statistics.

At first glance, judging by the main social and economic indicators on living standards (see, for example, *Sotsialnoye polozhenie*, 2013, Table 7.1), it could be argued that the return on social investment is high. For instance, in 2000–2013 such indicators as disposable income and the ratio between real wages and the subsistence wage (which increased from 189% in 2000 to 351% in 2013) clearly improved, while the proportion of people earning less than the subsistence wage declined from 29% to 11% of the total population, life expectancy at birth rose from 65.3 to 70.2 years, and so on. However, improvements in the indicators measuring living standards and quality of life are due to a general shift in the country's socioeconomic development away from a downward spiral to a robust recovery. It is economic growth that has led to higher wages and declining poverty, and has reversed the population decline.

As for social investment, it was so insignificant that it could not possibly have influenced macroeconomic indicators in any meaningful way. Moreover, the share of social investment against total investment (Figure 12.2c) and as a share of government spending on education and healthcare (Figure 12.2e) went down. Consequently, while the key indicators on living standards and quality of life improved, social investment moved in the opposite direction. Measuring the efficiency of social investment is not so much about overall living standards as it is about measuring the outcomes of concrete socially oriented projects and programmes.

Such projects and programmes have little in common with what businesses typically do, since their outcomes can't be evaluated using such conventional financial indicators as the net present value, payback period and the internal rate of return. For this reason, the Guidelines for Devising and Implementing State Programmes in the Russian Federation are based on the idea that such factors as the degree to which the objectives of subprogrammes and the state programme in general were achieved, and to what extent spending is efficient and if it is in line with initial projections. What follows is a review of existing approaches for measuring the efficiency of state programmes using the example of the state programme Education Development in 2013–2020 (Table 12.3).

Table 12.3 Criteria and methods for assessing the efficiency of state programme

Assessed area	*Indicators*	*Efficiency criteria*
1 Assessing the extent to which the general objectives and goals (PDC^{gen}) of the state programme (SP) were achieved	$PDC^{gen} = \frac{1}{n}\sum_{k=1}^{n} I_k^{gen}$ where: PDC^{gen} –is the value of the indicator showing to what extent the general objectives and goals of the state program were achieved; n – number of indicators on goals and objectives factored into the state programmes; I_k^{gen} - the ratio of the actual to the planned k indicator on the fulfillment of SP goal and objectives.	PDC^{gen}> 1 (1)
2 Assessing the extent to which the objectives and goals of SP's subprogrammes were achieved	$PDC_i^{Sub} = \frac{1}{n_i}\sum_{k=1}^{n_i} I_k^{Sub_i}$ where: PDC_i^{Sub} -is the value of the indicator showing to what extent the objectives and goals of an i subprogram were achieved; is the number of indicators factored into the i subprogramme; $I_k^{Sub_i}$ is the ratio of the actual to planned value of the k indicator on the fulfillment of SP goal and objectives.	$PDC_i^{Sub} > 1 (2)$
3 Assessing compliance with the projected spending targets and the public spending efficiency	$PSE = \frac{S^{bud}}{S^{ac}}$ Where PSE is an indicator of compliance of the projected spending targets with the efficiency of handling public funds when implementing SP.	PSE> 1 (3)
4 Overall SP efficiency and performance (EP)	$EP = \{PDC^{gen} + \frac{\sum_{i=1}^{M} PDC_i^{Sub}}{M}\} \times PSE$	EP> 1 (4)

Source: 'Rasporyazhenie Pravitel'stva Rossiyskoi Federatsii ot 22 noyabrya 2014 goda No. 2148-r Ob utverzhdenii gosudarstvennoy programi Rossiyskoi Federatsii Razvitie Obrazovaniya na 2013–2020 Gody' ('Directive of the Government of the Russian Federation No. 2148-r dated November 22, 2014 On the Approval of the State Program of the Russian Federation 'Development of Education in 2013–2020'). Available at: http://base.garant.ru/70265348/.

The main advantage of this system of indicators is its simplicity. In fact, it encompasses all the tools that are needed for evaluating the efficiency of the state programme on top of a straightforward comparison of the projected targets to the actual outcomes. However, would this bare-bones approach be up to the task of gauging the efficiency of state programmes? Could it eventually lead to groundless management decisions? For instance, the actual value of every indicator factored into a state programme or subprogramme does not have to be equal to or exceed the initial projections to ensure that the indicator showing whether the goals and objectives of a state programme (PDC^{gen}) or a subprogramme (PDC_i^{Sub}) is above 1 (formulas 1 and 2 in Table 12.3). Consequently, using this method a programme or subprogramme that fails to deliver on one of several objectives may be regarded as being efficient. The failure to deliver on some indicators does not make the whole programme inefficient and requires a deeper analysis of the reasons behind it. But when the programme is labelled as being efficient from the outset, such analysis will never take place.

It should be noted that the formula for evaluating the fulfillment of goals and objectives under state programmes or subprogrammes where PDC^{gen} and PDC_i^{Sub} are used as an arithmetic average of the ratio of the actual outcomes to target indicators is based on the assumption that all target indicators are equally important. However, in real life, this assumption is hardly acceptable. This is evident simply from looking at the list of target indicators factored into the subprogramme on Developing a System for Evaluating Education Quality and Information Transparency of the Education System:[9] (1) the number of education levels subject to external education quality assessment mechanisms; (2) the proportion of educational institutions with collegial management bodies involving community representatives (parents, employers) against the total number of education institutions; (3) the proportion of educational institutions providing statutory data on their activities through their official websites against the total number of educational institutions; and (4) the number of international comparative research studies in which the Russian Federation participates on a regular basis.

In accordance with the approved plan for the implementation of target indicators, the second and third indicators are expected to be fully implemented by 2014 and should remain at the 100% level throughout 2020. In this case, if these results are actually achieved in line with the initial projections, two out of four indicators will no longer affect the assessment of the subprogramme's efficiency after 2014, and will become negligible.

Using the EP indicator to evaluate the efficiency and performance under state programmes (formula 4, Table 12.3) could also lead to questionable results. If the target indicators factored into state programmes and subprogrammes are not achieved and the deviation is 10% and spending is 20% above the initial projections, it is evident that the outcomes of the programme are unsatisfactory. However, calculations made using formula 4 (Table 12.3) point the other way: $(0.9 + 0.9) \times 1 : 1.2 = 1.5$, that is EP >1. This, in turn, means that this method of assessment needs to be revised.

All in all, approaches to choosing criteria for assessing the efficiency of state programmes should be substantially improved. Simple solutions are not always the best ones. Using simplistic methods to designate the key indicators creates additional risks, since such decisions as whether to continue to provide financing for such programmes or not can be groundless. The PART method (Program Assessment Rating Tool) could be used to develop new approaches to evaluating the efficiency of state programmes.[10] This was first used in the USA and has since been tried and tested across the world. The fact that about 50% of federal programmes were declared inefficient after the PART method was implemented is quite telling. This proportion declined to 30% within a year, which means that the programmes had improved and become results-driven.

What lies ahead for social investment?

In order to evaluate social investment prospects objectively, the criteria for such an assessment should be accepted by the academic community. One possible approach could be to select the most important indicators on various social sectors (education, healthcare, provision of social services to the population, environmental protection etc.) and blend them together. However, it should be taken into account that these sectors are competing against each other for public financing, while the indicators that are supposed to reflect their development are often of little interest to businesses. For this reason, the private sector is not eager to promote social investment by engaging in corporate social responsibility initiatives as part of public–private partnerships. Finding an integrated criterion for assessing the future of social investment by blending diverging indicators related to social development is challenging. Selecting indicators is the most challenging task in this regard, since any consensus among experts on the importance of various development indicators, for example in education and healthcare, is unlikely.

In view of the above, using an integrated indicator that shows the level of trust among businesses and the population in the state generally and its social policy in particular could be an unbiased way of analysing social investment. In our opinion, the meaning of the trust criterion for social and economic research is underestimated. All things being equal, higher confidence in the state could directly translate into concrete economic effects such as lower commercial risks, leading to an increase in investment and higher returns from public–private partnerships, as well as creating new investment opportunities for businesses.

This approach could be implemented using the strategic matrix. Working along the same lines as the Boston Consulting Group (with its two-dimension matrix on 'market share/market growth'), the Ansoff Matrix (product–market matrix) and similar tools, we can build a matrix for evaluating social investment prospects using two dimensions: profitability and fairness. These two indicators shall have the following meaning:

a We can define profitability as the average annual change in per capita income against the subsistence level. Using the average per capita income would be less representative, since this metric may grow against the background of an even higher increase in the subsistence level and declining living standards.

b The fairness indicator is defined as the average annual change in income inequality. In this respect we will rely on the Federal State Statistics Service's income inequality ratio, which is the ratio of the average income of the richest 10% to the poorest 10%.

The strong points of these indicators are that they are not affected by inflation (being based on ratios, not absolute figures), and rely on conventional statistical indicators. Figure 12.3 shows a graphic representation of the social investment assessment matrix, featuring brief descriptions of its quadrants.

Let us now consider two crucial periods in recent Russian history, from 1992 to 2000 and from 2000 to 2013, and see how they compare to the quadrants of the proposed matrix using the retrospective indicators of profitability and fairness (see Table 12.4). According to the results, the profitability and justice indicators fell into the matrix's second quadrant in 1992–2000, when the levels of trust were low in all respects (trust of consumers and businesses in the state, as well as the trust of the state in businesses). Resources for social investment were non-existent, and even budget-sponsored socially oriented policies were usually mistrusted by the low-income groups that were supposed to benefit from such initiatives. The reason is quite evident: from the outset people suspected such projects of being driven by corrupt schemes.

The landscape changed considerably in 2000–2013, with the profitability and justice indicators shifting from the second to the third quadrant of the matrix. Average income grew more than four times faster than income inequality. This means that prerequisites were created for strengthening trust and attracting social investment from the private sector. Given that the Russian economy is known for its regional imbalances (see Chapter 11), we can test the abovementioned conclusions by analysing profitability and justice indicators in regions with diverging levels of social risk using the investment attractiveness ranking of the Russian regions in 2013 published by the Expert RA rating agency.[11] In accordance with the agency's internationally acclaimed method, the investment appeal can be analysed using a two-dimensional matrix by comparing investment potential with investment risks, where social risk is one of the key indicators.

The first stage consists of selecting representative regions. We decided to pick the Belgorod Region, the Stavropol Territory and the Republic of Buryatia as regions with low, average and high social risk, respectively. Since statistics on the regions have not been provided in a single format until recently, we use available statistical data to review the indicators in question for these regions, which basically correspond with the profitability and fairness indicators for 2002–2012.[12] The results are outlined in Table 12.5.

It is telling that results from regions with different levels of social risks are almost identical to those for the entire country. The profitability and fairness

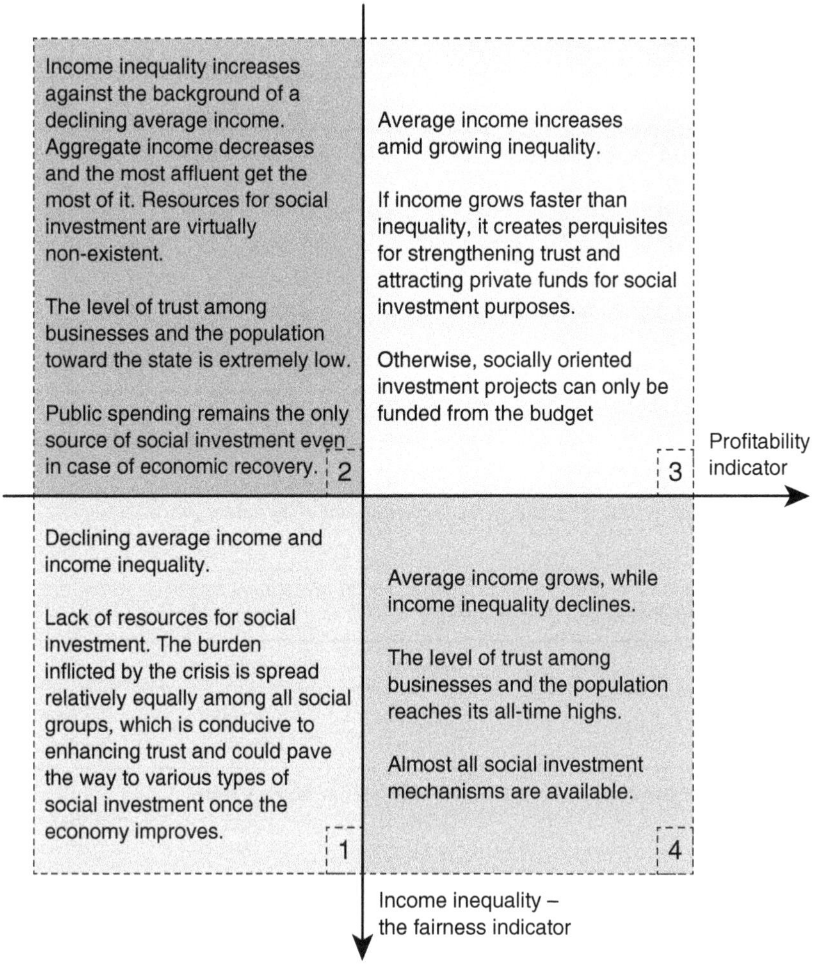

Figure 12.3 Social investment potential matrix.

Source: Research by the author.

indicators in this table correspond to the third quadrant of the social investment matrix. Since the social and economic processes in question take a lot of time to emerge, the fact that Table 12.4 examines data for 2000–2013 and Table 12.5 for 2002–2012 does not affect the obtained results.

On the one hand, the obtained data show that confidence is improving, which entails a number of positive consequences, the most important of which is perhaps the fact that the popularity rankings of President Vladimir Putin have reached historic highs amid growing foreign policy tensions due to the Ukraine conflict and various sanctions against Russia by the United States and some other countries

Table 12.4 Statistical information and calculated indicators for the matrix on social investment prospects for the periods in question

Indicators	*Years*		
	1992	*2000*	*2013*
Ratio of average per capita income to the subsistence level, *x* times	2.12	1.89	3.51
Income inequality ratio	8.0	13.9	16.2
Average annual rate of change in the key indicators, %	1992–2000		2000–2013
– Ratio of average per capita income to the subsistence level	−1.43		4.88
– Income inequality ratio	7.15		1.18

Source: *Sotsialnoye polozhenie i uroven zhisni naseleniya Rossii-2013* (*Social status and living standards in Russia*) (2013). Moscow: Rosstat, available at: http://www.gks.ru/bgd/regl/b13_44/Main.htm, and calculations by the author.

Note: Income inequality ratio is the ratio of the average income of the richest 10% to the poorest 10%.

Table 12.5 Calculated indicators for evaluating social investment prospects in regions with different levels of social risk

Indicator	*Regions*		
	Belgorod Region	*Stavropol Territory*	*Republic of Buryatia*
Ratio of average per capita income to the subsistence level, *x* times			
2002	1.76	1.425	1.497
2012	4.21	2.696	2.53
Income inequality ratio, *x* times			
2002	9.4	9.4	14.1
2012	15.3	13.1	15.2
Average annual rate of change in the key indicators in 2002–2012, %			
– Ratio of average per capita income to the subsistence level	9.1	6.6	5.4
– Income inequality ratio	5.0	3.4	0.8

Source: *Regiony Rossii. Sotsialno-economicheskie pokazateli-2013* (*Russian regions: Socioeconomic indicators, 2013*) (Moscow: Rosstat, 2013). Available at: http://www.gks.ru/bgd/regl/b13_14p/Main.htm, and calculations by the author.

that followed suit. This atmosphere of trust consolidates the elites as well as society in general and should be regarded as the prerequisite for efficient development and improving competitiveness against the backdrop of growing tensions in Russia's relations with the outside world.

On the other hand, the change in the profitability and fairness indicators provides new financing opportunities for social investment, as well as offers new mechanisms for implementing socially oriented projects. Specifically, there is already some positive experience in education and healthcare of using public–private partnerships in various forms. Among the examples of such initiatives is the transfer of a maternity hospital to a private clinic in Novosibirsk, under which the concession operator is expected to ensure that the facility is operated to the highest standards and carries out 48 costly in vitro fertilization operations to patients with state-funded mandatory medical insurance policies. The concession operator has economic incentives to participate in this project, being able to serve clients with private medical insurance policies or on a paid basis. It is evident that even seriously discussing such projects, let alone implementing them, could have been hardly envisaged in 1992–2000.

Conclusion

In this chapter, social investment has been defined as a non-recurrent investment of resources (financial, material or intellectual) in societal economic activity (education, healthcare, utilities, social and personal services) for achieving the investor's strategic social objectives. Despite a decline in investment in the 1990s, the trend reversed in the 2000s, and by 2013 the average annual investment volumes almost doubled compared to the mid-1990s. Social investment (especially in education) grew at a much slower pace than investment in general, so while the general trend to increase social investment is encouraging, the aggregate amount is so far insufficient. The same is also true for public spending on societal types of economic activities in general. That said, reviewing social development priorities could free up more resources for social investment. Additional investments in education and healthcare can be found. In this case, public spending could make social projects more attractive for private investors.

Providing an objective analysis of social investment efficiency remains problematic. Confining the analysis to following changes in such superficial indicators as increases in the disposable income and the ratio of real income to the subsistence level and life expectancy at birth in 2000–2013 could lead to the conclusion that the return on social investment was quite high. However, improvements in living standards and quality of life are actually attributable to the country's social and economic development, with economic growth coming on the heels of a protracted period of contraction. As for social investment, its size was so insignificant that it could not have possibly affected macroeconomic social indicators in any meaningful way. For this reason, the assessment of social investment efficiency should be not so much about comparing it with quality of life indicators, as about measuring the outcomes of concrete projects and programmes related to social investment. The PART method (Programme Assessment Rating Tool) could be used to develop new approaches to evaluating the efficiency of state programmes. It was developed in the United States and has been recognized around the world.

We propose an integrated tool for measuring business and consumer trust in the state in general and its social policy specifically as an unbiased instrument for analyzing the prospects of social investment. To this end, a strategic matrix could be used to gauge social investment prospects along profitability and fairness axes. This analytical tool is based on (a) the profitability indicator, which is defined as the average annual change in per capita income against the subsistence level, and (b) the fairness indicator defined as the average annual change in income inequality. The strong points of these indicators are that they are not affected by inflation, and rely on conventional statistical indicators.

It is quite telling that in the matrix measuring social investment prospects, profitability and fairness indicators for 1992–2000 fell into the quadrant that reflects an atmosphere of total mistrust (trust among consumers and businesses in the state, as well as the trust of the state in businesses) and a lack of social investment prospects. The landscape changed considerably in 2000–2013, with the profitability and fairness indicators shifting from the second to the third quadrant of the matrix. Average incomes grew more than four times faster than income inequality. Accordingly, prerequisites have been created for strengthening trust and attracting social investment from the private sector. Given that the Russian economy is known for its regional imbalances, it was important to substantiate these data. Statistics from regions with different levels of social risk (the Belgorod Region, the Stavropol Territory and the Republic of Buryatia) were analysed, and the results turned out to be nearly identical to the data for the entire country. This positive momentum in profitability and fairness indicators significantly expands funding opportunities for social investment, as well as ensures that more solutions for implementing social investment projects are available, including working with the private sector on social initiatives within the framework of public–private partnerships.

Notes

1 Both the state and private companies may act as investors.

2 For example, Yuri Blagov, Sergei Litovchenko and Yekaterina Ivanova (eds), *Doklad o sotsialnykh investitsiyakh v Rossii* (*Report on Social Investment in Russia*) (Moscow: Assotsiatsiya Menedherov, 2008); Natalia Ivanova, 'Sotsialnoye investirovanie: obzor zarubezhnykh praktik' ('Social Investment: A Review of Foreign Practices', *Grazhdanskoye obshchestvo v Rossii i za rubezhom* (*Civil Society in Russia and Abroad*), No. 3, 2013.

3 Directive of the Government of the Russian Federation No. 294, dated 15 April 2014, 'Ob utverzhdenii Gossudarstvennoi programmy Rossiyskoi Federatsii Razvitie Zdravokhraneniya' ('On the approval of the State Programme on Healthcare Development'), *Sobranie zakonodatelstva Rossiyskoi Federatsii* (Collected Legislation of the Russian Federation), No. 17, 2014, p. 2,057. See also 'Ob utverzhdenii Metodicheskikh ukazaniy po rasrabotke i realizatsii gosudarstvennykh program Rossiyskoi Federatsii' ('On the Approval of Methodological Recommendations Regarding the Development and Implementation of Russia's State Programme'), Order of Russia's Ministry of Economic Development No. 690, dated 20 November 2013. Available at: http://programs.gov.ru/Portal/programs/documents. [Accessed on: 17 June 2015].

4 Blagov et al., 2013.
5 Vladislav Lavrov and Nikita Krichevsky, 'Chto takoe sotsialnie investitsii?' (What is social investment), *Agentstvo politicheskikh novostei*, 2 February 2006. Available at: www.apn.ru/publications/article1776.htm. [Accessed on: 17 June 2015].
6 *Osnovnye pokazateli investitsionnoi i stroitelnoi deyatelnosti v Rossiyskoi Federatsii-2014* (*Key Indicators on Investment and Construction in Russia*) (Moscow: Rosstat, 2014). Available at: http://www.gks.ru/wps/wcm/connect/rosstat_main/rosstat/ru/statistics/publications/catalog/doc_1140096774766. [Accessed on: 17 June 2015].
7 Here and onward, fixed capital investment is analysed as a total of costs channelled into construction and renovation (except for expansion and modernization) of facilities to enhance their original value.
8 The table is drawn from *Sotsialnoye polozhenie i uroven zhisni naseleniya Rossii-2013* (*Social status and living standards in Russia, 2013*) (Moscow: Rosstat, 2013), http://www.gks.ru/bgd/regl/b13_44/Main.htm [Accessed on: 17 June 2015]; *Rossiya v tsifrakh: 2014* (*Russia in Figures*) (Moscow: Rosstat, 2014), http://www.gks.ru/bgd/regl/b14_11/Main.htm [Accessed on: 17 June 2015].
9 See Rasporiazhenie Pravitelstva Rossiyskoi Federatsii ot 22 noyabrya 2014 goda No. 2148-r 'Ob utverzhdenii gosudarstvennoy programmi Rossiiskoi Federatsii Razvitie Obrazovaniya na 2013–2020 Gody' (Directive of the Government of the Russian Federation No. No. 2148-r, dated 22 November 2014 'On the Approval of the State Programme of the Russian Federation Development of Education in 2013–2020'), 2014, Appendix 1, page 315, http://base.garant.ru/70265348/. [Accessed on: 17 June 2015].
10 See, for example, Programme Assessment Rating Tool Guidance No. 2008–01. Office of Management and Budget. January 2008.
11 'Investitsionnaya privlekatelnost regionov 2013: aktsent na infrastructuru' ('Investment Appeal of the Regions 2013: Focusing on Infrastructure], Expert RA rating agency, www.raexpert.ru/raitings/regions/2013/. [Accessed on: 17 June 2015].
12 *Regiony Rossii. Sotsialno-economicheskie pokazateli-2013* (*Russian Regions: Socioeconomic Indicators, 2013*) (Moscow: Rosstat, 2013), http://www.gks.ru/bgd/regl/b13_14p/Main.htm. [Accessed on: 17 June 2015].

13 The Russian elite's strategy of self-isolation

Boris Mezhuev

The aim of this chapter is to account for the alienation of Russian political elites (both in power and in the opposition) from the majority of the population, which is reflected in their beliefs and values as well as in the political conduct of their representatives. This alienation explains why liberal elites have lost political leadership. As I will seek to demonstrate, liberals are trying to regain leadership by recreating the perestroika model in which progressive elements in the government moved closer to the liberal intelligentsia. After feeling doomed to remain on the margins of society, the intelligentsia rode a powerful wave of public support and won over the majority for some time. However, I believe their new project will fail, as any new 'perestroika' will inevitably unfold in its own way.

Cultural hegemony from tsarist times to the Soviet era

In Eldar Ryazanov's immensely popular 1979 comedy *Garage*, a nasty character named Karpukhin constantly changes sides during a vote and utters the words 'I'm with the majority' to explain his seemingly erratic behaviour. Since then the word 'majority' has gradually acquired a pejorative connotation in Russian political discourse. Ten years after the film's release one of the leaders of the democratic opposition, Yury Afanasyev, called the delegates voting for the presidium 'the aggressively obedient majority' at the First Congress of People's Deputies of the USSR. By 1999, Gleb Pavlovsky, the former dissident who organized the first mass demonstration in Moscow in 1989, was talking about 'Putin's majority', which incorporated former opponents – both liberals and nationalists. Ten years later, Pavlovsky would remark on the disintegration of this unstable electoral coalition, which later reemerged as 'the overwhelming majority', in his words, by excluding the 'progressive minority'. The discourse on 'the majority' came full circle – once a symbol of national unity, it again became a euphemism for obedience and conformism.

The years 1989–2009 marked a brief period in Russian history when the liberal elite were able to rally 'the people' behind them and exercise political leadership. Of course, it could only maintain leadership with the support of the authorities, who had to meet the majority halfway from time to time, thereby showing solidarity. However, these symbolic steps in the interests of the majority did not contradict the interests of the elite initially. The flat tax rate was introduced in Russia in 2000, the same year the Soviet national anthem was revived. However, this in-between state could not last for long. Sooner or later the government would have to choose whether to focus primarily on the elite or the people. This choice could have been avoided if the elite had ensured popular support. By the early 2010s the elite had largely lost its ability to lead, partly due to its freely chosen 'strategy of self-isolation' from the people.

To understand this strategy, let us turn to the concept of 'cultural hegemony' – a popular term in social philosophy, first introduced into academic discourse by the Italian Marxist Antonio Gramsci, author of the influential *Prison Notebooks*. He used the concept to explain the mechanisms of power possessed by the ruling class in an exploitative society. Gramsci contrasted 'domination' based on coercion with 'hegemony'. As with violence, the lower classes had to tolerate the hegemony established by the upper classes, which relied on culture to espouse values, principles and views that legitimatized the existing system and their subordination in it. Power is derived not only from force but also culture. However, as a committed Marxist, Gramsci believed that culture reinforces political domination and that the ultimate aim of political domination is economic exploitation.[1]

Western historiography adopted the concept of 'cultural hegemony' in specific studies, but rid Gramsci's theory of its inherent rationalistic reductionism by recognizing the mutual influence between the culture of the 'bottom' and that of the 'top'. Such cross-pollination was typical of the Reformation and the early Enlightenment. In his book *Religion and the Decline of Magic*, the British historian Keith Thomas writes that the new rational, science-based mentality was being born at that time, while magical thinking about nature and man was receding into the past.[2] Nonetheless, according to Gramsci's approach, culture plays a functional role in the social system as a conscious or subconscious ally of the forces that ensure the unity of the system by suppressing notions of justice that differ from the dominant ones.[3] However, the problem is that cultural hegemony does not necessarily translate into political leadership for the class that achieves it, although leadership as such is not an indispensable prerequisite for political dominance or economic exploitation. Moreover, the goals of economic and cultural power do not always coincide: the special status of the nobility at the very top of the Russian Empire's pyramid of exploitation in the nineteenth century and its prevalence in the national culture of that time did not mean that the culture of the nobility was able to entrench and perpetuate the economic system of serfdom.[4]

Interestingly, the cultural hegemony achieved by the educated nobility in the middle of the nineteenth century in Russia destroyed, instead of strengthened, its political and economic power. The Western values of 'personal liberty' and 'individualism' embraced by the enlightened nobility paradoxically contributed to the dismantling of their system of social privileges. Cultural hegemony cannot be considered merely an auxiliary means of dominance and exploitation. This type of hegemony can help the class that holds dominant positions in culture to ensure its political leadership. Thus, in the early twentieth century Russia eventually accepted the leadership of the revolutionary intelligentsia largely because they destroyed the hegemony of the nobility and the clergy and managed to present themselves to some extent as the inheritor of the best cultural traits of all social strata. In the early twentieth century the upper class of the Russian Empire lost the ability to impose its tastes and views on the educated part of society. The loss of its role as 'cultural hegemon' predetermined not only the social isolation of the ruling aristocracy but also its subsequent departure from the historical stage.

The same applies to the Soviet Party elite, although, unlike the Russian aristocracy, it never claimed cultural hegemony in society – in the Soviet era there were no films or books that affectionately described the daily life of some party apparatchik. Nor would it occur to any approved Soviet author to write a novel about a Politburo member of the Brezhnev era. Party apparatchiks rooted their cultural legitimacy in the legacy of early Bolshevism. The high-ranking officials posing as the successors of Vladimir Lenin and Yakov Sverdlov – real members of the intelligentsia – had to reach an intellectual level appropriate for the elite. Incidentally, at about the same time western intellectuals observed the alienation of government officials from knowledge in their own countries. In a 1954 lecture, C. Wright Mills wrote ruefully that 'Knowledge and power are not truly united inside the ruling circles; and when men of knowledge do come to a point of contact with the circles of powerful men, they come not as peers but as hired men. The elite of power, wealth and celebrity are not of the elite of culture, knowledge and sensibility. Moreover, they are not in contact with it.'[5]

It is hard to say to what extent the upper crust of the Romanov monarchy accepted responsibility for their cultural defeat, which ultimately led to their political defeat. There is no document in which representatives of the tsarist dynasty or the nobility express concern over the fact that the last Russian emperor, Nicholas II, lacked the opportunity to rub elbows with the best writers and poets of his era (as Nicholas I and, to a lesser extent, Alexander II had). Indeed, at some point the upper crust of society becomes disconnected from the cultural trends of their time and self-isolation no longer seems like a risky or dangerous option. However, Russian intellectuals understood well that the monarchy's alienation from progressive trends in society was the regime's Achilles heel and that sooner or later the intelligentsia's cultural hegemony would lead to political leadership.[6] The monarchy's last attempt to gain cultural leadership was the so-called 'Russian style' of the Alexander III era. It was imposed from above and reflected the conservative attitudes of this era. Nicolas II stayed out of culture altogether. The Art Nouveau style that dominated his era was decidedly informal and had no connection to anything even remotely official. Putin's conservatism may suffer the same tragic fate if it fails to associate itself with progressive intellectual and artistic trends.

The same Russian intelligentsia that rejected the right of the ruling class to cultural hegemony over educated society acquired the political ambitions to assert its own cultural hegemony over the people – the third symbolic member of the Russian triad. It would be interesting to look at the culture of the late nineteenth and early twentieth centuries through the prism of the hidden struggle for influence over 'the silent majority' of the Russian people, which had been waged by the Russian government and the Russian revolutionary opposition with varying degrees of success. The so-called period of 'going to the people' was followed by an abrupt separation of the intelligentsia and the people. The intelligentsia concluded that the majority of people were not on their side and started looking for various strategies to gain both hegemony and leadership. In particular, they made an attempt to move closer to the people on the basis of religion – the atheism of the majority of intellectuals was one of the most vulnerable facets of their socio-cultural views.[7] The Russian intelligentsia resisted the strategy of dominance that worked best for the government, which by means of various tactics presented itself as the true defenders of the national interest – as distinct from the markedly hostile educated class that ostensibly tried to use popular discontent to blackmail those at the top and consolidate its own position as leaders.[8]

However, the situation changed substantially in the late Soviet era when a considerable part of the intelligentsia declared itself an obvious minority that was far removed from the people and quietly accepted as a norm its alienation both from political power and the majority. Curiously, this happened at a time when the intelligentsia enjoyed 'cultural hegemony' over the majority of people, which it could have parlayed into political leadership later on. However, 'the strategy of self-isolation' of the early 1970s played a role in how the intelligentsia made use of the benefits it accrued after finally gaining political power in the 1990s.

Loss of the minority

To understand the effects of this bizarre strategy, let us take a closer look at recent events. The confrontation between the authorities and the liberal opposition that reached its peak after the 2011–2012 winter protests is often described as a struggle between the pro-government 'majority' and the protesting 'minority'.[9] It should be noted that this characterization suits both sides equally well. Our main thesis is that during this confrontation 'the minority' that sought political power both in the government and the opposition actually gave up its bid for cultural hegemony of its own free will and chose what we consider an obviously losing strategy of 'self-isolation'. The liberal elite stopped fighting to win over the people, claiming even that the methods they would have to use to do so are flawed and morally dubious. Yet, they did not give up their claims to political leadership or their attempts to access the instruments of influence, such as the media.

Meanwhile, the authorities only feigned the impression that they were guided by the will of the majority. In reality they perceived the majority as a passive object to be manipulated, as illustrated by their attitude to the so-called party of the majority – United Russia. Political machinations raised the party's standing and gave it an electoral advantage. During the 2011 Duma election campaign, the party was not given a chance to become an independent political actor. On the contrary, it had no freedom to respond to any campaign issue. The party of the majority became 'a party of acclamation'. The forces bent on the regime's destruction immediately exploited the opening. United Russia had no more 'swindlers and thieves' than any other party, but its members were not allowed to defend themselves against this derogatory label.

The Duma elections killed the idea of the majority as the mute ward of the educated elite that was supposed to passively accept its slogans, tastes and views. However, the problem was not that the authorities wanted to keep the majority on its side, but that they didn't want the majority to become an independent political actor. Unfounded accusations were hurled at United Russia. Alexei Kudrin's supporters blamed the party for wanting to spend money from the Stabilization Fund, whereas his opponents accused it of supporting Kudrin's preferred fiscal policies. Meanwhile, United Russia had nothing to do with the Fund and yet did not respond to the accusations, limiting itself to statements about the 'real work' that was being done. When Vitaly Ivanov, a staunch supporter of the present system, called United Russia a 'saw' or 'shovel' in the hands of the executive branch, he probably did not realize what an apt metaphor this was for the party's main flaw.[10]

To justify their claims to exclusivity, representatives of the political elite often rely on undemocratic arguments about how the majority is uneducated or at best brainwashed by propaganda and therefore unable to make the right decisions in today's complex world. Therefore, power should be held not by representatives of this majority but the most worthy and competent representatives of the minority.[11] The majority is unable to rationally articulate its interests because it is captive to a media that pushes the positions of the government.[12]

To assess the political consequences of this 'strategy of self-isolation' let us compare two events: the 1905–1907 Russian revolution and the 'political awakening' of 2011 and 2012. Outwardly, these two events have something in common – both started with mass demonstrations in the capitals and led to a rapid revival of civic engagement after many years of political stagnation and unfulfilled hopes for a 'revolution from above'. In the first case, the protests were sparked by the strike at the Putilov plant and the arrest of its organizers, while the recent protests were a response to the State Duma elections that some in the opposition denounced as fraudulent. In both cases the protests came after the authorities prohibited demonstrations in the city centre. Initially both seemed massive and threatened to develop into prolonged periods of unrest. Despite the radically different tactics employed by the opposition in these two cases, the volatile combination of several simultaneous but not directly linked expressions of discontent accounted for the significant impact of both protests. In 1905 peasants set fire to the manors of the nobility to protest ruinous agrarian policies, liberals in the provinces were grumbling and the proletariat were dissatisfied with their working conditions. At that time the left-wing intelligentsia nurtured revolutionary socialist dreams and tried to harness all these forms of discontent to realize them.

While the centres of resistance in 2011–2012 were less diverse and widespread than in 1905, they were not as homogeneous or scarce as both sides would later claim. The protests could have remained strictly local if the revolt of 'the creative class' – already incensed by the Putin–Medvedev job swap at the United Russia party conference in September 2011 – had not been amplified by the party's unpopularity in the country's regions with a predominantly ethnic Russian population. People saw United Russia as an alliance of corrupt local officials and state-supported businesses. According to the Central Election Committee, United

Russia received 49.3% of votes, significantly lower than the 64.3% it received in 2007 when the party won a constitutional majority to the State Duma. It was this relative failure in 2011 that allowed the protests in Moscow to reach a national scale.[13] Members of the opposition, supporters of the current government and experts with varying degrees of bias endlessly repeated the refrain that the events of the winter of 2011–2012 were the work of the urban privileged class. It was derisively dubbed 'the mink revolution'. It is clear why opponents of the protests on Moscow's Bolotnaya Square played down the national reach of the protests, but supporters also basically conceded the point, as if in cahoots with the opposing side, which only reinforced the impression that the 'creative class' was confined to enclaves in Russia's cities. This minority believes that its defeatism and lack of interest in success is a mark of moral virtue.[14]

In light of this, the political tactics of the opposition in the winter of 2011 seem very strange. Given the fortuitous alignment of the opposition in Moscow with the aspirations of at least one-third of Russia's regions where United Russia received less than 40% of the vote, the creative class should have placed its bets on the social forces and political movements that could bridge the gap between them. The spontaneous crowd of opposition members that formed on Bolotnaya Square included such forces, primarily, the Left Front. The demonstrations enjoyed substantial support from students who were upset about their economic wellbeing and professional prospects.[15] It was clear that the continuation of liberal reforms in education and science would undercut the social standing of this group, which played into the hands of the Left Front. Incidentally, its leaders, especially Sergei Udaltsov, managed to see its potential and at one point took charge of the street opposition, leaving behind the rest of the protest leaders.

Alexei Navalny also had some chance of emerging as a national leader. He used his unquestioned authority in the beginning of the protest movement to considerably expand the base of the street opposition, co-opting left-wing and nationalist politicians to lead it. Later, however, the leaders of the opposition's liberal wing did all they could to dramatically reduce their reliance on the masses by following the self-isolation strategy. Incidentally, the Russian authorities did not pay attention to the widespread protest sentiment at the grassroots level that was unrelated to the attitudes of the Moscow revolutionaries, and managed to successfully push the opposition to the socio-cultural ghetto that is 13% of the population at most. The remaining 87% that subsequently rallied around the president over events in Ukraine and the West's response came together organically, as illustrated by the solidary voting of all parliamentary parties in the Duma and United Russia's de facto renunciation of its exclusive right to be 'the ruling party' or 'the party of the majority'. The entire Duma became a kind of a symbolic pro-presidential majority, which paradoxically reduced rather than enhanced its legitimacy in the eyes of the majority. According to the polling agency VTsIOM, on 4 March 2013 less than half of all Russians approved of the Duma, which was actually an improvement compared to 2012.[16]

Subsequently, the authorities actively worked with representatives of the liberal minority who were ready to give up radical slogans but shut down any attempts by certain public figures to gain the support of the ‘overwhelming’ (or ‘Crimean’) majority with ideas that contradicted, even slightly, the semi-official line on reformatting the ideology of the ‘Russian Spring’. Sergei Udaltsov, who strongly supported reunification with Crimea and the uprising in Donbass, was the only leader of the Bolotnaya Square opposition to land in prison. Hero of the Sevastopol uprising and ‘people’s mayor’ Alexei Chaly was forced out of politics by bureaucrats and had to bow out of the governor’s race despite his triumph in the elections to the Legislative Assembly in September 2014. Military leader of the Donetsk People’s Republic Igor Strelkov was dismissed from his post but still remains a prominent figure and is covered by the media owing to the support he gets from influential ultra-right business groups. What was true under Alexander III remains true today: the authorities prefer to deal with either an obedient majority or with a self-isolated and self-satisfied minority that holds no appeal whatsoever for the majority. Needless to say, given this unilateral approach, the authorities run the risk of simply losing the people at some point, having become convinced of their inherent conservatism. Meanwhile, history teaches us that the people are unlikely to remain silent forever.

An ‘iron curtain’ for personal use

In 2011 sociologist Natalya Zubarevich introduced her concept of the four Russias, each with its own voting preferences.[17] The political context of this concept was clear: according to Zubarevich, Putin continues to be supported by voters of Russia-2 in the country’s gradually degrading industrial periphery and hydrocarbon regions. Residents of the large metropolitan areas in Russia-1 form the potential base of voters for a candidate from the liberal opposition, with Just Cause (Pravoe Delo) leader Mikhail Prokhorov filling that role at the time. Zubarevich draws a clear dividing line between the sources of discontentment for the advanced and backward segments of society. The Bolsheviks described similar tactics employed by the proletariat during the Russian revolution as ‘menshevist-sky’, which came to be used to denote the proletariat’s strategy of self-isolation from the poorest peasantry, although the origins of the terms ‘Bolshevism’ and ‘Menshevism’ were determined by completely different historical circumstances.

Representatives of the elites did their best to present the 2011–2012 protests not as the expression of demands by different segments of the population but the voice of the progressive minority that claimed for itself the right to priority access to sources of power and cultural influence by virtue of their radical positions on social issues and relative economic independence. Playing right into the administration’s political strategy to undermine the protests, opposition members aligned themselves with counter-cultural social movements, which immediately emphasized their marginality and put them at odds with the traditional moral values of the majority. This primarily applies to their support for the members of Pussy Riot, who were sentenced to prison for their outrageous conduct in Christ the Saviour Cathedral. What began as an acceptable level of indignation at an overly harsh and unjustified verdict quickly turned into an anti-clerical campaign, causing many believers to turn away from the opposition. Needless to say, the authorities continuously exploited the cultural divisions between the urban class and the country's more traditional population. However, unlike all other eras of political awakening in Russia, the leaders of the most recent one did not fight back vigorously and instead adhered to the self-isolation strategy described above.[18]

On 6 May 2012, the day before Putin's inauguration, Udaltsov led people to Bolotnaya Square for the March of Millions. Liberal intellectuals wearing white ribbons were joined by left-wing youth sporting red and black anarchist flags who came to Moscow from the provinces largely just to show the 'effete intellectuals from the capital' what a real protest looks like. Clashes between such demonstrators and law enforcement led to criminal proceedings against the organizers of the march and those who fought with the police. It would seem that the required unity of the country's centre and regions had been achieved, but opposition media glossed over the participation of 'provincials' in the 6 May events even more than pro-government outlets. The liberal minority thus demonstrated its complete lack of interest in fighting for cultural hegemony and political leadership over the social groups and movements whose presence in the square made it the largest opposition rally to date. Apparently, the liberals felt they didn't need this majority (which is to say, they didn't need their own people). They were only interested in a specific set of values shared by a minority of Russians.

This self-isolation strategy can be explained, in part, by the liberal political leanings of a segment of both pro-government and opposition elites in Russia. During the 1905 revolution the liberals had to make a tactical alliance with socialists and accept part of their programme, but the elite also adopted a line of socio-cultural and economic isolation from the majority. In this sense the opposition was completely in synch with the government's pro-Western liberal wing, for which the participation of leftists and nationalists provided a reason (or excuse) to stay away from the protests. But the strategy was not based on a rational foundation. Liberal intellectuals perhaps hoped that the progressive minority's growing alienation from the government would sooner or later lead to frustration among government officials, whose children would seek symbolic legitimization among the ardent opponents of their fathers.[19] Maybe they also hoped to play on the divisions between Russia and the West, posing as Russia's 'internal West', which would act as the government's broker during any attempts to liberalize the country that would enjoy the support of the wider world. To achieve both these goals, the opposition doesn't need the support of all four Russias (to use Zubarevich's framework) – it is enough to dominate in Russia-1.

The problem is that neither of these goals were realistic. If the opposition is alienated from the people and dismissive of cultural hegemony and political leadership, it cannot bargain with the government from a position of strength. Simply put, the opposition's lack of appeal among voters has not been helpful. Even if the West compels the Russian government to work more closely with the minority, it is not clear how this minority will manage to retain political leadership at a critical moment without the kinds of authoritarian tools that liberals used to implement economic reforms in the early 1990s. But any authoritarian rule would rely on the security establishment, which is now being accused of switching its allegiance to great-power patriotism and anti-Western policy.[20] In other words, there is good reason to believe that if the political crisis predicted by the opposition comes to pass, history will come full circle once again and the triumph of liberalism in Russia will give way to an authoritarian regime that eventually will have to seek the support of the majority at the expense of Russia-1.

Likewise, it is reasonable to assume that the children of today's rulers will seek the company of critics such as Lyudmila Ulitskaya and Andrei Makarevich over loyal cultural figures like Iosif Kobzon and Nikita Mikhalkov, whose prestige pales in comparison to that of their rebellious colleagues. But if the children of the elite, who are drawn to the progressive minority, come to occupy the positions of their parents, they will also have to seek common ground with the majority by asking cultural figures who express the majority's interests and aesthetic preferences for their symbolic support. Any government that ignores the preferences of its people risks losing power.

We believe that the main motivators of the self-isolation strategy are irrational. Following the method of rational choice elaborated by Viktor Sergeyev and Vadim Tsymbursky, the emergence of this self-isolation strategy can be explained by the 'behavioural scenario' of perestroika.[21] In my recent book *Perestroika-2: Repetition Experience* (Moscow: Ves Mir, 2014) I analysed the popular view in Putin's Russia that perestroika is a specific scenario that may repeat itself in the future. Some experts are waiting for perestroika-2 with horror, fearing it may lead to another national catastrophe. They believe that the entire liberal reformation of the Soviet system was fraught with disaster from the very start.

Former French Prime Minister Georges Clemenceau said that the French revolution should be viewed as a whole, without dividing it into bad and good stages. Those who fear another perestroika take the view advanced by Clemenceau. This is why these experts fear that even weak and timid liberal movements could lead the country to ruin. But the segment of society that is pleased with the results of the reforms in the late 1980s to early 1990s also take a holistic view of this era. So for them the behaviour of the intelligentsia in the 1970s–1980s provides an example to follow, a blueprint for future revolutionaries. In Solzhenitsyn's famous essay 'The Smatterers', published in 1974 as part of the collection *From Under the Rubble*, he pointed to numerous articles by liberal members of the dissident movement who spoke of their special mission as the right-thinking minority in a country with a passive and unreflective majority. He expressed grave concerns over the intelligentsia's alienation from its own people, which was not true of the intelligentsia in past eras.[22]

Solzhenitsyn was absolutely right. Such attitudes were prevalent among the liberal intelligentsia, as expressed in many works of art at the time. In 1971 the Strugatsky brothers published one of their most popular books, *The Inhabited Island*. More than a mere pamphlet against the totalitarian Soviet system, it was primarily a critique of the courageous but senseless dissidents who sought to end the tyranny of the KGB and CPSU then and there, either single-handedly or with the help of some dark forces in the Brezhnev leadership. But instead of engaging in a dangerous struggle that could be exploited by the real enemies of peace and freedom, the dissidents in the intelligentsia were being offered an alliance with the educated autocrats in charge of scientific research and counter-intelligence. People at the time read the book as an anti-totalitarian story, but in reality it was probably the most overt justification of the need to preserve the chosen minority's totalitarian control of the majority.

However, the ideas of the science fictions writers, the Strugatsky brothers, who were at the peak of their popularity in the 1970s–1980s, were not the only example of the self-isolation strategy of dissident intellectuals in the late Soviet era. The problem of the lonely intellectual in an alien and indifferent environment became the main subject of essays by one of Solzhenitsyn's main opponents – the philosopher Grigory Pomerants.[23] Dissident intellectuals typically wrote in coded language. When Pomerants wrote about India, his readers understood that he meant the Soviet Union. He defended Buddhism as a movement of lonely, doubt-ridden, reflective intellectuals who were harassed both by the radical and ascetic Jains and the new conservatives, the Hindus.[24] This is Pomerants writing in code about a small group of like-minded allies, the first Soviet dissidents, who would not accept the Bolshevist ideocracy or the Russian Orthodox nationalism that had already started to manifest itself by that time. The philosopher believed the ideologies of both the radical reformers and the counter-revolutionaries were bound to lead to violence. Both movements were led by angels foaming at the mouth. Intellectuals were told not to fall for one-sided doctrines, to stay in their marginal position in society, and to keep a distance from the majority of their compatriots.

The first dissidents revelled in their small numbers, as the intelligentsia always does. This feeling naturally grew stronger after the direct heirs of these dissidents – the so-called first-wave democrats – led hundreds of thousands of people into the streets. Unlike in 1968, when only seven people protested on Red Square against the occupation of Czechoslovakia, roughly half a million people protested against the deployment of Soviet tanks in Vilnius. It seemed that the moral minority would inexorably win over the initially passive majority sooner or later. The liberal intelligentsia predicted this would happen, including in Ryazanov's movie *Garage* that was mentioned earlier, which depicts a protesting minority in which morality trumps self-interest for only one woman (the role made actress Liya Akhedzhakova a symbol of moral conviction among the liberal fronde). But when the corrupt leadership wavers, the minority defeats the powerful majority of conformists. This model seemed to work brilliantly in the late 1980s when the protests of a handful of dissidents developed into mass collective action of intellectuals, miners and retired party officials. However, there is no reason to believe that the future will see a remake of this old movie.

History does not repeat itself

The way in which perestroika played out convinced the intelligentsia that the tactic of liberal alienation from the majority employed in the Brezhnev era – which

Solzhenitsyn was too quick to denounce in 'The Smatterers' – is not only morally justified but also politically effective. The expectation was that popular protest movements would eventually emerge from the self-isolated minority, like a butterfly from its cocoon, and elevate the liberal elite to political leadership, bringing perestroika-2 to the same victorious conclusion as perestroika-1, or so the intelligentsia argues. Why are bets that paid off in the 1980s no longer relevant today? Why is this self-isolated minority doomed to remain an eternal outsider in big time politics? Why can't the marginalized intelligentsia hope for a perestroika-2 to yield political advantage? I believe the main reason is the Soviet intelligentsia's cultural hegemony over the majority of the population, which it has since squandered.

In the 1960s–1980s the intelligentsia that produced and disseminated scientific knowledge was actually a privileged class of Soviet society. The most interesting books and movies were about this group. Soviet futurology as expressed in the science fiction and, to an extent, philosophy of the time promoted the advantages of free labour, as exemplified by scientists selflessly devoted to their work. Soviet philosophy conceived of socialism as one big academic city where there is no division between work and free time. The best example of this genre is *Space Apprentice* by the Strugatsky brothers, in which the happy residents of a communist paradise are contrasted with workers made miserable by the focus on material abundance in the hell of capitalism.

The intelligentsia democrats easily won unquestioned political leadership in Russian society in the 1980s because almost everyone belonged to the intelligentsia at that time. All of perestroika's political battles were won during the stagnation era when the intelligentsia briefly managed to impose its tastes and preferences on the whole country. The Strugatsky brothers were possibly the most popular Soviet writers, the whole country laughed together at the shows of Gennady Khazanov and Mikhail Zhvanetsky, while singer Vladimir Vysotsky became a national poet. But so long as singers of romantic pop ballads like Stas Mikhailov (hated by Moscow progressives) remain hugely popular in the provincial backwaters, Moscow intellectuals will find it difficult to win the support of millions. They have no one but themselves to blame for the situation they now find themselves in, because it was their political victory in the 1990s that led to the mass commercialization of culture and the loss of their almost indisputable cultural hegemony in the Brezhnev era. Today's unsophisticated TV audience, which is criticized from time to time by representatives of the creative elite, is mainly the result of the commercialization of television, followed by state censorship.

In his famous 1970 article 'Dual Mentality of the Intelligentsia', which Solzhenitsyn criticized in his essay 'The Smatterers', the writer and philosopher Vladimir Kormer points out that the Soviet intelligentsia was called on to replace the entire elite that disappeared with the Russian Empire. It culturally suppressed and imposed its values and tastes on the party bureaucracy (the nomenklatura, the ruling class under real socialism according to Milovan Djilas and Mikhail Voslensky). Kormer writes:

> Potential merchants and the nobility unwillingly become members of the intelligentsia for lack of opportunities to use their talents. People with the temperament of travelling salesmen are getting involved in research; someone who might have been a tavern keeper is instead making an academic career, while unfulfilled priests are writing articles for scientific magazines. In general, any person with higher education is automatically counted as a member of the intelligentsia. Strange as it may seem, this is fair because all of them share almost the same culture and extremely miserable lifestyle. Legally all of them are in the same position of powerless slaves in a totalitarian state . . . Usually the party bureaucracy, or 'the new class' to quote Djilas, rises out of this amorphous conglomerate. Apparently, this differentiation is justified but it is important to remember that this bureaucracy is largely aligned with the intelligentsia. As distinct from the former nobility, the clergy or the merchant class, the bureaucracy does not have a distinct culture and its own productive capacity – it has the transformed capacity of the intelligentsia. In this sense, the party bureaucracy represents the polarization of the intelligentsia.[25]

The latent, inorganic nature of the intelligentsia noticed by Kormer (not only in his essays but also in his novel *The Legacy*) was reflected in the borderline hysterical self-abnegation that was so pronounced in works of art even before perestroika. As Kormer predicted, political and economic changes in the USSR led to a situation where the intelligentsia began to produce a new class after artificially embracing all other professional strata in the Soviet era and imposing on them its own culture in its simplest form, that is Vladimir Vysotsky songs rather than Alfred Schnittke's symphonies. This class was meant to become the hegemon of new Russia and include entrepreneurs and their top managers, economic analysts, stockbrokers and lowly cubicle dwellers. I would describe them collectively as the 'new capitalist class'. Some cultural trends of the 1980s made it clear that the old intellectual class was no longer inclined to fight for cultural hegemony and was ready to cede it to a successor as soon as one is allowed to emerge on the historical stage. However, the liberal elite hoped that representatives of the 'new capitalist class' would maintain close ties with it and will be more like the intellectuals from books by Strugatsky brothers than the heroes of *The Team* television show, not to mention the characters of the *TASS is Authorized to Announce* series.

As I do not have certain sociological data available, I will instead cite two films that were released in the Soviet Union around the same time: Sergei Solovyev's *Los Elegidos* (1982) and Eldar Ryazanov's famous *Cruel Romance* (1984). Both deal with the moral depravity of naval-gazing intellectuals against the backdrop of ordinary lives of ordinary people bounded by their private interests. In the first movie (one of Solovyev's very best, in my opinion), the hero played by Leonid Filatov is displeased with the earthly, egoistic interests of the people that surround him, but ultimately reveals himself to be worse than any of them when he betrays the woman he loves in order to save his own life. In the long-standing dispute between the exalted intellectuals and narrow-minded philistines Solovyev cautiously sides with the latter. Two years later Ryazanov raised the same problem in a grotesque caricature of a poor and honest intellectual who does not take bribes and despises philistines. However, it is revealed that he is motivated entirely by his envy of the strong and the rich. The movie makes it clear that the city's best people deserve what they have, although, alas, sometimes beautiful women and inconspicuous bureaucrats fall victim to their good time.

Needless to say, the intelligentsia became more open in expressing such attitudes after the Soviet system's disintegration, the final collapse of the socialist intellectual ethos and the beginning of sweeping privatization when large chunks of property started to go to the heirs of Knurov and Vozhevatov who were so lovingly depicted by Ryazanov in his adaptation of Alexander Ostrovsky's *Without a Dowry*. What matters is not that this was bad, morally or economically. The intellectual class simply handed over its right to cultural hegemony to other segments of society that had been deprived of a strong cultural voice before, as Kormer rightly observed. These included salespeople, members of the security establishment and, at worst, the criminal world that succeeded in imposing its cultural hegemony in much of the provinces. Russian pop ballads and whodunnit TV shows are a good example.

Looking ahead

To conclude, the liberal opposition's moderately successful self-isolation strategy in the 1980s was largely made possible by the intelligentsia's clear cultural hegemony over a considerable segment of what was a relatively homogenous society. But the intelligentsia's unofficial ideologues were somewhat embarrassed about the hegemony they possessed and even denied it. Now that society is less homogenous, this kind of political alienation from the people and complete neglect of their interests and values will only further marginalize liberal political elites both in power and in the opposition, even if they manage to compel 'the external West' to recognize them as 'the internal West', that is its only legitimate representative in Russia. (In the history of social democracy in Russia, this resembles Trotskyism's hopes that the proletarian dictatorship would keep power by relying on the working class of advanced countries.) The growing self-alienation of the elites from the majority, based on the hope that the people will join them sooner or later, follows the script of the first perestroika, when cultural hegemony was easily converted into the political leadership of the liberal opposition for two reasons – the prestige of the upper echelon of the intelligentsia among the progressive circles of the party apparatchiks and the low cultural heterogeneity of Soviet society.

As demonstrated by the media outcry over the funding of Bolotnaya Square leaders by agencies of the Moscow city government, prestige is still a factor; but the social homogeneity of that period no longer exists. The liberal intellectuals that were critical of the party-built political structure lost their cultural connection to the people in the 1990s and lost touch with their interests and values. Moreover, they missed a good chance to find a common language with the majority over the nation-wide frustration with the ruling party, bureaucracy and corruption.

But instead of creating a national protest movement, the pro-Western elite limited itself to expressing anti-Putinism in riots directed against a supposedly culturally ossified government. For conservatives, this was perhaps the best possible outcome. But it is bound to complicate any attempts to liberalize society from above.

Active rapprochement with liberals would carry electoral and rating risks for those in power. It is hard to say whether the minority's temptation to move closer to the West will outweigh the risk of finding itself isolated at home as a result. The self-isolation strategy of the creative minority has led it to gradual extinction on the social reservation rather than political leadership. The energy behind the protests will find another channel sooner or later, but future crises are likely to differ considerably from what we remember of the 2011–2012 era of political awakening.

Notes

1 'It is possible to determine how "organic" different strata of the intelligentsia are and their more or less close link with the main social group by conducting a structurally functional analysis of superstructures from the bottom up (that is, starting from the foundation of a structure and moving up). At this stage it is possible to identify two main "floors" in superstructures: the first floor that incorporates the entire complex of institutions that are roughly defined as "private" and may be called "civil society", while the second floor may be referred to as "political society or a state". On the first floor the dominant group exercises "hegemony" over the entire society and on the second floor the state machinery and the "judicial" government carry out the function of "direct dominance" or management. Both functions are of an organizational, binding character. Intellectuals are "managers" of the dominant group, which fulfill auxiliary functions that are linked with the exercise of social hegemony and political power by that group, notably: 1) they help ensure the "spontaneous" consent of the popular masses to the line imposed on society by the main dominant group; moreover, this consent emerges "historically" owing to the prestige (and hence trust) enjoyed by the dominant group owing to its role in production; 2) the state machinery of coercion is formed from among them and is designed to keep a tight rein on those who do not express "consent" either passively or actively. It may embrace the whole society in anticipation of a management and leadership crisis when spontaneous consent disappears. As a result of such an arrangement, the concept of an "intellectual" is interpreted very broadly. However, this is the only way to approach the real state of things.' See Antonio Gramsci, 'Emergence of the Intelligentsia' in Antonio Gramsci, *Arts and Politics* (Moscow: Iskusstvo, 1991), pp. 436–437.

2 Keith Thomas, *Religion and the Decline of Magic* (New York: Penguin, 1971).

3 For a very interesting analysis of various transformations of the idea of cultural hegemony in Western historiography, see T. J. Jackson Lears, 'The Concept of Cultural Hegemony: Problems and Possibilities', *American Historical Review*, Vol. 90, June 1985.

4 Alexander Etkind concluded with good reason that 'the cultural power of literature demonstrated a complicated dialectic: the more productive a literary text was in exercising cultural hegemony, the more critical and eventually destructive it became for the machinery of dominance'. See Alexander Etkind, *Vnutrennyaya kolonizatsiya: Impersky opyt Rossii* (*Internal Colonization: Russia's Imperial Experience*) (Moscow: Novoye Literaturnoye Obozreniye, 2013), p. 9.

5 C. Wright Mills, *The Politics of Truth: Selected Writings of C. Wright Mills*, ed. John H. Summers (Oxford: Oxford University Press, 2008), p. 130.

6 This idea is a leitmotif in the famous 1964 article by the historian of Russian social-democracy Leopold Haimson, 'The Problem of Social Stability in Urban Russia, 1905–1917', *Slavic Review*, Vol. 23, December 1964, pp. 620–642; Vol. 24, March 1965, pp. 1–22.

7 Modest Kolerov, 'Ob obrashchenii k religii kak priyome revolyutsionnoi strategii' ('Using Religion as a Method of Revolutionary Strategy'), in *Problemy idealizma*' [1902] (*Problems of Idealism*), *Istoriya i kontekst: Seriya: Issledovaniya po istorii russkoi mysli* (*History and Context. Series: Studies of the History of Russian Thought*) (Moscow: Tri Kvadrata, 2002). 'It is even possible to say that practical Russian "Christian socialism" that has developed from the socially failed "idealistic trend" was a desire to copy Gapon's success, to saddle the revolutionary-religious mass that he brought to life; *to replace a superficial and accidental leader with an ideological one*, to replace Gapon with Bulgakov', p. 202.

8 In 1986 I happened to attend my first and only lecture by historian Natan Eidelman, who was very popular in the 1980s. He spoke about Faddei Bulgarin. According to Eidelman, the Bulgarian actually created the new ideology of Russia under Nicolas II, according to which the tsar and the people who loved him opposed the upper crust of the nobility that had been corrupted by Western ideas. This ideology was very different from the official ideology of enlightenment according to which the tsarist regime was protecting the educated minority from uneducated Asian people.

9 See the entire discussion of 'the overwhelming majority' at http://gefter.ru/archive/9438. [Accessed on: 17 June 2015].

10 See Vitaly Ivanov, 'Yedinaya Rossiya – partiya chisto instrumentalnaya' ('United Russia is Merely an Instrument'), *Russky zhurnal: tema nedeli* (*Russian Magazine: Theme of the Week*), Issue 1 (43), 2010, p. 8, http://www.intelros.ru/pdf/Rus_Jornal/43/5.pdf. [Accessed on: 17 June 2015].

11 See 'Izgnaniye meritov: Chem grozit prizyv popolanov i porka nobilei' ['Expulsion of Meritocrats: A Threat from the Appeal to Craftsmen and Trade Guilds and the Beating of Nobles']. Interview with Gleb Pavlovsky in *Moskovskiye Novosti*, 3 June 2013.

12 These ideas are regularly expressed in the Russian press by Svetlana Babayeva, the editor-in-chief of the Gazeta.ru website. See, for example: http://fox.ivlim.ru/show article.asp?id=3616. [Accessed on: 17 June 2015].

13 Russia's Central Election Committee announced the official results of the State Duma elections, 9 December 2014; http://top.rbc.ru/politics/09/12/2011/629226.shtml. [Accessed on: 17 June 2015].

14 See, for example, this typical statement by sociologist Olga Zdravomyslova: 'As for public actions that are called "perestroika" without adequate grounds, they came as a surprise unlike Gorbachev's perestroika, which had been brewing in post-Stalinist soviet society since the twentieth party congress. The main point is that these protests are moral rather than political in nature . . . It is very difficult to turn a moral protest into a political one: it cannot be expressed on a mass scale; it does not compel anyone to anything; it has no ideology, programme or a common leader. But a moral protest is deeper than a political one because it exerts a stronger influence on the feelings of people and transforms their consciousness'. 'Idei 80-kh v kontekste novoi perestroika: Reinkarnatsiya kontseptov' ('The ideas of the 1980s in the Context of the New Perestroika: Reincarnation of Concepts'), transcript of the joint meeting of the Gefter.ru Community and the John Locke Intellectual Club on 10 December 2012; http://gefter.ru/archive/7484). [Accessed on: 17 June 2015].

15 After the protests of students from the Russian Trade and Economic University in late 2012, the author of these words expressed the view that student protestors, whose numbers would diminish as a result of education reforms, may become a 'dangerous class' that acts as the midwife of Russia's new social democracy: 'No doubt, now these students will be joined by representatives of various political forces. Everyone understands that if one "ineffective" university has staged a protest, it will be joined, sooner or later, by more and more. Then all universities ousted by the Ministry of Education and Science will link up. Sooner or later specific demands will develop into broader grievances and a full neo-liberal agenda. Sooner or later the fact that students, especially in the regions, have no options in life except to become police, taxi drivers or gangsters will come in for heavy criticism. Sooner or later all this fermentation will produce genuine social democracy in Russia which will demand from the government greater opportunities to get an education and a good job rather than public assistance and protection.' See Boris Mezhuev, 'Rozhdeniye opasnogo klassa' ('The Birth of the Dangerous Class'), *Izvestiya*, 19 December 2012, http://izvestia.ru/news/541884#ixzz3IYYXK3J3. [Accessed on: 17 June 2015].

16 See *Parlamentskaya gazeta*, 4 March 2013.

17 See Natalya Zubarevich, 'Chetyre Rossii' ['Four Russias'], *Vedomosti*, 30 December 2011, http://russialist.org/four-very-different-russias-moving-in-four-very-different-directions-zubarevich-says/. [Accessed on: 17 June 2015].

18 I wrote about this surprising phenomenon of alienation from the interests of the majority in a column after the events of 6 May 2012 and the formation of an opposition tent camp on Chistoprudny Boulevard: 'On 6 May the columns of people with white ribbons were joined by many tough-looking young guys who had apparently come from the provinces. They despised white ribbons, rallies and conversation, and did not wish to take part in any claptrap. They were not interested in public speakers at all. They were obviously willing to clash with riot police and show a rotten and weak Moscow what real fighting is all about. They were not seen on Chistye Prudy. Those who did not remove white ribbons returned to their creative ghetto to talk dreamily about Tahrir Square and Pussy Riot. Needless to say, these amiable people pose no threat except to the environment. I hope that the three girls from the punk group will soon be released from prison. That said, I must admit that their role in Russian politics is by no means commensurate with their importance. Their act is of no serious interest for residents of the Moscow suburbs who are primarily concerned about rising utility fees and dubious prospects for the future in the event of another crisis and job losses. A group of prosperous Moscow writers who went for a walk in the city is hardly capable of engendering another Tahrir. The walk looks nice to observers, is pleasant for the participants, poses little threat to the authorities and is completely pointless.' See Boris Mezhuev, 'Moskovsky protest, bessmyslenny i bezopasny' ('Moscow Protest: Pointless and Safe'), *Izvestia*, 15 May 2012, http://izvestia.ru/news/524411#ixzz3IYeHtzEV. [Accessed on: 17 June 2015].

19 See Alexander Birman, 'Druzya i deti: pomogut li Rotenbergi mladshiye otmenit "zakon Rotenberga"' ('Friends and Children: Will the Younger Rotenbergs Help Dismantle "Rotenberg's Law"?'), *Forbes*, 15 October 2014, http://www.forbes.ru/mneniya-column/vertikal/270549-druzya-i-deti-pomogut-li-rotenbergi-mladshie-otmenit-zakon-rotenberga. [Accessed on: 17 June 2015].

20 See, for instance, Pavel Sheremet, 'Nebolshaya, pobedonosnaya' ('Small, Victorious'), Colta.ru, 18 November 2014, http://www.colta.ru/articles/society/5376. [Accessed on: 17 June 2015].

21 On the peculiar model of target-rational action and deviations from it, including those determined by unconscious imitation of past scenarios, see Vadim Tsymbursky, 'Chelovek prinimayet resheniye' ('Man Makes Decision'), in *Konyektury zemli i vremeni: Geopoliticheskiye i khronologicheskiye intellektualnyye rassledovaniya* (*Conjectures of Land and Time: Geopolitical and Chronological Studies*) (Moscow: Yevropa, 2011), pp. 320–345.

22 Arguing with Altayev (the pen name of philosopher and writer Vladimir Kormer), Solzhenitsyn wrote: ' . . . the pre-revolutionary intelligentsia (in *Vekhi*'s interpretation) did not think it was alienated from its people; to the contrary, it was convinced of its absolute right to speak on their behalf; the modern intelligentsia is by no means alienated from the modern state; those who feel like this – by themselves or in a narrow circle, inhibited and depressed, fatefully and devoutly – not only keep the state going with their daily intellectual activities but accept and fulfill even a more horrible condition of the state: to involve their souls in mandatory, common lies.'

23 In 'The Smatterers' Solzhenitsyn quotes Pomerants' revealing line of reasoning: 'The intelligentsia is a measure of public forces – both progressive and reactionary. Set against the intelligentsia, all people are reduced to a reactionary mass.' 'It is a part of the educated segment of society that is developing spiritually, destroying old values and establishing new ones, and taking one more step from the beast to the Lord . . . The intelligentsia is what it was trying to find in the people, proletariat, etc. – the ferment that is moving history forward.' Moreover: 'Love of the people is much more dangerous (than love of animals); there is no barrier that prevents one from standing on all fours.' And simply: 'Here . . . the spine of a new people is taking shape,' 'something new will replace the people,' 'people of creative intellectual labor are becoming a chosen nation of the twentieth century'!!!

24 See Grigory Pomerants, 'O prichinakh upadka buddizma v srednevekovoi Indii' ('On the Reasons for the Decline of Buddhism in Medieval India'), in Grigory Pomerants, *Vykhod iz transa* (*Coming out of a Trance*), a collection of early essays (Moscow: Yurist, 1995), http://www.pomeranz.ru/p/pub_buddizm.htm. [Accessed on: 17 June 2015].

25 Vladimir Kormer, 'Dvoinoye soznaniye intelligentsii i presvdokultura' ('The Dual Mentality of the Intelligentsia and Pseudo-Culture'), *Vestnik russkogo studencheskogo khristianskogo dvizhenia*, No. 97, Paris and New York, 1970.

14 Conclusion

Bringing the people back in

Richard Sakwa

This book has examined the many dimensions of what it means to be someone living in Russia today. What is overwhelmingly clear is that no single feature captures the many dimensions of the contemporary Russian individual. Equally, it is not always clear what turns an individual into a citizen, someone conscious of political rights and interested in exercising these rights in a non-discriminatory and equal manner. Russian political discourse is full of dismissive terms for the 'masses', and even some of the most energetic 'democrats' have been known to make disparaging comments about what is after all meant to be the subject of a modern democracy, the people. One of the profound reasons for the dissolution of the Communist order in the late 1980s was the sense that a system that ruled in the name of the people had become an unaccountable power hierarchy insulated from the real concerns of the citizenry over which they ruled. As Mikhail Gorbachev's glasnost (openness) took hold, the revelations about the luxurious life styles of Party officials discredited the system as a whole, while the mass of the population endured ever-lengthening queues for even basic goods. This in the end provoked a wave of anger that swept the old system away. Today the question of elite privileges and the grotesque inequality in Russian society is once again a factor that raises questions about the legitimacy of the present system.

This book has explored the many dimensions of inequality, and at the same time raised some fundamental questions about the resilience of the political system that rules over such a society. At the same time, it is clear that there is no immediate 'legitimacy crisis' of the sort that toppled the Soviet regime. There is gross inequality, injustice and major developmental problems, but these issues are, as it were, aligned along different planes, and thus do not reinforce each other to the degree that they can represent a coherent challenge to the political system. The regime so far has been able to avoid a coalescence of grievances target on itself, although such an eventuality cannot be ruled out. As we know all too well from Russian history, a system that appears solid and eternal one day, can dissolve in a blink of historical time.

In the 2000s the administration led by Vladimir Putin was able to present itself not only as the champion of the people, but its own discursive framework suggested that in some way it was leading a revolt against the privileges and distortions of the 1990s. In that first post-Soviet decade, as several chapters in this book make clear, the foundations of a liberal capitalist system were established, but this was accompanied by the repudiation not only of the planned economy of the Soviet years, but also of many of the positive aspects of the Soviet system, including a high degree of social equality (although this did not encompass the top elite) and universal access to education, health and welfare provision. Although perhaps not of the highest quality, the Soviet system in the post-Stalin years had become a type of authoritarian welfare state. All this was now swept away, and many of the old elite representatives of the old Soviet ruling class, the nomenklatura, now transformed themselves into the new capitalist class, now freed of restrictions imposed by Soviet norms and Party control.

A large proportion of the population was reduced to penury as a small group of 'oligarchs' gained ownership of great swathes of the industry and enterprises that had been created by the labour of the Soviet people. This oligarch class was not hesitant in asserting its political power against the presidency of Boris Yeltsin. The state and the oligarchy effectively fused. There was no end of contradictions and tensions, but as far as the liberal reformers of the time were concerned, an irreversible shift had taken place away from the Soviet system to capitalism. The foundations were created for a capitalist economic system, but the whole process was an inverted form of Soviet-style economism, and once again the quality of social and political relations was subordinated to the teleological goal of creating a new economic order.

On coming to power in 2000 Putin launched a remedial programme to challenge what came to be presented as the dark 1990s. This is just one of the paradoxes of the Putin-style of rule: a powerful insider presenting himself as the leader of a poplar insurgency against the excesses of a system that itself had sponsored his rise to office. On coming to power, Putin swiftly set about limiting the political privileges of the oligarchs, although part of his new 'social contract' allowed them to accumulate wealth as long as they kept out of independent politics. Indeed, part of the new deal meant that the business class should support the various endeavours of the regime as the price for capital accumulation. When Mikhail Khodorkovsky sought to break away from this system, he was arrested in October 2003 and soon after his Yukos oil company was transferred into state hands. Putin also tamed the autonomy of regional governors, and with the abolition of gubernatorial elections in 2005 they effectively became part of Putin's system of managed democracy.

Although the coherence of the so-called 'power vertical' has been greatly exaggerated, nevertheless something like it exists. The United Russia party was created in the early Putin years to become one of the pillars of the system, and when that provoked a backlash, Putin in 2011 created the Russian Popular Front as yet another mechanism to coordinate the power system with societal interests. Civil society has thrived in the Putin years, but of a peculiar sort. Independence and autonomy is constrained, although it is far from destroyed (hence the Putin system is at most a type of soft authoritarianism), but the regime itself sponsors forms of civil society activism that advances its goals. Even official channels of civic activism, such as the Civic Chamber and its regional counterparts, can influence public policy, although within poorly defined limits.

The focus of this book, however, is less civil society but society itself. And here the question posed by Dutkiewicz in the Introduction is fundamental: why has there been so little discussion on social needs, structures and demands? Subsequent chapters show that such a debate is certainly not absent, but it has lacked a clearly articulated format. The Communist Party of the Russian Federation (CPRF), like its predecessor in the Soviet period, talks constantly of the needs of the people, but too much of this is little more than artificial sloganeering, while a real debate about social priorities and social policy more broadly is notable by its absence.

The Just Russia party was sponsored by the regime precisely to provide a more traditional type of social democratic party, and to a degree the party has fulfilled this task. However, its lack of genuine independence has weakened its potential ability to mobilise political constituencies in support of social democratic goals. Just Russia has become one of the four 'systemic' parties, along with the CPRF, United Russia and Vladimir Zhirinovsky's Liberal Democratic Party of Russia. These parties have been represented in parliament (the State Duma) for as long as they have existed. Outside of parliament are the 'non-systemic' parties. Notable among them is the social liberal party Yabloko, one of the longest-established groupings that was represented in parliament until 2003. Yabloko does have a clearly formulated social policy, including a condemnation of inequality and the residual power of the oligarchy, but in the Putin years this party, like all the others critical of the regime, has become increasingly marginalized.

The needs and concerns of the state are much discussed, but the concerns and aspirations of the people, of society, are less well examined. There are plenty of public opinion polls on issues of public policy, but fewer examinations of the complex dynamics of the social structure and the articulations of society. The Putin system has tried to depoliticize the conduct of public management, presenting itself as the neutral and supreme arbiter of the public good. Such a claim is not necessarily false, since the Putin administrations have devoted considerable resources to maintaining and developing public welfare, health, education and other social provision. The question is whether some more conventional system of competitive party politics could have delivered these same goods at less cost and of higher quality and sustainability.

This is where the point made by Dutkiewicz about the statist foundations of the Russian polity comes in. In the Soviet era the Communist Party claimed a 'leading role' in managing society and the country's development. The Party-state dominated all social and political processes, becoming the successor to the patrimonial features of the Tsarist system that it had displaced. Equally, in the post-communist era this pattern of displaced popular sovereignty was perpetuated, now in the form of the regime-state. Once again, the reformed administrative system claimed tutelary powers over society and political processes. This is what Dutkiewicz calls the system of 'trusteeship', with the regime claiming leadership over society in a time of revolutionary transformation.

This has once again given rise to what I have called elsewhere the 'dual state', with two systems operating side by side. On the one hand, the constitutional state operates within the bounds of law and the limits set by the regulations of the system itself. However, this is balanced by the administrative regime, which mostly operates within the framework of the constitutional state, but it has the power to rule *by* law rather than within the framework of law. These arbitrary powers allow the administrative system to control elections rather than allowing itself to become subject to the vicissitudes of electoral popularity. However, the duality of the system means that there are distinct limits to the exercise of prerogative powers by the regime. Their excessive use would destroy the delicate tissues linking the two types of power, undermine the popular legitimacy of the regime, and threaten to isolate the power system in a recreated citadel of authoritarianism.

This is why this book places Boris Kapustin's chapter on 'a people in the absence of a people' right at the front. Article 3.1 of the Russian constitution of December 1993 proclaims that 'The holder of sovereignty and the sole source of authority in the Russian Federation is its multinational people', but it is not clear how 'the people' can be represented to shape the government and the polity. The question is a fundamental one, and helps place all the succeeding analyses in context. Kapustin questions linear and teleological interpretations of 'the transition' from communism to capitalism, and instead argues that the process of change is open-ended and indeterminate. Ultimately, the anti-communist revolutions of 1989 to 1991 were intended to place 'the people' back into the driving seat, after decades in which popular sovereignty had arguably been usurped by the communist authorities and their ruling elites. Instead, a new form of usurpation took place, but this time with the driving force inverted. No longer was the aim to build socialism, with all of its bureaucratic distortions accompanied by an emancipatory project to achieve social justice and political equality. The transition to capitalism turned out to be as much a historicist project as the building of socialism. Both assumed that they knew the purpose and end point of history, and thus it was only a matter of getting there.

In the end, both displaced 'the people' from the throne, in the name of the exigencies of the transition itself. In other words, a type of 'transitional progressivism' reigned in both cases, which determined the peculiar quality to historical time in both Soviet and post-communist Russia. While 'the people', as Kapustin notes, may be a 'fiction', as always, fictions are a useful device for conveying some deeper fact. While a people can never directly exercise sovereignty, in contemporary democratic societies the popular will is considered the basis of political legitimacy. The question then becomes how to aggregate and express the popular will, and what is considered to be genuinely popular as opposed to mistaken, populist or deviant. Thus the people are not only divided, but too often absent as the real source of political agency. Kapustin's rich and sophisticated dissection of the concept of the people raises issues that are amplified and examined in later chapters.

The chapter by Vladimir Popov and Piotr Dutkiewicz returns us to the 1990s, and the devastating effect that the reforms had on society. This really was a 'matter of life and death', with a massive increase in mortality rates, inequality and corruption accompanied by the largest fall in economic activity in a developed state in modern history. Society endured an unprecedented demographic collapse. The figures are shocking, and help explain the continuing popularity of Putin's remedial programme. Government expenditure as a proportion of GDP fell sharply as the state was unable to tax the new oligarch class, and the state withdrew from many of its normal activities. Under Putin the state was restored to its central place in society. For many, this looks too much like traditional Russian statism; for others, it offers a lifeline for basic security and welfare.

In these conditions, Vladimir Popov examines the strange puzzle of the enduring support for market reforms, even though they benefitted a relatively small proportion and created a massively wealthy oligarch class. The absence of an alternative programme that could ameliorate living standards and the social status of the mass of the population is remarkable. In part, the answer lies in the negative trends of the late Soviet years, allowing the post-communist changes to be seen as an improvement and opening up prospects for further improvement. Visions of the future were extrapolated from the past, but above all the new wealthy class was able to shape public preferences that excluded a coherent alternative. In light of my comments above, we can add that Putin was able to offer a glimpse of an alternative, but one tamed and constrained by the needs of the regime itself. The Putin system dealt with some of the earlier excesses, while its own distortions and contradictions were screened from the public domain.

These themes are taken up by Leonid Grigoryev, asking whether the transformation served the people or the elite. Grigoryev is both one of the outstanding analysts of the post-communist changes, and at the same time he is also an active participant in the reforms. An important element in his analysis is the role of cultural factors in shaping the perceptions and discourses of the changes. The impetus to return to some sort of normative normality after the Soviet period helped sustain belief in the programme of change. He identifies the developmental failures of the Soviet system and the challenges facing the reformers in the early 1990s – one of whom was Grigoryev himself. Above all, he identifies the macroeconomic imbalances that forced the pace of change, above all the emerging scarcity of goods in the last Soviet years. His study exposes the ebbs and flow of the reform impetus, with a period of consolidation under Yevgeny Primakov's leadership after the economic collapse of August 1998. This was a foretaste of the Putinite consolidation, although under Primakov this was a direct political challenge against the power of the oligarchs. Under Putin the state's fiscal extractive capacity was greatly enhanced, allowing the steady payment of improved pensions and welfare payments, which effectively neutralized politically a significant proportion of the population. However, the energy rent model of development and popular pacification is clearly running out of steam, especially in conditions of falling oil prices and sanctions. Grigoryev identifies the challenges emanating from the West, accompanied by the alienation of the intelligentsia. The picture he paints is of a system under extreme strain, in which the old social bargain is no longer sustainable, accompanied by the absence of new developmental ideas.

Popular attitudes towards the decades of post-communist change are traced by Mikhail Gorshkov, who as director of Institute of Sociology has his finger close to the pulse of Russian life. He shows how Yeltsin and the radical reformers quickly lost their social base, a finding confirmed by the December 1993 and subsequent parliamentary elections. He traces how society became increasingly polarized between the liberals and conservatives, with a large indeterminate group of 'indifferent' people in between. He vividly demonstrates the major concerns of the Russian people as Putin assumed the presidency in 2000, along with a startling lack of confidence in the future and the impossibility to plan one's life. It was precisely this issue that Putin addressed, but after a decade and half at the helm some of the old concerns are beginning to re-emerge. By contrast with the relatively closed Soviet system, people in Russia today can compare their condition not only with the past but also with standards abroad, and on this count Russia is increasingly found wanting. However, material issues are tempered by an extraordinary popular commitment to Russia as a great power. This means that any Russian leader would have to respond to this deep 'patriotic' aspiration, and to that degree, contrary to the common Western view that support for Putin's foreign policy is manufactured and artificial, it in fact responds to deep popular orientations. This is more profound than everyday opinions or views but reflects a deeper hierarchy of values.

Nevertheless, Natalya Tikhonova is right to talk of the 'Russian roller coaster'. The society has undergone deep changes, in terms not only of income differentiation, employment patterns and the like, but also the incomplete disaggregation of power and property. The Soviet system represented the fusion of power and property, and the intention of the reforms of the 1990s was to create a new class of owners who were envisaged to act as a counter-balance to the old power system. In practice, the concentration of wealth in the hands of a tiny elite once again allowed the state to be captured by the new property owners. Under Putin this worked the other way, with a high degree of business capture to create once again a unified system. The power elite is largely synonymous with the business elite, although not without points of tension and contradiction. In the Putin years inequality stopped growing, but the space for the development of a vibrant small and medium business sector was stymied. The subjective model of status perception shows a growing 'middle class' bulge, yet the economic and social data show a more complex picture, above all a squeezed middle and a bottom section that increasingly finds the path of upward social mobility blocked. Although Russians are relatively tolerant of inequality, there is an accumulating sense of dissatisfaction that bodes ill for long-term political stability.

A quarter century of public opinion polling is traced by Valery Fyodorov, at the head of Russia's longest-established polling agency, the Russian Public Opinion Research Centre (VTsIOM). He follows the ups and downs of popular concerns and views of the changes. He confirms the pattern outlined in earlier chapters, noting that the golden age of the Putin leadership came to a rude end with the onset of the great recession in late 2008. Although economic growth rates quickly recovered, the crisis exposed some deep vulnerabilities that have once again been exposed in the declining growth rates that had set in even before the fall in oil prices and sanctions. Readiness to emigrate as a response to crisis is one of the key indices of a deepening malaise of the social system. The popular mobilization in response to Putin's return to the presidency and the flaws in the parliamentary election of December 2011 was one sign of a growing sense of alienation from the power system. The heavy-handed tutelage of the administrative system had become increasingly dysfunctional. The regime responded with an expensive and partially effective electoral transparency campaign and a package of political reforms. Data provided by Fyodorov demonstrate that although there remain points of tension, this is balanced by quite strong figures showing a strong satisfaction with one's life. Thus all discussions about the vulnerability of the system need to be seen in the context of a population that is broadly satisfied with present conditions. Putin's turn to a more conservative ideology has broad popular support, although a significant number are not sympathetic to the ideas of conservatism. The Putin system is deeply attentive to public opinion, and as the various outbreaks of contentious politics demonstrate, societal views are ignored at the regime's peril.

Elena Shestopal examines images of authority, reflecting the point just made about the symbiotic relationship between the regime and society. Shestopal applies a range of political psychology measures to trace the evolving pattern of interaction. Her data are particularly telling in examining popular views of democracy and authority. She shows how socialist affiliations have declined, and contrary to much commentary, how the proportion of those who identify as liberals has quadrupled since 1993 to reach 20% by 2013. This is balanced by an increasing proportion that takes a positive view of the Soviet system, rising from 30% in 2000 to 44% in 2013. A key finding is that the fragmentation of values that characterize the early post-communist years is gradually giving way to elements of consolidation, although there remains a high degree of ideological and political pluralism. This allows the regime to appear as the aggregator of a diffuse popular will.

Natalya Gribanova turns our attention to Russia's ethnic and religious profile. She notes that in contrast to the Soviet passports, the new Russian system has now deleted the infamous 'Point 5' that denoted a person's ethnicity (called 'nationality' in Soviet parlance). This aroused deep concerns in some of Russia's ethnic regions, notably in Tatarstan. Although ethnic Russians comprise 80% of the population, Russia remains a deeply *pluricultural* society. While multiculturalism seeks to address the problem of integration and adaptation of incoming communities, a pluricultural society is one that has several autochthonous peoples who are native to the country. Chief among them are the Tatars, who make up 3.9% of the population according to the 2010 census. Although Gribanova notes the 'ethnic revival' in Russia since the fall of the communist system, not all have a conflict-creating potential, but the border between ethnic patriotism and nationalism is a fine one. Only a few regions have descended into ethnic conflict, typically provoked by economic crisis, historical factors and poor political leadership. Above all, the 'Russian question' has still not been resolved, and, like the 'English question', national grievances are susceptible to exploitation by adventuristic elites. As for religious factors, Russia has undergone a renaissance in religious affiliation, although regular attendance at religious services is far lower. There is a looming cleavage between defenders of traditional secularism and the trend for Russia to become a post-secular society. It is clear, as Gribanova argues in the light of the Ukraine conflict, that attempts to consolidate society on the basis of enmity to an alleged hostile outsider is fraught with danger.

Zubarevich shifts our attention to the regions. She examines the various strata making up society, stressing that the centre–periphery divide is the most important cleavage. The various geographical divisions are complemented by regions in which ethnic Russians predominate as opposed to those where there are titular ethnic groups based on some sort of ethno-federal unit. The balance of power between the centre and the regions has undergone major change, with the Yeltsinite devolution of power being sharply reversed in the 2000s as Putin consolidated the vertical of power. Above all, regions are sharply differentiated on the basis of socio-economic indicators and level of development. A mass of data show the precise level of differentiation, as well as the various patterns of migration. Thus, the way that a population adapts to the changing social and political change depends above all on the level of economic development and the standard of living.

Andrei Margolin looks at the issue of social investment, providing some important definitions and above all examining the criteria for investment in education, healthcare, social services, environmental protection and much else. He provides a methodology on which such investments can be made. In the final chapter by Boris Mezhuev we return to political questions. His focus is on the alienation of Russian political elites from what he considers to be the values and opinions of the mass of the population. Above all, he argued that the alliance between the liberals and popular aspirations coincided for only a relatively short period in the final period of perestroika in the early 1990s, and thereafter the liberals were effectively alienated from the people. The outbreak of contentious politics in 2011–2012 once again promised to bring 'minority' avant-garde views into alignment with the people. In fact, Mezhuev argues that what by then had become a disparate opposition not only failed to achieve a degree of cultural hegemony, but also effectively pursued a strategy of 'self-isolation' because of inability to engage with the real concerns of the population. The liberal intellectuals had lost their grounding in society.

This brings us full-circle. Whereas in most of the East European countries liberalism became hegemonic, in Russia it was isolated from society and was unable to reflect the concerns of 'the people'. The argument can be taken further to suggest that this gulf has become systemic and reflects the deeper inability of any political force to achieve hegemony in post-communist Russia. Instead, there is a deep ideational pluralism, with various varieties of traditionalism ranged against liberals, and none has been able to achieve predominance. Putin has been able to draw strength from all the tendencies, but his regime remains independent of all. This reinforces the regime's tutelary role, and prevents capture by any one group. This allows the regime to insulate itself from social forces, but in the long term it is threatened with isolation. It also means that public policy becomes the product of an endless process of triangulation, and ultimately encourages policy stalemate and developmental stasis. The symptoms of this have been analysed in this book. The post-communist administrations have transformed Russian society, but some deep patterns have re-asserted themselves. The Putin system is responsive to public demands, values and aspirations, but ultimately it needs to articulate a clear developmental strategy and positive agenda for the country and its people.

15 Afterword to the Russian edition

Vladimir Yakunin

The beginning of the twenty-first century has been marked by powerful tectonic shifts in world politics, which an army of academics and experts, mostly from Western schools of scholarship, have been hard at work describing and analysing. It would not be an exaggeration to say that this whirlwind of geopolitical change was triggered by the sociopolitical developments that have unfolded on the one-third of the global landmass occupied by the former Soviet Union following the superpower's collapse.

Prior to the disintegration of the USSR, Western political scientists, culture experts, sociologists and others tended not so much to analyse the contemporary state of the USSR and Soviet society as to identify the defects of the state machine and to study the few dissidents who openly opposed the Soviet system. At the same time, the ideology-driven Soviet social sciences lacked the necessary impartiality and critical attitude, which is why their theories described a nonexistent country, Tlön (as discovered by Jorge Luis Borges), rather than the real trends and cause-and-effect relationships that formed the rich palette of Soviet society. I think it is fair to say that the well-known statement in the early 1980s by Communist Party Politburo member and USSR KGB Chairman Yury Andropov that 'We don't know the country that we rule' could be applied to describe many of the studies of Russia today. This perpetuates the negative stereotypes of the country, which exacerbate the international tensions that have the potential to wipe out all the achievements of humanity.

To be fair, in Russia itself there have been far too few attempts to create a coherent picture of the country's social history, despite the publication of a number of relatively good history books. Without belittling the importance of recent studies in this field, I would like to stress that the present study is a unique attempt to create a collective monograph that employs some of the most advanced methods of analysis to understand the processes at work in this huge country over the last few decades. I am convinced that unless we continue this work in a systematic manner, not only will we soon see a dramatic contraction of scholarly knowledge about Russian society, but we will also lose the academic tools and the depth of thought appropriate for the study of our distinctive national intellectual heritage. We cannot afford to lose our capacity to study the future, however vague and indistinct the trends may appear today.

Our conscious decision to avoid using the term 'population' to describe the people we ourselves belong to is significant. The winners and losers of the last

30 years of reforms are the people of the same great nation, as convincingly shown by the majority of chapters in this book. The country survives thanks to the hard work of the Russian people, their sense of fairness and their ability to meet daily challenges, endure hardships and nurture the next generation, and not to the ingenious plans of competing elite groups in the interregnum period.

While the leading European sociologist Zygmunt Bauman, who contributed to the volume of discussions, published with our support, edited by Piotr Dutkiewicz and Richard Sakwa, *22 Ideas to Fix the World: Conversations with the World's Foremost Thinkers*, a joint publication of the Social Science Research Council and New York University Press published in 2014, uses the term 'interregnum' to characterize the state of European society, I actually see the situation in Russian society as a chain of crises in an epoch of global transformations. In real life, this crisis of the transition to the future is expressed in a number of socio-cultural cleavages provoked by generational differences in views that are dramatic enough to constitute a topic of research in their own right. The crisis is exacerbated by an ill-defined neo-liberal conception of the future that has practically become the leading idea of our time.

I am convinced that only a socially oriented economic model can create the conditions for higher living standards and greater efficiency and competitiveness in strategic sectors of the economy. This progress too often is alien to the general state of academic and political discourse, which has become sharply antagonistic as a result of economic crises, outside pressure on the country and the absence of a sufficiently developed culture of 'fundamental pragmatism'. The Centre for the Study of Society in Crisis, which was created many years ago and which I lead, has published a large number of in-depth studies and held dozens of conferences on this question.

I would like to stress the special role played by the Political Science Department of Moscow State University in preparing this book for publication, as the initial idea was suggested at one of its conferences. Russian political scientists and sociologists, and representatives of the business community – all of us have high hopes for the recently established Russian Society of Political Scientists (ROP). Perhaps its most important task is systematically to fill in the gaps in knowledge of our own country. Superficial views of Russia too often predominate in government agencies and among large numbers of Russian analysts, and for years foreign analysts have had to rely on the lopsided and biased interpretations of developments in Russia that this produced. There is no direct, meaningful dialogue in Russia between groups of researchers with different views, a feature which traditionally has been a distinguishing feature of Russian scholarship. I believe this trend has become particularly pronounced during the tragic events in Ukraine.

In conclusion, I hope readers will enjoy this collection of high-quality scholarship, contributed by leading Russian researchers from different fields in the social sciences. The authors are not bound by corporate solidarity or the closeness of their views on Russia's development prospects; in fact, they sometimes hold opposing viewpoints. Our aim was to present a diversity of perspectives that together could contribute to a deeper understanding of the complex processes shaping Russian society.

Index

Page numbers followed by an 'f' refer to figures; page numbers followed by a 't' refer to tables

For Product Safety Concerns and Information please contact our EU representative GPSR@taylorandfrancis.com
Taylor & Francis Verlag GmbH, Kaufingerstraße 24, 80331 München, Germany

www.ingramcontent.com/pod-product-compliance
Ingram Content Group UK Ltd.
Pitfield, Milton Keynes, MK11 3LW, UK
UKHW020019200926
475702UK00014B/1963
* 9 7 8 1 1 3 8 4 7 7 1 1 7 *